Business Ethics 03/04

Fifteenth Edition

EDITOR

John E. Richardson

Pepperdine University

Dr. John E. Richardson is professor of marketing in the George L. Graziadio School of Business and Management at Pepperdine University. He is president of his own consulting firm and has consulted with organizations such as Bell and Howell, Dayton-Hudson, Epson, and the U.S. Navy, as well as with various service, nonprofit, and franchise organizations. Dr. Richardson is a member of the American Management Association, the American Marketing Association, the Society for Business Ethics, and Beta Gamma Sigma honorary business fraternity.

McGraw-Hill/Dushkin

530 Old Whitfield Street, Guilford, Connecticut 06437

Visit us on the Internet
http://www.dushkin.com

Credits

1. **Ethics, Values, and Social Responsibility in Business**
   Unit photo—© 2003 by PhotoDisc, Inc.
2. **Ethical Issues and Dilemmas in the Workplace**
   Unit photo—TRW, Inc. photo.
3. **Business and Society: Contemporary Ethical, Social, and Environmental Issues**
   Unit photo—© 2003 by PhotoDisc, Inc.
4. **Ethics and Social Responsibility in the Marketplace**
   Unit photo—© 2003 by PhotoDisc, Inc.
5. **Developing the Future Ethos and Social Responsibility of Business**
   Unit photo—© 2003 by PhotoDisc, Inc.

Copyright

Cataloging in Publication Data
Main entry under title: Annual Editions: Business Ethics. 2003/2004.
1. Business Ethics—Periodicals. I. Richardson, John E., *comp.* II. Title: Business Ethics.
ISBN 0–07–283847–7   658'.05   ISSN 1055–5455

Fifteenth Edition

Cover image © 2003 PhotoDisc, Inc.
Printed in the United States of America   1234567890BAHBAH543   Printed on Recycled Paper

Editors/Advisory Board

Members of the Advisory Board are instrumental in the final selection of articles for each edition of ANNUAL EDITIONS. Their review of articles for content, level, currentness, and appropriateness provides critical direction to the editor and staff. We think that you will find their careful consideration well reflected in this volume.

EDITOR

John E. Richardson
Pepperdine University

ADVISORY BOARD

Donald J. Beelick
Wright State University

Archie B. Carroll
University of Georgia

James G. Coe
Taylor University

Clifford E. Darden
Pepperdine University

Gerald R. Ferrera
Bentley College

William J. Kehoe
University of Virginia

Robert A. Larmer
University of New Brunswick

Tom Mahaffey
St. Francis Xavier University

Tim Mazur
Anthem, Inc.

Thomas Mulligan
Brock University

Patrick E. Murphy
University of Notre Dame

Lisa H. Newton
Fairfield University

Donald P. Robin
Wake Forest University

Andrew Sikula
Marshall University Graduate College

Roberta Snow
West Chester University

Marc D. Street
University of Tulsa

Michael van Breda
Southern Methodist University

David Vogel
University of California

Jon West
University of Miami

Staff

Jeffrey L. Hahn, Vice President/Publisher

EDITORIAL STAFF

Theodore Knight, Ph.D., Managing Editor
Roberta Monaco, Managing Developmental Editor
Dorothy Fink, Associate Developmental Editor
Addie Raucci, Senior Administrative Editor
Robin Zarnetske, Permissions Editor
Marie Lazauskas, Permissions Assistant
Lisa Holmes-Doebrick, Senior Program Coordinator

TECHNOLOGY STAFF

Richard Tietjen, Senior Publishing Technologist
Jonathan Stowe, Executive Director of eContent
Marcuss Oslander, Sponsoring Editor of eContent
Christopher Santos, Senior eContent Developer
Janice Ward, Software Support Analyst
Angela Mule, eContent Developer
Michael McConnel, eContent Developer
Ciro Parente, Editorial Assistant
Joe Offredi, Technology Developmental Editor

PRODUCTION STAFF

Brenda S. Filley, Director of Production
Charles Vitelli, Designer
Mike Campbell, Production Coordinator
Eldis Lima, Graphics
Juliana Arbo, Typesetting Supervisor
Julie Marsh, Project Editor
Jocelyn Proto, Typesetter
Cynthia Powers, Typesetter

To the Reader

In publishing ANNUAL EDITIONS we recognize the enormous role played by the magazines, newspapers, and journals of the public press in providing current, first-rate educational information in a broad spectrum of interest areas. Many of these articles are appropriate for students, researchers, and professionals seeking accurate, current material to help bridge the gap between principles and theories and the real world. These articles, however, become more useful for study when those of lasting value are carefully collected, organized, indexed, and reproduced in a low-cost format, which provides easy and permanent access when the material is needed. That is the role played by ANNUAL EDITIONS.

Recent events have brought ethics to the forefront as a topic of discussion throughout our nation. And, undoubtedly, the area of society that is getting the closest scrutiny regarding its ethical practices is the business sector. Both the print and broadcast media have offered a constant stream of facts and opinions concerning recent unethical goings-on in the business world. Insider trading scandals on Wall Street, the marketing of unsafe products, money laundering, and questionable contracting practices are just a few examples of events that have recently tarnished the image of business.

As corporate America struggles to find its ethical identity in a business environment that grows increasingly complex, managers are confronted with some poignant questions that have definite ethical ramifications. Does a company have any obligation to help solve social problems such a poverty, pollution, and urban decay? What ethical responsibilities should a multinational corporation assume in foreign countries? What obligation does a manufacturer have to the consumer with respect to product defects and safety?

These are just a few of the issues that make the study of business ethics important and challenging. A significant goal of *Annual Editions: Business Ethics 03/04* is to present some different perspectives on understanding basic concepts and concerns of business ethics and to provide ideas on how to incorporate these concepts into the policies and decision-making processes of businesses. The articles reprinted in this publication have been carefully chosen from a variety of public press sources to furnish current information on business ethics.

This volume contains a number of features designed to make it useful for students, researchers, and professionals. These include the *table of contents* with summaries of each article and key concepts in italics, a *topic guide* for locating articles on specific subjects related to business ethics, and a comprehensive *index*. Also, included in this edition are selected *World Wide Web* sites that can be used to further explore article topics.

The articles are organized into five units. Selections that focus on similar issues are concentrated into subsections within the broader units. Each unit is preceded by an overview that provides background for informed reading of the articles, emphasizes critical issues, and presents key points to consider that focus on major themes running through the selections.

Your comments, opinions, and recommendations about *Annual Editions: Business Ethics 03/04* will be greatly appreciated and will help shape future editions. Please take a moment to complete and return the postage-paid *article rating form* on the last page of this book. Any book can be improved, and with your help this one will continue to be.

John E. Richardson
Editor

Contents

UNIT 1
Ethics, Values, and Social Responsibility in Business

Seven selections provide an introduction to business ethics and social responsibility.

The concepts in bold italics are developed in the article. For further expansion, please refer to the Topic Guide and the Index.

UNIT 2
Ethical Issues and Dilemmas in the Workplace

Sixteen selections organized within seven subsections examine crucial employee-related issues and their ethical implications for management's decision-making practices and policies.

The concepts in bold italics are developed in the article. For further expansion, please refer to the Topic Guide and the Index.

UNIT 3
Business and Society: Contemporary Ethical, Social, and Environmental Issues

Ten articles organized within three subsections provide an analysis of important ethical, social, and environmental issues affecting both domestic and global workplaces.

The concepts in bold italics are developed in the article. For further expansion, please refer to the Topic Guide and the Index.

The concepts in bold italics are developed in the article. For further expansion, please refer to the Topic Guide and the Index.

UNIT 4
Ethics and Social Responsibility in the Marketplace

Six selections organized within two subsections describe the practice of incorporating ethics into the marketplace.

The concepts in bold italics are developed in the article. For further expansion, please refer to the Topic Guide and the Index.

UNIT 5
Developing the Future Ethos and Social Responsibility of Business

Seven selections consider guidelines and principles for developing the future ethos and social responsibility of business.

The concepts in bold italics are developed in the article. For further expansion, please refer to the Topic Guide and the Index.

Topic Guide

This topic guide suggests how the selections in this book relate to the subjects covered in your course. You may want to use the topics listed on these pages to search the Web more easily.

On the following pages a number of Web sites have been gathered specifically for this book. They are arranged to reflect the units of this *Annual Edition*. You can link to these sites by going to the DUSHKIN ONLINE support site at *http://www.dushkin.com/online/*.

ALL THE ARTICLES THAT RELATE TO EACH TOPIC ARE LISTED BELOW THE BOLD-FACED TERM.

Brands
36. Designing a Trust-Based e-Business Strategy

Business and government
18. A Hero—and a Smoking-Gun Letter

Codes of ethics
6. Doing Well by Doing Good
7. Best Resources for Corporate Social Responsibility
11. Unjust Rewards
26. Adding Corporate Ethics to the Bottom Line
27. Corporate Social Audits—This Time Around
32. Values in Tension: Ethics Away From Home
33. Global Standards, Local Problems
37. Managing for Organizational Integrity
42. Wanted: Ethical Employer

Conflicts of interest
3. Defining Moments: When Managers Must Choose Between Right and Right
5. Improper Behavior
20. Where Do You Draw the Line?
23. The Parable of the Sadhu
24. Trust in the Marketplace
28. Scandals Shred Investors' Faith
41. After Enron: The Ideal Corporation

Consumer protection
6. Doing Well by Doing Good
31. Virtual Morality: A New Workplace Quandary
34. The Perils of Doing the Right Thing
35. Ethical Marketing for Competitive Advantage on the Internet
41. After Enron: The Ideal Corporation
45. Profits From Principle: Five Forces Redefining Business

Discrimination
13. Is Wal-Mart Hostile to Women?
14. Racism in the Workplace
15. The Unifying Force of Diversity
24. Trust in the Marketplace
27. Corporate Social Audits—This Time Around
30. America Addresses Work Force Diversity
32. Values in Tension: Ethics Away From Home

Diversity
14. Racism in the Workplace
15. The Unifying Force of Diversity
16. The Kindest Cut
27. Corporate Social Audits—This Time Around
30. America Addresses Work Force Diversity
39. 100 Best Corporate Citizens
43. Old Ethical Principles: The New Corporate Culture
46. Executive Women and the Myth of Having It All

Downsizing
16. The Kindest Cut
17. Downsize With Dignity
38. Industrial Evolution
45. Profits From Principle: Five Forces Redefining Business

Employee responsibility
14. Racism in the Workplace
20. Where Do You Draw the Line?
31. Virtual Morality: A New Workplace Quandary

Employee rights
1. Thinking Ethically: A Framework for Moral Decision Making
2. Appreciating, Understanding, and Applying Universal Moral Principles
3. Defining Moments: When Managers Must Choose Between Right and Right
4. Managing by Values
7. Best Resources for Corporate Social Responsibility
8. HR Must Know When Employee Surveillance Crosses the Line
9. Cut Loose
13. Is Wal-Mart Hostile to Women?
17. Downsize With Dignity
19. Speaking Out Has High Cost
30. America Addresses Work Force Diversity
31. Virtual Morality: A New Workplace Quandary
33. Global Standards, Local Problems
44. Do It Right
45. Profits From Principle: Five Forces Redefining Business
46. Executive Women and the Myth of Having It All

Environmental disregard
6. Doing Well by Doing Good
7. Best Resources for Corporate Social Responsibility
11. Unjust Rewards
24. Trust in the Marketplace
25. Ethics in Cyberspace
27. Corporate Social Audits—This Time Around
32. Values in Tension: Ethics Away From Home
33. Global Standards, Local Problems
34. The Perils of Doing the Right Thing
37. Managing for Organizational Integrity
38. Industrial Evolution
39. 100 Best Corporate Citizens
43. Old Ethical Principles: The New Corporate Culture
45. Profits From Principle: Five Forces Redefining Business

Environmental pollution
6. Doing Well by Doing Good
7. Best Resources for Corporate Social Responsibility
11. Unjust Rewards
24. Trust in the Marketplace
25. Ethics in Cyberspace
27. Corporate Social Audits—This Time Around
32. Values in Tension: Ethics Away From Home
33. Global Standards, Local Problems
37. Managing for Organizational Integrity
38. Industrial Evolution
39. 100 Best Corporate Citizens
43. Old Ethical Principles: The New Corporate Culture

Equal employment opportunities
12. Harassment Grows More Complex
14. Racism in the Workplace
15. The Unifying Force of Diversity
30. America Addresses Work Force Diversity

World Wide Web Sites

The following World Wide Web sites have been carefully researched and selected to support the articles found in this reader. The easiest way to access these selected sites is to go to our DUSHKIN ONLINE support site at *http://www.dushkin.com/online/*.

AE: Business Ethics 03/04

The following sites were available at the time of publication. Visit our Web site—we update DUSHKIN ONLINE regularly to reflect any changes.

General Sources

American Civil Liberties Union (ACLU)
http://www.aclu.org/issues/worker/campaign.html

The ACLU provides this page in its "Campaign for Fairness in the Workplace." Papers cover such privacy issues as lifestyle discrimination, drug testing, and electronic monitoring.

Center for the Study of Ethics in the Professions
http://www.iit.edu/departments/csep/

Sponsored by the Illinois Institute of Technology, this site links to a number of world business ethics centers.

Harvard Business School (HBS)
http://www.hbs.edu/educators.html

Surf through the many valuable links attached to this Educators and Research News site to preview upcoming issues of the *Harvard Business Review*.

Markkula Center
http://www.scu.edu/SCU/Centers/Ethics/

Santa Clara University's Markkula Center strives to heighten ethical awareness and to improve ethical decision making on campus and within the community. A list of published resources, links to ethical issues sites, and other data are provided.

Murray G. Bacon Center for Ethics in Business
http://www.public.iastate.edu/~BACON_CENTER/homepage.html

This Iowa State University site was developed to aid businesses to understand and come to grips with ethical dilemmas.

U.S. Department of Labor
http://www.dol.gov

Browsing through this site will lead you to a vast array of labor-related data and discussions of issues affecting employees and managers, such as the minimum wage.

U.S. Equal Employment Opportunity Commission (EEOC)
http://www.eeoc.gov

The EEOC's mission "is to ensure equality of opportunity by vigorously enforcing federal legislation prohibiting discrimination in employment." Consult this site for facts about employment discrimination, enforcement, and litigation.

Wharton Ethics Program
http://ethics.wharton.upenn.edu/

The Wharton School of the University of Pennsylvania provides an independently managed site that offers links to research, cases, and other business ethics centers.

UNIT 1: Ethics, Values, and Social Responsibility in Business

Association for Moral Education (AME)
http://www.amenetwork.org/

AME is dedicated to fostering communication, cooperation, training, and research that links moral theory with educational

practices. From here it is possible to connect to several sites of relevance in the study of business ethics.

Business for Social Responsibility (BSR)
http://www.bsr.org/

The 9 core topic areas covered by BSR are listed on this page. They cover everything from Corporate Social Responsibility to Business Ethics to Community Investment to the Environment to Governance and Accountability to Human Rights to Marketplace to Mission, Vision, Values, and finally Workplace. New information is added on a regular basis. For each topic or subtopic there is an introduction, examples of large and small company leadership practices, sample company policies, links to helping resources, and other information.

Business Policy and Strategy
http://www.aom.pace.edu/bps/bps.html

This site of the Business Policy and Strategy Division of the Academy of Management is full of information about various topics in business theory and practice.

Enron Online
http://www.enron.com/corp/

Explore the Enron Web site to find information about Enron's history, products, and services. Go to the "Press Room" section for Enron's spin on the current investigation.

Ethics Updates/Lawrence Hinman
http://ethics.acusd.edu

This site provides both simple concept definitions and complex analysis of ethics, original treatises, and sophisticated search engine capability. Subject matter covers the gamut, from ethical theory to applied ethical venues.

Institute for Business and Professional Ethics
http://commerce.depaul.edu/ethics/

This site is interested in research in the field of business and professional ethics. It is still under construction, so check in from time to time.

National Center for Policy Analysis
http://www.ncpa.org

This organization's archive links lead you to interesting materials on a variety of topics that affect managers, from immigration issues, to affirmative action, to regulatory policy.

Who We Are
http://enron.com/corp/

At this site, the Enron Corporation explains itself from its early history to its present day problems.

UNIT 2: Ethical Issues and Dilemmas in the Workplace

American Psychological Association
http://www.apa.org/books/homepage.html

Search this site to find references and discussion of important ethics issues for the workplace of the 1990s, including the impact of restructuring and revitalization of businesses.

www.dushkin.com/online/

We highly recommend that you review our Web site for expanded information and our other product lines. We are continually updating and adding links to our Web site in order to offer you the most usable and useful information that will support and expand the value of your Annual Editions. You can reach us at: *http://www.dushkin.com/annualeditions/*.

UNIT 1

Ethics, Values, and Social Responsibility in Business

Unit Selections

1. **Thinking Ethically: A Framework for Moral Decision Making**, Manuel Velasquez, Claire Andre, Thomas Shanks, and Michael J. Meyer
2. **Appreciating, Understanding, and Applying Universal Moral Principles**, Judy Cohen
3. **Defining Moments: When Managers Must Choose Between Right and Right**, Joseph L. Badaracco Jr.
4. **Managing by Values**, Ken Blanchard
5. **Improper Behavior**, Ronald Berenbeim
6. **Doing Well by Doing Good**, *The Economist*
7. **Best Resources for Corporate Social Responsibility**, Karen McNichol

Key Points to Consider

- Do you believe that corporations are more socially responsible today than they were 10 years ago? Why or why not?

- In what specific ways do you see companies practicing social responsibility? Do you think most companies are overt or covert in their social responsibility activities? Explain your answer.

- What are the economic and social implications of "management accountability" as part of the decision-making process? Does a company have any obligation to help remedy social problems, such as poverty, urban decay, and pollution? Defend your response.

- Using the recent examples of stock, financial, and accounting debacles, discuss the flaws in America's financial system that allow companies to disregard ethics, values, and social responsibility in business.

 **Links: www.dushkin.com/online/**
These sites are annotated in the World Wide Web pages.

Association for Moral Education (AME)
http://www.amenetwork.org/

Business for Social Responsibility (BSR)
http://www.bsr.org/

Business Policy and Strategy
http://www.aom.pace.edu/bps/bps.html

Enron Online
http://www.enron.com/corp/

Ethics Updates/Lawrence Hinman
http://ethics.sandiego.edu/index.html

Institute for Business and Professional Ethics
http://commerce.depaul.edu/ethics/

National Center for Policy Analysis
http://www.ncpa.org

Who We Are
http://enron.com/corp/

Ethical decision making in an organization does not occur in a vacuum. As individuals and as managers, we formulate our ethics (that is, the standards of "right" and "wrong" behavior that we set for ourselves) based upon family, peer, and religious influences, our past experiences, and our own unique value systems. When we make ethical decisions within the organizational context, many times there are situational factors and potential conflicts of interest that further complicate the process.

Decisions do not only have personal ramifications—they also have social consequences. Social responsibility is really ethics at the organizational level, since it refers to the obligation that an organization has to make choices and to take actions that will contribute to the good of society as well as the good of the orga-

nization. Authentic social responsibility is not initiated because of forced compliance to specific laws and regulations. In contrast to legal responsibility, social responsibility involves a voluntary response from an organization that is above and beyond what is specified by the law.

The seven selections in this unit provide an overview of the interrelationships of ethics, values, and social responsibility in business. The first four essays offer practical and insightful principles and suggestions to managers, enabling them to approach the subject of business ethics with more confidence. The next three selections point out the complexity and the significance of making ethical decisions.

thinking ethically

A FRAMEWORK FOR MORAL DECISION MAKING

DEVELOPED BY MANUEL VELASQUEZ, CLAIRE ANDRE, THOMAS SHANKS, S.J., AND MICHAEL J. MEYER

Moral issues greet us each morning in the newspaper, confront us in the memos on our desks, nag us from our children's soccer fields, and bid us good night on the evening news. We are bombarded daily with questions about the justice of our foreign policy, the morality of medical technologies that can prolong our lives, the rights of the homeless, the fairness of our children's teachers to the diverse students in their classrooms.

Dealing with these moral issues is often perplexing. How, exactly, should we think through an ethical issue? What questions should we ask? What factors should we consider?

The first step in analyzing moral issues is obvious but not always easy: Get the facts.

The first step in analyzing moral issues is obvious but not always easy: Get the facts. Some moral issues create controversies simply because we do not bother to check the facts. This first step, although obvious, is also among the most important and the most frequently overlooked.

But having the facts is not enough. Facts by themselves only tell us what *is*; they do not tell us what *ought* to be. In addition to getting the facts, resolving an ethical issue also requires an appeal to values. Philosophers have developed five different approaches to values to deal with moral issues.

The Utilitarian Approach

Utilitarianism was conceived in the 19th century by Jeremy Bentham and John Stuart Mill to help legislators determine which laws were morally best. Both Bentham and Mill suggested that ethical actions are those that provide the greatest balance of good over evil.

To analyze an issue using the utilitarian approach, we first identify the various courses of action available to us. Second, we ask who will be affected by each action and what benefits or harms will be derived from each. And third, we choose the action that will produce the greatest benefits and the least harm. The ethical action is the one that provides the greatest good for the greatest number.

The Rights Approach

The second important approach to ethics has its roots in the philosophy of the 18th-century thinker Immanuel Kant and others like him, who focused on the individual's right to choose for herself or himself. According to these philosophers, what makes human beings different from mere things is that people have dignity based on their ability to choose freely what they will do with their lives, and they have a fundamental moral right to have these choices respected. People are not objects to be manipulated; it is a violation of human dignity to use people in ways they do not freely choose.

Of course, many different, but related, rights exist besides this basic one. These other rights (an incomplete list below) can be thought of as different aspects of the basic right to be treated as we choose.

- *The right to the truth*: We have a right to be told the truth and to be informed about matters that significantly affect our choices.
- *The right of privacy*: We have the right to do, believe, and say whatever we choose in our personal lives so long as we do not violate the rights of others.

---

the case of
maria elena

Maria Elena has cleaned your house each week for more than a year. You agree with your friend who recommended her that she does an excellent job and is well worth the $30 cash you pay her for three hours' work. You've also come to like her, and you think she likes you, especially as her English has become better and you've been able to have some pleasant conversations.

Over the past three weeks, however, you've noticed Maria Elena becoming more and more distracted. One day, you ask her if something is wrong, and she tells you she really needs to make additional money. She hastens to say she is not asking you for a raise, becomes upset, and begins to cry. When she calms down a little, she tells you her story:

She came to the United States six years ago from Mexico with her child, Miguel, who is now 7 years old. They entered the country on a visitor's visa that has expired, and Maria Elena now uses a Social Security number she made up.

Her common-law husband, Luis, came to the United States first. He entered the country illegally, after paying smugglers $500 to hide him under piles of grass cuttings for a six-hour truck ride across the border. When he had made enough money from low-paying day jobs, he sent for Maria Elena. Using a false green card, Luis now works as a busboy for a restaurant, which withholds part of his salary for taxes. When Maria Elena comes to work at your house, she takes the bus and Luis baby-sits.

In Mexico, Maria Elena and Luis lived in a small village where it was impossible to earn more than $3 a day. Both had sixth-grade educations, common in their village. Life was difficult, but they did not decide to leave until they realized the future would be bleak for their child and for the other children they wanted to have. Luis had a cousin in San Jose who visited and told Luis and Maria Elena how well his life was going.

After his visit, Luis and Maria Elena decided to come to the United States.

Luis quickly discovered, as did Maria Elena, that life in San Jose was not the way they had heard. The cousin did not tell them they would be able to afford to live only in a run-down three-room apartment with two other couples and their children. He did not tell them they would always live in fear of INS raids.

After they entered the United States, Maria Elena and Luis had a second child, Jose, who is 5 years old. The birth was difficult because she didn't use the health-care system or welfare for fear of being discovered as undocumented. But, she tells you, she is willing to put up with anything so that her children can have a better life. "All the money we make is for Miguel and Jose," she tells you. "We work hard for their education and their future."

Now, however, her mother in Mexico is dying, and Maria Elena must return home, leaving Luis and the children. She does not want to leave them because she might not be able to get back into the United States, but she is pretty sure she can find a way to return if she has enough money. That is her problem: She doesn't have enough money to make certain she can get back.

After she tells you her story, she becomes too distraught to continue talking. You now know she is an undocumented immigrant, working in your home. What is the ethical thing for you to do?

This case was developed by Tom Shanks, S.J., director of the Markkula Center for Applied Ethics. Maria Elena is a composite drawn from several real people, and her story represents some of the ethical dilemmas behind the immigration issue.

This case can be accessed through the Ethics Center home page on the World Wide Web: http://www.scu.edu/Ethics/. You can also contact us by e-mail, ethics@scu.edu, or regular mail: Markkula Center for Applied Ethics, Santa Clara University, Santa Clara, CA 95053. Our voice mail number is (408) 554-7898. We have also posted on our homepage a new case involving managed health care.

- *The right not to be injured*: We have the right not to be harmed or injured unless we freely and knowingly do something to deserve punishment or we freely and knowingly choose to risk such injuries.

- *The right to what is agreed*: We have a right to what has been promised by those with whom we have freely entered into a contract or agreement.

In deciding whether an action is moral or immoral using this second approach, then, we must ask, Does the action respect the moral rights of everyone? Actions are wrong to the extent that they violate the rights of individuals; the more serious the violation, the more wrongful the action.

The Fairness or Justice Approach

The fairness or justice approach to ethics has its roots in the teachings of the ancient Greek philosopher Aristotle, who said that "equals should be treated equally and unequals unequally." The basic moral question in this approach is: How fair is an action? Does it treat everyone in the same way, or does it show favoritism and discrimination?

Favoritism gives benefits to some people without a justifiable reason for singling them out; discrimination imposes burdens on people who are no different from those on whom burdens are not imposed. Both favoritism and discrimination are unjust and wrong.

The Common-Good Approach

This approach to ethics presents a vision of society as a community whose members are joined in the shared pursuit of values and goals they hold in common. This community comprises individuals whose own good is inextricably bound to the good of the whole.

The common good is a notion that originated more than 2,000 years ago in the writings of Plato, Aristotle, and Cicero. More recently, contemporary ethicist John Rawls defined the common good as "certain general conditions that are… equally to everyone's advantage."

In this approach, we focus on ensuring that the social policies, social systems, institutions, and environments on which we depend are beneficial to all. Examples of goods common to all include affordable health care, effective public safety, peace among nations, a just legal system, and an unpolluted environment.

Appeals to the common good urge us to view ourselves as members of the same community, reflecting on broad questions concerning the kind of society we want to become and how we are to achieve that society. While respecting and valuing the freedom of individuals to pursue their own goals, the common-good approach challenges us also to recognize and further those goals we share in common.

The Virtue Approach

The virtue approach to ethics assumes that there are certain ideals toward which we should strive, which provide for the full development of our humanity. These ideals are discovered through thoughtful reflection on what kind of people we have the potential to become.

Virtues are attitudes or character traits that enable us to be and to act in ways that develop our highest potential. They enable us to pursue the ideals we have adopted.

Honesty, courage, compassion, generosity, fidelity, integrity, fairness, self-control, and prudence are all examples of virtues.

Virtues are like habits; that is, once acquired, they become characteristic of a person. Moreover, a person who has developed virtues will be naturally disposed to act in ways consistent with moral principles. The virtuous person is the ethical person.

In dealing with an ethical problem using the virtue approach, we might ask, What kind of person should I be? What will promote the development of character within myself and my community?

Ethical Problem Solving

These five approaches suggest that once we have ascertained the facts, we should ask ourselves five questions when trying to resolve a moral issue:

- What benefits and what harms will each course of action produce, and which alternative will lead to the best overall consequences?
- What moral rights do the affected parties have, and which course of action best respects those rights?
- Which course of action treats everyone the same, except where there is a morally justifiable reason not to, and does not show favoritism or discrimination?
- Which course of action advances the common good?
- Which course of action develops moral virtues?

This method, of course, does not provide an automatic solution to moral problems. It is not meant to. The method is merely meant to help identify most of the important ethical considerations. In the end, we must deliberate on moral issues for ourselves, keeping a careful eye on both the facts and on the ethical considerations involved.

FOR FURTHER READING

Frankena, William. *Ethics*, 2nd ed. (Englewood Cliffs, N.J.: Prentice Hall, 1973).

Halberstam, Joshua. *Everyday Ethics: Inspired Solutions to Real Life Dilemmas* (New York: Penguin Books, 1993).

Martin, Michael. *Everyday Morality* (Belmont, Calif: Wadsworth, 1995).

Rachels, James. *The Elements of Moral Philosophy*, 2nd ed. (New York: McGraw-Hill, 1993).

Velasquez, Manuel. *Business Ethics: Concepts and Cases*, 3rd ed. (Englewood Cliffs, N.J.: Prentice Hall, 1992) 2–110.

This article updates several previous pieces from Issues in Ethics *by Manuel Velasquez—Dirksen Professor of Business Ethics at SCU and former Center director—and Claire Andre, associate Center director. "Thinking Ethically" is based on a framework developed by the authors in collaboration with Center Director Thomas Shanks, S.J., Presidential Professor of Ethics and the Common Good Michael J. Meyer, and others. The framework is used as the basis for many Center programs and presentations.*

Appreciating, understanding and applying universal moral principles

Judy Cohen

Associate Professor, Marketing Department, Rider University, Lawrenceville, New Jersey, USA

Keywords *Marketing, Ethics, Moral responsibility.*

Abstract *Interest in business ethics has soared over the past ten to 15 years. Lacking in the literature are normative approaches that provide guidelines for managers to evaluate their behavior in order to determine whether that behavior is in fact ethical. This paper makes a contribution to normative research, by offering a graded task approach to applying certain principles based on the philosophy of ethics (referred to as universal moral principles). These principles include utilitarianism, the categorical imperative, rights, and justice. First, some arguments against the use of universal moral principles are discussed, and rebutted. Next, the principles themselves are explained. Finally, a worksheet is presented. This worksheet offers a step-by-step approach to applying each of the principles.*

Interest in business ethics

Interest in business ethics has soared over the past ten to 15 years (Vitell and Ho, 1997). Two streams of research have emerged. Empirical research describes ethical behavior in business, with the goal of understanding and predicting that behavior. Normative research is prescriptive; it focuses on what businesses should do in order to be ethical (Donaldson and Dunfee, 1994). Smith (1995) points out that most research on marketing ethics has been descriptive. Lacking in the literature, however, are normative approaches that provide guidelines for managers to evaluate their behavior in order to determine whether that behavior is in fact ethical. This paper concentrates on making a contribution to normative research, by offering a graded task approach to applying certain principles based on the philosophy of ethics (which will be referred to as universal moral principles). These principles include utilitarianism (which deems a behavior ethical if it results in the greatest good for the greatest number), the categorical imperative (which asks whether a universal law can be made from the behavior); rights theory (both human rights and consumer rights), and justice (i.e. is everyone treated equally).

First, some arguments against the use of universal moral principles will be discussed, and rebutted. Next, the principles themselves will be explained. Finally, a worksheet will be presented. This worksheet offers a step-by-step approach to applying each of the four principles.

The debate concerning an ethical framework appropriate for marketers

Universal moral principles (based on the philosophy of ethics) have come under fire by researchers in business ethics in general, and in marketing in particular. With respect to frameworks borrowed from the philosophy of ethics, Smith (1995, p. 3) says:

[t]hese frameworks make a valuable contribution to the marketing ethics literature, but they presuppose a familiarity with moral philosophy that few managers have… Unless managers can

be philosophers as well as businesspeople, normative marketing ethics frameworks must be more accessible.

Valuable tools

The purpose of this paper is to make these frameworks more accessible. While philosophy may be perceived as unintelligible, in fact the principles offered by the philosophy of ethics are valuable tools that managers can use just as they use other tools for analysis.

Perhaps an even more pessimistic outlook comes from Donaldson and Dunfee (1994, p. 3), who write:

… using abstract, universal concepts of ethics to solve specific ethical dilemmas is notoriously difficult, and as business ethics instructors frequently remark, the course that never moves beyond a discussion of Utilitarian or Kantian ethics (with appeals to "apply" them to business problems) is doomed to disaster.

True, a discussion of *any* principle that is not applied to business problems is likely to be considered worthless by students of marketing (with the possible exception of doctoral students) and marketing managers alike. This paper offers a method for applying universal moral principles to business problems.

Certain constraints

Several authors have criticized the principles themselves, and offered alternative frameworks. Their arguments will next be discussed and evaluated. Robin and Reidenbach (1993) feel that universal moral principles are not appropriate for marketers because they do not take into account history, time and context in order to determine what is ethical. Owing to history, time and context, certain constraints are imposed on marketing: from society; capitalistic objectives; and human capacities and limitations.

Robin and Reidenbach (1993) point out that society imposes constraints on marketers in the form of laws. While this is true, this simply limits the behaviors that marketers can engage in. Those behaviors that are still legally available can then be analyzed using universal moral principles. A second constraint that the authors categorize as societal refers to the consumer orientation of marketers, especially focusing on consumers who are willing and able to pay. However, it seems more pertinent to include this issue with capitalistic objectives, since such a consumer orientation is the logical strategy to use for any organization that has a profit motive.

Profit motive

Robin and Reidenbach cite Bowie (1991) as an ethicist who criticizes the profit motive. They conclude that for an ethical framework to be useful to marketers, the profit motive must be considered legitimate. However, the issue of the profit motive is not a problem with the ethical principles themselves. It seems that Robin and Reidenbach's concerns stem from the fact that some persons (namely Bowie, 1991) feel that marketers should make a positive contribution to society, rather than be concerned about the profit motive.

There are three ways of approaching the issue of the profit motive. First, is to feel there should not be a profit motive; marketers should only enhance society's interests. However, universal moral principles should not be rejected just because a few philosophers have socialistic tendencies. An opposite approach is that the only interest of marketers should be profit. In fact, if one is to believe that marketing is truly "value in exchange" then one should believe that both sides can benefit—the marketer and the consumer. However, if this is the correct stance, then we may as well forget about ethics altogether, and agree with Gaski (1985) that the only responsibility of marketers is to meet the needs of consumers in order to maximize profit.

Extremes that miss the issue

Both of these approaches are extremes that miss the issue. Universal moral principles do not require that marketers become social reformers. On the other hand, marketers cannot assume that they and their consumers exist in a vacuum; other stakeholders are impacted by their decisions. For example, marketers can do an excellent job marketing pesticides to golf courses, which in turn market perfect lawns to golfers. The golfers, pesticide manufacturers and the golf course marketers are happy. Unfortunately, the rest of the population suffers from tainted groundwater. If marketers are going to care at all about ethics, they need to realize that both profits and ethics matter, and in fact both can be considered and both can be satisfied.

A third constraint for marketers which Robin and Reidenbach (1993) identify is that of human capacities and limitations. This concept reflects psychological egoism, i.e. "that each human being acts to maximize his or her own good and minimize his or her own discomfort as he or she perceives it" (Robin and Reidenback, 1993, p. 5). To the extent that this is true, it is a constraint on all human beings, not just marketers. Furthermore, the purpose of having ethical principles is not to force people to care about ethics. Rather, the purpose is to give marketers who already care about ethics and profit the tools to analyze behaviors. Universal moral principles provide such tools.

Other critics of universal moral principles are Donaldson and Dunfee (1994). They offer one minor criticism that universal moral principles are not appropriate for business because, even a master of moral theories would not be able to define unethical employee compensation. However, that is not the purpose of these principles. Rather, the purpose is to determine whether a specific behavior (in this case, a specific type of employee compensation) is unethical.

Specific context of business situations

On a more profound level, Donaldson and Dunfee (1994) claim that moral theories such as utilitarianism and Kant's deontological principle (i.e. the categorical imperative) do not take into account the specific context of business situations. These specific concepts can be culture- or industry-specific. However, this is not a fair evaluation of all universal moral principles. While it is true that the categorical imperative is quite rigid, other principles are more flexible. Utilitarianism focuses on the outcome of behaviors; it is necessary to understand the context of the behavior to predict the outcome. Ironically, Donaldson and Dunfee (1994, p. 4) also feel that people have a hard time applying moral theories because they "confront their own finite capacity to comprehend and absorb all details relevant to ethical contexts". This indicates that one does in fact need to understand the context in order to apply universal moral principles. While it is true that such knowledge is necessary, it is also true that knowledge of both the industry and the cultural environment is necessary to make any good business decision.

These critics of universal moral principles have offered alternative ethical frameworks. Smith (1995) suggests the consumer sovereignty test. This test is basically a subset of right's theory. Smith focuses on the right to be informed and the right to choose, as well as capability (i.e. the extent of vulnerability of a consumer). Smith himself admits

there are problems with focusing on consumer rights, such as broader social issues (e.g. the environment).

Consumer sovereignty

It is this author's contention that focusing on the right to be informed and the right to choose is insufficient. The importance of other stakeholder groups cannot be ignored. For example, college students can buy research papers from a variety of sources, to submit to professors as if they had written the papers themselves. These students are making a choice and are well informed of what they are doing. Does this mean that marketing papers that promote plagiarism is ethical? Other stakeholders are involved, including students who write their own papers. These legitimate works may not be able to compete with papers written by experts. The honest students' grades will suffer in comparison. In another type of example, AOL Time Warner Inc.'s Cartoon Network decided to pull certain cartoons from a Bugs Bunny retrospective because they included negative portrayals of certain minority groups (Beatty, 2001). The cartoons would have offended some consumers. But others felt it unfair to censor materials that reflect the thinking of their time. Which consumers should have sovereignty in this situation? The consumer sovereign test is just one test to determine whether a marketing behavior is ethical. Sometimes it is the most appropriate principle to use in evaluating the ethics of a behavior, but sometimes other principles are more relevant.

Donaldson and Dunfee (1994) offer, as an alternative to universal moral principles, the social contract. Microsocial contracts are acceptable (what the authors call "authentic" but not "obligatory") for local economic communities. As long as they do not negatively affect other economic communities, only local communities can say what is right for them. However, even these microsocial contracts require informed consent and the right of exit. Donaldson and Dunfee admit that people in an economic community often do not have the right of exit (e.g. to leave one's job in a poor economy). The authors do not have a solution to this problem.

Hypernorms

For microsocial contracts to be obligatory, and for macrosocial contracts, the contracts must not violate hypernorms. Hypernorms are "principles so fundamental to human existence that they serve as a guide in evaluating lower level moral norms" (Donaldson and Dunfee, 1994, p. 16). However, since these are so fundamental, is it necessary to put them in a formal framework? Furthermore, most of the hypernorms identified by Donaldson and Dunfee, e.g. murder, torture and tyranny, are not usually behaviors that marketers engage in. True, deceit is another hypernorm identified; this is certainly a practice that marketers may engage in. However, this hypernorm apparently is not so universal, since Donaldson and Dunfee also feel that deception in negotiations is acceptable, as long as all parties realize that deception may happen (an attitude reminiscent of Carr (1968)). Donaldson and Dunfee (1994) say that many theorists consider rights as hypernorms. If so, then this is in fact an argument for the use of universal moral principles.

Donaldson and Dunfee (1994) use bribery as a classic example of a behavior that universal moral principles cannot evaluate correctly, because they do not take into account the context of the behavior. They imply that the social contract is a better way to determine whether bribery is ethical, based on the norms of the social/economic environment in which it takes place. They give the example of Lockheed's $13 million payment to Japanese Prime Minister Tanaka in the 1970s as failing the hypernorm test, because it distorted the democratic process and therefore, violated the right to political participation. Yet, the universal moral principles of utilitarianism and rights would have reached the same conclusion, i.e. that this specific case of bribery was unethical. For a lesser bribe, e.g. a women's cooperative in a developing country giving gifts to army personnel to maintain their contract to provide military uniforms, utilitarianism could have concluded that the behavior was not unethical, depending on the specific facts of the case.

Understanding universal moral principles

In this section, each of the universal moral principles will be described. Shortcomings of each principle will be discussed.

Seven dimensions of pleasure/pain

A teleological principle: utilitarianism
In a teleological analysis, a behavior is evaluated in terms of its results. The most well-known type of teleological analysis is utilitarianism, developed by Jeremy Bentham (1748-1832). Bentham evaluated all actions in terms of their ability to produce utility (i.e. "benefit, advantage, pleasure, good, or happiness" (Bentham, 1989, p. 137) and prevents "mischief, pain, evil, or unhappiness" (Bentham, 1989, p. 137)). A behavior is ethical if it results in the greatest good for the greatest number. Bentham felt that pain and pleasure can be measured quantitatively (which he called hedonistic calculus). The action that has the highest pleasure value and the lowest pain value is the most ethical action. Bentham suggested seven dimensions of pleasure/pain:

1. Intensity, i.e. the strength of the pain or pleasure.
2. Duration, i.e. how long the pain or pleasure will last.
3. Certainty or uncertainty, i.e. how sure we are of the outcome.
4. Propinquity or remoteness, i.e. how soon the pleasure/pain starts.
5. Fecundity, i.e. the probability that pleasure will be followed by more pleasure and that pain will be followed by more pain.
6. Purity, i.e. the probability that pleasure will be followed by pain in the long run, and vice versa.
7. Extent, i.e. the number of people who experience the pain or pleasure.

This is an integral factor in determining the greatest good for the greatest number. Because animals can feel both pleasure and pain, Bentham recognized animals as legitimate stakeholders (Rachels, 1986).

Utilitarianism shortcomings

Utilitarianism has been criticized for several shortcomings. The biggest shortcoming is the problem of the "greatest bad for the smallest number". Take the example of Rimadyl (Adams, 2000). Rimadyl is an anti-arthritic drug for dogs. While most dogs are greatly helped by Rimadyl, a small percentage die. According to utilitarianism, marketing this product is the greatest good for the greatest number. Yet, those who are hurt (both dogs and their owners, who witness their dogs failing health and ultimately grieve their deaths) are very badly hurt.

A second shortcoming of utilitarianism is predicting the outcome of the behavior being analyzed, and whether this will result in pain or pleasure. This includes two considerations: predicting the outcome itself, and predicting the pain/pleasure associated with that outcome. It is true that one can never be absolutely sure of an outcome. But marketers, more than most people, should be able to make decisions based on predictions of outcomes, since this is required of marketing decisions. The second issue is whether that outcome would be associated with pleasure or pain. John Stuart Mill stated in 1863:

> There is no difficulty in proving any ethical standard whatever to work ill, if we suppose universal idiocy to be conjoined with it; but on any hypothesis short of that, mankind must by this time have acquired positive beliefs as to the effects of some actions on their happiness; and the beliefs which have thus come down are the rules of morality for the multitude (Mill, 1989, p. 152–3).

"Backwards looking reasons"

A third shortcoming of utilitarianism is its lack of "backwards looking reasons" (a concern to Robin and Reidenbach (1993) and Donaldson and Dunfee (1994)). However, as discussed above, a thorough utilitarian analysis would take into account history and context, for they would affect the outcome of a behavior. Suppose, for example, the owner of a dry cleaner has been purchasing perchlorethylene, a chemical used in dry cleaning, from the same supplier for ten years. The sup-

plier has helped the owner by extending credit when needed. Now the owner has been offered a better price deal by a competitor. By passing part of the lower price to his customers, both the customers and the owner (as well as the new supplier) benefit. The only stakeholder who experiences pain is the former supplier. To conclude that this is the greatest good for the greatest number, however, fails to take into account all the facts of the case. The owner of the dry cleaner has a history of financial difficulties; he will no doubt need credit again. The new supplier, a discounter, does not offer credit. The dry cleaner will fail, and his customers will suffer the pain of finding a new dry cleaner that is as good as their original choice. While these outcomes are not guaranteed, they are logical, based on the history of those involved.

Of the three criticisms of utilitarianism, the most logical one is the first one, i.e. that utilitarianism does not take into account the greatest bad for the smallest number. Because of this shortcoming, utilitarianism is not the most logical tool to use in all situations. Let us now consider several other ethical principles.

Three deontological principles

Deontological principles
Deontological principles focus on whether the behavior itself is ethical, regardless of outcome. There is confusion about what constitutes a deontological principle. While it is true that deontological principles are rule-based, this does not mean that a behavior is ethical simply because it conforms to a rule. After all, marketers could go by the rule "lie to customers, as long as you make the sale". Therefore, the rules that deontological principles follow must themselves reflect universal moral principles. In this paper, I will describe three deontological principles: Kant's categorical imperative, rights, and justice.

Kant's categorical imperative. The basic rule for Kant's categorical imperative states "[a]ct as if the maxim of your action were to become through your will a universal law of nature" (Kant, 1989, p. 122). In other words, what would happen if everyone acted according to the same principle as the behavior in question? Would the behavior be self-defeating? Kant gives the example of lying. Why does a person lie? They hope to deceive the person(s) they are lying to. Under what conditions would they succeed? People can succeed in deceiving people only if their intended victim(s) believes their lies. The victim is only likely to believe a liar if the victim is used to hearing people tell the truth, and therefore, has reason to believe that the liar is also telling the truth. But suppose lying became a universal rule of nature, that is, everyone lied all the time. There would be no victims, because everyone would know not to believe anyone else. If everyone were to lie, the act of lying becomes self-defeating. Thus, liars free ride on the fact that most people do not lie. To free ride means to take advantage of the fact that others are behaving differently. Take the example of an advertisement for margarine that emphasizes that it has no cholesterol. What is the purpose of doing this? It is to imply that this margarine has a competitive advantage over other brands of margarine. In fact, because it is a vegetable-derived product, all brands of margarine have no cholesterol, and therefore could make the same claim. What would happen of all brands made this claim? No brand would have a competitive advantage; all brands would appear to be the same, which in fact they are (with respect to cholesterol). According to the categorical imperative, the no-cholesterol claim is unethical.

Situational variables

As with the utilitarian principle, the categorical imperative principle is not perfect. One shortcoming of the categorical imperative is that it does not allow for situational variables to "interfere" with determining whether a behavior is ethical or unethical. To Kant, lying is unethical, even if done to save a life. Kant would argue that it is better to tell the truth, because we can never be certain of an outcome, but we do know what a lie is (Kant, 1989).

Another shortcoming of the categorical imperative is that it does not recognize that certain intuitively unethical behaviors are actually more successful if everyone engages in the same behavior. For example, used car dealers have a reputation for using hard sell techniques and for being deceptive. It is easier for them to use these techniques if all used car dealers behave the same way. If some dealers were honest, it would be more difficult for others to continue to be dishonest, because they would lose customers. Another example is when one marketer in an industry raises prices. It is easier to raise prices when everyone in the industry raises prices; otherwise, the individual marketer will lose customers to lower-priced competitors. Again, the categorical imperative is not violated, although the behavior does not appear to be ethical, either intuitively or according to other principles.

In other situations, the categorical imperative concludes that a behavior is unethical, although it appears to be ethical, either intuitively or according to other principles. Take the example of lowering prices. The purpose of lowering prices is to gain market share. But suppose all competitors in a mature industry (i.e. one in which the market is saturated) lower price. Because the market is saturated, one can only gain customers at the expense of competitors. So everyone can not gain market share. The categorical imperative would say that lowering prices is unethical. As we saw above, the categorical imperative reached the conclusion that raising prices is ethical. But price competition benefits the consumer.

One piece of evidence

As with utilitarianism, the categorical imperative does not give the best answer in all situations. Rather, it is one piece of evidence that a manager should use to make a final decision regarding the ethics of a behavior.

Rights principle. Wasserstrom (1964) states that because rights are entitlements, having a right means one does not need to request that right—it is just there. If one acts in such a way as to exercise a right, one does not need any justification. On the other hand, if someone violates another's right, the violator is open to criticism. This does not mean that there are never any good reasons to violate a right. A prima facie right "… is a nonabsolute right whose weight in competition with other considerations is not fully specified" (Nickel, 1987, p. 14). Different rights have different weights; an absolute right can outweigh a prima facie right. Similarly, the utilitarian consequences of a behavior can outweigh the importance of rights in certain situations. For example, one can argue that consumers' right to choose a vehicle that is highly polluting is outweighed by the fact that this is not the greatest good for the greatest number, and violates others' right to a clean environment.

Liberty rights

Nickel (1987, p. 17) says that rights "… specify who is entitled to receive a certain model of treatment (the rightholders) and who must act on specific occasions to make that treatment available (the addressees)". Rights can be positive (i.e. the addressee must do something to ensure the rights of the rightholders) or negative (i.e. the addressee must refrain from doing something that would infringe on the rights of the rightholders.) Rights that are pertinent to marketers include human rights and consumer rights. Although philosophers have recognized a variety of human rights, we will deal with eight basic human rights. These rights can be categorized as welfare rights and liberty rights. Welfare rights are positive rights. The basic welfare rights are employment, food, housing, and education. It is generally accepted that it is government's responsibility to provide people under their jurisdiction with welfare rights (Bowie, 1990). Businesses must be concerned with liberty rights (Bowie, 1990), which include the right to:

- *Privacy.* For example, Double Click came under fire for planning to sell information linking e-mail addresses to demographic information (*Houston Chronicle*, 2000).
- *Free speech.* For example, some marketers have tried to silence consumers who make negative comments about their product on the Internet (Schmitt, 1999).

- *Free consent.* In other words a person should not be forced to do something that he or she considers unethical. For example, waitresses at some riverboat casinos are pressured to give free drinks to customers even if they are already inebriated and must then drive home (Hallinan 2000).
- *Freedom of conscience (i.e. freedom of religion).* An example of an organization that has made a special effort to avoid violating the freedom of conscious is Educational Testing Service (ETS). ETS offers tests on days other than Saturdays (the Jewish sabbath), so that orthodox Jewish people can take them.

Four consumer rights

Marketers must also respect consumer rights. Four consumer rights were identified by John Kennedy in his 1962 presidential message. These are:

1. *The right to be informe*d. For example, in their advertising for the weight loss drug Xenical, Roche Group avoided the FDA's requirement that full-length advertisements for pharmaceuticals must include negative side effects. Instead, Roche group used two shorter advertisements (separated by at least one advertisement). They were then able to avoid mentioning possible side effects, which include loss of control over bowel movements (Adams, 2001).
2. *The right to choose.* For example, only recently has the controversial abortion pill been made available in this country. Also, the right to choose can be violated when consumers do not have information in order to make an informed choice, as in the Xenical example.
3. *The right to safety.* An example is the Ford Explorer with Firestone tires, whose defects caused many accidents and deaths (Simison *et al.*, 2000).
4. *The right to be heard.* Consumers should be able to voice their grievances to marketers.

Rights are certainly compelling. In the USA, we place a strong emphasis on rights. However, rights are not always absolute; other concerns may override rights.

"Veil of ignorance"

Justice principle. The principle of justice requires that everyone be treated equally, by making decisions under the "veil of ignorance". This means that when making decision, "no one knows his place in society, his class position or social status, nor does any one know his fortune in the distribution of natural assets and abilities, his intelligence, strength, and the like" (Rawls, 1971, p. 236). Since this requirement is impossible to meet in the real world, decisions should be made as if the decision maker did not know his/her own identity. The lack of such a veil is evident in an upper-level official at a chemical company, discussing chlorinated drinking water: "[a]s long as those people can't be *identified*, as long as they are not *specific* people, it's OK. Isn't that strange? So you put a filter on your own house and try to protect yourself" (Jackall, 1988, p. 127). If this person could not tell the difference between his/her loved ones and the faceless, crowds, he/she would be more careful about contaminating water.

The principle of justice deals with treating groups of stakeholders equally. However, we need to consider two ways to treat people equally, i.e. the justice of process and the justice of outcome. Consider the example of a professor assigning grades to her students (i.e. her customers). She could make sure she achieves justice of outcome, i.e. that every student's grade has the same outcome—the same grade. Or she could make sure she achieves justice of process, i.e. every student's grade is determined by the same process. In this case, it is obvious that justice of process is most appropriate. On the other hand, take the case of a restaurant that bans dogs, with the exception of seeing-eye dogs. In this case, justice of process is not attained; some people are allowed to bring in their dogs and some are not. However, justice of outcome is achieved; both sighted and blind people can enjoy being in the restaurant. This is the more logical application of justice in this situation. When there are different conclusions regarding justice of process versus outcome, we must determine which conclusion is more appropriate for that situation. However, in many situations, the two will not conflict.

Treat people equally
For the principle of justice to be made, it is necessary, but not sufficient, to treat people equally. Take the Xenical example. All consumers are treated equally; all are cheated (out of information) equally. Intuitively, it seems not to be just. It is necessary to add to the concept of justice a second requirement, i.e. "[a]n action is just if, and only if, it is prescribed exclusively by regard for the rights of all whom it affects substantially" (Vlastos, 1962, p. 53). For justice to prevail, stakeholder groups need to be treated equally, and no rights can be violated.

Universal moral principles—conclusions

The universal moral principles described above take very different approaches to determining whether a behavior is ethical. One criticism of universal moral principles is that there is no single ethical principle that can be applied to all situations. Steidlmeier (1987) says this has been considered the "scandal of philosophy". His approach to philosophy is that "… [philosophy] is a human search for meaning and, therefore, will always inherently be unfinished" (Steidlmeier, 1987, p. 106). Even Robin and Reidenbach (1993, p. 4), who argue against the use of universal moral principles, offer a definition of ethics as "an attempt by human beings to use their intelligence and capacity for reasoning to improve on the 'law of the jungle' conditions from which they evolved". Marketing managers succeed in their jobs only to the extent that they have intelligence and capacity to reason. There is no reason why they cannot apply this capacity to using universal moral principles to determine the ethics of behaviors.

Managerial implications

Decision-making tools
The universal moral principles described in this paper are useful, utilizable, applicable, and effective. Marketing managers should use these principles as decision-making tools, just as they use other decision-making tools, to help them evaluate current and planned marketing activities. Unlike other decision-making tools, which may be more oriented to profit or market share, universal moral principles can help marketers evaluate activities in order to determine whether they are ethical. In order to become proficient in understanding and applying these principles, practice is necessary. It is suggested that readers use these principles to evaluate the ethics not only to their own marketing activities, but also of other marketers' activities. These activities can be found in a variety of business and more general publications.

Applying universal moral principles

A worksheet for applying each of the four universal moral principles is shown in the Appendix. Note that, because the worksheet was developed for use in the classroom, the user is asked to explain the reasoning behind each conclusion. It is suggested that the marketer still explain his/her reasoning, to make sure that reasoning is logical.

How principles will be applied
First, however, a few words will be said to clarify further how the principles will be applied. Utilitarianism, as stated above, is based on Bentham's (1989) concept of "the greatest good for the greatest number". However, Bentham was concerned with identifying the most ethical alternative. For the marketing manager, the goal is to determine whether a behavior is ethical at all. Therefore, the utilitarian rule will be simplified somewhat, to "good for the greatest number". If the marketing manager needs to choose between several ethical decisions, and wants to choose the most ethical decision, he/she can then evaluate which of the decisions offers the "greatest good". Also simplified is

Bentham's quantitative analysis of seven dimensions. In the suggested application of utilitarianism, qualitative analysis is used. This is because determining specific numbers for each dimension can be rather difficult. There is also the possibility that, after such numbers have been assigned, they will be considered "hard" numbers, and fixed. A third simplification will be of the seven dimensions themselves. We will be concerned about short-term versus long-term outcomes (which reflect Bentham's propinquity or remoteness, fecundity and purity). We will also combine intensity and duration, because these are related. For example, the intense pain of disfigurement as a result of a Ford Explorer rollover is long-term; this increases the intensity. We will also be concerned with certainty, which is of concern to marketing managers for regarding the outcome of any decision they make.

For the principle of justice, we will assume that it is logical to treat stakeholders differently when they are in different roles. Marketing managers will always treat customers differently than employees; it would not make sense to treat them the same. Therefore, we will be concerned with treating stakeholders of the same kind (e.g. consumers, salespersons) equally.

Hypothetical case
In order to make clearer the applications of the principles, let us first consider a hypothetical case that concerns product testing. Suppose a pharmaceutical company (Wellness, Inc.) has developed what appears to be a very potent drug that lowers cholesterol. High cholesterol can lead to serious health problems, such as heart attacks. The drug has no serious side effects. Based on preliminary research, this drug appears to be much more effective and safe than competitive products. The company is now doing human trials, in order to determine if the drug really works, and get the drug approved by the FDA. The human trials consist of two groups of people with high cholesterol, with 100 people in each group. One group, the treatment group, receives the new drug. The second group, the control group, receives a placebo. All participants take no other drug to help their cholesterol while they are participating in the research. At the end of the one-year trial, the progress of each group will be measured.

Because high cholesterol is so dangerous, some people feel it is unfair to give a group a placebo, when they could be taking a drug that helps them. A grassroots organization, People for Ethical Medicine, has protested this study. Their protests have been reported in several major newspapers. There is particular concern about Emma Goldsmith, 70 years old, who takes care of her husband with cancer. She only has a 50 percent chance of being in the treatment group.

Given this scenario, which is standard in the pharmaceutical industry, let us apply the four ethical principles. Included in the worksheet (see Appendix) are common mistakes to avoid. These are listed. Applications of the principles to the hypothetical case are italicized. See Table AI in the Appendix.

References
Adams, C., 2000, "Drug bites man: most arthritic dogs do great on this pill, except those that die", *The Wall Street Journal*, May 13, A1.

Adams, C., 2001, "Xenical ads avoid listing unpleasant side effects", *The Wall Street Journal*, April 3, B1.

Beatty, S., 2001, "Bunny in blackface: why cartoon network won't run 12 bugs pix", *The Wall Street Journal*, May 4, A1.

Bentham, J., 1989, "An introduction to the principles of morals and legislation", rev. ed., Goldberg, D.T., *Ethical Theory and Social Issues*, Holt Rhinehart and Winston, New York, NY.

Bowie, N., 1990, Lecture given at the Arthur Andersen Seminar for Teaching Business Ethics.

Bowie, N., 1991, "Challenging the egoistic paradigm", *Business Ethics Quarterly*, 1, 1, 1–21.

Carr, A. Z., 1968, "Is business bluffing ethical?", *Harvard Business Review*, 46, 1, 145–53.

Donaldson, T., Dunfee, T.W., 1994, "Toward a unified conception of business ethics", *The Academy of Management Review*, 19, 2, 252–84.

Gaski, J.F., 1985, "Dangerous territory: the societal marketing concept revisited", *Business Horizons*, 28, 4, 42–7.

Hallinan, J.T., 2000, "High rollers: at riverboat casinos; the free drinks come with a tragic toll", *The Wall Street Journal*, 23 October, A1.

Houston Chronicle, 2000, "Privacy groups: latest effort by Double Click rings hollow", *Houston Chronicle*, 15 February, 4.

Jackall, R., 1988, *Moral Mazes*, Oxford University Press, New York, NY.

Kant, I., 1989, "Groundwork of the metaphysic of morals", trans. H.J. Paton, Goldberg, D.T., *Ethical Theory and Social Issues*, Holt Rhinehardt and Winston, New York, NY.

Mill, J.S., 1989, *Utilitarianism*, Goldberg, D.T., *Ethical Theory and Social Issues*, Holt Rhinehart and Winston, New York, NY.

Nickel, J.W., 1987, *Making Sense of Human Rights: Philosophical Reflections on the Universal Declaration of Human Rights*, University of California Press, Berkeley, CA.

Rachels, J., 1986, *The Elements of Moral Philosophy*, Temple University Press, Philadelphia, PA.

Rawls J., 1971, *A Theory of Justice*, The Belknap Press, Cambridge, MA.

Robin, D.P., Reidenbach, R.E., 1993, "Searching for a place to stand: toward a workable ethical philosophy for marketing", *Journal of Public Policy and Marketing*, 12, 1, 97–108.

Schmitt, R.B., 1999, "Terminix suit aims to mute a Web critic", *The Wall Street Journal*, 3 December, B1.

Simison, R.L., Lundegaard, Shirouzu, N., Heller, J., 2000, "Blowout: how the tire problem turned into a crisis for Firestone and Ford", *The Wall Street Journal*, 10 August, A1.

Smith, N.C., 1995, "Marketing strategies for the ethics era", *Sloan Management Review*, 36, 4, 85–97.

Steidlmeier, P., 1987, "Business ethics: reconciling economic values with human values", Prakash, S.S., Falbe, C.M., *Business and Society*, Lexington Books, Lexington, MA.

Vitell, S.J., Ho, F.N., 1997, "Ethical decision making in marketing: a synthesis and evaluation of scales measuring the various components of decision making in ethical situations", *Journal of Business Ethics*, 16, 7, 699–717.

Vlastos, G., 1962, "Justice and equality", Brandt, R.B., *Social Justice*, Prentice-Hall, Englewood Cliffs, NJ.

Wasserstrom, R., 1964, "Rights, human rights, and racial discrimination", *The Journal of Philosophy*, 61, 20, 628–41.

Appendix. Worksheet for analyzing ethics of a marketing behavior

I. Describe the behavior being analyzed
Common mistakes to avoid:

• describing the behavior generically (e.g. risking lives).

Using a treatment group and a control group to test the safety and efficacy of a new drug for lowering cholesterol. The drug appears to be powerful, with no harmful side effects.

II. Stakeholder identification

Who are the major stakeholders in this situation? Stakeholders are any individual or group affected by the (potential) behavior of the company:

1. Direct stakeholders: those individuals who are directly affected by the actions of the organization. In this case, the direct stakeholders would include the people in the study. However, we can be more specific. For example, we need to divide stakeholders into those who are in the treatment group and those who are in the control group. Also included are Wellness, Inc. itself.

2. Indirect stakeholders: this includes individuals who are indirectly affected by the actions of the organization. These include:
   • *people not in the study who have high cholesterol;*
   • *the FDA;*
   • *families of people with high cholesterol;*
   • *physicians;*
   • *newspapers reporting on the protests;*
   • *families of people in the treatment group; and*
   • *families of people in the control group.*

3. Empathic stakeholders: this includes individuals who have not been affected themselves by the behavior of the organization, but who have chosen to take an interest in the issue because they think it is

important. In this case, People for Ethical Medicine is an empathic stakeholder.

Common mistakes to avoid with stakeholder identification:

• Ignoring major stakeholders. For example, all people with high cholesterol are stakeholders, because ultimately the study will determine whether this drug is safe and effective for them.

• If individuals are identified as belonging to a larger stakeholder group, do not list them separately. For example, Emma Goldsmith is included in the placebo group.

III. Apply four ethical principles to the behavior you have identified in Step I

A. Utilitarian analysis:

1. What is the outcome of the proposed behavior on each of the stakeholders listed above?
   • For each stakeholder, put a plus (+) for each way they are positively affected and a minus (–) for each way they are negatively affected. The size of the + or – should indicate how much pleasure or pain results. For each + or –, explain how they are positively and or negatively affected. If there is a difference in short term or long term outcome, indicate which + or – is short term or long term. If an outcome is very uncertain, the size of the + or – should be smaller.
   • If there is more than one + or – for any stakeholder group:
     - list all of the +s together, and all of the –s together;
     - indicate whether the net effect for that group is + or –, and the size of that + or –.

Common mistakes to avoid:

• Feeling this step if finished if you have identified one + or -, instead of brainstorming on all the potential ways that stakeholder group may be affected.

• Discounting pains; emphasizing pleasures. Be objective about both pains and pleasures.

• Not making the size of the +'s or -'s reflect how much pain or pleasure there is.

• Switching the behavior your are analyzing. Make sure you keep referring to the behavior you have described in Step I for every application of every ethical principle in your analysis. (e.g., you should not, in the same step, be applying any principle to two opposite behaviors of having a control group and giving everyone the new drug.)

Direct stakeholders:

The treatment group
Lare + *they are receiving a new drug that is likely to help them medium – they are foregoing other, already proven drugs (although these drugs are probably not as safe or effective)*
Net *medium +*

Control group
Large – *they are foregoing other, already proven drugs. The are running the risk of a heart attack*
small + *they may experience that "placebo effect", and get better because they think they are taking an effective drug*
small + *in the long run, they will have a safe and effective drug available*
Net *medium –*

Wellness, Inc. itself
Large + *this study is the final step needed to market this drug, which promises to be a blockbuster.*
small – *have to deal with People for Ethical Medicine, which is giving them some negative publicity*
Net *large +*

Indirect stakeholders
People not in the study who have high cholesterol
Large + *will have a proven drug available that is safe and effective*

FDA

Medium + *will be able to make a well-informed decision on allowing the drug to be marketed*

Families of people with high cholesterol, not in study

Large + will have a healthier family member

Families of people in treatment group

Large + will have healthier family member

Families of people in the control group

Large – their family member has no medication for the course of the study; runs the risk of a heart attack

Physicians

Large + will have a safe and effective drug to offer patients

Newspapers reporting on the protests

Small + something to write about

Empathic stakeholders

People for Ethical Medicine

Large – they are upset that this study is taking place

2. Make two columns. Label column 1 "+" and column 2 "–." Under column 1, list all of the stakeholders that are affected positively; under column 2 list all stakeholders which are affected negatively (see Table AI).

3. Taking into consideration how many individuals are included in each stakeholder group, analyze whether this behavior results in the greatest good for the greatest number. Explain how you reached this conclusion.

Common mistakes to avoid:

• Counting the number of stakeholders in the "+" column and comparing it with the number of stakeholders in the "–" column. Remember you are comparing the total number of individuals represented by the stakeholders. A stakeholder may have one individual in it, or it may have millions.

• Not explaining how you reached your conclusion. Do not just say, for example, "more stakeholders are negatively affected than positively, so it is not the greatest good for the greatest number".

• Note that the number of employees is rarely greater than the number of customers for a firm. Therefore, a behavior that benefits the employees but hurts customers is not likely to be the greater good for the greatest number, if the analysis is based on these two stakeholder groups.

There are more individual stakeholders in the positive column. The number of people in the control group and their families is balanced by the number of people in the treatment group and their families. The membership of People for Ethical Medicine is not likely to be higher than the number of people in Wellness, Inc. In any case, the one group that is larger than all negatively affected groups combined consists of people with high cholesterol, who are positively affected. Therefore, this is the greatest good for the greatest number.

4. a. If your analysis showed that the behavior is not the greatest good for the greatest number, state: <ldquo>this behavior violates the utilitarian principle"; otherwise, state: <ldquo>this behavior does not violate the utilitarian principle".

Table A1	
Positively affected stakeholders (+)	*Negatively affected stakeholders* (–)
People in treatment group	*People in control group*
Families of people in treatment group	*Families of people in control group*
Wellness, Inc.	*People for Ethical Medicine*
People with high cholesterol	
Physicians	
Newspaper	

Common mistakes to avoid:

• Your conclusion must follow logically from whether the behavior results in the greatest good for the greatest number. Sometimes a behavior may seem blatantly unethical but still result in the greatest good for the greatest number (if, for example, the minority that is harmed is harmed quite badly.). In this case, you should conclude that utilitarianism does not show that the behavior is unethical. However, since (presumably) other principles will conclude the behavior is unethical, ultimately you will conclude that utilitarianism is not the most appropriate principle for deciding the ethics of this particular behavior.

This behavior does not violate the utilitarian principle.

4. b. Given your conclusion in 4a, state either "according to the utilitarian principle, the behavior is unethical" or "according to the utilitarian principle, the behavior is ethical"

According to the utilitarian principle, the behavior is ethical.

Deontological analyses

B. Categorical Imperative:

1. State the core behavior being evaluated.

Common mistakes to avoid:

• As with Step 1, do not make the mistake of describing the behavior generically. This is especially true when a behavior is deceptive. Do not describe the core behavior as "lying" unless the behavior is an outright lie.

Using a treatment group and a control group to test the safety and efficacy of a new drug for lowering cholesterol. The drug appears to be powerful, with no harmful side effects.

2. Ask: "What would happen if everyone engaged in _____?" (Fill in the blank with the core behavior you gave for step 1.) What is you answer to this question? Would the behavior be self defeating? The behavior is self-defeating if it would be *harder* for the organization to engage in the behavior if everyone does it. The behavior is not self-defeating if it would be *easier* for the organization to engage in if everyone did it. *Explain* your answer.

Common mistakes to avoid:

• Self-defeating means defeating to the organization engaging in the behavior, not negative to some other stakeholder group (e.g. customers). Can the *organization* successfully engage in the behavior if everyone does it?

• Make sure your explanation does not just repeat back the concept that the behavior would or would not be self-defeating; make sure you explain why.

• Do not fail to distinguish between one person or organization engaging in a behavior, versus if all persons or (similar) organizations engaged in that behavior. For example, suppose an individual marketer raised prices 100 percent. We would not argue that this behavior is self defeating because it would lower sales to the point that they would go out of business (and therefore would not be able to raise prices any more) because the issue is what would happen if all marketers raised prices.

What would happen if all pharmaceutical companies tested new drugs by using a treatment group and a control group? The behavior would not be self-defeating because this is what all pharmaceutical companies do now. In fact, it is expected and demanded of them.

3. Given your answer to (2), decide if the behavior is ethical according to the categorical imperative principle. Your decision will be either "the behavior violates the categorical imperative principle" (if behavior would be self-defeating) or "the behavior does not violate the categorical imperative principle" (if the behavior would not be self defeating).

The behavior does not violate the categorical imperative.

4. Given your answer to (3), state either "according to the categorical imperative, the behavior is unethical" or "according to the categorical imperative, the behavior is ethical".

According to the categorical imperative, the behavior is ethical.

C. Rights theory:

11

1. Are there any rights that this behavior violates for any of the stake-holders? Identify the rights. Explain how these right(s) have been violated. You can use liberty or consumer rights.

Common mistakes to avoid:

- Do not confuse business rights with consumer or human rights. Businesses do not have freedom of speech because a business is not a human. They can not say whatever they want in advertising. Similarly, do not confuse the right to choose with the right for business to do whatever they want. The right to choose is a consumer right. (Businesses do have the right to choose in their role as consumers.)

- Consumers' right to choose is also not the right to choose absolutely anything they want. For example, consumers do not have the right to choose to buy a BMW for $100.

- The right to be heard is not the same as the right to be obeyed. Consumers have the right to voice their opinions to businesses, but businesses do not always have to respond. Sometimes consumers' demands are unreasonable.

- If more than one right is violated, do not just discuss one. This is because when a final decision must be made, if there are conflicts among the principles, knowing all rights that are violated will help you make a final decision.

- On the other hand, sometimes no rights are violated, even though other principles show the behavior is unethical. If this is true, do not try to be creative and find a right that is violated.

In the pharmaceutical case, we can make an argument that three rights have been violated for those in the control group: the right to be informed, the right to choose, and the right to safety. Although the subjects can choose whether or not to participate in the study at all, they do not know whether they are just being given a placebo, and can not make the choice to be given the treatment, although obviously they are in the study because they want the treatment. In addition, because only taking a placebo creates a risk to their health, the right to safety is violated.

2. Decide whether the behavior is ethical from a rights theory perspective, i.e. decide "Acording to right theory, the behavior is unethical because ____ rights have been violated", or "Acording to right theory, the behavior is ethical because no rights have been violated".

Acording to right theory, the behavior is unethical because the right to choose, to be informed, and safety rights have been violated.

D. Justice principle:

1. Is everyone treated equally in this behavior? Explain.

Common mistakes to avoid:

- Justice does not mean people getting what they deserve. It only means whether people are treated equally.

- Do not conclude that because all stakeholders in one group are treated the same as others in their group, that everyone is treated equally. For example, it would be incorrect to say that everyone in the treatment group is treated equally and everyone in the control group is treated equally.

- On the other hand, do not mix apples and oranges. For example, we would not conclude that justice is violated because people in the study are treated differently than Wellness, Inc. treats the FDA. The justice principle deals with whether stakeholders in the same role are treated differently.

2. If everyone has not been treated equally, state "The principle of justice has been violated".

3. If everyone has been treated equally, but everyone's' rights have been violated, explain what rights have been violated, and state "The principle of justice has been violated".

4. If neither (2) nor (3) hold, state "The principle of justice has not been violated".

Wellness, Inc. is treating people in the treatment group differently than people in the control group. The people in the treatment group get a potentially safe and effective drug for their health problem; the people in the control group not only do no get help, but risk a heart attack.

5. Conclude either "according to the principle of justice, the behavior is ethical" or "according to the principle of justice, the behavior is unethical."

According to the principle of justice, the behavior is unethical.

IV. Final decision – is the behavior ethical?

1. Are there conflicting conclusions, based on the four principles? Explain.

2. If there are conflicts, which principles give better reasoning in terms of whether the behavior is ethical? If the utilitarian principle does not show that the behavior is unethical, think about the stakeholders who are hurt by the behavior. How much are they hurt? Think about the stakeholders who benefit. In what ways do they benefit? When considering the deontological principles, what situational factors might lead you to think one principle is more appropriate in this case than another?

Common mistakes to avoid:

- Do not just repeat back "the behavior is (un)ethical because the ____ principle is violated." Explain why that principle gives better reasoning than those principles that resulted in opposite conclusions.

According to the utilitarian principle and the categorical imperative, the behavior is ethical. According to the rights and justice principles, the behavior is unethical. In this case, the utilitarian principle offers the best reasoning. It is necessary to have a treatment and a control group in order to determine the effectiveness and safety of a drug. If everyone were in the treatment group, and improved during the study, it would not be clear if the improvement were due to an effective drug or due to the placebo effect. Patients could end up paying for a drug that is totally ineffective, and lose the opportunity to take drugs that actually help their condition. It is true those in the control group have their rights violated in the short run, because they are taking no effective medicine. However, there would be no known effective medicine to take if no one had ever been part of a treatment group to test the safety and efficacy of other medicines.

3. After addressing any conflicting conclusions based on the different principles, give your final decision—is the behavior ethical or not? Explain.

Common mistakes to avoid:

- Do not assume that because rights are violated that the behavior is unethical, when other principles say the behavior is ethical. Rights are not necessarily the most important factor in any one case.

The behavior is ethical because it is necessary to have a treatment group in order to see whether drugs are truly safe and effective.

The research register for this journal is available at
http://www.mcbup.com/research_registers

The current issue and full text archive of this journal is available at **http://www.emerald-library.com/ft**

From *Journal of Consumer Marketing*, Vol. 18, No. 7, 2001, pp. 578-594. © 2001 by Journal of Consumer Marketing.

Defining Moments:
WHEN MANAGERS MUST CHOOSE BETWEEN
RIGHT and RIGHT

By Joseph L. Badaracco Jr.

THOUGHTFUL MANAGERS SOME-times face business problems that raise difficult, deeply personal questions. In these situations, managers find themselves wondering: Do I have to leave some of my values at home when I go to work? How much of myself—and of what I really care about—do I have to sacrifice to get ahead? When I get to the office, who am I?

Difficult questions like these are often matters of right versus right, not right versus wrong. Sometimes, a manager faces a tough problem and must choose between two ways of resolving it. Each alternative is the right thing to do, but there is no way to do both. There are three basic types of right-versus-right problems: those that raise questions about personal integrity and moral identity; conflicts between responsibilities for others and important personal values; and, perhaps the most challenging, those involving responsibilities that a company shares with other groups in society.

Most companies are now en-meshed in networks of ongoing rela-tionships. Strategic alliances link organizations with their customers and suppliers, and even competitors. Many companies also have complicated dealings with the media, government regulators, local communities and various interest groups. These networks of relationships are also networks of managerial responsibility. Taken together, a company's business partners and stakeholders have a wide range of legitimate claims, but no company can satisfy all of them. At times, stakeholder responsibilities conflict with managers' personal and organizational obligations. When these conflicts occur, managers confront this third type of right-versus-right problem.

A particularly stark example of this occurred in the pharmaceutical industry nearly a decade ago. Late in 1988, the senior management of Paris-based Roussel-Uclaf had to decide where and how to market a new drug, called RU 486. Early tests had shown that the drug was 90 to 95 percent effective in causing a miscarriage during the first five weeks of pregnancy. The drug came to be known as "the French abortion pill," and Roussel-Uclaf and its managers found themselves at the vortex of the abortion controversy.

The chairman of Roussel-Uclaf, Edouard Sakiz, was a physician with a longstanding personal commitment to RU 486. He would make the final decisions on introducing the drug. Earlier in his career, while working as a medical researcher, Dr. Sakiz had helped develop the chemical compound on which RU 486 was based. He believed strongly that the drug could help thousands of women, particularly in poor countries, avoid injury or death from botched abortions. In the developed world, he believed, RU 486 would provide women and physicians with a valuable alternative to surgical abortions.

But Dr. Sakiz couldn't base his decision on RU 486 solely on his personal values. As the head of a company, he had other important obligations. Some were to his share-holders; from this perspective, RU 486 was a serious problem. Revenues from the drug were likely to be quite small, particularly in the early years. Yet, during this period, anti-abortion groups would mount an international boycott of products made by Roussel-Uclaf and Hoechst, the German chemical giant that was Roussel-Uclaf's largest shareholder. A successful boycott would cost the two companies far more than they would earn from RU 486. At worst, a boycott could imperil Roussel-Uclaf's survival, for it was a relatively small company with weak profits.

Like any executive, Dr. Sakiz also had responsibilities for the people in his company. He had to assess the seriousness of the threats of violence against Roussel-Uclaf and its employees.

At a personal level, Dr. Sakiz faced a version of the question, Who am I? Was he, first and foremost, a medical doctor, a scientific researcher, an advocate of women's rights, or a corporate executive with responsibilities to shareholders and employees? In addition, his decision on RU 486 would commit his company to some values rather than others, thereby answering the organizational question, Who are we?

The prospect of introducing RU 486 placed Dr. Sakiz at the center of a network of responsibilities to important groups and institutions outside Roussel-Uclaf. Among these were the French Government, which owned 36 percent of Roussel-Uclaf, and the French Ministry of Health, which closely regulated the company, thus shaping its business opportunities.

Hoechst, which owned 55 percent of Roussel-Uclaf, also made strong ethical claims on the company. Its chairman was a devout Roman Catholic, who opposed abortion on moral grounds and had repeatedly stated his position in public. Moreover, Hoechst had a mission statement committing the company to lofty goals, which was put in place partly in reaction to its role in producing a poison gas used at Auschwitz.

China was another powerful actor in the drama. It wanted access to RU 486 for population control. The moral ground for China's position was avoiding the misery and risks of starvation resulting from its surging population.

Roussel-Uclaf's network of relationships and responsibilities raised extremely difficult questions for Dr. Sakiz and his company. What, in fact, were the company's obligations to women? To the Government laboratory that helped develop the steroid molecule on which RU 486 was based? To the larger medical and research communities? Were the unborn a stakeholder group? Could Roussel-Uclaf introduce the drug both in the West, citing a woman's right to choose, and in China, where women had apparently been coerced into abortions, even near the end of their pregnancies?

Dr. Sakiz's decision would define his company's role in society and its relationships with stakeholders. Everyone was watching him intently because his actions would be decisive, for RU 486 and for the company. In addition, he would be revealing, testing and in some ways shaping his own ethics. In short, Dr. Sakiz also had to make a personal choice that would become an important part of his life and career.

In late October 1988, a month after the French Government approved RU 486, Dr. Sakiz met with the executive committee of Roussel-Uclaf. Dr. Sakiz asked for a discussion of RU 486. After several hours, he called for a vote. When he raised his own hand in favor of suspending distribution of RU 486, it was clear that the pill was doomed.

The company's decision, and Dr. Sakiz's role in it, sparked astonishment and anger. The company and its leadership, some critics charged, had doomed a promising public health tool and set an example of cowardice. Other critics suggested sarcastically that the decision was no surprise, because Roussel-Uclaf had decided, in the face of controversy

during the 1960's, not to produce contraceptive pills.

Three days after Roussel-Uclaf announced that it would suspend distribution, the French Minister of Health summoned the company's vice chairman to his office and said that if it did not resume distribution, the Government would transfer the patent to a company that would. After the meeting, Roussel-Uclaf announced that it would distribute RU 486 after all.

These events suggest that the RU 486 episode was something considerably less than a profile in courage. Edouard Sakiz seemed to have protected his job by sacrificing his convictions. There was, to be sure, strong opposition to RU 486, both inside and outside the company, but Dr. Sakiz made no effort to mobilize and lead his allies. He gave up without a fight. At a defining moment for the company, Dr. Sakiz's message seemed to place political caution and returns to shareholders above research and "the service of Life," as the company's mission statement put it.

But the surprising reversal of Roussel-Uclaf's original decision caused suspicion among some observers, who began to ask whether Dr. Sakiz had figured out a way to get what he wanted with a minimum of damage to himself and his company. Indeed, some wondered if the company and the Government had choreographed the entire episode. Others noted that Government science and health officials and Roussel-Uclaf managers and researchers had worked together for years—on RU 486, on other products and on many other regulatory issues—making it easy for them to anticipate each other's reactions.

What had Dr. Sakiz accomplished? More specifically, had he protected and advanced his own position? Had he contributed to the strength and security of his company? And had he defined its role in society in a creative way?

In personal terms, Dr. Sakiz succeeded in making good on his own commitment to RU 486—Roussel-Uclaf would distribute the drug. At the same time, he protected his job against the chairman of Hoechst. Because the French Government had effectively ordered Roussel-Uclaf to distribute the drug, Hoechst would accomplish little by replacing Dr. Sakiz with an opponent of RU 486. For Roussel-Uclaf employees, the period of uncertainty and speculation was over, and the company decision was clear.

ARISTOTLE COUNSELS MODERATION AND CAUTION PRECISELY BECAUSE HE IS GIVING ADVICE FOR SITUATIONS IN WHICH IMPORTANT ETHICAL CLAIMS STAND IN OPPOSITION.

Dr. Sakiz seems to have defined Roussel-Uclaf's role in society in a remarkable, perhaps even daring way. It would be a political activist and catalyst. The company worked to stimulate and then shape media coverage; it invited its allies to mobilize after dismaying them by suspending distribution; it acceded to Government intervention that it may have encouraged or even arranged; and it tried to blur responsibility for the introduction of RU 486.

Roussel-Uclaf was committed to "the service of Life" following an original, complex and audacious strategy. Roussel-Uclaf would distribute RU 486, first in France and then elsewhere, but neither Dr. Sakiz nor his company had volunteered for martyrdom.

Clearly, there is an urgent need to find other lessons for managers who face choices like Dr. Sakiz's. The writings of Aristotle, who developed the foremost theory of human virtue, are an excellent place to find such lessons. Aristotle counsels moderation and caution precisely because he is giving advice for situations in which important ethical claims stand in opposition. He wants to discourage men and women who find tension or conflict among their duties, commitments, responsibilities and virtues from veering too sharply in one direction or another and trampling on some fundamental human values as they pursue others. This is why Stuart Hampshire has written that, for Aristotle, "balance represents a deep moral idea in a world of inescapable conflicts."

The ideal of balance provides valuable guidance for managers who must resolve right-versus-right conflicts—especially those like Edouard Sakiz's, that pit so many important values and responsibilities against each other. Aristotle's question for managers would be this: Have you done all you can to strike a balance, both morally and practically? By Aristotle's standard of balance, Dr. Sakiz performed quite well.

Joseph L. Badaracco Jr. is the John Shad Professor of Business Ethics at the Harvard Business School. He has taught courses on strategy, general management, business-government relations and business ethics in the school's M.B.A. and executive programs. Mr. Badaracco is a graduate of St. Louis University, Oxford University, where he was a Rhodes scholar, and the Harvard Business School, where he earned his M.B.A. and doctorate.

Reprinted from *strategy+business*, First Quarter 1998, pp. 4-6. Originally from *Defining Moments: When Managers Must Choose Between Right and Right*, by Joseph L. Badaracco, Jr., Boston, 1997. ©1997 by Harvard Business School Press. Reprinted by permission.

Managing by Values

Where there is alignment between core values and common practices, financial results will follow.

KEN BLANCHARD

A FORTUNATE 500 COMPANY IS one determined by: the quality of life available to its employees; the quality of service provided to its customers; and the quality of its products and their placement in the marketplace. If a company excels in these things, the hard numbers of sales revenues and profitability will directly follow.

Three Precepts

In a book that I co-authored with Michael O'Connor entitled *Managing by Values*, we explain how you can become a Fortunate 500 company by learning how to define, communicate, and align your values with your practices. Unless values are prioritized, you have nothing but situational ethics where anything goes.

1. Identifying core values. Many companies claim they have a set of core values, but what they mean is a list of business beliefs that everyone would agree with, such as having integrity, making a profit, and responding to customers. Such values have meaning only when they are further defined in terms of how people actually behave and are rank-ordered to reveal priority.

For example, Disney's four core values are safety, courtesy, the show (performing your particular role well), and efficiency. If these values aren't carefully ordered, people are left to their own devices. For example, a bottom-line-oriented manager might overemphasize efficiency and thus jeopardize the three higher-ranking values.

Fortunate 500 companies first emphasize the beliefs, attitudes, and feelings that top management have about employees, customers, quality, ethics, integrity social responsibility, growth, stability, innovation, and flexibility. Organizations today must know what they stand for and on what principles they operate. Values-based behavior is a requisite for survival. Once you have a clear picture of your mission and values, you have a basis for evaluating your management practices and bringing them into alignment.

Ethics means doing the right thing by being honest, acting in a legally and socially responsible manner, being fair in our treatment of others, and acting in ways that result in feeling good about ourselves and our company.

2. Communicating core values. Make sure that your values are evident to all stakeholders-employees, customers, suppliers, stockholders, and the community. For example, if your core values are to be ethical, responsive, and profitable, you then need to look for ways to implement these values with your major stakeholders. Provide people with what you know, when you know it—especially when it is information about company finances, new products, competitive practices, and pending changes in policies. This interests most employees. Involve employees in decisions that affect them—or better yet—whenever possible let them make the decisions.

3. Aligning values and practices. Once your values have been broadly communicated, you need to assess how well these values are practiced. To be effective, values and strategies need to unite the energies of all people, especially those dealing with the company's various publics. Without some way of identifying gaps between values and behavior, a set of core values is nothing more than a wish list.

In Fortunate 500 companies, the behavior of the leaders is aligned with corporate values. Management "walks its talk." For example, if executives indicate that they value innovation and flexibility but then have an authoritarian-based bureaucracy, there is an alignment problem.

Or, if executives say that they value the full development of people's potential but then have a performance review system that forces managers to rate people on a normal distribution curve, again there is an alignment problem. Misalignment between values and practices creates an energy drain that sabotages productive behavior. Alignment liberates energy and empowers people to act congruently. That makes for loyal customers and employees and a productive environment.

Closing the Values Gap

In using our values, we have to make some hard decisions that may not, in the short run, enhance our bottom line. And yet, since ethics and relationships are our first two values, we would not be walking our talk if we acted as if we were only in business to make money.

Michael has developed two simple but powerful problem-solving tools called People-Oriented Problem Solving (POPS) and Technical-Oriented Problem Solving (TOPS). Through the use of these tools, anyone in our company can shout out "gap" if they or anyone else is being treated by someone in a way that is inconsistent with our values, or when something in our system-compensation, performance review, space use—is causing a values conflict. In the first case, POPS would come into play and, in the second case, TOPS would be appropriate.

When a gap occurs, a series of problem-solving questions are asked of the people involved in the situation to reduce the gap and get our actions back in alignment with our values. No one should get away with treating anyone in an unethical or unloving way. When all is said and done, it's all about love—who loves you and who you love. Remember, your business is important, but it's not who you are—not your reason for being.

Ken Blanchard is the author of the One-Minute Manager *series and chairman of Blanchard Training and Development; 800-728-6000.*

Improper Behavior

by Ronald Berenbeim

ENRON IS THE most compelling business ethics case in a generation. I will focus on the issues raised by the conduct of its directors, officers, accountants, and lawyers.

My outline is taken from the syllabus of 10 classes that I teach in Professional Responsibility at the Stern School of Business, New York University.

Class 1 focuses on how market failure gives rise to professional dilemmas. There is nothing wrong with patents (temporary monopolies) and the use of unique expertise. Yet, certain forms of market failure are so egregious that they unreasonably interfere with the rights of others and endanger the credibility of all legitimate transactions. Information asymmetries occur when the business decision-makers know something that the person at the other end of the transaction does not. At times this asymmetry is a threat to the rights of others. Insider trading is one of the indefensible exploitations of information asymmetries. Enron officers and directors should have been far more alert than they were to the perception that they engaged in this practice. Ethical literacy is not about giving large sums of money to charity—it is about recognizing potential ethical issues before they become legal problems.

Class 2 focuses on truth and disclosure. "Falsehood ceases to be falsehood, when the truth is not expected to be spoken" wrote Henry Taylor. Exaggeration and bluffing are part of the business game, but how much is too much? The Taylor rule does not apply to audited financial statements or statements made to employees who are also shareholders (60 percent of the 401-(k) holdings were in Enron stock). While the employees were given the soothing balm of e-mail reassurance, the author of the missive and his colleagues were selling their stock. Enron's accountants and analysts are making the case for Enron deception, but if the truth is not expected to be spoken, then it is their job to pierce the veil. No potential client thinks otherwise. The role of accountants and analysts is to serve shareholders in rectifying the information asymmetries that exist when shareholders deal directly with the company.

Class 3 is on gifts, side deals, and payoffs. Here we need to dwell on the recipients of Enron beneficence. John Mendelssohn was president of the University of Texas MD Anderson Cancer Center. Enron donated more than $600,000 to this center since 1996. Wendy Gramm is director of the Mercatus Center at George Mason University. Enron gave this center $50,000. Drs. Mendelssohn and Gramm are on the Audit Committee of Enron's Board.

There are so many beneficiaries of Enron's generosity that it is difficult to find critics who are free from any appearance of conflict of interest.

Such potential conflicts of interest and incidental benefits inherent in gifts to board member's favorite charities are all too common.

Class 4 is on whistle-blowing. Suffice it to say that Enron had its whistle-blowers. At least one was fired. On the question of just how thoroughly the allegations of a second were investigated, the future of one of Houston's most influential law firms may hang.

Class 5 is on the fiduciary duties of managers and directors. Twice the Enron board "waived" the company's own ethics code requirements to allow the company's CFO to serve as general partner of the partnerships that it was using as a conduit for much of its business. The fiduciary duty that is owed is one of good faith and full disclosure. There is no evidence that when Enron's CEO told the employees that the stock would probably rise that he also disclosed he was selling stock. Moreover, the employees could not have learned that he was doing so in a few days because the stock was sold to the company to repay money that the CEO owed Enron. Officer sales of stock to the company qualify as an exception to the ordinary disclosure requirement. Such transactions need not be reported until 45 days after the end of the fiscal year. In relying on this technicality, the Enron CEO cast serious doubt on his claim that he still thought that the stock would increase in value.

The concern with a fiduciary's appearance of impropriety is based upon the fiduciary's role in assuring that the enterprise will observe the spirit and letter of the law. Extra measures of prudence are necessary to ensure that core legal requirements are not violated. The fiduciary's role is to erect and to guard those fences—not to test just how far in from their original position the fences can be moved.

Class 6 is devoted to social responsibility. Enron's social beneficence created intolerable conflicts of interest for its directors. It's generosity enmeshed Enron in controversies with which the company did not have the competence to deal. Even those who are strongly committed to the principle of corporate social responsibility would have difficulty defending Enron's approach to this form of stakeholder relations.

Class 7 deals with moral standards across borders. Any global company needs to sort out the issues regarding the rules of engagement between the company and developing economies. India is a country where Enron was especially active. Enron confronted many issues in this area.

Class 8—control by law—reviews the terms, conditions, and requirements of the U.S. Organizational Sentencing Guidelines. In the interest of "erecting fences round the law," the Guidelines provide incentives in the form of mitigation of primal fines and penalties for companies that have strong compliance programs and can demonstrate that misfeasances were the work of a few rogue actors. Further relief may be available to companies that cooper-

ate in prosecutorial investigations of bad practices. A company whose board waived its own code of ethics to permit a senior officer to serve as a general partner for partnerships that were dealing with the company and which may have shredded documents when a federal investigation was imminent, is not a candidate for sentencing guidelines leniency.

Arthur Andersen's approval of financial statements can't insulate Enron from liability—particularly since the company was the source of the information in the first place.

Class 9 also covers sales ethics in financial markets. Here we might ask whether it was appropriate to engorge the company's 401(k) plan with company stock—particularly in circumstances where the plan's shares were less liquid than the holdings of directors and senior officers.

Class 10 discusses insider trading. It is unlawful for directors, as the Enron chairman was, who have

inside price sensitive information, to trade stock—until the public has had the same information for a time.

Issues of right to privacy, patterns of discrimination and termination, and downsizing have also been raised. When everything goes wrong due to a seismic failure, employees are bound to use these legal rights as vehicles for their grievances.

Enron is a perfect instrument for teaching a course in business ethics. Enron was deemed to be the company of the future, but Enron rejected progressive innovation and sought to circumvent systems that were designed to protect the company and its shareholders and to bolster the credibility of its dealings.

Ronald Berenbeim is director of Global Business Ethics Programs, The Conference Board. This article is adapted from his speech to Members' Briefing, New Delhi, India, and used with permission of Vital Speeches of the Day.

From *Executive Excellence*, June 2002, pp. 12-13. © 2002 by Executive Excellence.

Doing well by doing good

Anti-globalisation protesters see companies as unethical as well as exploitative. Firms demur, of course, but face an awkward question: Does virtue pay?

TO MANY people the very concepts of "business" and "ethics" sit uneasily together. Business ethics, to them, is an oxymoron—or, as an American journalist once put it, "a contradiction in terms, like jumbo shrimp." And yet, in America and other western countries, companies increasingly wonder what constitutes ethical corporate behaviour, and how to get their employees to observe it. Management schools teach courses on the subject to their students. Business ethics is suddenly all the rage.

Fashionable perhaps—but also vague. Protesters in Washington, DC, were this week railing against corporate immorality as well as the IMF. But plenty of people retort that companies should not be in the business of ethics at all—let alone worrying about social responsibility, morals or the environment. If society wants companies to put any of these ahead of the pursuit of shareholder value, then governments should regulate them accordingly. Thirty years ago Milton Friedman, doyen of market economics, summed up this view by arguing that "there is one and only one social responsibility of business—to use its resources and engage in activities designed to increase its profits."

Even those who think companies do have wider responsibilities argue about the best way to pursue them. Ulrich Steger, who teaches environmen-

tal management at the International Institute for Management Development in Lausanne, says that companies cannot possibly hope to pursue a single abstract set of ethical principles and should not try. No universal set of ethical principles exists; most are too woolly to be helpful; and the decisions that companies face every day rarely present themselves as ethics versus economics in any case. He says that companies should aim instead for "responsible shareholder-value optimisation": their first priority should be shareholders' long-term interests, but, within that constraint, they should seek to meet whatever social or environmental goals the public expects of them.

Certainly companies, which increasingly try to include their ethical principles in corporate codes, stumble over how to write in something about the need for profitability. Or, to put the dilemma more crudely: when money and morality clash, what should a company do? Most firms try to resolve this with the consoling belief that such clashes are more imagined than real, and that virtue will pay in the end. Yet they cannot always be right.

Indeed, companies face more ethical quandaries than ever before. Technological change brings new debates, on issues ranging from genetically modified organisms to privacy on the Internet. Globalisation brings companies into contact with

other countries that do business by different rules. Competitive pressures force firms to treat their staff in ways that depart from past practice. Add unprecedented scrutiny from outside, led by non-governmental organisations (NGOs), and it is not surprising that dealing with ethical issues has become part of every manager's job.

Don't lie, don't cheat, don't steal

In America, companies have a special incentive to pursue virtue: the desire to avoid legal penalties. The first attempts to build ethical principles into the corporate bureaucracy began in the defence industry in the mid-1980s, a time when the business was awash with kickbacks and $500 screwdrivers. The first corporate-ethics office was created in 1985 by General Dynamics, which was being investigated by the government for pricing scams. Under pressure from the Defence Department, a group of 60 or so defence companies then launched an initiative to set up guidelines and compliance programmes. In 1991, federal sentencing rules extended the incentive to other industries: judges were empowered to reduce fines in cases involving companies that had rules in place to promote ethical behaviour, and to increase them for those that did not.

But the law is not the only motivator. Fear of embarrassment at the hands of NGOs and the media has given business ethics an even bigger push. Companies have learnt the hard way that they live in a CNN world, in which bad behaviour in one country can be seized on by local campaigners and beamed on the evening television news to customers back home. As non-governmental groups vie with each other for publicity and membership, big companies are especially vulnerable to hostile campaigns.

One victim was Shell, which in 1995 suffered two blows to its reputation: one from its attempted disposal of the Brent Spar oil rig in the North Sea, and the other over the company's failure to oppose the Nigerian government's execution of Ken Saro-Wiwa, a human-rights activist in a part of Nigeria where Shell had extensive operations. Since then, Shell has rewritten its business principles, created an elaborate mechanism to implement them, and worked harder to improve its relations with NGOs.

Remarkably, Shell's efforts had no clear legal or financial pressure behind them. Neither of the 1995 rows, says Robin Aram, the man in charge of Shell's policy development, did lasting damage to the company's share price or sales—although the Brent Spar spat brought a brief dip in its market share in Germany, thanks to a consumer boycott. But, he adds, "we weren't confident that there would be no long-term impact, given the growing interest of the investment community in these softer issues." And he also concedes that there was "a sense of deep discomfort from our own people." People seem happier working for organisations they regard as ethical. In a booming jobs market, that can become a powerful incentive to do the right thing.

The quest for virtue

In America there is now a veritable ethics industry, complete with consultancies, conferences, journals and "corporate conscience" awards. Accountancy firms such as PricewaterhouseCoopers offer to "audit" the ethical performance of companies. Corporate-ethics officers, who barely existed a decade ago, have become *de rigueur*, at least for big companies. The Ethics Officer Association, which began with a dozen members in 1992, has 650 today. As many as one in five big firms has a full-time office devoted to the subject. Some are mighty empires: at United Technologies, for example, Pat Gnazzo presides over an international network of 160 business-ethics officers who distribute a code of ethics, in 24 languages, to people who work for this defence and engineering giant all round the world.

For academic philosophers, once lonely and contemplative creatures, the business ethics boom has been a bonanza. They are employed by companies to run "ethics workshops" and are consulted on thorny moral questions. They also act as expert witnesses in civil lawsuits "where lawyers usually want to be able to tell the judge that their client's behaviour was reasonable. So you are usually working for the defendants. They want absolution," says Kirk Hanson, a professor at Stanford Business School.

Outside America, few companies have an ethics bureaucracy. To some extent, observes IMD's Mr Steger, this reflects the fact that the state and organised labour both still play a bigger part in corporate life. In Germany, for example, workers' councils often deal with issues such as sexual equality, race relations and workers' rights, all of which might be seen as ethical issues in America.

In developing a formal ethics policy, companies usually begin by trying to sum up their philosophy in a code. That alone can raise awkward questions. The chairman of a large British firm recalls how his company secretary (general counsel) decided to draft an ethics code with appropriately lofty standards. "You do realise", said the chairman, "that if we publish this, we will be expected to follow it. Otherwise our staff and customers may ask questions." Dismayed, the lawyer went off to produce something more closely attuned to reality.

Not surprisingly, codes are often too broad to capture the ethical issues that actually confront companies, which range from handling their own staff to big global questions of policy on the environment, bribery and human rights. Some companies use the Internet to try to add precision to general injunctions. Boeing, for instance, tries to guide staff through the whole gamut of moral quandaries, offering an online quiz (with answers) on how to deal with everything from staff who fiddle their expenses on business trips to suppliers who ask for kickbacks.

The best corporate codes, says Robert Solomon of the University of Texas, are those that describe the way everybody in the company already behaves and feels. The worst are those where senior executives mandate a list of principles—especially if they then fail to "walk the talk" themselves. However, he says, "companies debate their values for many months, but they always turn out to have similar lists." There is usually something about integrity; something about respect for the individual; and something about honouring the customer.

The ethical issues that actually create most problems in companies often seem rather mundane to outsiders. Such as? "When an individual who is a wonderful producer and brings in multiple dollars doesn't adhere to the company's values," suggests Mr Gnazzo of United Technologies: in other words, when a company has to decide whether to sack an employee who is productive but naughty. "When an employee who you know is about to be let go is buying a new house, and you're honour-bound not to say anything," says Mr Solomon. "Or, what do you do when your boss lies to you? That's a big one."

Issues such as trust and human relations become harder to handle as companies intrude into the lives of their employees. A company with thousands of employees in South-East Asia has been firing employees who have AIDS, but giving them no explanation. It now wonders whether this is ethical. Several companies in America scan their employees' e-mail for unpleasant or disloyal material, or test them to see if they have been taking drugs. Is that right?

Even more complicated are issues driven by conflicts of interest. Edward Petry, head of the Ethics Officer Association, says the most recent issue taxing his members comes from the fad for Internet flotations. If a company is spinning off a booming e-commerce division, which employees should be allowed on to the lucrative "friends-and-family" list of share buyers?

Indeed, the revolution in communications technologies has created all sorts of new ethical dilemmas—just as technological change in medicine spurred interest in medical ethics in the 1970s. Because it is mainly businesses that develop and spread new technologies, businesses also tend to face the first questions about how to use them. So companies stumble into such questions as data protection and customer privacy. They know more than ever before about their customers' tastes, but few have a clear view on what uses of that knowledge are unethical.

Foreigners are different

Some of the most publicised debates about corporate ethics have been driven by globalisation. When companies operate abroad, they run up against all sorts of new moral issues. And one big problem is that ethical standards differ among countries.

Reams of research, says Denis Collins in an article for the *Journal of Business Ethics*, have been devoted to comparing ethical sensitivities of people from different countries. As most of this work has been North American, it is perhaps not surpris-

ing that it concluded that American business people are more "ethically sensitive" than their counterparts from Greece, Hong Kong, Taiwan, New Zealand, Ukraine and Britain. They were more sensitive than Australians about lavish entertainment and conflicts of interest; than French and Germans over corporate social responsibility; than Chinese in matters of bribery and confidential information; and than Singaporeans on software piracy. Given such moral superiority, it is surprising that American companies seem to turn up in ethical scandals at least as often as those from other rich countries.

Many companies first confronted the moral dilemmas of globalisation when they had to decide whether to meet only local environmental standards, even if these were lower than ones back home. This debate came to public attention with the Bhopal disaster in 1984, when an explosion at a Union Carbide plant in India killed at least 8,000 people. Most large multinationals now have global minimum standards for health, safety and the environment.

These may, however, be hard to enforce. BP Amoco describes in a recent environmental and social report a huge joint venture in inland China. "Concerns remain around the cultural and regulatory differences in risk assessment and open reporting of safety incidents," the report admits. "For instance, deference to older and more senior members of staff has occasionally inhibited open challenging of unsafe practices." BP Amoco thinks it better to stay in the venture and try to raise standards. But Shell claims to have withdrawn from one joint venture because it was dissatisfied with its partner's approach. Most companies rarely talk about these cases, creating the suspicion that such withdrawals are rare.

Bribery and corruption have also been thorny issues. American companies have been bound since 1977 by the Foreign Corrupt Practices Act. Now all OECD countries have agreed to a convention to end bribery. But

many companies turn a blind eye when intermediaries make such payments. Only a few, such as Motorola, have accounting systems that try to spot kickbacks by noting differences between what the customer pays and what a vendor receives.

Some corruption is inevitable, say companies such as Shell, which work in some of the world's nastiest places. "If someone sticks a Kalashnikov through the window of your car and asks for 20 naira, we don't say that you shouldn't pay," says Mr Aram. "We say, it should be recorded." United Technologies' Mr Gnazzo takes a similar view: "We say, employees must report a gift so that everybody can see it's a gift to the company, and we can choose to refuse it. Every year we write to vendors, saying that we don't want gifts, we want good service."

Rights and wrongs

Human rights are a newer and trickier problem. Shell has written a primer on the subject, in consultation with Amnesty International. It agonises over such issues as what companies should do if they have a large investment in a country where human rights deteriorate; and whether companies should operate in countries that forbid outsiders to scrutinise their record on human rights (yes, but only if the company takes no advantage of such secrecy and is a "force for good").

The force-for-good argument also crops up when companies are accused of underpaying workers in poor countries, or of using suppliers who underpay. Such problems arise more often when there are lots of small suppliers. At Nike, a sporting-goods firm, Dusty Kidd, director of labour practices, has to deal with almost 600 supplier-factories around the world. The relationship is delicate: "They are independent businesses, but we take responsibility," says Mr Kidd. When, last year, Nike insisted on a rise in the minimum wage paid by its Indonesian suppliers, it claims to have absorbed much of the cost.

NGOs have berated firms such as Nike for failing to ensure that workers are paid a "living wage". But that can be hard, even in America. "I once asked a university president, do you pay a living wage on your campus?" recalls Mr Kidd. "He said that was different. But it isn't." In developing countries, the dilemma may be even greater: "In Vietnam, our workers are paid more than doctors. What's the social cost if a doctor leaves his practice and goes to work for us? That's starting to happen."

Stung by attacks on their behaviour in the past, companies such as Shell and Nike have begun to see it as part of their corporate mission to raise standards not just within their company, but in the countries where they work. Mr Kidd, for instance, would like Nike's factories to be places where workers' health actually improves, through better education and care, and where the status of women is raised. Such ideals would have sounded familiar to some businessmen of the 19th century: Quaker companies such as Cadbury and Rowntree, for instance, were founded on the principle that a company should improve its workers' health and education. In today's more cynical and competitive world, though, corporate virtue no longer seems a goal in its own right.

When, in the late 1980s, companies devoted lots of effort to worrying about the environment, they told themselves that being clean and green was also a route to being profitable. In the same way, they now hope that virtue will bring financial, as well as spiritual, rewards. Environmental controls can, for instance, often be installed more cheaply than companies expect. Ed Freeman, who teaches ethics at the Darden Business School at the University of Virginia, recalls how the senior executive of a big chemical company announced that he wanted "zero pollution". His engineers were horrified. Three weeks later, they returned to admit that they could end pollution and save money. "The conflict between ethics and business may be a lot less than we think," he argues.

Most academic studies of the association between responsible corporate ethics and profitability suggest that the two will often go together. Researchers have managed to show that more ethically sensitive sales staff perform better (at least in America; the opposite appears to be the case in Taiwan); that share prices decline after reports of unethical conduct; and that companies which state an ethical commitment to stakeholders in their annual reports do better financially. But proving a causal link is well-nigh impossible.

What of the growing band of ethical investors? "I don't know of a single one of these funds which looks at the effectiveness of a company's internal ethics programme," says the EOA's Mr Petry, sadly. So a defence firm scores bad marks for being in a nasty industry, but no offsetting good marks for having an elaborate compliance programme.

And then there is the impact on employees. It may be true that they like working for ethically responsible companies. But, says Stanford's Mr Hanson, "I see a lot of my graduate students leaving jobs in not-for-profits to go and work for dot.coms." Few dot.coms would know a corporate ethics code if it fell on their heads. Small firms, in particular, pay far less attention than bigger rivals to normalising ethical issues and to worrying about their social responsibilities. Yet employment is growing in small companies and falling in big ones.

There may still be two good reasons for companies to worry about their ethical reputation. One is anticipation: bad behaviour, once it stirs up a public fuss, may provoke legislation that companies will find more irksome than self-restraint. The other, more crucial, is trust. A company that is not trusted by its employees, partners and customers will suffer. In an electronic world, where businesses are geographically far from their customers, a reputation for trust may become even more important. Ultimately, though, companies may have to accept that virtue is sometimes its own reward. One of the eternal truths of morality has been that the bad do not always do badly and the good do not always do well.

Reprinted with permission from *The Economist*, April 22, 2000, pp. 65–67. © 2000 by The Economist, Ltd. Distributed by the New York Times Special Features.

Best Resources for Corporate Social Responsibility

RESEARCH BY KAREN McNICHOL

What most of us lack these days isn't data but time. The World Wide Web is a marvelous research tool, but the sheer amount of information available can be overwhelming. How do you weed through it to find the very best sites, where someone has already synthesized masses of material for you? Well, consider the offerings below a garden without the weeds: a selection of the best of the best sites in corporate social responsibility (CSR).

1. Best Practices and Company Profiles

www.bsr.org—This may well be the best CSR site of all. Run by the business membership organization Business for Social Responsibility, its focus is on giving business hands-on guidance in setting up social programs, but data is useful to researchers as well, particularly because of "best practice" examples. Topics include social auditing, community involvement, business ethics, governance, the environment, employee relations, and corporate citizenship. New topics are being researched all the time. One recent report, for example, looked at companies linking executive pay to social performance, while others have looked at how to implement flexible scheduling, or become an "employer of choice." Visitors can create their own printer-friendly custom report on each topic, selecting from sections like Business Importance, Recent Developments, Implementation Steps, Best Practices, and Links to Helping Resources. To receive notices about updates, plus other CSR news, subscribe to BSR Resource Center Newsletter by sending a message to centerupdates@bsr.org with "subscribe" in the subject line.

www.ebnsc.org—You might call this the BSR site from Europe. It is sponsored by Corporate Social Responsibility Europe, whose mission is to help put CSR into the mainstream of business. This site includes a databank of best practices from all over Europe on topics like human rights, cause-related marketing, ethical principles, and community involvement. To give just one example of the site's capability, a search on the topic "reporting on CSR" came up with a dozen news articles available in full, plus a case study, and a list of 20 books and reports on the topic. One unique feature is the "CSR Matrix," which allows visitors to call up a complete social report on companies like IBM, Levi Strauss, or Procter & Gamble. The "matrix" is a grid, where the visitor clicks on one box to view the company's code of conduct, another box to see how the company interacts with public stakeholders, a third box to access the company's sustainability report, and so forth.

www.worldcsr.com is a World CSR portal offering one-stop access to the leading business-led organizations on corporate social responsibility in Europe and the U.S., including the two sites mentioned above. Another site on the portal—www.businessimpact.org—offers a useful databank of links to related organizations, such as the Global Reporting Initiative, Institute for Global Ethics, and World Business Council for Sustainable Development. Readers can also subscribe to the Business Impact News e-mail newsletter.

www.responsibleshopper.org For individuals wishing to shop with or research responsible companies, Responsible Shopper from Co-op America offers in-depth social profiles on countless companies. A report on IBM, for example, looks at everything from Superfund sites, toxic emissions, and worker benefits to laudatory activities. Different brand names for each company are listed, and social performance is summarized in letter ratings—as with IBM, which got an "A" in Disclosure, and a "B" in the Environment.

quite small, particularly in the early years. Yet, during this period, anti-abortion groups would mount an international boycott of products made by Roussel-Uclaf and Hoechst, the German chemical giant that was Roussel-Uclaf's largest shareholder. A successful boycott would cost the two companies far more than they would earn from RU 486. At worst, a boycott could imperil Roussel-Uclaf's survival, for it was a relatively small company with weak profits.

Like any executive, Dr. Sakiz also had responsibilities for the people in his company. He had to assess the seriousness of the threats of violence against Roussel-Uclaf and its employees.

At a personal level, Dr. Sakiz faced a version of the question, Who am I? Was he, first and foremost, a medical doctor, a scientific researcher, an advocate of women's rights, or a corporate executive with responsibilities to shareholders and employees? In addition, his decision on RU 486 would commit his company to some values rather than others, thereby answering the organizational question, Who are we?

The prospect of introducing RU 486 placed Dr. Sakiz at the center of a network of responsibilities to important groups and institutions outside Roussel-Uclaf. Among these were the French Government, which owned 36 percent of Roussel-Uclaf, and the French Ministry of Health, which closely regulated the company, thus shaping its business opportunities.

Hoechst, which owned 55 percent of Roussel-Uclaf, also made strong ethical claims on the company. Its chairman was a devout Roman Catholic, who opposed abortion on moral grounds and had repeatedly stated his position in public. Moreover, Hoechst had a mission statement committing the company to lofty goals, which was put in place partly in reaction to its role in producing a poison gas used at Auschwitz.

China was another powerful actor in the drama. It wanted access to RU 486 for population control. The moral ground for China's position was avoiding the misery and risks of starvation resulting from its surging population.

Roussel-Uclaf's network of relationships and responsibilities raised extremely difficult questions for Dr. Sakiz and his company. What, in fact, were the company's obligations to women? To the Government laboratory that helped develop the steroid molecule on which RU 486 was based? To the larger medical and research communities? Were the unborn a stakeholder group? Could Roussel-Uclaf introduce the drug both in the West, citing a woman's right to choose, and in China, where women had apparently been coerced into abortions, even near the end of their pregnancies?

Dr. Sakiz's decision would define his company's role in society and its relationships with stakeholders. Everyone was watching him intently because his actions would be decisive, for RU 486 and for the company. In addition, he would be revealing, testing and in some ways shaping his own ethics. In short, Dr. Sakiz also had to make a personal choice that would become an important part of his life and career.

In late October 1988, a month after the French Government approved RU 486, Dr. Sakiz met with the executive committee of Roussel-Uclaf. Dr. Sakiz asked for a discussion of RU 486. After several hours, he called for a vote. When he raised his own hand in favor of suspending distribution of RU 486, it was clear that the pill was doomed.

The company's decision, and Dr. Sakiz's role in it, sparked astonishment and anger. The company and its leadership, some critics charged, had doomed a promising public health tool and set an example of cowardice. Other critics suggested sarcastically that the decision was no surprise, because Roussel-Uclaf had decided, in the face of controversy

during the 1960's, not to produce contraceptive pills.

Three days after Roussel-Uclaf announced that it would suspend distribution, the French Minister of Health summoned the company's vice chairman to his office and said that if it did not resume distribution, the Government would transfer the patent to a company that would. After the meeting, Roussel-Uclaf announced that it would distribute RU 486 after all.

These events suggest that the RU 486 episode was something considerably less than a profile in courage. Edouard Sakiz seemed to have protected his job by sacrificing his convictions. There was, to be sure, strong opposition to RU 486, both inside and outside the company, but Dr. Sakiz made no effort to mobilize and lead his allies. He gave up without a fight. At a defining moment for the company, Dr. Sakiz's message seemed to place political caution and returns to shareholders above research and "the service of Life," as the company's mission statement put it.

But the surprising reversal of Roussel-Uclaf's original decision caused suspicion among some observers, who began to ask whether Dr. Sakiz had figured out a way to get what he wanted with a minimum of damage to himself and his company. Indeed, some wondered if the company and the Government had choreographed the entire episode. Others noted that Government science and health officials and Roussel-Uclaf managers and researchers had worked together for years—on RU 486, on other products and on many other regulatory issues—making it easy for them to anticipate each other's reactions.

What had Dr. Sakiz accomplished? More specifically, had he protected and advanced his own position? Had he contributed to the strength and security of his company? And had he defined its role in society in a creative way?

In personal terms, Dr. Sakiz succeeded in making good on his own

Defining Moments:
WHEN MANAGERS MUST CHOOSE BETWEEN
RIGHT and RIGHT

By Joseph L. Badaracco Jr.

THOUGHTFUL MANAGERS SOME-times face business problems that raise difficult, deeply personal questions. In these situations, managers find themselves wondering: Do I have to leave some of my values at home when I go to work? How much of myself—and of what I really care about—do I have to sacrifice to get ahead? When I get to the office, who am I?

Difficult questions like these are often matters of right versus right, not right versus wrong. Sometimes, a manager faces a tough problem and must choose between two ways of resolving it. Each alternative is the right thing to do, but there is no way to do both. There are three basic types of right-versus-right problems: those that raise questions about personal integrity and moral identity; conflicts between responsibilities for others and important personal values; and, perhaps the most challenging, those involving responsibilities that a company shares with other groups in society.

Most companies are now enmeshed in networks of ongoing rela-tionships. Strategic alliances link organizations with their customers and suppliers, and even competitors. Many companies also have compli-cated dealings with the media, govern-ment regulators, local communities and various interest groups. These networks of relationships are also networks of managerial responsibil-ity. Taken together, a company's business partners and stakeholders have a wide range of legitimate claims, but no company can satisfy all of them. At times, stakeholder re-sponsibilities conflict with managers' personal and organizational obliga-tions. When these conflicts occur, managers confront this third type of right-versus-right problem.

A particularly stark example of this occurred in the pharmaceutical industry nearly a decade ago. Late in 1988, the senior management of Paris-based Roussel-Uclaf had to de-cide where and how to market a new drug, called RU 486. Early tests had shown that the drug was 90 to 95 percent effective in causing a miscar-riage during the first five weeks of pregnancy. The drug came to be known as "the French abortion pill," and Roussel-Uclaf and its managers found themselves at the vortex of the abortion controversy.

The chairman of Roussel-Uclaf, Edouard Sakiz, was a physician with a longstanding personal commit-ment to RU 486. He would make the final decisions on introducing the drug. Earlier in his career, while working as a medical researcher, Dr. Sakiz had helped develop the chem-ical compound on which RU 486 was based. He believed strongly that the drug could help thousands of women, particularly in poor coun-tries, avoid injury or death from botched abortions. In the developed world, he believed, RU 486 would provide women and physicians with a valuable alternative to surgical abortions.

But Dr. Sakiz couldn't base his decision on RU 486 solely on his personal values. As the head of a company, he had other important obligations. Some were to his share-holders; from this perspective, RU 486 was a serious problem. Reve-nues from the drug were likely to be

www.worldcsr.com offers one-stop access to the leading business-led organizations on corporate social responsibility in Europe and the U.S.

2. Social Investing

www.socialfunds.com—Run by SRI World Group, Social Funds is the best social investing site on the web. A staff of reporters researchers breaking news and posts it without charge. For socially responsible mutual funds, the site offers performance statistics plus fund descriptions. There's an investing center where you can build your own basket of social companies, plus a community banking center with information on savings accounts and money market funds with responsible banking organizations. A shareholder activism section offers a status report on social resolutions and is searchable by topic (equality, tobacco, militarism, etc.). Also available is a free weekly e-mail newsletter, SRI News Alert—which goes beyond social investing. One recent issue, for example, looked at new labeling programs for clean-air office construction, an Arctic Wildlife Refuge resolution against BP Amoco, and why greener multinationals have higher market value. A new service from SRI World Group, offered jointly with Innovest Strategic Advisors, offers subscribers ($100 annually) ratings of companies in various industries, based on environmental and financial performance.

www.socialinvest.org—This is the site of the nonprofit professional membership association, the Social Investment Forum, and is a useful pair to the above site. One unique feature is the collection of Moskowitz Prize-winning papers on research in social investing. The 2000 winner, for example, was "Pure Profit: The Financial Implications of Environmental Performance." Also available is a directory to help visitors find a financial adviser anywhere in the country; a mutual funds chart; a guide to community investing (showing resources by state and by type); and materials on SIF's campaign to end predatory

lending. You can also access the Shareholder Action Network-which shows how to submit shareholder resolutions, and offers information on both current campaigns and past successes.

www.goodmoney.com.—Offering some unique investing features of its own is the Good Money site, which showcases the Good Money Industrial Average: a screened index which outperformed the Dow in 2000. Also available are social profiles and performance data for a variety of public companies—including the 400 companies in the Domini Social Index, companies with the best diversity record, the Council on Economic Priorities "honor roll" list, and signers of the CERES Principles (a voluntary environmental code of conduct). Another section on Eco Travel has dozens of links and articles.

3. Corporate Watchdogs

www.corpwatch.org—For activists, this may be the best site of all. Calling itself "The Watchdog on the Web," Corp-Watch offers news you may not find elsewhere on human rights abuses abroad, public policy; and environmental news—plus on-site reporting of protests. Its director Josh Karliner was nominated by Alternet.org (an alternative news service) as a Media Hero 2000, for using the web to fight the excesses of corporate globalization. CorpWatch puts out the bimonthly Greenwash Awards, and runs a Climate Justice Initiative, as well as the Alliance for a Corporate-Free UN. An Issue Library covers topics like the WTO and sweatshops, while the Hands-on Guide to On-line Corporate Research is useful for research ideas. A free twice-monthly e-mail newsletter updates readers on recent Corp-Watch headlines. One recent issue of "What's New on Corp-Watch" looked at topics like the World Bank's record, the

For activists, www.corpwatch.org may be the best site of all.

protests at the World Economic Forum, California's deregulation troubles, plus the regular "Take Action" feature urging readers to send e-mails or faxes on a specific issue. To subscribe to the e-letter, send blank message to corp-watchers-subscribe @igc.topica.com.

www.corporatepredators.org—Featuring Russell Mokhiber, editor of the weekly newsletter *Corporate Crime Reporter*, this site offers a compilation of weekly e-mail columns called "Focus on the Corporation," written by Mokhiber and Robert Weissman. They offer a valuable, quirky voice in corporate responsibility. Taking on topics not covered elsewhere, the columns have looked at how the chemical industry responded to Bill Moyers TV program on industry coverup, how little academic research focuses on corporate crime, and why it's inappropriate to legally view corporations as "persons." At this site (which also features the book *Corporate Predators* by Mokhiber and Weissman), readers can access weekly columns back through 1998. Subscribe free to the column by sending an e-mail message to corp-focus-request@lists.essential.org with the text "subscribe."

4. Labor and Human Rights

http://oracle02.ilo.org/vpi/welcome—Sponsored by the International Labor Organization, this web site offers a new Business and Social Initiatives Database, compiling Internet sources on employment and labor issues. It covers topics like child labor, living wage, dismissal, investment screens, monitoring, international labor standards, glass ceilings, safe work, and so forth. It features information on corporate policies and reports, codes of conduct, certification criteria, labeling and other programs. A search feature allows visitors to retrieve information on specific companies, regions, and business sectors. This is one of the most comprehensive labor sites out there.

www.summersault.com/~agj/clr/—Sponsored by the Campaign for Labor Rights, this site keeps activists up to date on anti-sweatshop struggles and other pro-labor activities around the world. Particularly useful is the free e-mail newsletter Labor Alerts, which updates readers on recent news about trade treaties, plant shutdowns, labor organizing, job postings, upcoming protests, recent books, and so forth. One recent issue contained a "webliography" of sites about the pending creation of the Free

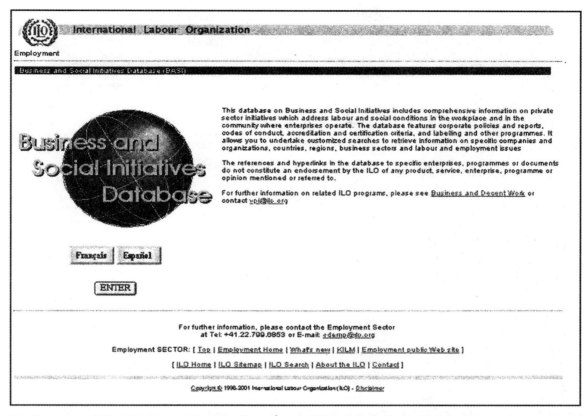

The Business and Social Initiatives Database (http://oracle02.ilo.org/vpi/welcome) is one of the most comprehensive labor compilations out there.

Trade Area of the Americas (FTAA). To subscribe contact clrmain@afgj.org.

5. Progressive Economics

www.epn.org—For the best thinking in progressive economic policy, this site managed by *The American Prospect* magazine is a one-stop source. It's the Electronic Policy Network, an on-line consortium of over 100 progressive policy centers nationwide, like the Center for Public Integrity, the Brookings Institution, the Financial Markets Center, and many more. (The focus of member groups is heavily though not exclusively economic.) A feature called Idea Central offers online bibliographies on topics like globalization, poverty, and livable cities. Certain topics get "Issues in Depth" treatment: One, for example, looks at campaign finance reform—including history, alternatives, and legal background, with numerous links to sites like a database of soft-money contribution, research from the Center for Responsive Politics, ACLU factsheets, and more. Another feature, "What's New," looks at recent reports and research papers by member policy centers—like a recent report from the Economic Policy Institute on privatization, or a report on state initiatives for children from the National Center for Children in Poverty. Readers can receive summaries of new research reports by subscribing to the e-mail EPN News; send an e-mail to majordomo@epn.org with "subscribe epnnews" in the message body.

www.neweconomics.org—This valuable site is run by The New Economics Foundation (NEF), a UK nonprofit think tank created in 1986 to focus on "constructing a new economy centered on people and the environment." Different areas on the site focus on powerful tools for economic change, like alternative currencies, social investment, indicators for sustainability, and social accounting. A monthly web-based newsletter reports on topics like Jubilee 2000 (the movement to cancel the debt of developing nations), May Day plans, an "indicator of the month," and more. A new bimonthly e-briefing is called "mergerwatch," which looks at the hidden costs behind mergers, and who pays the price. Its first issue in April 2001 reported, for example, that a 1999 KPMG study showed 53 percent of mergers destroy shareholder value, and a further 30 percent bring no measurable benefit.

6. Employee Ownership

http://cog.kent.edu—For researchers in employee ownership, the Capital Ownership Group site is indispensable. COG is a virtual think tank of individuals—including academics, employee ownership specialists, and business leaders worldwide—who aim to promote broadened ownership of productive capital. The site's library allows visitors to browse ongoing discussions, on topics like promoting employee ownership globally, getting economists more involved in issues of capital ownership, the role of labor in employee ownership, and more. The library of-

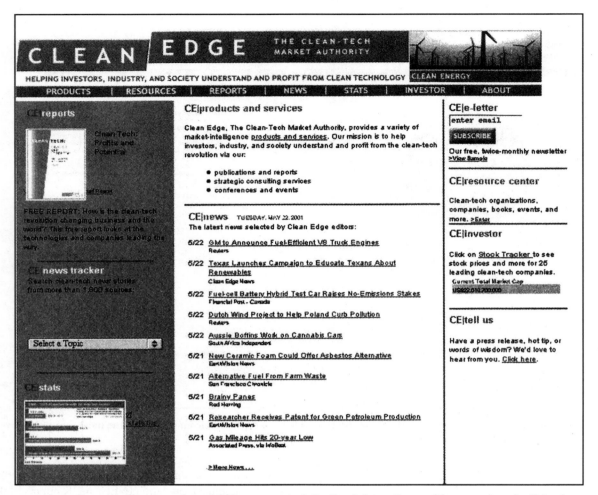

www.cleanedge.com offers news from 1,800 sources, stock trading information on 25 companies, plus lists of conferences, trade associations and research centers.

fers hundreds of papers and research reports, on topics like labor-sponsored venture capital, employee governance, case studies, and much more.

www.nceo.org—This is the site of the National Center for Employee Ownership, a nonprofit research and membership organization that is one of the best sources for employee ownership information. Its web library features a valuable introduction to the history of Employee Stock Ownership Plans (ESOPs), plus information on open book management, stock options, and alternatives to ESOPs. An "Interactive Introduction to ESOPs" lets visitors "chat" with an expert in the same way as if they spent fifteen minutes on the phone with a lawyer. Also available are a wealth of links to related sites, plus news and statistics on employee ownership.

www.fed.org—The sponsor of this site is the Foundation for Enterprise Development—a nonprofit started by Robert Beyster, founder of employee-owned SAIC—which is an organization that aims to promote employee ownership. Its focus is not ESOPs but stock options and other forms of equity ownership. A monthly online magazine features profiles of employee ownership at specific companies, articles on developing an owner-ship culture, plus news. An e-mail service updates readers on headlines.

www.the-esop-emplowner.org—From the ESOP Association—a membership and lobbying organization—this site offers a resource library, news of events, reports on legislative victories, and information on legislative initiatives. The site also offers information on the ESOP Association's political action committee, which since 1988 has helped candidates for federal office who support ESOPs and ESOP law.

7. Sustainability

www.GreenBiz.com—Run by Joel Makower, editor of *The Green Business Letter*, Green Biz is the best site on progressive environmental business activities. It enables visitors to discover what companies are doing, and to access citations of countless web resources and reports, on topics like sustainable management, green auditing, EPA programs, pending legislation, clean technologies, recycling, and all things green. A new service features free job listing for environmental professionals. Get regular updates from a free e-mail newsletter, GreenBiz, published every other week.

www.rprogress.org—Run by the nonprofit Redefining Progress—which produces the Genuine Progress Indicator (as a counterpoint to GDP)—this site offers news on topics like climate change, forest-land protection, tax reform, and congressional influence peddling. Recent stories featured a proposal to promote market-based policies for reducing sprawl, a better way to return the government surplus, plus a look at Living Planet 2000—calculating the ecological footprints of the world's largest 150 countries. Numerous studies on environmental justice, tax fairness, and community indicators are available, plus links to other climate change sites.

www.sustainablebusienss.com—The monthly on-line magazine Sustainable Business offers news on the "green economy," covering recycling, product take-back, legislative developments, and so forth. Other features are a database of "Green Dream Job" openings; plus a section to help green businesses find venture capital. A library features web sites, reports, and books.

www.cleanedgess.com—The new organization Clean Edge focuses on helping investors, industry, and society understand and profit from clean technology, like wind, solar, energy efficiency, and alternative fuels. The site offers news from 1,800 sources, stock trading information on 25 companies, plus lists of conferences, trade associations and research centers. The group's premier publication, "Clean Tech: Profits and Potential," reports that clean energy technologies will grow from less than $7 billion today to $82 billion by 2010.

8. Ethics

www.depaul.edu/ethics—Sponsored by the Institute for Business and Professional Ethics at DePaul University, this site offers a large compilation of ethics resources on the web, categorized by topic; educational resources for teachers and trainers, including syllabi; faculty position announcements; calls for papers; a calendar of events; a list of other ethics institutes, and much more.

www.ethics.ubc.ca—From the Center for Applied Ethics at the University of British Columbia in Canada, this site offers a particularly valuable compilation about ethics codes—featuring sample codes, guidance on writing a code, plus books and articles on the topic. Other features are links to ethics institutes, consultants, course materials, publications, and collections of articles.

www.ethics.org/businessethics.html—Sponsored by the **Ethics Resource Center**, this site features valuable data from several business ethics surveys 1994–2000, information on character education for youth, a compendium of codes (coming soon), plus links to many ethics centers and organizations. A research bibliography covers topics like measuring success in an ethics program, or ethics in a global economy. And a provocative "Ethics Quick Test" can be taken on-line, with results available by e-mail.

Reprinted with permission from *Business Ethics*, Summer 2001, pp. 16-18. © 2001 by Business Ethics, PO Box 8439, Minneapolis, MN 55408 (612) 879-0695.

UNIT 2
Ethical Issues and Dilemmas in the Workplace

Unit Selections

Key Points to Consider

- What ethical dilemmas do managers face most frequently? What ethical dilemmas do employees face most often?

- What forms of gender and minority discrimination are most prevalent in today's workplace? In what particular job situations or occupations is discrimination more widespread and conspicuous? Why?

- Whistle-blowing occurs when an employee discloses illegal, immoral, or illegitimate organizational practices or activities. Under what circumstances do you believe whistle-blowing is appropriate? Why?

- Given the complexities of an organization, where an ethical dilemma often cannot be optimally resolved by one person alone, how can an individual secure the support of the group and help it to reach a consensus as to the appropriate resolution of the dilemma?

 **Links: www.dushkin.com/online/**
These sites are annotated in the World Wide Web pages.

American Psychological Association
   http://www.apa.org/books/homepage.html

Annenberg Washington Program in Communications Policy Studies of Northwestern University
   http://www.annenberg.nwu.edu/pubs/downside/

Fortune
   http://www.pathfinder.com/fortune/bestcompanies/intro.html

International Labour Organization (ILO)
   http://www.ilo.org

What You Can Do in Your Workplace
   http://www.connectforkids.org/info-url1564/info-url_list.htm?section=Workplace

LaRue Tone Hosmer, in *The Ethics of Management,* lucidly states that ethical problems in business are truly managerial dilemmas because they represent a conflict, or at least the possibility of a conflict, between the *economic performance* of an organization and its *social performance.* Whereas the economic performance is measured by revenues, costs, and profits, the social performance is judged by the fulfillment of obligations to persons both within and outside the organization.

Units 2 to 4 discuss some of the critical ethical dilemmas that management faces in making decisions in the workplace, in the marketplace, and within the global society. This unit focuses on the relationships and obligations of employers and employees to each other.

Organizational decision makers are ethical when they act with equity, fairness, and impartiality, treating with respect the rights of their employees. An organization's hiring and firing practices, treatment of women and minorities, allowance of employees' privacy, and wages and working conditions are areas in which it has ethical responsibilities.

The employee also has ethical obligations in his or her relationship to the employer. A conflict of interest can occur when an employee allows a gratuity or favor to sway him or her in selecting a contract or purchasing a piece of equipment, making a choice that may not be in the best interests of the organization. Other possible ethical dilemmas for employees include espionage and the betrayal of secrets (especially to competitors), the theft of equipment, and the abuse of expense accounts.

The articles in this unit are broken down into seven sections representing various types of ethical dilemmas in the workplace. The initial article in this first section analyzes the debate over Internet monitoring in the workplace. "Cut Loose" discloses some sad examples of how some companies have tricked retiring employees out of their health benefits.

In the subsection entitled *Organizational Misconduct and Crime,* two articles explore white-collar crime and disclose that the government has awarded billions of dollars to companies that have repeatedly broken the law.

The two selections under *Sexual Treatment of Employees* take a close look at how women are treated in the workplace and how recent court decisions are attempting to clarify sexual harassment.

The two readings in the *Discriminicial and Prejudicial Employment Practices* section scrutinize racism and ageism in the workplace and explore the importance of using diversity as a unifying force in the work environment.

In the next subsection, *Downsizing of the Work Force,* two articles suggest the importance of management's seriously thinking about the specific reasons for considering layoffs, creative alternatives to downsizing, ways to handle terminations with dignity, and possible strategies to be used in assisting survivors of downsizings.

The first selection included under the heading *Whistle-Blowing in the Organization* analyzes the ethical dilemma and possible ramifications of whistle-blowing. The second article describes whistle-blowing in Japan, which often leads to retaliation, but may be changing.

The article "Where Do You Draw the Line?," which opens the last subsection of *Handling Ethical Dilemmas at Work,* offers possible approaches to some ethical dilemmas supply managers face. The next article provides a case presenting the dilemma an editor faces in regard to running a story that could have a costly aftermath. "Leaders as Value Shapers" delineates the importance of managers fully understanding their values as they face serious ethical dilemmas at work. "The Parable of the Sadhu" presents a real-world ethical dilemma for the reader to ponder.

HR Must Know
When Employee Surveillance Crosses the Line

The debate over Internet monitoring at work rages on, and HR not only must know the issues, but should be part of the decisions on whether (and how) to monitor.

By Eilene Zimmerman

John Fox is a senior technical analyst at Sapphire Technologies, an IT placement firm in Woburn, Massachusetts. He's the man to call when the server is down, the network fails, or the system crashes. He's also the guy to call if someone at the company is sending harassing e-mails or viewing porn sites.

Fox is Sapphire's tech-enabled Big Brother. A year and a half ago, the company installed both e-mail and Internet monitoring systems from Elron Software in Burlington, Massachusetts. The e-mail product, Message Inspector, is set up using triggers—certain words, video files, or attachments—that, when detected, forward the message immediately to Fox for review. The Web component of the monitoring system automatically blocks graphically explicit sites, and if an employee tries to go to a blocked site, Fox is notified. Using parameters given to him by human resources, essentially to block hardcore porn and violence sites, Fox can veto the block, which sometimes occurs automatically because a certain word, say "naked," appears on a Web page too many times.

The majority—57 percent—of U.S. companies now monitor their employees' e-mail and Internet use, according to IDC, a technology research and analysis firm in Framing-

ham, Massachusetts. And the number is expected to rise substantially in the next couple of years. Large companies are more likely to monitor their employees than small ones: at the end of 2001, 70 percent of firms with 1,000 or more employees had implemented electronic monitoring systems. For companies of any size, the decision on whether or not to read an employee's e-mail and monitor his or her Internet activity is highly emotional and intensely controversial.

Employers say they monitor to increase productivity and to protect themselves from potentially disastrous computer viruses, harassment lawsuits, and leaks of confidential information to competitors. An IDC survey conducted in the fall of 2001 reports that 48 percent of the employers who monitor employees say that their intention is to protect against viruses and the loss of information; 21 percent as a way to limit legal liability.

Many employees, privacy rights experts, and workers' rights advocates, however, are angered and offended by the monitoring trend. They argue that privacy is a guaranteed human right—at home and at work. They say workplace monitoring is an unnecessary infringement on that right. A recent Privacy Foundation study found that 14 million U.S. workers are already subject

to continuous monitoring while online. The nonprofit Denver-based organization studies communications, technologies, and services that may pose a threat to privacy.

Lewis Maltby, president of The National Workrights Institute Inc., in Princeton, New Jersey, says the most frequent complaint his organization hears from workers is that employers don't distinguish between personal and workplace communications. "They look at everything," he says.

George Baroudi is vigorously opposed to the use of electronic monitoring. He is chief technology officer and an Internet security expert at iLabyrinth, a company that develops network security systems headquartered in Hockessin, Delaware. "The Internet is a tool for learning, not a way to invade privacy," he says. "Just as the United States Postal Service is permitted to deliver your mail but not open it, e-mail is the property of the recipient, not the message carrier."

Proponents of monitoring challenge that point of view, and insist that they are only looking at e-mails that signal a problem—such as sexual harassment or a predilection for child porn, and are not endorsing personal snoop squads.

Composing Risk-Free E-mails

TOOLS

One of the easiest and most effective ways for employers to reduce electronic risk is simply to require that employees use appropriate, businesslike language in all electronic communications, says Nancy Flynn, author of *The ePolicy Handbook* (AMACOM, 2001).

Here are some of the guidelines she recommends in composing a business e-mail:

• **Use a conversational tone.** Flynn says to imagine you are attending a dinner party with colleagues, supervisors, and customers. Use the same language and tone in an e-mail that you would use at that kind of event.

• **Don't be overly rigid with grammar use.** In business the rules have changed. Feel free to use contractions, to end sentences with prepositions, and to use pronouns like I, we, and you. If grammar is too stiff, readers won't know what the message is about.

• **No sexist language.** This isn't just harassing or discriminatory jokes and comments, but also the overuse of masculine pronouns. Given the increasing number of women in the workforce, it's important for electronic writers to avoid language that could rankle clients or colleagues.

• **Don't incorporate jokes into electronic business writing.** Because e-mail is impersonal and lacks inflection or body language, your joke is likely to fall flat or to be misconstrued.

• **Limit the use of abbreviations** and use only legitimate and recognizable ones, not your own personal shorthand. An excess of abbreviations can be annoying and confusing for the reader.

• **Don't try to warm up business writing with "smileys"**—also known as emoticons—using keyboard characters to represent smiles and similar facial expressions. Smileys are the equivalent of e-mail slang and have no place in business communications.

• **If you have trouble getting employees to adhere to a business writing standard,** you can always apply a technological solution to the problem, Flynn says, by installing software programmed to detect and report the use of "trigger" words in e-mails sent by employees. That software can usually be programmed to track competitors' names as well, alerting management to communication that is taking place between employees and the company's competition.

For many corporate decision-makers, a potential violation of privacy rights and the possibility of stunting creativity are minor concerns compared to the advantages of monitoring. That's why the market for monitoring and filtering software is growing by about 36 percent a year, and revenue in the industry is expected to triple in the next three years, according to IDC.

Although companies have different reasons for monitoring, Fox says Sapphire began the practice as a way of preventing potential legal problems. If one employee makes allegations about another employee's behavior, for example, checking e-mail correspondences can substantiate the charge.

Fox notes that, despite company warnings, three people at Sapphire have been fired for spending time surfing adult-oriented Web sites. The company reminds its 350 employees that they are being monitored each time they log on to the network. Fox says that no one has quit because of the monitoring, and that he has heard only a few complaints from employees about violations of privacy rights. "Generally, people know that if they aren't doing anything wrong, they have nothing to worry about."

Bart Lazar, a partner in the high-tech group at the Seyfarth Shaw law firm in Chicago, says smart employers do monitor e-mail and Internet use in "some way, shape, or form." Lazar was lead counsel for GeoCities in 1998 in the country's first Internet privacy suit. The Federal Trade Commission sued GeoCities, arguing that the company took consumer information collected on its Web site and disclosed that information to a direct mail marketing company. (GeoCities eventually settled with the FTC.)

Lazar advises his clients—which include Fortune 1000 companies in the financial services, high- and low-tech manufacturing, media and education industries—to use filtering or monitoring systems. Many do, largely to protect computer systems from viruses and junk e-mails, some of which could be offensive to certain employees, prompting hostile-work-environment lawsuits.

Employers also use monitoring to protect trade secrets and prevent other proprietary information from getting out. "Suppose you're a loyal employee in a chat room on the Internet and you see someone bashing the company's profits," Lazar notes. "The employee sends a message saying, 'No, you're wrong. In fact, we're about to announce our best quarter ever.' Well-intentioned sure, but what they did is illegal."

"If you find that someone who never works after 6 p.m. is suddenly showing up at the office in the middle of the night and going online, that should raise eyebrows."

Nancy Flynn, founder of the ePolicy Institute in Columbus, Ohio, and author of *The ePolicy Handbook* (AMACOM, 2001), says a company can also set up its monitoring system to alert management to suspicious behavior. "If you find that someone who never works after 6 p.m. is suddenly showing up at the office in the middle of the night and going online, that should raise eyebrows. Why is this employee online? Is she downloading proprietary information?"

Even if employees aren't conversing in chat rooms, leaking trade secrets, or furtively looking at porn, they may be active recreational surfers, day traders, or radio listeners who are wasting a lot of company time and bandwidth.

Judi Epstein, product manager for iPrism, an Internet monitoring and blocking system from St. Bernard Software in San Diego, says her clients typically find that an employee goes online for business purposes and then gets unintentionally sidetracked, sometimes for a few hours. "At other times it is intentional," Epstein says. "At my last job, I worked with a woman who ran a side business on eBay Inc. while at the office—eight hours a day."

For all of the pros and cons, knowing what electronic monitoring systems cost and how much money they save is an obvious concern. But is it possible to figure out the ROI of monitoring software?

Vendors such as iPrism say yes. Companies use gains in productivity to calcu-

Essentials of Internet and E-mail Monitoring Policies
TOOLS

Businesses throughout the country are clamoring for electronic-monitoring software, but the biggest mistake they make in implementing the technology is not having a policy to back it up.

"The cleanest approach is to notify employees up front, put the policy in the handbook, and keep records of how often you remind employees they are being monitored," says attorney Wayne Hersh, a partner specializing in labor and employment law at Berger Kahn in Irvine, California. "Employees have a much harder time suing successfully for violated privacy rights if they've been notified."

Nancy Flynn, author of *The ePolicy Handbook* (AMACOM, 2001) and founder of the ePolicy Institute in Columbus, Ohio, agrees, and adds that employers must have a training program in place to educate employees about electronic liabilities and the importance of compliance. "The only way to reduce workplace risk is through training. You can't expect all of your employees to understand and comply with policies without an ongoing training program," Flynn says.

Here are some guidelines to follow in establishing electronic-monitoring policies:

• **Ban e-mail language that could negatively affect your organization's business relationships,** damage your corporate reputation, or trigger a lawsuit. Ban sexist or racist language; ban jokes. Employees should try to keep e-mail language gender-neutral.

• **Include corporate guidelines such as how you want employees to refer to the company,** how to sign off, and what kinds of salutations to use. Banish emoticons. That kind of visual shorthand has no place in business writing.

• **Ban inappropriate Web sites**—usually those that are sexually explicit or violent, or contain otherwise objectionable images or language.

• **To conserve bandwidth, outlaw Net surfing for personal information,** gameplaying online, chat rooms, gambling, shopping, and any other electronic activity not directly related to professional duties. (Many employers do allow some personal use of the Web during lunchtime.)

• **Prohibit employees from posting or transmitting material that is obscene,** hateful, harmful, malicious, threatening, hostile, abusive, vulgar, defamatory, profane, or racially, sexually, or ethnically objectionable.

late the ROI, Epstein says. iPrism's software, for example, costs about $20 per employee per year, or about a nickel a day. Websense, a provider of Internet blocking and monitoring software located in San Diego, cites the same cost for its product. Vice president of marketing Andrew Meyer says the firm's research shows that the average employee spends about three hours a week on personal surfing. If monitoring helps cut that wasted time down to one hour, and the average employee earns about $20 per hour, the investment in Websense is paid back in a week.

Epstein is, of course, an advocate of monitoring. Still, she says the majority of workers who use the Internet are not overtly malicious. Most of iPrism's clients still allow their employees a lot of latitude in using the Internet, she says.

Even the most vociferous proponents of corporate snooping agree that the rules and morality now governing electronic monitoring are far from clear. Bruce Kasanoff, a former partner at marketing consultancy Peppers and Rogers Group and author of *Making It Personal* (Perseus, 2001), finds electronic monitoring frightening. His book discusses how technology enables companies to play Big Brother.

He is concerned not only about what companies are doing today, but also about what they will be able to do in the very near future. In the next year or two, states will

begin implementing a system called e911, which will require cell phones to send the location of a call to their phone-service carrier. Pinpointing the location of a cell phone user in the event of an emergency could save lives, but the technology could be used for more ominous purposes.

"Today companies read what you write in e-mails, where you go on the Web," Kasanoff says. "Two years from now they will be able to track, for example, where their salespeople go and what they do. Where will it end?"

Many of these same concerns are receiving a great deal of attention in boardrooms and courtrooms. In May, Federal Appeals Court Judge Alex Kozinski and other judges ordered the shutdown of software that tracked the online activities of all employees in the Ninth Circuit Court of Appeals. In an open letter to federal judges published in the *Wall Street Journal* on September 4th, Kozinski likened the monitoring of judiciary employees to the treatment that prison inmates receive. "The proposed policy tells our 30,000 dedicated employees that we trust them so little we must monitor all their communications... How did we get to the point of even considering such a draconian policy?"

In September, the Judicial Conference of the United States, which sets policy for the courts, approved a revised version of the monitoring program, allowing only

limited tracking of Web surfing and no e-mail monitoring.

Chris Hoofnagle, legislative counsel for the Electronic Privacy Information Center in Washington D.C., hopes that because the judges themselves want privacy, they will be more apt to uphold privacy rights in worker-versus-employer cases coming before the courts. Regardless of a company's position on monitoring, he says, it's still imperative that all businesses have a written Internet-use and e-mail policy and that they notify employees regularly if monitoring occurs.

> **"All sorts of problems arise if you do monitor. Workplace studies on productivity show a detrimental effect on employee morale and an increase in employee stress."**

"Right now the law heavily favors employers' right to monitor," he says. "But all sorts of problems arise if you do monitor. Workplace studies on productivity show a detrimental effect on employee morale and an increase in employee stress."

A Websense random survey of U.S. companies conducted last fall found that one third of those surveyed had fired an employee for Internet misuse; and over 60 percent had disciplined an employee.

Andrew Schulman, chief researcher with the Privacy Foundation, says employers falsely defend the use of electronic monitoring by saying it protects the company against lawsuits. But in all the hostile-work-environment cases he has seen, none began with an offensive e-mail. Instead, they started as sexual-discrimination cases in which female employees were not promoted but male employees were. "And as one piece of evidence used to show gender bias, the women's lawyer says, 'Look, this guy thinks it's funny to trade e-mails with his buddy about why beer is better than women.' But the lawsuit wasn't triggered by the e-mail," he relates.

Attorney Ann Kiernan is a solo practitioner in New Brunswick, New Jersey, who specializes in preventive law for employers and is also one of the principals in Fair Measures Corporation, a group of attorneys who train executives and managers on how to prevent employee lawsuits. She says that monitoring may actually *increase* a company's potential liability. Right now, the law states that employers aren't liable for harassment unless they are made aware that harassment is occurring. Once the company becomes aware of the problem, it must take prompt corrective action. But if a company monitors employees, Kiernan says that business assumes responsibility for everything it sees and everything it monitors on the Internet, whether an employee brings it to the company's attention or not. "You suddenly have a duty to investigate everything," she says.

Schulman and other privacy-rights advocates say electronic monitoring may be warranted in specific cases if there is suspected wrongdoing, but that monitoring should always be used as narrowly as possible to prevent abuse and misuse.

A reoccurring problem is that companies often make a snap decision about how

White Papers on Web Use at Work

TOOLS

Wavecrest Computing (www.wavecrest.net) has collected several white papers on aspects of appropriate Web use, including managing Web use, determining the "appropriateness" of Web site visits, and one employee's perspective on Internet use and abuse. You can read all of them at: http://wavecrest.net/library/whitePapers/

they are going to use monitoring software. One story circulated by analysts and researchers tells of a CEO who read a Sunday newspaper article linking lost productivity at work to too much Internet use. Convinced that it was a problem at his own company, the CEO took the article to work on Monday and went straight to IT—rather than HR—and ordered the department to immediately install an electronic-monitoring system.

The story also is a reminder of why HR—and not IT—should be responsible for creating a monitoring policy and carrying it out. "When you have the IT department saying to the CEO, 'Everyone is doing all this browsing on CNN and we have to put a stop to this,' you have the cops making the laws, and that's not good," says Bill Gassman, research director for Gartner, a business consulting firm specializing in IT infrastructure operations.

It's also problematic to ask employees to give informed consent to a policy of surveillance when they aren't able to view the data collected about them. Schulman says if they can't see the data, they can't verify that the information is accurate.

One service—FastTracker—puts out reports that resemble a telephone bill and allow employees to see their own usage. FastTracker, a product of Fatline Corporation in Boulder, Colorado, analyzes its clients' Internet traffic and sends reports back to the company for examination by both management and employees.

When employees have access to their own Web usage statistics—where they've been and how long they were there—they become responsible for managing their own time, says Bob Silk, FastTracker's vice president of sales. "When you block sites, you treat employees like children. You don't give them any responsibility. Our product makes each employee responsible for his or her actions."

Ultimately, an employee who wants to break the rules will break the rules, those close to the issue say. Sexual harassment was occurring long before the Internet existed, and confidential information can just as easily leave a company in a face-to-face conversation as it can in an e-mail.

Attorney Ann Kiernan says she thinks employers who e-monitor should ask themselves why they don't also monitor phone calls, mail, and faxes.

"How much time do you, as an employer, want to spend policing your employees?" she asks. "From a practical point of view, isn't it better to have someone who is skilled in information technology or human resources doing something productive, rather than playing nanny?"

For more info on:
Privacy
Download two sample Internet and e-mail usage policies.
workforce.com/02/01/feature 1

Eilene Zimmerman is a freelance writer based in San Diego. To comment, e-mail editors@workforce.com.

CUT LOOSE

Companies Trick Retirees out of Health Benefits

by Anne-Marie Cusac

Fran Asbeck worked for IBM for thirty-two years. He retired at age fifty-six in 1994, secure in the knowledge that IBM would cover health care for himself and his wife. "The thing is, we were promised all this would be free," he says. "They said we had all the deferred money coming on down the line—a fat pension with yearly COLAs [Cost-of-Living Allowances], free lifetime health care. Those were the verbal promises made."

Two years ago, says Asbeck, IBM went back on its promises. "They just sent a letter saying, 'You've got to start paying for it'" or get less coverage, he recalls.

Asbeck, a former computer programmer who lives in Boyds, Maryland, relied on the excellent health care insurance that IBM offered. But now it's not as attractive. "Since I retired, in order to keep it at zero cost, I have had to take lower and lower levels of health insurance," he says. So Asbeck moved out of what to him was an ideal plan into IBM's preferred provider organization. He no longer gets to choose his doctors freely.

Earlier this year, Asbeck discovered that accepting a lower level of health coverage for himself and his wife wasn't going to work anymore. Worried about the risks of emergency hospitalization, he decided to start paying $80 each month.

It sounds relatively cheap as far as health insurance goes. But Asbeck says he can't afford the cost, in part because his pension has not kept up with the cost of living. That's why he's had to get another job.

"I'm just going to have to work until I'm in the box and hear the dirt hit the lid," he says.

Many IBM employees share Asbeck's plight.

The retirees were told "in department meetings, by their managers, in handbooks, that they would have free health insurance for life," says Lee Conrad, an IBM retiree who is now an organizer with Alliance@IBM, which is connected to the Communications Workers of America and based in Endicott, New York. "Now they've got to pay. This has been a real culture shock for people."

IBM defends its practice. "Back in the early '90s, the company set a limit and a cap" on the amount it would pay for retiree health care and informed the retirees that it wouldn't pay more than that, says Jana Weatherbee, a spokesperson for IBM. "That limit has been reached."

Weatherbee says she "can't speak to any verbal promises." However, she does say that the company repeatedly informed retirees in writing that, "once you reach this limit, you will start helping in the contribution for that coverage."

And the IBM insurance brochure does include this statement: "The company reserves the right, at its discretion, to amend, change, or terminate any of its benefits plans, programs, or policies, as the company requires. Nothing contained in this Enrollment Guide shall be construed as creating an expressed or implied obligation on the part of the company to maintain such benefits plans, programs, practices, or policies."

"They're covered legally," says Asbeck. But he feels betrayed. And he and other IBM retirees say they're suffering while IBM's Chairman and CEO Louis V. Gerstner Jr. is raking it in. Gerstner made $2 million in salary in 1999 and $5.25 million in bonuses, according to the company's 1999 proxy statement. The bonuses are based partly on cash flow and stock market gains. Companies can boost both by cutting retiree health benefits.

"Lou Gerstner has only been at IBM for seven years," says Conrad. "He's affecting the lives of retirees who put thirty, forty years in. They're the ones who built the company and created the wealth that Lou Gerstner is now pillaging. When you have people who are ill, on fixed income, the increased costs are going to create serious problems. That's unconscionable. How can you do this to people? IBM has their own personal piggy bank right now. And it's not their money. It's the employees' and the retirees' money."

Asbeck puts it another way: "He's getting fat on our blood."

It's not just IBM. Many other companies renege on health insurance promises made to retirees. According to a December 2000 study by William M. Mercer, Inc., a human resources and benefits firm, only 31 percent of companies with 500 or more employees now provide health care coverage to retirees under the age of sixty-five (the age that people qualify for Medicare). This is down from 35 percent in 1999 and 46 percent in 1993. The number of larger companies covering insurance for seniors ages sixty-five and older also fell, from 28 percent to 24 percent. This was the seventh year in a row that retiree insurance coverage declined.

Telephone company retirees make up probably the largest single group that has seen cuts in coverage or faced increases in monthly insurance costs, says C. William Jones, president of the Association of BellTel Retirees. The former Bell system retirees number more than one million, he says. The BellTel retirees' insurance costs have risen up to 500 percent.

"Many of the large corporations are involved," says Paul Edwards, chairman of the Coalition for Retirement Security, a grassroots organization that works on pension and retiree health insurance issues and is based in Springfield, Massachusetts. "It has become an acceptable practice. These aren't just isolated events. Just name your top corporations: IBM, GE's had some benefit reductions. We're talking millions of employees."

Michael Gordon is a D.C.-based lawyer who is working with the BellTel Retirees. In the last decade, says Gordon, five million retirees or their spouses nationwide have lost or had substantially reduced health benefits. "This is a national problem," he says. "It affects just about every retiree who has had some type of health coverage under their employers."

"We think it's a great concern," says Gerry Smolka, senior policy adviser for the Public Policy Institute of the American Association of Retired Persons. "People plan based on what they know. Health benefits are one of the things that give you financial security in retirement. It can completely erode your savings if you're not adequately covered."

Some retirees are more vulnerable than others. After age sixty-five, Medicare pays about 80 percent of medical bills, usually excluding pharmaceuticals. It can be extremely difficult for older retirees, who sometimes live on a pension that inflation has sharply reduced, to pay the remaining 20 percent.

But people who retire early, often as the result of pressure from their employers, can be in even more serious trouble. Those who are not yet eligible for Medicare may have to rely solely on their promised benefits. When their companies snip the strings, these retirees come down hard.

Some early retirees "have lost their benefits and can't get replacement insurance because they have a pre-existing condition now that is so severe no one will insure them, or because the costs are so high that they'll just eat up their pension," says Gordon. "If you're not Medicare-eligible, you're in a black hole if you've got a medical condition that requires expensive treatment and the employer pulls out the rug."

Companies have an incentive to take back retiree health benefits: They can get richer that way.

On October 25, 2000, *The Wall Street Journal* published an article entitled "Companies Transform Retiree-Medical Plans into Source of Profits." The reporter, Ellen E. Schultz, revealed that a little-known accounting rule, called the Financial Accounting Standard (FAS) 106, forced companies in the early 1990s to report the lifetime benefits they owed to future retirees as a liability.

Few companies want large liabilities on their balance sheets. So, by decreasing the amounts they owe on health insurance, they appear better off. Some companies overestimated their retiree health benefits at first. By downscaling their estimates and by cutting coverage, they improved their balance sheets.

"The kicker is that at numerous companies… the paper gains not only erased the retiree benefit expenses, but exceeded them," wrote Schultz. "And that is how benefit plans came to boost the bottom line."

"Companies that have boosted their bottom lines by this method," wrote Schultz, include R. R. Donnelly and Sons, Sears, Sunbeam, Tektronix, and Walt Disney.

One of the most egregious cases involves BWX Technologies, Inc., based in Lynchburg, Virginia. The company is a subsidiary of McDermott International, which describes itself as "a leading worldwide Energy Services Company."

In the mid-1990s, say employees, the company's naval nuclear fuel division began to push people into early retirement. "They said, 'If you retire early, you can keep your insurance,'" recalls William McKenna, a retiree from the company. But if you don't retire early, they said you'll have no insurance when you do. "About 400 people jumped on that bandwagon."

Richard Mull, a former chief electrician, says that management told him, "The most your health insurance will be for the rest of your life will be $16" per month. From 1996 through 1998, he says, "they really pressed this point. They got rid of a lot of older employees that way."

Mull left in 1997, at age sixty-two, having worked for BWX Technologies for thirty years. "I was anxious to get out of the plant," he says, mentioning a supervisor who he says died of a brain tumor thirty days after diagnosis. "They wanted to know if he'd been exposed to radiation or asbestos. Uranium 235, enriched uranium, we worked with every day. You had all these poisons around you."

When he heard about his supervisor's death, Mull decided to leave. "I said, 'I'm getting out of this place.'"

Mull got out. Then his insurance costs started to soar. In April 1998, the company segregated the retirees out from the insurance policies of the active workers. In a document entitled "Employee Information 1376" (released only to active employees, but leaked to the retirees), the company warned, "Beginning April 1, 1998, retirees enrolled in the Health Care and Life Insurance Plans will be responsible for most of the cost of those coverages."

In that document, the company explains the new charges: "The current cost of providing Health Care and Life Insurance Plans for retirees is very high and continues to increase. Changing the structure of the plans lowers the cost to the company, which helps improve the company's cash flow and its profitability."

In August 1998, Mull says he received a letter that stated the retirees would be charged between $250 and $750 per month, according to age and state of health. At that point, he says, because his health was good, his insurance costs rose to only $285 per month. By October, he says, the company had gotten rid of coverage for prescriptions and doubled the deductible for hospital visits. "They dropped about 50 percent of your coverage," says Mull.

From then on, every six months, the retirees were reassessed. "I eventually went up to $795 a month for me and my wife," says Mull. "No general, no doctor's visits, just for 70 percent hospitalization after we paid a $1,500 deductible." By April 1999, Mull says the company informed him that, at the rate he was paying, his insurance would not cover prior illnesses.

"Now, you work at a chemical or a nuclear plant for thirty years, you've got priors," he says. "I myself have mild asbestosis." Three months ago, Mull learned that he also has basal skin cancers. "The doctor said there could be a link, or there might not," he says. "I got a lot of high density radiation burns from welding."

Last July came another note from BWX Technologies' parent corporation. The premium had risen to $1,113 per month for Mull and his wife. Further, the letter said, coverage was guaranteed only if at least 85 percent of the retirees agreed to participate in the plan. "If this level of participation is not attained, it is highly likely that no alternative plan can be identified, and the company will no longer be able to provide you access to

any medical coverage plan," says the document.

"People dropped their health coverage. They withdrew money from their 401(k)s, they went and got home equity loans," says McKenna, who worked for the company as a darkroom technician developing X-ray film, as a welder, and as an accountability technician. Then, after local press attention from reporter Chris Flores of the Lynchburg, Virginia, *News and Advance*, "all of a sudden, [the company] found a nice policy" for just over $600, says McKenna. Even so, he says, "After twenty, thirty years of work, it's taking your whole retirement check to pay for your health insurance."

McKenna has pulmonary illness. He says he was exposed to many hazardous chemicals and asbestos, as well as raw, unprocessed uranium. "I can no longer breathe on my own without daily doses of Prednisone and asthma medications and aerosol breathing treatments every four to six hours," he wrote to former Energy Secretary Bill Richardson on April 13, 2000, in response to Richardson's proposal to compensate sick nuclear workers.

In separate interviews, Mull and McKenna mention a recent asbestos screening organized by the retirees. "Sixty percent tested positive for lung scarring," says McKenna. "194 took the test. 150 were retirees. Our lawyer made sure the doctor read these real strict." Those that tested positive, says McKenna, "were real bad. You should have heard all the stories that retirees told about all the stuff they were exposed to."

McKenna claims that he is also in the beginning stages of asbestosis. "I went and had my test back in July. I was positive," he says. "The lady that did the lung screening said, 'They exposed you to asbestos, and now they're going to dump you in the street and take away your insurance.'"

Both Mull and McKenna now get their insurance from other sources: Mull from the Veteran's Administration, McKenna from his wife's employer.

"These are loyal, twenty-five to thirty-year employees," says Gary Kendall, general counsel to the Virginia AFL-CIO. "The amount of insurance in some cases is equal to, or maybe even

more than, their monthly pensions. Nobody can afford to carry it. Had they known that, they never would have retired."

Ron Hite, director of government and public relations for BWX Technologies, blames increasing medical costs for the surge in charges these retirees now face. "The costs are going up at just an exponential rate," he says. He also blames accounting rule FAS 106. "Companies really have no incentive to provide health care coverage," he says. But "our company tried very vigorously to keep retirees with some type of affordable insurance."

Hite says that BWX Technologies continues to contribute "a reasonable level of support" to the retirees' health care costs, but he refuses to say how much. "That's information that's proprietary," he says.

Hite also says that he cannot discuss alleged medical conditions for individual employees. "What I can tell you is we are one of the most highly regulated industries in the country," he says. "Throughout our history, we have complied with all federal and state laws."

McKenna can't get over the company's duplicity. "The bottom line is, 'We don't care about the retirees no more. We need cash flow,'" he says.

Corporations are not the only ones reneging. Unions are doing it, too. Robert Devlin was vice president of the Transportation Communications International Union for sixteen years before he retired. He is a fifty-six-year member of the union. Now he's involved with the Retired Employees Protective Association, based in River Edge, New Jersey.

"We are all retired officers or employees of a railroad union that has cut our benefits," says Devlin. "For thirty-three years, we've had health insurance, just as the railroad employees had, including cost-free insurance into retirement—not only for the rest of our lives, but to our surviving spouse. A new group of officers came in, and they decided that these old retirees are getting treated too well."

The union decided to charge retirees $100 per month, or else they would have to forfeit their insurance.

Devlin feels double-crossed. "If the railroads had done this to their employees, they would have had a strike on their hands," he says.

The union did not respond to several requests for comment.

Many retirees are outraged to learn that companies are acting legally when they do away with health benefits.

"It's a particularly nasty problem because courts have held that employers are free to end or reduce retiree health coverage almost regardless of the circumstances—whether they need to or not," says Gordon. "Even if there was an understanding when the retirees retired that these are lifetime benefits, courts have held that retirees are helpless to protect them. Every federal court in the country has had this issue litigated. It's the same problem over and over again."

The crux of the problem is that, even when companies make promises to retirees, they shield themselves with written statements claiming the right to modify or terminate the benefits at any time.

Gordon calls *GM vs. Sprague* "the most shocking case of all." About 50,000 GM employees were offered an early retirement package in the mid-1990s. The company assured them they would get the same benefits they had as employees as retirees. This, the retirees later claimed, was part of what induced them to take early retirement. Then GM backed out. The retirees went to court and eventually lost. The U.S. Supreme Court denied the case a review. "These guys are out of luck—some 50,000 of them," says Gordon.

The appellate court took a generous view of GM's side of the story. "GM's failure, if it may properly be called such, amounted to this: The company did not tell the early retirees at every possible opportunity that which it had told them many times before—namely, that the terms of the plans were subject to change," said Judge David A. Nelson in

his 1998 ruling for the United States Court of Appeals for the Sixth Circuit. "There is, in our view, a world of difference between the employer's deliberate misleading of employees… and GM's failure to begin every communication to plan participants with a caveat."

But the dissent to this decision, from Chief Judge Boyce F. Martin Jr., is scathing in its evaluation of GM's behavior. "This is a classic case of corporate shortsightedness," Martin wrote. "When General Motors was flush with cash and health care costs were low, it was easy to promise employees and retirees lifetime health care. Later, when General Motors was trying to sweeten the pot for early retirees, health care was another incentive to get employees off General Motors's groaning payroll. Of course, many of the executives who promised lifetime health care to early and general retirees are probably long since gone themselves. Rather than pay off those perhaps ill-considered promises, it is easier for the current regime to say those promises never were made…. Seemingly, any reservation of rights, no matter how weakly worded or unconnected to the grant of rights, will inure a company from having to live up to its obligations in the future."

Representative John Tierney, Democrat of Massachusetts, believes retirees won't be adequately protected unless the law is changed. That's why he introduced the Emergency Retiree Health Benefits Protection Act of 2001.

"Obviously, if you don't have to show an obligation to pay out retiree health benefits, there's more cash on hand" and the company is more financially attractive, Tierney says. "Many of these companies are extraordinarily healthy financially. It has not been a hardship thing." Tierney lists several companies: "General Electric, you don't get much stronger than that. The telephone companies are surviving and doing well, for the

most part. General Motors is a strong company. Sears Roebuck."

The bill, which Tierney submitted along with three other Democrats (Robert E. Andrews of New Jersey, Dale E. Kildee of Michigan, and Carolyn McCarthy of New York), would require employers to restore any post-retirement reductions or cancellations of health benefits, unless to do so would cause financial hardship. And it sets up an emergency loan guarantee of $5 billion for those employers who need financial help to give their retirees benefits.

Retirees of many corporations—including the former Bell Telephone companies, General Electric, U.S. West, SNET, Prudential, Johns Manville, the New York Transit Police, Greyhound, and Grumman Aircraft—have signed on to the legislation. Other supporters are the Institute of Electrical and Electronics Engineers and the Pension Rights Center.

But in a Republican Administration, the bill's chance of passage appears bleak, despite President Bush's pledge that health care for seniors is a top priority.

Mike Kucklinca, executive vice president of the BellTel Retirees, was a loyal employee: "I went into the company because I thought I would have job and benefit security both during my tenure and into retirement," he says. His father, a power company employee, drilled that ethic into his head, he says.

"Who would disbelieve a company that you've worked for for thirty and more years? It was like Mother Bell would take care of us. Well, she didn't. I never thought I'd be spending all this time and energy organizing to get what I and the other retirees feel we worked for all our lives. I'm going to fight until I leave this world."

Anne-Marie Cusac is Managing Editor of The Progressive.

ENOUGH IS ENOUGH

WHITE-COLLAR CRIMINALS: THEY LIE THEY CHEAT THEY STEAL AND THEY'VE BEEN GETTING AWAY WITH IT FOR TOO LONG

BY CLIFTON LEAF

Arthur Levitt, the tough-talking former chairman of the Securities and Exchange Commission, spoke of a "multitude of villains." Red-faced Congressmen hurled insults, going so far as to compare the figures at the center of the Enron debacle unfavorably to carnival hucksters. The Treasury Secretary presided over a high-level working group aimed at punishing negligent CEOs and directors. Legislators from all but a handful of states threatened to sue the firm that bollixed up the auditing, Arthur Andersen. There was as much handwringing, proselytizing, and bloviating in front of the witness stand as there was shredding behind it.

It took a late-night comedian, though, to zero in on the central mystery of this latest corporate shame. After a parade of executives from Enron and Arthur Andersen flashed on the television monitor, Jon Stewart, anchor of *The Daily Show*, turned to the camera and shouted, "Why aren't all of you in jail? And not like white-guy jail—*jail* jail. With people by the weight room going, 'Mmmmm.'"

It was a pitch-perfect question. And, sadly, one that was sure to get a laugh.

Not since the savings-and-loan scandal a decade ago have high crimes in the boardroom provided such rich television entertainment. But that's not for any lack of malfeasance. Before Enronitis inflamed the public, gigantic white-collar swindles were rolling through the business world and the legal system with their customary regularity. And though they displayed the full creative range of executive thievery, they had one thing in common: Hardly anyone ever went to prison.

Regulators alleged that divisional managers at investment firm Credit Suisse First Boston participated in a "pervasive" scheme to siphon tens of millions of dollars of their customers' trading profits during the Internet boom of 1999 and early 2000 by demanding excessive trading fees. (For one 1999 quarter the backdoor bonuses amounted to as much as a fifth of the firm's total commissions.) Those were the facts, as outlined by the SEC and the National Association of Securities Dealers in a high-profile news conference earlier this year. But the January news conference wasn't to announce an indictment. It was to herald a settlement, in which CSFB neither admitted nor denied wrongdoing. Sure, the SEC concluded that the investment bank had failed to observe "high standards of commercial honor," and the company paid $100 million in fines and "disgorgement," and CSFB itself punished 19 of its employees with fines ranging from $250,000 to $500,000. But whatever may or may not have happened, no one was charged with a crime. The U.S. Attorney's office in Manhattan dropped its investigation when the case was settled. Nobody, in other words, is headed for the hoosegow.

A month earlier drugmaker ICN Pharmaceuticals actually pleaded guilty to one count of criminal fraud for intentionally misleading investors—over many years, it now seems—about the FDA approval status of its flagship drug, ribavirin. The result of a five-year grand jury investigation? A $5.6 million fine and the company's accession to a three-year "probationary" period. Prosecutors said that not only had the company deceived investors, but its chairman, Milan Panic, had also made more than a million dollars off the fraud as he hurriedly sold shares. He was never charged with insider trading or any other criminal act. The SEC is taking a firm stand, though, "seeking to bar Mr. Panic from serving as a director or officer of any publicly traded company." Tough luck.

And who can forget those other powerhouse scandals, Sunbeam and Waste Management? The notorious Al "Chainsaw" Dunlap, accused of zealously fabricating Sunbeam's financial statements when he was chief executive, is facing only civil, not criminal, charges. The SEC charged that Dunlap and his minions made use of every accounting fraud in the book, from "channel stuffing" to "cookie jar reserves." The case is now in the discovery phase of trial and likely to be settled; he has denied wrongdoing. (Earlier Chainsaw rid himself of a class-

Schemers and scams: a brief history of bad business

It takes some pretty spectacular behavior to get busted in this country for a white-collar crime. But the business world has had a lot of overachievers willing to give it a shot.

by Ellen Florian

1920: The Ponzi scheme

Charles Ponzi planned to arbitrage postal coupons—buying them from Spain and selling them to the U.S. Postal Service at a profit. To raise capital, he outlandishly promised investors a 50% return in 90 days. They naturally swarmed in, and he paid the first with cash collected from those coming later. He was imprisoned for defrauding 40,000 people of $15 million.

1929: Albert Wiggin

In the summer of 1929, Wiggin, head of Chase National Bank, cashed in by shorting 42,000 shares of his company's stock. His trades, though legal, were counter to the interests of his shareholders and led to passage of a law prohibiting executives from shorting their own stock.

1930: Ivar Krueger, the Match King

Heading companies that made two-thirds of the world's matches, Krueger ruled—until the Depression. To keep going, he employed 400 off-the-books vehicles that only he understood, scammed his bankers, and forged signatures. His empire collapsed when he had a stroke.

1938: Richard Whitney

Ex-NYSE president Whitney propped up his liquor business by tapping a fund for widows and orphans of which he was trustee and stealing from the New York Yacht Club and a relative's estate. He did three years' time.

1961: The electrical cartel

Executives of GE, Westinghouse, and other big-name companies conspired to serially win bids on federal projects. Seven served time—among the first imprisonments in the 70-year history of the Sherman Antitrust Act.

1962: Billie Sol Estes

A wheeler-dealer out to corner the West Texas fertilizer market, Estes built up capital by mortgaging nonexistent farm gear. Jailed in 1965 and paroled in 1971, he did the mortgage bit again, this time with nonexistent oil equipment. He was re-jailed in 1979 for tax evasion and did five years.

1970: Cornfeld and Vesco

Bernie Cornfeld's Investors Overseas Service, a fund-of-funds outfit, tanked in 1970, and Cornfeld was jailed in Switzerland. Robert Vesco "rescued" IOS with $5 million and then absconded with an estimated $250 million, fleeing the U.S. He's said to be in Cuba serving time for unrelated crimes.

1983: Marc Rich

Fraudulent oil trades in 1980–1981 netted Rich and his partner, Pincus Green, $105 million, which they moved to offshore subsidiaries. Expecting to be indicted by U.S. Attorney Rudy Giuliani for evading taxes, they fled to Switzerland, where tax evasion is not an extraditable crime. Clinton pardoned Rich in 2001.

1986: Boesky and Milken and Drexel Burnham Lambert

The Feds got Wall Streeter Ivan Boesky for insider trading, and then Boesky's testimony helped them convict Drexel's Michael Milken for market manipulation. Milken did two years in prison, Boesky 22 months. Drexel died.

1989: Charles Keating and the collapse of Lincoln S&L

Keating was convicted of fraudulently marketing junk bonds and making sham deals to manufacture profits. Sentenced to 12½ years, he served less than five. Cost to taxpayers: $3.4 billion, a sum making this the most expensive S&L failure.

(continued)

Schemers and Scams (continued)

1991: BCCI	1991: Salomon Brothers	1995: Nick Leeson and Barings Bank	1995: Bankers Trust	1997: Walter Forbes
The Bank of Credit & Commerce International got tagged the "Bank for Crooks & Criminals International" after it came crashing down in a money-laundering scandal that disgraced, among others, Clark Clifford, advisor to four Presidents.	Trader Paul Mozer violated rules barring one firm from bidding for more than 35% of the securities offered at a Treasury auction. He did four months' time. Salomon came close to bankruptcy. Chairman John Gutfreund resigned.	A 28-year-old derivatives trader based in Singapore, Leeson brought down 233-year-old Barings by betting Japanese stocks would rise. He hid his losses—$1.4 billion—for a while but eventually served more than three years in jail.	Derivatives traders misled clients Gibson Greetings and Procter & Gamble about the risks of exotic contracts they entered into. P&G sustained about $200 million in losses but got most of it back from BT. The Federal Reserve sanctioned the bank.	Only months after Cendant was formed by the merger of CUC and HFS, cooked books that created more than $500 million in phony profits showed up at CUC. Walter Forbes, head of CUC, has been indicted on fraud charges and faces trial this year.
1997: Columbia/HCA	1998: Waste Management	1998: Al Dunlap	1999: Martin Frankel	2000: Sotheby's and Al Taubman
This Nashville company became the target of the largest-ever federal investigation into healthcare scams and agreed in 2000 to an $840 million Medicare-fraud settlement. Included was a criminal fine—rare in corporate America—of $95 million.	Fighting to keep its reputation as a fast grower, the company engaged in aggressive accounting for years and then tried straight-out books cooking. In 1998 it took a massive charge, restating years of earnings.	He became famous as "Chainsaw Al" by firing people. But he was then axed at Sunbeam for illicitly manufacturing earnings. He loved overstating revenues—booking sales, for example, on grills neither paid for nor shipped.	A financier who siphoned off at least $200 million from a series of insurance companies he controlled, Frankel was arrested in Germany four months after going on the lam. Now jailed in Rhode Island—no bail for this guy—he awaits trial on charges of fraud and conspiracy.	The world's elite were ripped off by years of price-fixing on the part of those supposed bitter competitors, auction houses Sotheby's and Christie's. Sotheby's chairman, Taubman, was found guilty of conspiracy last year. He is yet to be sentenced.

action shareholder suit for $15 million, without admitting culpability.) Whatever the current trial's outcome, Dunlap will still come out well ahead. Sunbeam, now under bankruptcy protection, gave him $12.7 million in stock and salary during 1998 alone. And if worse comes to worst, he can always tap the stash he got from the sale of the disemboweled Scott Paper to Kimberly-Clark, which by Dunlap's own estimate netted him a $100 million bonanza.

Sunbeam investors, naturally, didn't fare as well. When the fraud was discovered internally, the company was forced to restate its earnings, slashing half the reported profits from fiscal 1997. After that embarrassment, Sunbeam shares fell from $52 to $7 in just six months—a loss of $3.8 billion in market cap. Sound familiar?

The auditor in that case, you'll recall, was Arthur Andersen, which paid $110 million to settle a civil action. According to an SEC release in May, an Andersen partner authorized unqualified audit opinions even though "he was aware of many of the company's accounting improprieties and disclosure failures." The opinions were false and misleading. But nobody is going to jail.

At Waste Management, yet another Andersen client, income reported over six years was overstated by $1.4 billion. Andersen coughed up $220 million to shareholders to wipe its hands clean. The auditor, agreeing to the SEC's first antifraud injunction against a major firm in more than 20 years, also paid a $7 million fine to close the complaint. Three partners were assessed fines, ranging from $30,000 to $50,000, as well. (You guessed it. Not even home detention.) Concedes one former regulator familiar with the case: "Senior people at Andersen got off when we felt we had the goods." Andersen did not respond to a request for comment.

The list goes on—from phony bookkeeping at the former Bankers Trust (now part of Deutsche Bank) to allegations of insider trading by a former Citigroup vice president. One employee of California tech firm nVidia admitted that he cleared

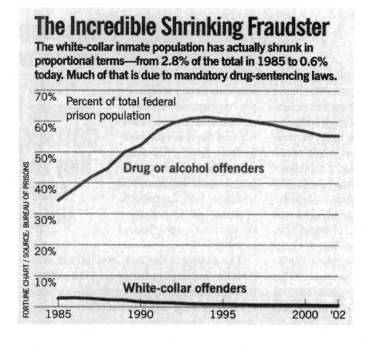

The Incredible Shrinking Fraudster

The white-collar inmate population has actually shrunk in proportional terms—from 2.8% of the total in 1985 to 0.6% today. Much of that is due to mandatory drug-sentencing laws.

FORTUNE CHART / SOURCE: BUREAU OF PRISONS

Percent of total federal prison population

Drug or alcohol offenders

White-collar offenders

nearly half a million dollars in a single day in March 2000 from an illegal insider tip. He pleaded guilty to criminal charges, paid fines, and got a 12-month grounding at home.

The problem will not go away until white-collar thieves face a consequence they're actually scared of: time in jail.

While none of those misbehaviors may rise to Enronian proportions, at least in terms of salacious detail, taken en masse they say something far more distressing. The double standard in criminal justice in this country is starker and more embedded than many realize. Bob Dylan was right: Steal a little, and they put you in jail. Steal a lot, and you're likely to walk away with a lecture and a court-ordered promise not to do it again.

Far beyond the pure social inequity—and that would be bad enough, we admit—is a very real dollar-and-cents cost, a doozy of a recurring charge that ripples through the financial markets. As the Enron case makes abundantly clear, white-collar fraud is not a victimless crime. In this age of the 401(k), when the retirement dreams of middle-class America are tied to the integrity of the stock market, crooks in the corner office are everybody's problem. And the problem will not go away until white-collar thieves face a consequence they're actually scared of: time in jail.

The U.S. regulatory and judiciary systems, however, do little if anything to deter the most damaging Wall Street crimes. Interviews with some six dozen current and former federal prosecutors, regulatory officials, defense lawyers, criminologists, and high-ranking corporate executives paint a disturbing pic-

ture. The already stretched "white-collar" task forces of the FBI focus on wide-ranging schemes like Internet, insurance, and Medicare fraud, abandoning traditional securities and accounting offenses to the SEC. Federal securities regulators, while determined and well trained, are so understaffed that they often have to let good cases slip away. Prosecutors leave scores of would-be criminal cases referred by the SEC in the dustbin, declining to prosecute more than half of what comes their way. State regulators, with a few notable exceptions, shy away from the complicated stuff. So-called self-regulatory organizations like the National Association of Securities Dealers are relatively toothless; trade groups like the American Institute of Certified Public Accountants stubbornly protect their own. And perhaps worst of all, corporate chiefs often wink at (or nod off to) overly aggressive tactics that speed along the margins of the law.

LET'S START WITH THE NUMBERS. WALL STREET, AFTER ALL, IS about numbers, about playing the percentages. And that may be the very heart of the problem. Though securities officials like to brag about their enforcement records, few in America's top-floor suites and corporate boardrooms fear the local sheriff. They know the odds of getting caught.

The U.S. Attorneys' Annual Statistical Report is the official reckoning of the Department of Justice. For the year 2000, the most recent statistics available, federal prosecutors say they charged 8,766 defendants with what they term white-collar crimes, convicting 6,876, or an impressive 78% of the cases brought. Not bad. Of that number, about 4,000 were sentenced to prison—nearly all of them for less than three years. (The average time served, experts say, is closer to 16 months.)

But that 4,000 number isn't what you probably think it is. The Justice Department uses the white-collar appellation for virtually every kind of fraud, says Henry Pontell, a leading criminologist at the University of California at Irvine, and co-author of *Big-Money Crime: Fraud and Politics in the Savings and Loan Crisis.* "I've seen welfare frauds labeled as white-collar crimes," he says. Digging deeper into the Justice Department's 2000 statistics, we find that only 226 of the cases involved securities or commodities fraud.

And guess what: Even those are rarely the highfliers, says Kip Schlegel, chairman of the department of criminal justice at Indiana University, who wrote a study on Wall Street law-breaking for the Justice Department's research wing. Many of the government's largest sting operations come from busting up cross-state Ponzi schemes, "affinity" investment scams (which prey on the elderly or on particular ethnic or religious groups), and penny-stock boiler rooms, like the infamous Stratton Oakmont and Sterling Foster. They are bad seeds, certainly. But let's not kid ourselves: They are not corporate-officer types or high-level Wall Street traders and bankers—what we might call *starched*-collar criminals. "The criminal sanction is generally reserved for the losers," says Schlegel, "the scamsters, the low-rent crimes."

Statistics from the Federal Bureau of Prisons, up to date as of October 2001, make it even clearer how few white-collar criminals are behind bars. Of a total federal inmate population of

The SEC's Impressive Margins

Did someone say "resource problem"? The SEC is, in fact, a moneymaking machine. The U.S. Treasury keeps fees and penalties. Disgorgements go into a fund for fraud victims.

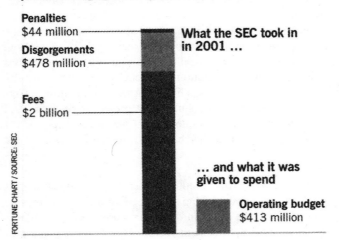

Penalties $44 million

Disgorgements $478 million

Fees $2 billion

What the SEC took in in 2001 ...

... and what it was given to spend

Operating budget $413 million

FORTUNE CHART / SOURCE: SEC

156,238, prison authorities say only 1,021 fit the description—which includes everyone from insurance schemers to bankruptcy fraudsters, counterfeiters to election-law tamperers to postal thieves. Out of those 1,000 or so, well more than half are held at minimum-security levels—often privately managed "Club Feds" that are about two steps down the comfort ladder from Motel 6.

And how many of them are the starched-collar crooks who commit securities fraud? The Bureau of Prisons can't say precisely. The Department of Justice won't say either—but the answer lies in its database.

Susan Long, a professor of quantitative methods at the school of management at Syracuse University, co-founded a Web data clearinghouse called TRAC, which has been tracking prosecutor referrals from virtually every federal agency for more than a decade. Using a barrage of Freedom of Information Act lawsuits, TRAC has been able to gather data buried in the Justice Department's own computer files (minus the individual case numbers that might be used to identify defendants). And the data, which follow each matter from referral to the prison steps, tell a story the Justice Department doesn't want you to know.

In the full ten years from 1992 to 2001, according to TRAC data, SEC enforcement attorneys referred 609 cases to the Justice Department for possible criminal charges. Of that number, U.S. Attorneys decided what to do on about 525 of the cases—declining to prosecute just over 64% of them. Of those they did press forward, the feds obtained guilty verdicts in a respectable 76%. But even then, some 40% of the convicted starched-collars didn't spend a day in jail. In case you're wondering, here's the magic number that did: 87.

FIVE-POINT TYPE IS SMALL PRINT, SO TINY THAT ALMOST everyone who remembers the Bay of Pigs or the fall of Saigon will need bifocals to read it. For those who love pulp fiction or

the crime blotters in their town weeklies, however, there is no better place to look than in the small print of the *Wall Street Journal*'s B section. Once a month, buried in the thick folds of newsprint, are bullet reports of the NASD's disciplinary actions. February's disclosures about alleged misbehavior, for example, range from the unseemly to the lurid—from an Ohio bond firm accused of systematically overcharging customers and fraudulently marking up trades to a California broker who deposited a client's $143,000 check in his own account. Two senior VPs of a Pittsburgh firm, say NASD officials, cashed out of stock, thanks to timely inside information they received about an upcoming loss; a Dallas broker reportedly converted someone's 401(k) rollover check to his personal use.

In all, the group's regulatory arm received 23,753 customer complaints against its registered reps between the years 1997 and 2000. After often extensive investigations, the NASD barred "for life" during this period 1,662 members and suspended another 1,000 or so for violations of its rules or of laws on the federal books. But despite its impressive 117-page *Sanction Guidelines*, the NASD can't do much of anything to its miscreant broker-dealers other than throw them out of the club. It has no statutory right to file civil actions against rule breakers, it has no subpoena power, and from the looks of things it can't even get the bums to return phone calls. Too often the disciplinary write-ups conclude with a boilerplate "failed to respond to NASD requests for information."

"That's a good thing when they default," says Barry Goldsmith, executive vice president for enforcement at NASD Regulation. "It gives us the ability to get the wrongdoers out quickly to prevent them from doing more harm."

Goldsmith won't say how many cases the NASD passes on to the SEC or to criminal prosecutors for further investigation. But he does acknowledge that the securities group refers a couple of hundred suspected insider-trading cases to its higher-ups in the regulatory chain.

Thus fails the first line of defense against white-collar crime: self-policing. The situation is worse, if anything, among accountants than it is among securities dealers, says John C. Coffee Jr., a Columbia Law School professor and a leading authority on securities enforcement issues. At the American Institute of Certified Public Accountants, he says, "no real effort is made to enforce the rules." Except one, apparently. "They have a rule that they do not take action against auditors until all civil litigation has been resolved," Coffee says, "because they don't want their actions to be used against their members in a civil suit." Lynn E. Turner, who until last summer was the SEC's chief accountant and is now a professor at Colorado State University, agrees. "The AICPA," he says, "often failed to discipline members in a timely fashion, if at all. And when it did, its most severe remedy was just to expel the member from the organization."

Al Anderson, senior VP of AICPA, says the criticism is unfounded. "We have been and always will be committed to enforcing the rules," he says. The next line of defense after the professional associations is the SEC. The central role of this independent regulatory agency is to protect investors in the financial markets by making sure that publicly traded companies

The Odds Against Doing Time

Regulators like to talk tough, but when it comes to actual punishment, all but a handful of Wall Street cheats get off with a slap on the wrist.

What Really Happens
In the ten-year period from 1992 to 2001, SEC officials felt that 609 of its civil cases were egregious enough to merit criminal charges. These were referred to U.S. Attorneys.

Of the initial 609 referrals, U.S. Attorneys have disposed of **525**:

👤👤👤👤👤👤👤👤👤👤👤👤👤👤👤👤👤👤👤👤👤👤👤👤👤👤
👤👤👤👤👤👤👤👤👤👤👤👤👤👤👤👤👤👤👤👤👤👤👤👤👤👤

187 defendants were prosecuted:

👤👤👤👤👤👤👤👤👤👤👤👤👤👤👤👤👤👤👤

142 were found guilty:

👤👤👤👤👤👤👤👤👤👤👤👤👤👤

87 went to jail:

👤👤👤👤👤👤👤👤👤

👤 = ten defendants

SOURCE: TRANSACTIONAL RECORDS ACCESS CLEARINGHOUSE

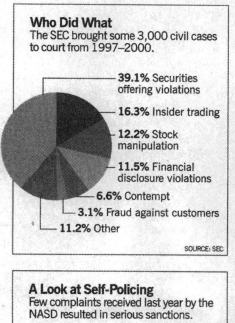

Who Did What
The SEC brought some 3,000 civil cases to court from 1997–2000.

- **39.1%** Securities offering violations
- **16.3%** Insider trading
- **12.2%** Stock manipulation
- **11.5%** Financial disclosure violations
- **6.6%** Contempt
- **3.1%** Fraud against customers
- **11.2%** Other

SOURCE: SEC

A Look at Self-Policing
Few complaints received last year by the NASD resulted in serious sanctions.

Registered reps	675,821
Customer complaints received	5,155
Individuals barred	466
Individuals suspended	346

SOURCE: NASD REGULATION

play by the rules. With jurisdiction over every constituent in the securities trade, from brokers to mutual funds to accountants to corporate filers, it would seem to be the voice of Oz. But the SEC's power, like that of the Wizard, lies more in persuasion than in punishment. The commission can force companies to comply with securities rules, it can fine them when they don't, it can even charge them in civil court with violating the law. But it can't drag anybody off to prison. To that end, the SEC's enforcement division must work with federal and state prosecutors—a game that often turns into weak cop/bad cop.

Nevertheless, the last commission chairman, Arthur Levitt, did manage to shake the ground with the power he had. For the 1997–2000 period, for instance, attorneys at the agency's enforcement division brought civil actions against 2,989 respondents. That figure includes 487 individual cases of alleged insider trading, 365 for stock manipulation, 343 for violations of laws and rules related to financial disclosure, 196 for contempt of the regulatory agency, and another 94 for fraud against customers. In other words, enough bad stuff to go around. What would make them civil crimes, vs. actual handcuff-and-fingerprint ones? Evidence, says one SEC regional director. "In a civil case you need only a preponderance of evidence that there was an intent to defraud," she says. "In a criminal case you have to prove that intent beyond a reasonable doubt."

When the SEC does find a case that smacks of criminal intent, the commission refers it to a U.S. Attorney. And that is where the second line of defense often breaks down. The SEC

has the expertise to sniff out such wrongdoing but not the big stick of prison to wave in front of its targets. The U.S. Attorney's office has the power to order in the SWAT teams but often lacks the expertise—and, quite frankly, the inclination—to deconstruct a complex financial crime. After all, it is busy pursuing drug kingpins and terrorists.

And there is also the key issue of institutional kinship, say an overwhelming number of government authorities. U.S. Attorneys, for example, have kissing-cousin relationships with the agencies they work with most, the FBI and DEA. Prosecutors and investigators often work together from the start and know the elements required on each side to make a case stick. That is hardly true with the SEC and all but a handful of U.S. Attorneys around the country. In candid conversations, current and former regulators cited the lack of warm cooperation between the law-enforcement groups, saying one had no clue about how the other worked.

THIRTEEN BLOCKS FROM WALL STREET IS A DIFFERENT KIND of ground zero. Here, in the shadow of the imposing Federalist-style courthouses of lower Manhattan, is a nine-story stone fortress of indeterminate color, somewhere in the unhappy genus of waiting-room beige. As with every federal building these days, there are reminders of the threat of terrorism, but this particular outpost has taken those reminders to the status of a four-bell alarm. To get to the U.S. Attorney's office, a visitor must wind his way through a phalanx of blue police barricades, stop by a kiosk manned by a U.S. marshal, enter a giant white tent with police and metal detectors, and proceed to a bulletproof visitors desk, replete with armed guards. Even if you make it to the third floor, home of the Securities and Commodities Fraud Task Force, Southern District of New York, you'll need an electronic passkey to get in.

This, the office which Rudy Giuliani led to national prominence with his late-1980s busts of junk-bond king Michael Milken, Ivan Boesky, and the Drexel Burnham insider-trading ring, is one of the few outfits in the country that even know how to prosecute complex securities crimes. Or at least one of the few willing to take them on. Over the years it has become the favorite (and at times lone) repository for the SEC's enforcement hit list.

And how many attorneys are in this office to fight the nation's book cookers, insider traders, and other Wall Street thieves? Twenty-five—including three on loan from the SEC. The unit has a fraction of the paralegal and administrative help of even a small private law firm. Assistant U.S. Attorneys do their own copying, and in one recent sting it was Sandy—one of the unit's two secretaries—who did the records analysis that broke the case wide open.

Even this office declines to prosecute more than half the cases referred to it by the SEC. Richard Owens, the newly minted chief of the securities task force and a six-year veteran of the unit, insists that it is not for lack of resources. There are plenty of legitimate reasons, he says, why a prosecutor would choose not to pursue a case—starting with the possibility that there may not have been true criminal intent.

But many federal regulators scoff at such bravado. "We've got too many crooks and not enough cops," says one. "We could fill Riker's Island if we had the resources."

And Owens' office is as good as it gets in this country. In other cities, federal and state prosecutors shun securities cases for all kinds of understandable reasons. They're harder to pull off than almost any other type of case—and the payoff is rarely worth it from the standpoint of local political impact. "The typical state prosecution is for a standard common-law crime," explains Philip A. Feigin, an attorney with Rothgerber Johnson & Lyons in Denver and a former commissioner of the Colorado Securities Division. "An ordinary trial will probably last for five days, it'll have 12 witnesses, involve an act that occurred in one day, and was done by one person." Now hear the pitch coming from a securities regulator thousands of miles away. "Hi. We've never met, but I've got this case I'd like you to take on. The law that was broken is just 158 pages long. It involves only three years of conduct—and the trial should last no more than three months. What do you say?" The prosecutor has eight burglaries or drug cases he could bring in the time it takes to prosecute a single white-collar crime. "It's a completely easy choice," says Feigin.

That easy choice, sadly, has left a glaring logical—and moral—fallacy in the nation's justice system: Suite thugs don't go to jail because street thugs have to. And there's one more thing on which many crime experts are adamant. The double standard makes no sense whatsoever when you consider the damage done by the offense. Sociologist Pontell and his col-

leagues Kitty Calavita, at U.C. Irvine, and Robert Tillman, at New York's St. John's University, have demonstrated this in a number of compelling academic studies. In one the researchers compared the sentences received by major players (that is, those who stole $100,000 or more) in the savings-and-loan scandal a decade ago with the sentences handed to other types of nonviolent federal offenders. The starched-collar S&L crooks got an average of 36.4 months in the slammer. Those who committed burglary—generally swiping $300 or less—got 55.6 months; car thieves, 38 months; and first-time drug offenders, 64.9 months. Now compare the costs of the two kinds of crime: The losses from all bank robberies in the U.S. in 1992 *totaled* $35 million, according to the FBI's Uniform Crime Reports. That's about 1% of the estimated cost of Charles Keating's fraud at Lincoln Savings & Loan.

"Nobody writes an e-mail that says, 'Gee, I think I'll screw the public today.' There's never been a fraud of passion."

"OF ALL THE FACTORS THAT LEAD TO CORPORATE CRIME, NONE comes close in importance to the role top management plays in tolerating, even shaping, a culture that allows for it," says William Laufer, the director of the Zicklin Center for Business Ethics Research at the Wharton School. Laufer calls it "winking." And with each wink, nod, and nudge-nudge, instructions of a sort are passed down the management chain. Accounting fraud, for example, often starts in this way. "Nobody writes an e-mail that says, 'Gee, I think I'll screw the public today,'" says former regulator Feigin. "There's never been a fraud of passion. These things take years." They breed slowly over time.

So does the impetus to fight them. Enron, of course, has stirred an embarrassed Administration and Congress to action. But it isn't merely Enron that worries legislators and the public—it's *another* Enron. Every day brings news of one more accounting gas leak that for too long lay undetected. Wariness about Lucent, Rite Aid, Raytheon, Tyco, and a host of other big names has left investors not only rattled but also questioning the very integrity of the financial reporting system.

And with good reason. Two statistics in particular suggest that no small degree of executive misconduct has been brewing in the corporate petri dish. In 1999 and 2000 the SEC demanded 96 restatements of earnings or other financial statements—a figure that was more than in the previous nine years combined. Then, in January, the Federal Deposit Insurance Corp. announced more disturbing news. The number of publicly traded companies declaring bankruptcy shot up to a record 257, a stunning 46% over the prior year's total, which itself had been a record. These companies shunted $259 billion in assets into protective custody—that is, away from shareholders. And a record 45 of these losers were biggies, companies with assets greater than $1 billion. That might all seem normal in a time of burst bubbles and economic recession. But the number of nonpublic bankruptcies has barely risen. Regulators and plaintiffs lawyers say both restatements and sudden public bankruptcies often signal the presence of fraud.

The ultimate cost could be monumental. "Integrity of the markets, and the willingness of people to invest, are critical to us," says Harvey J. Goldschmid, a professor of law at Columbia since 1970 and soon to be an SEC commissioner. "Widespread false disclosure would be incredibly dangerous. People could lose trust in corporate filings altogether."

So will all this be enough to spark meaningful changes in the system? Professor Coffee thinks the Enron matter might move Congress to take action. "I call it the phenomenon of crash-then-law," he says. "You need three things to get a wave of legislation and litigation: a recession, a stock market crash, and a true villain." For instance, Albert Wiggin, head of Chase National Bank, cleaned up during the crash of 1929 by short-selling his own company stock. "From that came a new securities law, Section 16(b), that prohibits short sales by executives," Coffee says.

But the real issue isn't more laws on the books—it's enforcing the ones that are already there. And that, says criminologist Kip Schlegel, is where the government's action falls far short of the rhetoric. In his 1994 study on securities law-breaking for the Justice Department, Schlegel found that while officials were talking tough about locking up insider traders, there was little evidence to suggest that the punishments imposed—either the incarceration rates or the sentences themselves—were more severe. "In fact," he says, "the data suggest the opposite trend. The government lacks the will to bring these people to justice."

DENNY CRAWFORD SAYS THERE'S AN ALL-TOO-SIMPLE REASON for this. The longtime commissioner of the Texas Securities Board, who has probably put away more bad guys than any other state commissioner, says most prosecutors make the crimes too complicated. "You've got to boil it down to lying, cheating, and stealing," she says, in a warbly voice that sounds like pink lemonade. "That's all it is—the best way to end securities fraud is to put every one of these crooks in jail."

Reprinted from the March 18, 2002, issue of *Fortune*, pp. 62-65 by special permission. © 2002 by Time, Inc.

Unjust Rewards

The government continues to award federal business worth billions to companies that repeatedly break the law. A *Mother Jones* investigation reveals which major contractors are the worst offenders.

By Ken Silverstein

IN 1989, AN EXPLOSION RIPPED through a Phillips Petroleum chemical plant in Pasadena, Texas, killing 23 workers and injuring more than 100. Federal officials fined the company $4 million, citing "clear evidence that the explosion was avoidable had recognized safety practices been followed." In 1999 and 2000, two more explosions at the plant left another 3 workers dead and 73 injured. Phillips was hit with an additional $2.3 million in fines for ignoring safety hazards.

In 1994, a worker was killed in an explosion at an Arizona factory run by TRW, the nation's leading maker of air bags. The company, which had a record of violating workplace laws at the plant, settled criminal charges in the case for $1.7 million. Officials later discovered that TRW, in a move "clearly approved by management," was illegally dumping chemical waste from the plant at landfills in three states. Last year, the company paid a record $24 million in civil and criminal penalties.

In 1999, a jury found Koch Industries guilty of negligence in the deaths of two teenagers killed in a fire caused by a corroded pipeline. The following year, the Kansas-based energy giant paid $30 million—the largest civil penalty in the history of the Clean Water Act—for illegally discharging 3 million gallons of crude oil in six states. Last year, Koch paid $25 million to settle charges that it lied about how much oil it was pumping out of federal lands, cheating the government in nearly 25,000 separate transactions.

Phillips, TRW, and Koch have more in common than a history of repeatedly violating workplace and environmental laws. They also rank among the nation's largest government contractors. Between 1995 and 2000, the three corporations received a combined total of $10.4 billion in federal business—at the same time that regulatory agencies and federal courts were citing the companies for jeopardizing the safety of their employees, polluting the nation's air and water, and even defrauding the government.

That's not supposed to happen. Federal contracting officers are charged with reviewing the record of companies that do business with the government and barring those that fail to demonstrate "a satisfactory record of integrity and business ethics." But officials are given no guidelines to follow in making such decisions, and there's no centralized system they can consult to inform them of corporate wrongdoing. As a result, a government report concluded in 2000, those responsible for awarding federal contracts are "extremely reluctant" to take action, even when they are aware of violations. And in the rare instances when the rule is enforced, it is almost always employed against small companies with little clout in Washington.

Shortly before leaving office, President Clinton issued a new order to provide clear guidelines for deciding which firms share in the roughly $200 billion in federal contracts awarded each year. The new "contractor responsibility rule"—championed by Vice President Al Gore and developed after two years of congressional testimony and public hearings—specified that federal officials should weigh "evidence of repeated, pervasive, or significant violations of the law." Officials were told to consider whether a company has cheated on prior contracts or violated laws involving the environment, workplace safety, labor rights, consumer protection, or antitrust activities.

President Bush quietly killed a rule requiring officials to ban federal contractors with a record of "repeated, pervasive, or significant" violations of workplace safety and other laws.

The measure was never implemented. In one of his first acts as president, George W. Bush put the rule on hold after only 11 days in office, saying the issue needed further study. With big business suing to block the new guidelines, Bush revoked the rule 11 months later.

Some 80,000 contractors do at least $25,000 in business with the federal government each year, and the great majority comply with the law. But a six-month investigation by *Mother Jones* of the nation's 200 largest contractors found that the government continues to award lucrative contracts to dozens of companies that it has repeatedly cited for serious violations of workplace and environmental laws. The government's own database of contractors was matched with lists of the worst violations documented by the Environmental Protection Agency (EPA) and the Occupational Safety and Health Administration (OSHA) between 1995 and 2000. Among the findings:

- Forty-six of the biggest contractors were prosecuted by the Justice Department and ordered to pay cleanup costs after they refused to take responsibility for dumping hazardous waste and other environmental violations. General Electric—which received nearly $9.8 billion from the government, making it the nation's 10th-largest contractor—topped the list with 27 cases of pollution for which it was held solely or jointly liable.

- Fifty-five of the top contractors were cited for a total of 1,375 violations of workplace safety law that posed a risk of death or serious physical harm to workers. Ford Motor, which ranks 177th among contractors with $442 million in federal business, led the OSHA list with 292 violations deemed "serious" by federal officials. In 1999, six workers were killed and dozens injured when a boiler exploded at Ford's River Rouge Complex in Dearborn, Michigan. The company was hit with a $1.5 million fine after an internal memo revealed that Ford had decided not to replace safety equipment on the aging boilers because it would then have to fully upgrade them to meet "all present safety standards."

- Thirty-four leading contractors were penalized for violating both environmental and workplace safety rules. The firms were hit with a total of $12.6 million in EPA penalties and $5.9 million in OSHA fines—costs more than covered by the $229 billion in federal contracts they were awarded during the same period.

"It is clear that, in many cases, the government continues to do business with contractors who violate laws, sometimes repeatedly," concludes a 2000 report by the Federal Acquisition Regulatory Council, the agency that oversees federal contractors. Others put it more bluntly. "Government should not do business with crooks," says Rep. George Miller (D-Calif.), who has demanded that the White House make public any closed-door meetings it had with corporate lobbyists to discuss killing the contractor responsibility rule. Bush's decision, Miller says, "sends a message to contractors that the government doesn't care if you underpay your workers, or expose them to toxic hazards, or destroy the public lands—the government will do business with you anyway."

DURING BILL CLINTON'S second term in office, a coalition of labor, civil rights, and consumer groups lobbied the government to crackdown on contractor misconduct. Backed by Miller and other congressional allies, they pointed to numerous studies documenting the extent of the problem. A 1995 report by the Government Accounting Office revealed that 80 major federal contractors had violated the National Labor Relations Act by seeking to suppress unions. Another GAO report found that in 1994 alone, OSHA imposed fines of $15,000 or more on each of 261 companies that had received a combined $38 billion in federal contracts. Noting that some contractors place workers "at substantial risk of injury or illness," the report added that the "prospect of debarment or suspension can provide impetus for a contractor to undertake remedial measures to improve working conditions."

> Two contractors who settled charges that they **defrauded the government** on prior contracts received $38 billion in **new federal business** between 1995 and 2000.

In July 1999, Clinton declared his support for the reform coalition and announced plans to revise the rule. What emerged over the next two years was a set of specific guidelines for federal contracting officers to follow in determining a company's eligibility. The new rule created a hierarchy of violations to be considered, topped by convictions for contract fraud. It stipulated that only repeated and serious wrongdoing, not administrative complaints, should be weighed. And it acknowledged a need for flexibility, noting that companies with serious violations might continue to receive contracts if they "correct the conditions that led to the misconduct."

"We view this fundamentally as empowering the government to do what every business in the world does, which is not to be forced to do business with people it doesn't trust," said Joshua Gotbaum, who helped draft the rule as controller of the Office of Management and Budget.

Clinton's move generated a fast and furious reaction from business and industry. The Business Roundtable, the U.S. Chamber of Commerce, and the National Association of Manufacturers launched a fierce lobbying campaign against the new rule. Despite a provision stating that only a pattern of "pervasive" and "significant" abuses would be considered, business opponents argued that the guidelines gave contracting officers excessive discretion to arbitrarily torpedo a contractor. "The proposed rules would allow contract officers to blacklist firms without regard to the number, nature, or severity of violations," said the National Center for Policy Analysis, a business-backed think tank. "Suspicions raised by rivals or disgruntled employees could cost firms millions, if not billions, of dollars."

To fight the measure, the business coalition hired Linda Fuselier of the Capitol Group, a high-powered lobbyist who had previously helped insurance firms avoid cleanup costs at Superfund waste sites. Opponents flooded officials with hundreds of comments opposing the guidelines. And when Clinton formally issued the new rule in December 2000, they went to federal court seeking to get the provision thrown out.

The court never had to decide the issue. A month later, when Bush took office, he immediately moved to postpone the rule. On January 31, 2001, federal agencies were quietly ordered to delay implementing it for six months—without issuing a public notice or soliciting comment. The Congressional Research Service issued an opinion concluding that the secret suspension of the rule was probably illegal, but the move went virtually unreported in the media. When Bush finally revoked the rule while vacationing at his Texas ranch last December, corporate executives and their allies in Congress hailed the decision. "There was never any rational basis or need for additional standards, since existing regulations already ensure the government does not do business with unethical companies," declared Rep. Thomas Davis III, a Republican from Virginia.

In reality, the government makes little effort to review contractors' records—and even the most diligent contracting officer would find it almost impossible to do so. The government does not maintain a central database to store information on contractors' records of compliance with the law. The EPA and OSHA maintain their own lists of corporate violations, but parent compa-

The Dirty Dozen: Federal contractors with both EPA and OSHA violations, ranked by penalties (1995–2000)

	CONTRACTS (IN MILLIONS)	RANK AS CONTRACTOR	EPA VIOLATIONS	OSHA VIOLATIONS	TOTAL PENALTIES
FORD MOTOR	$442	177	12	292	$6,082,271
TRW	10,267	9	3	79	5,745,234
ARCHER DANIELS MIDLAND	471	168	4	93	1,676,850
EXXONMOBIL	2,173	43	20	5	1,481,400
E.I. DU PONT DE NEMOURS	446	175	17	23	956,700
AVONDALE INDUSTRIES	1,347	66	1	73	759,100
GENERAL MOTORS	4,854	18	21	14	418,393
GENERAL ELECTRIC	9,777	10	27	48	369,363
OLIN CORP.	1,310	68	7	4	168,500
ATLANTIC RICHFIELD	675	138	10	1	150,600
DAIMLERCHRYSLER	1,575	54	7	166	130,121
TEXTRON	5,507	17	4	78	111,215

ABOUT THE DATA

The "contractor responsibility rule" revoked by President Bush required officials to review a company's recent history of violating federal laws. To determine which contractors have the worst records in two significant areas covered by the rule—the environment and workplace safety—*Mother Jones* compiled a list of 200 corporations that did the most business with the government between 1995 and 2000. The list was then matched to two federal databases: a list of companies prosecuted by the Justice Department and found liable for environmental violations, and a list of firms cited by the Occupational Safety and Health Administration for posing a serious risk of injury or death to workers. Database work was conducted by Ron Nixon of Investigative Reporters and Editors, a nonprofit organization based in Columbia, Missouri. Additional reporting was provided by George Sanchez, with documentation from the Project on Government Oversight, a research group based in Washington, D.C. A complete list of violations committed by the top 200 contractors is available online at *www.motherjones.com*.

nies are not linked to their subsidiaries, which can number in the hundreds. OSHA makes some of its records available online, but the EPA and many other agencies do not. "There's no process built into the review system," says Gary Bass, executive director of OMB Watch, a Washington-based advocate of government accountability. "Just finding the right information is complicated and time-consuming."

As a result, even contractors that commit the most obvious violations are never suspended or debarred. One GAO study found that the government continues to award business to defense contractors that have committed fraud on prior contracts. General Dynamics, the nation's fifth-largest contractor, paid the government nearly $2 million in 1995 to resolve charges that it falsified employee timecards to bill the Pentagon for thousands of hours that were never worked on a contract for testing F-16 fighters. Northrop Grumman, the nation's fourth-largest contractor, paid nearly $6.7 million in 2000 to settle two separate cases in which it was charged with inflating the costs of parts and materials for warplanes. Yet the two defense giants continue to receive federal contracts, collecting a combined total of $38 billion between 1995 and 2000.

Opponents argue that the government already has the power to force contractors to clean up their act, without cutting them off from federal business. In addition, some contractors can be difficult to replace. The Pentagon, for example, maintains that it cannot afford to ban large defense contractors who provide specialized services and products, and the government is reluctant to take away contracts from nursing homes that commit Medicare fraud, fearing that patients will be hurt. "Debarment and suspension isn't practical," says Steven Schooner, a lawyer in the Office of Federal Procurement Policy under Clinton. "If the government needs the goods they produce, it's the only one that loses."

But while big contractors are all but immune from scrutiny, the government has no qualms about denying business to smaller operations that violate the law. Some 24,000 contractors are currently barred from government work, and almost all are small firms or individuals like Kenneth Hansen, a Kansas dentist banned from receiving federal funds to provide care for low-income patients because he defaulted on $164,800 in student loans. "We never takedown the big guys," concedes Schooner, now a government-contracts

law professor at George Washington University.

THE REVIEW OF environmental and workplace violations by *Mother Jones* reveals that many big contractors could have been forced to forfeit federal business had Bush not interceded on their behalf. Consider the record of ExxonMobil, which became the nation's 43rd-largest contractor when the two oil giants merged in 1999. Between 1995 and 2000, the firms received a total of $2.2 billion from the government for everything from renting fuel storage space to the Pentagon to selling oil to the Commerce Department. At the same time, they were openly disregarding the law. ExxonMobil has been held liable, either on its own or with other companies, in 20 cases in which it refused to clean up Superfund sites or take responsibility for air and water violations. The company is a partner in Colonial Pipeline, an Atlanta-based firm that the Justice Department sued in 2000 for multiple spills in nine states. In one incident, a pipeline rupture poured 950,000 gallons of diesel fuel into the Reedy River in South Carolina, killing 35,000 fish and other wildlife. In 1995, Mobil was hit with a $98,500 fine for its failure to inspect equipment at a refinery in Torrance, California, where 28 workers were injured in an explosion. In 1999, authorities discovered that Exxon had knowingly contaminated water supplies near a refinery in Benicia, California, with benzene and toluene, both of which cause cancer and birth defects.

One of the federal contractors with the worst record of workplace violations is Avondale Industries, which builds ships for the Navy. Between 1990 and 1996, nine workers died at Avondale's shipyard outside New Orleans, a death rate nearly three times that at other Navy shipyards. In 1999, OSHA inspectors uncovered hundreds of violations of safety and health standards, including Avondale's failure to provide safe scaffolding or training for employees who work at dangerous heights. OSHA hit the company with $717,000 in fines, among the largest ever imposed on a shipbuilder. "The stiff penalties are warranted," said then-Secretary of Labor Alexis Herman. "Workers should not have to risk their lives for their livelihood."

Yet just a month after the fines, the government awarded Avondale $22 million to work on amphibious assault ships at the New Orleans yard. The following year, three more workers were killed in accidents at the Avondale yard. One of the victims, 33-year-old Faustino Mendoza, died of head injuries when he fell 80 feet from scaffolding that lacked required safety features—the same problem that had been found during the most recent inspection. OSHA fined Avondale $49,000 for the "repeat" violation, but the penalty amounted to a tiny fraction of the $1.3 billion the firm received in federal business between 1995 and 2000. (Last year, Avondale became a subsidiary of Northrop Grumman.)

Another contractor with a pattern of workplace abuses is Tyson Foods, which received more than $163 million between 1995 and 2000, mostly for supplying poultry to government agencies. In 1999, seven workers died at plants run by Tyson or its independent operators. One of the victims was a 15-year-old boy—hired in violation of child-labor laws—who was electrocuted at a Tyson plant in Arkansas. The company has also attempted to buy influence with federal officials. In 1997, Tyson pleaded guilty to giving former Agriculture Secretary Michael Espy more than $12,000 in "gratuities" while the firm had issues before his department.

Even though the current federal rule requires contractors like Tyson, Avondale, and ExxonMobil to demonstrate "integrity and business ethics," they are in no danger of being barred from receiving federal business under the current standard. Indeed, the government continues to award major contracts to companies that have both defrauded the government *and* violated environmental and workplace laws.

TRW, the nation's ninth-largest contractor, supplies the government with everything from military satellites and spacecraft to autoparts and hand tools. Yet the company's subsidiaries have been cited for cheating the government on defense contracts, and last year it settled two cases in which it forced its employees to work off the clock and mishandled pension payments. In 1997, TRW was also listed in a "rogues' gallery" of OSHA violators in a study by *Business and Management Practices*. In just two years, the magazine found, the company racked up 67 violations and $113,202 in fines. In a single inspection in December 1999, OSHA cited TRW for 43 serious and repeat violations at an auto-parts plant in Michigan.

Some of TRW's most egregious offenses took place at two air-bag plants that lie at the foot of the Superstition Mountains near Mesa, Arizona. Within two years after they opened in 1989, the factories had experienced dozens of fires and explosions, and were the target of at least six investigations by state regulators. "There were explosions so big that they felt like earthquakes," says Bunny Bertleson, who lives less than two miles from one of the plants. "Then clouds would come blowing out of the stacks."

The cause of the blasts was sodium azide, a highly volatile chemical that triggers the explosion that inflates air bags upon impact. Sodium azide is also highly toxic. It can damage the heart, kidneys, and nervous system if it is inhaled or comes into contact with the skin or eyes. Acute exposure can cause death.

A string of injuries suffered by workers at the Mesa plants drew the attention of state regulators. Employees frequently reported feeling queasy and dizzy, a condition they dubbed the "azide buzz," but say the company failed to address the problem. "There was constant pressure to get the production numbers up," recalls Felipe Chavez, a former employee. "That was the only priority." TRW insists that such expo-

sure is rare, and that employee safety is "our highest priority." But in 1994, a spark detonated a small quantity of sodium azide, killing one worker and injuring six. The following year, the Mesa fire chief shut down one of the plants for two days, calling it an "imminent threat to both life and property."

The Arizona attorney general's office had already taken TRW to court and won consent orders requiring it to halt the fires, which were releasing sodium azide into the air, and to properly manage hazardous waste at the plants. In 1995, after the company failed to take safety steps it had promised to make to settle prior charges, a state superior court ordered TRW to pay $1.7 million—the largest corporate criminal consent judgment in state history.

But neither court-ordered fines nor injuries to workers prompted TRW to clean up its act. In 1997, an anonymous caller informed a state environmental agency that TRW was illegally storing wastewater laced with sodium azide at one of its Mesa plants. Following up on the tip, state investigators discovered that the company had illegally disposed of hundreds of thousands of gallons of chemical wastewater at landfills in Arizona, Utah, and California. The Arizona attorney general's office determined that the dumping was not "the work of low-level employees" but involved the "approval or acquiescence" of management.

Given the scope of the illegal dumping and TRW's history of breaking its promises, the state pressed criminal charges against the company. In a statement, TRW said that "the errors that occurred did not result in harm to the environment, local residents, or our employees." But last year, the company agreed to pay $24 million to the government for the illegal dumping—the largest such consent agreement in history.

Yet the company's pattern of lawbreaking has not harmed its ability to do business with the government. Between 1995 and 2000, when most of the illegal dumping and other abuses took place, TRW received nearly $10.3 billion in federal contracts—more than 400 times the amount it agreed to pay for its environmental crimes. After the company was caught dumping sodium azide, federal officials reviewed its violations and decided that it should remain eligible to work for the government. Last year, TRW received another $2.5 billion in federal contracts.

From *Mother Jones*, May/June 2002, pp. 68-73, 86. © 2002 by Foundation for National Progress. Reprinted by permission.

Legal Intelligence

Harassment Grows More COMPLEX

BY CAROLE O'BLENES

Aside from gender, harassment claims are being asserted based on other protected characteristics, including race, religion, age, disability and national origin.

Sexual harassment complaints filed with the EEOC have more than doubled since 1991, and some recent Supreme Court decisions provide new guidance to employers.

In addition to damage awards, harassment complaints carry many intangible costs, such as adverse publicity and reduced morale. Retaliation claims also are a risk.

Develop a comprehensive policy that addresses all forms of unlawful harassment, outlines procedures for reporting and investigating complaints and prevents retaliation.

Awareness of sexual harassment in the workplace has reached unprecedented levels as President Clinton's sexual encounters—Monica Lewinsky, Paula Jones and others—have made sexual harassment a common topic in the news. For employers, this heightened awareness often results in additional sexual harassment complaints as employees develop higher expectations about what behavior is appropriate and conclude that their workplaces fall short of those expectations.

In 1998, more than 15,000 sexual harassment charges were filed with the U.S. Equal Employment Opportunity Commission (EEOC), up from about 6,900 in 1991. Amounts paid out by employers charged with sexual harassment in EEOC proceedings and actions alone exploded from $7.1 million in 1990 to $49.5 million in 1997.

But unlawful workplace harassment is not limited to sexual harassment of women by men. Men also can be (and are) sexually harassed. And harassment claims are being asserted based on protected characteristics other than gender, such as race, age, religion, disability and national origin. Such recent cases include a black Muslim correction officer who claimed he was subjected to racial and religious harassment by coworkers and supervisors; a disabled employee who asserted she was ridiculed about "the disability being in her mind only"; and an Italian-American who claimed he was subjected to racist comments, slurs and jokes based on his national origin. Lifestyle issues also can lead to harassment claims, as in the case of a gay employee offended by a "born-again Christian" coworker's views on homosexuality.

RISK REDUCTION

Every employee falls into at least one of the protected categories, and many belong to several. Therefore, it's essential to prevent incidents that might lead to harassment claims and respond effectively when they do arise. This will reduce your exposure to liability and maximize workplace productivity.

The litigation costs associated with the rise in harassment complaints are enormous and increasing. As a result of the Civil Rights Act of 1991, jury trials are now available in federal harassment cases, and the remedies available to plaintiffs in such cases have expanded to include not just equitable relief, such as reinstatement and back pay, but also compensatory and punitive damages.

Last year, a federal jury awarded nearly $5.7 million to the family of a former U.S. Postal Service engineer who complained of sexual harassment prior to committing suicide. A male dude ranch wrangler was awarded $300,000 by a federal jury based on his claim that he was sexually harassed by his female supervisor. In California, the average jury verdict in employment cases in 1998 was $2.5 million. Equally important are the intangible damages associated with harassment claims, such as absenteeism, employee turnover, low morale and low productivity.

WHAT IS UNLAWFUL HARASSMENT?

The concept of unlawful harassment grew out of sexual harassment claims, but it has been applied in cases involving other protected characteristics as well. The EEOC's "Guidelines on Discrimination Because of Sex" define sexual harassment as "unwelcome sexual advances, requests for sexual favors, and other verbal or physical conduct of a sexual nature." The EEOC, commentators and courts have identified two types of harassment: "quid pro quo" and "hostile environment."

Employees who are subjected to harassment tend to assume it's because of a protected characteristic.

In two cases last summer, *Faragher v. City of Boca Raton* and *Ellerth v. Burlington Indus.*, the Supreme Court clarified the definition of sexual harassment. The court explained that quid pro quo harassment occurs when a "tangible employment action," such as termination, demotion or a significant change in assignment or benefits, results from a refusal to submit to a supervisor's sexual demands. If there is no tangible employment action, an employee may still be a victim of sexual harassment if he or she is subjected to unwelcome sexual conduct that is sufficiently severe or pervasive to unreasonably interfere with his or her work performance or create an intimidating, hostile or offensive work environment.

Quid pro quo claims are limited to the sexual harassment context. Not so for the hostile work environment standard, which the courts have applied to other types of harassment claims. Regardless of the protected characteristic relied on by the plaintiff, in these cases the courts look to the severity and pervasiveness of the alleged harassment. To prevail on a hostile environment claim, the plaintiff must also show that he or she was subjected to severe and offensive conduct *because* of his or her protected characteristic.

When a company can show that the alleged harasser treated all employees in the same negative manner—sometimes referred to as an "equal opportunity harasser"—the harassment would not be unlawful because it is not related to the plaintiff's membership in a protected class. In *Pavone v. Brown*, for example, the court held that a disabled plaintiff could not prove unlawful harassment because other, nondisabled employees complained of the same mistreat-

BRIEF CASES

THE ADA AND CORRECTIVE DEVICES

Two cases currently before the Supreme Court will resolve a difference of opinion among the courts as to whether an individual can be considered "disabled," and thus protected by the Americans with Disabilities Act (ADA), if his or her medical condition is corrected with medication or assistive devices. The two cases involve employees who were denied jobs because of medical conditions—twin pilots who are nearsighted in *Sutton v. United Airlines*, and a truck mechanic with high blood pressure in *Murphy v. United Parcel Service*. In both cases, the 10th Circuit ruled that the employees were *not* disabled because their conditions were corrected with lenses and medication, respectively.

NEW GUIDANCE ON 'REASONABLE ACCOMMODATIONS'

The EEOC issued new Guidance in February that addresses some tough questions about the reasonable accommodation requirements of the ADA. Among those questions: When must you provide an accommodation? What type is required? Under what circumstances can you claim that a requested accommodation would impose an undue hardship? According to the EEOC, once an employee indicates that her medical condition is affecting some aspect of her work, the employer is obligated to clarify her needs and identify an appropriate accommodation. Reasonable accommodations may include restructurings of some job functions, leaves of absence, modified or part-time work schedules, modified workplace policies and job reassignments.

EEOC CHALLENGES AN ENGLISH-ONLY POLICY

A federal district court recently denied an employer's motion to dismiss a lawsuit filed by the EEOC that challenges the company's brief use of an English-only policy. The employer, Synchro-Start, had established a policy requiring employees to speak only English during work hours, allegedly in response to complaints that multilingual employees were harassing and insulting coworkers in their native tongues. It rescinded the policy within nine months. The EEOC suit claims the policy discriminates on the basis of national origin because it focuses on employees whose primary language is not English. EEOC Guidelines express a presumption that English-only rules create a discriminatory environment based on national origin.

ment by the plaintiff's supervisor. But companies need to be aware that employees who are subjected to verbal abuse and other harassment tend to assume that it is because of a protected characteristic. Thus, such behavior (particularly by supervisors) presents risks of claims, litigation costs and workplace disruption even if the employer may ultimately prevail on an "equal opportunity abuser" theory.

Proof that harassment was because of a protected characteristic was the pivotal issue in a case decided by the Supreme Court last year. In *Oncale v. Sundowner Offshore Services, Inc.*, the plaintiff, a male employee alleged, among other things, that he was grabbed by his male supervisor and a male coworker who physically abused him while threatening rape. The Supreme Court concluded that a heterosexual can state a viable claim of sexual harassment against another heterosexual of the same gender (i.e., same-sex harassment), but remanded the case to the lower court to determine whether Oncale was in fact harassed *because of his sex.*

EMPLOYER LIABILITY

The Supreme Court's recent decisions in *Ellerth* and *Faragher* also clarified the circumstances under which an employer can be held liable for harassment by a supervisor. When an immediate (or successively higher) supervisor's harassment culminates in a tangible employment action, such as discharge, demotion or undesirable reassignment, the employer will be liable for the supervisor's actions.

When the harassment does not result in a tangible employment action, the employer may raise an "affirmative defense" to liability or damages. This defense is made up of two parts: First, that the employer exercised reasonable care to prevent and correct promptly any harassing behavior. Second, that the plaintiff employee unreasonably failed to take advantage of any preventive or corrective opportunities provided by the employer or to avoid harm otherwise.

The reasonableness of an employer's response also determines liability in hostile environment cases involving harassment by a coworker, nonsupervisory employee or nonemployee (such as a vendor, customer, consultant or client). For example, a local Pizza Hut franchise was held liable for $200,000 in compensatory damages plus nearly $40,000 in attorney's fees and costs because it failed to prevent two of its customers from sexually harassing a waitress. In *Lockard v. Pizza Hut, Inc.*, the waitress claimed that her manager forced her to wait on two customers who pulled her hair and sexually assaulted her. The customers had engaged in other abusive conduct in prior visits and the plaintiff had complained to her manager. A federal appeals court upheld the verdict, observing that the manager had been given notice of the harassing conduct and had unreasonably failed to remedy or prevent the harassment.

• POINTS OF POLICY

Here are the hallmarks of an effective nondiscrimination and anti-harassment policy:
• Introductory statement that expresses a commitment to a work environment that is free of discrimination and harassment.
• Equal employment opportunity statement.
• Definitions of harassment, with examples of behaviors that may constitute harassment.
• Coverage extending to all applicants, employees and third parties, such as outside vendors, consultants or customers, and to all conduct in a work-related setting—including social occasions such as client lunches and holiday parties.
• Prohibition of retaliation, enforced through disciplinary action.
• Complaint procedure designating several different "avenues of complaint" and strongly urging the reporting of all incidents.
• Assurance of a prompt investigation of complaints.
• Confidentiality maintained to the extent consistent with adequate investigation and appropriate corrective action.
• Corrective action upon a finding of misconduct, with specific examples of possible actions.
—*C.O.*

In light of the Supreme Court's recent decisions, it is critical for employers to take affirmative steps to prevent and remedy harassment. At a minimum, they should:
• Develop a written nondiscrimination and anti-harassment policy (see box).
• Ensure that the policy provides employees with effective avenues to bring complaints forward (not just through their supervisor, who may in fact be the harasser).
• Include the policy in a prominent place in an employee handbook (if there is one).
• Widely disseminate the policy (independent of the handbook) throughout the workplace on a periodic basis to make sure all employees know of its existence and understand the complaint procedure.
• Train appropriate segments of the workforce, such as senior management, managers/supervisors and complaint-receivers, to understand and apply the policy.
• Promptly respond to complaints brought under the policy by thoroughly investigating them to determine if policy violations have occurred.
• Take prompt, effective remedial action to respond to violations.

PREVENTING RETALIATION

In addition to distributing an anti-harassment policy, companies need to develop policies and procedures to prevent retaliation against individuals who file complaints of harassment or discrimination or who participate in their investigation. Charges of retaliation are on the rise, with more than 19,000 claims filed with the EEOC in 1998 alone.

Retaliation is an independent basis for employer liability under the federal discrimination laws. All too often, companies are finding that even after a discrimination or harassment claim has been dismissed for lack of evidence, the courts are ordering them to proceed to trial on claims of unlawful retaliation. This is because adverse action taken against an employee who opposes unlawful practices (by filing or threatening to file a complaint) can be considered unlawful retaliation.

For example, a federal appellate court recently reinstated a retaliation claim filed against Wal-Mart, while affirming the dismissal of the plaintiff's claims of racial harassment and discrimination. The plaintiff had alleged that within the two months after she filed a discrimination complaint with the EEOC, she was listed as a "no-show" on a scheduled day off, twice reprimanded by her manager and then given a one-day suspension. In addition, she claimed, her manager began soliciting negative statements about her from coworkers. The court held that this conduct was sufficient to support a claim of retaliation, especially because the plaintiff had not received any reprimands in the 11 months before she filed her EEOC charge.

To minimize the risk of liability for such claims, employers need to incorporate a strong prohibition against retaliation in their anti-harassment policies. They also should advise employees at all levels that retaliation will not be tolerated and will result in disciplinary action up to and including termination. Then make sure the policies are fully enforced.

After filing a charge of harassment or discrimination, employees often perceive any adverse actions as related to their complaint. Therefore, a human resources officer or other appropriate manager should carefully monitor a complainant's work environment and work with his or her supervisor to avoid even the appearance of retaliation. Further, ensure that the complainant is not shunned by his or her coworkers, and counsel managers to make a conscious effort to include complainants in appropriate workplace meetings or events.

If a complainant is a candidate for discipline for performance-related reasons, his or her manager should consult with human resources before any discipline is imposed to verify that it is warranted and consistent with comparable situations. Similarly, decisions involving raises and promotional opportunities in the complainant's department should be discussed with HR to ensure the complainant received appropriate consideration and was treated even-handedly.

Carole O'Blenes, a partner in the New York office of Proskauer Rose LLP, has practiced labor and employment law since 1976. She has represented employers in collective bargaining, arbitration, administrative proceedings and employment litigation. She also provides advice and guidance to clients on a wide range of employment and labor law matters. E-mail: coblenes@proskauer.com. Tracey I. Levy, an associate at Proskauer Rose, also contributed to this article.

LITIGATION

IS WAL-MART HOSTILE TO WOMEN?

Female workers paint a picture of a harsh, sexist culture

Ocala, Fla., was no boomtown bursting with jobs in 1991. So when Wal-Mart Stores Inc. subsidiary Sam's Club came to town, hundreds of applicants dressed in suits sweated in the sun for hours to apply. Kim Miller was excited when she got the chance to join the late Sam Walton's team. Finally, she would have a great company to work for, an employer whose motto "respect for the individual" led her to believe she could build a career there.

Kim Miller, a plaintiff in a suit against Wal-Mart, claims she complained of discrimination to higher-ups several times but only got retaliation

It didn't turn out that way. Over the next nine years, Miller says, her job as a sales associate turned into a frat-house nightmare. She claims her male supervisors referred to her as "bitch" and talked about which female customers they would like to get into bed. The sexual talk allegedly turned her way, too, and included offers to get her pregnant. Once, when Miller was working in the tire-and-mounting unit, she claims she walked in on her male co-workers huddled over a porn video in the customer lounge. The worst of it, though, was that despite glowing performance reviews, an Employee-of-the-Year award, and many commendations from customers, Miller claims she was passed over time and again for pay raises and promotions.

Instead, jobs like team leader in tire-and-mounting were given to men such as a forklift repairman who had never even worked in the department.

Miller, 36, says she complained more than a dozen times to bosses at all levels but was retaliated against for doing so. When she got pregnant, she alleges she was transferred to a greeter position and not allowed by her manager to sit down until she got a doctor's note. "I worked there longer than most people are married these days," says Miller, who is no longer with the company. "And I never got a promotion."

WIDE NET. Wal-Mart isn't commenting on the allegations lodged by Miller and the other five women who filed a sexual discrimination class action in U.S. District Court for Northern California on June 19. Yet the suit could turn out to be the largest such case ever against a private employer if plaintiffs' attorneys win nationwide class-action status. The Bentonville (Ark.)-based company employs 960,000 people nationwide.

But even if lawyers fail to sweep in the company's entire U.S. employee roster, the case casts a wide net among Wal-Mart's 46,000 workers in California. The plaintiffs paint a picture of a harsh, anti-woman culture in which complaints go unanswered and the women who make them are targeted for retaliation. Based on filings Wal-Mart made to the Equal Employment Opportunity Commission, the claim details how 72% of the company's sales staff are women but only one-third of them

make it into management, despite Wal-Mart's promote-from-within policy. That means, according to EEOC data, that Wal-Mart doesn't just rank below its current retailing peers, which have an average of 56% women managers, but it also ranks below rivals' levels of 25 years ago.

SHOPTALK
Wal-Mart says the number of its women managers is growing

Wal-Mart denies the allegations about a systematic practice of discrimination, noting it has explicit policies forbidding such behavior. The company says that because it is the nation's largest employer, it is an attractive target for lawsuits. Says spokesman Jay Allen: "When you have a million people, you're going to have a few people out there who don't do things right." Still, "there's no doubt we need to continue to do a better job of promoting and developing women and minorities."

The sexual discrimination suit is the latest in a string of recent legal problems at the company. Wal-Mart has taken an aggressive, no-holds-barred litigation stance for years that has drawn the ire of courts nationwide. Judges have sanctioned the company more than 130 times, in 40,000 cases in the past decade, for discovery abuses. Now its employment-related problems are growing, too. Last month, a U.S. District Court in Tucson slapped the company with a contempt motion for violating a court order in an EEOC disability bias

WELCOME TO WAL-MART'S WOES

The sex-discrimination lawsuit isn't Wal-Mart's only problem. The company has also gotten into trouble with:

• The EEOC—for failing to comply with the Americans with Disabilities Act
    Wal-Mart says it has implemented training

• Judges—who have sanctioned the company 130 times for abusive litigation
    Wal-Mart says it has made "significant progress" on the issue

• Washington state—for delaying payment on workers' compensation benefits
    Wal-Mart is appealing and says it has worked with the state on the issues

• The National Labor Relations Board—for allegedly violating federal labor laws
    Wal-Mart says such charges are "easy to make"

Data: *BusinessWeek*

case. The court ordered it to pay $750,200 in fines for not following through on the terms of the settlement, which included creating training materials for hearing-impaired employees, providing disability training for managers, and allowing government disability and EEOC officials to visit stores to verify compliance.

Indeed, since 1994, the EEOC has filed 16 suits against Wal-Mart for disability discrimination. That is the most Americans with Disabilities Act-related EEOC suits of any U.S. company, according to the EEOC. "I have never seen this kind of blatant disregard for the law," says EEOC lawyer Mary Jo O'Neill. "You get the impression that Wal-Mart is an employer that, at the top, isn't committed to taking the [ADA] and federal employment laws seriously." Wal-Mart has asked for a rehearing but says it has instituted training. "Hopefully, our managers understand better now what kind of capabilities disabled people have," says spokesman Bill Wertz.

The company also has worker-related problems in Washington state, which last December issued an order revoking Wal-Mart's authority to administer its own workers' compensation claims because of mistreatment of injured workers and "repeated" and "unreasonable delays" in giving them benefits they were owed. Wal-Mart has since won a stay of that order, saying it has a "good and improving record" and has worked conscientiously with the state.

UNFAIR? The company says it has also worked on diversity issues by regularly tracking the number of women and minor-

ities in management and that the numbers are improving, though it declined to detail what percentage of senior managers are women. What's more, comparisons with other retailers are unfair, notes Wertz, because they may classify their managerial jobs differently. If Wal-Mart included department managers—hourly employees who have several layers of supervision above them—among management positions, women would make up 60% of the managerial ranks, the company says.

But Wal-Mart employees involved in the suit, even those who have been promoted, such as former personnel manager Micki Earwood, say that number is misleading. In her job, Earwood says, she had access to promotion and pay records for her store in Urbana, Ohio. These revealed, she alleges, that male workers were given most of the promotions and raises and that men were sometimes paid higher than women who ranked above them.

For plaintiffs' lawyers, the next hurdle is convincing the U.S. District Court judge that a company so centralized that it can keep tabs on every last lightbulb in its more than 3,100 stores can't claim ignorance about its alleged problems with women. The court may be reluctant to grant nationwide class-action status because the suit involves a potentially unprecedented number of people. But if it does, this could turn into the No. 1 legal problem for the No. 1 retailer.

By Michelle Conlin in New York and Wendy Zellner in Dallas

RACISM IN THE WORKPLACE

In an increasingly multicultural U.S., harassment of minorities is on the rise

By Aaron Bernstein

When Wayne A. Elliott was transferred in 1996 from a factory job to a warehouse at Lockheed Martin Corp.'s sprawling military-aircraft production facilities in Marietta, Ga., he says he found himself face to face with naked racism. Anti-black graffiti was scrawled on the restroom walls. His new white colleagues harassed him, Elliott recalls, as did his manager, who would yell at him, call him "boy," and tell him to "kiss my butt." He complained, but Elliot says the supervisor was no help. Instead, he assigned Elliott, now 46, to collecting parts to be boxed, which involves walking about 10 miles a day. Meanwhile, the eight whites in his job category sat at computer terminals and told him to get a move on—even though Elliott outranked them on the union seniority list.

The atmosphere got even uglier when Elliott and a few other blacks formed a small group in 1997 called Workers Against Discrimination, which led to the filing of two class actions. One day, he and the other two black men among the 30 warehouse workers found "back-to-Africa tickets" on their desks, he says, which said things like "Just sprinkle this dingy black dust on any sidewalk and piss on it, and, presto! hundreds of n-----s spring up!" They reported this, but the Lockheed security officials who responded took the three victims away in their security cars as if they were the wrongdoers, he says, and interrogated them separately.

Then, one day in 1999, according to Elliott, a hangman's noose appeared near his desk. "You're going to end up with your head in here," Elliott recalls a white co-worker threatening. Another noose appeared last November, he says. He and the other whites "hassle me all the time now, unplugging my computer so I lose work, hiding my bike or chair; it's constant," says Elliott, who gets counseling from a psychologist for the stress and says he has trouble being attentive to his two children, ages 7 and 8, when he's at home.

Lockheed spokesman Sam Grizzle says the company won't comment on any specific employee. But regarding the suits, which Lockheed is fighting, he says, "we do not tolerate, nor have we ever tolerated, harassment or discrimination of any form. We take such complaints very seriously, and we always have investigated them and taken appropriate action when needed."

The alleged incidents at Lockheed are part of an extensive pattern of charges of racial hatred in U.S. workplaces that *BusinessWeek* investigated over a two-month period. Nearly four decades after the Civil Rights Act of 1964 gave legal equality to minorities, charges of harassment at work based on race or national origin have more than doubled, to nearly 9,000 a year, since 1990, according to the Equal Employment Opportunity Commission (charts).

The problem is not confined to small Southern cities such as Marietta. In addition to high-profile suits at Lockheed, Boeing, and Texaco, dozens of other household names face complaints of racism in their workforce. Noose cases have been prosecuted in cosmopolitan San Francisco and in Detroit, with a black population among the largest in the nation.

It's true that minorities' share of the workforce grew over the decade, which could have led to a corresponding rise in clashes. Yet racial harassment charges have jumped by 100% since 1990, while minority employment grew by 36%. What's more, most charges involve multiple victims, so each year the cases add up to tens of thousands of workers—mostly blacks, but also Hispanics and Asians.

It's hard to reconcile such ugly episodes with an American culture that is more accepting of its increasing diversity than ever before. Today, immigrants from every ethnic and racial background flock to the U.S. There is a solid black middle class, and minorities are active in most walks of life, from academia

to the nightly news. When we do think about race, it's usually to grapple with more subtle and complex issues, such as whether affirmative action is still necessary to help minorities overcome past discrimination, or whether it sometimes constitutes reverse discrimination against whites.

Lockheed Martin employee Wayne Elliott says he found "back-to-Africa tickets" on his desk and was called "boy" by his manager. He complained, he says, to no avail. Then came the hangman's noose.

To some extent, the rise in harassment cases may actually reflect America's improved race relations. Because more minorities believe that society won't tolerate blatant bigotry anymore, they file EEOC charges rather than keep quiet out of despair that their complaints won't be heard, says Susan Sturm, a Columbia University law professor who studies workplace discrimination. Many cases involve allegations of harassment that endured for years.

Multimillion-dollar settlements of racial discrimination or harassment claims at such companies as Coca-Cola Co. and Boeing Co. also give victims greater hope that a remedy is available. Such suits became easier in 1991, after Congress passed a law that allowed jury trials and compensatory and punitive damages in race cases. "It's like rape, which everyone kept silent about before," says Boeing human resources chief James B. Dagnon. "Now, prominent individuals are willing to talk publicly about what happened, so there's a safer environment to speak up in."

But many experts say they are seeing a disturbing increase in incidents of harassment. Minority workers endure the oldest racial slurs in the book. They're asked if they eat "monkey meat," denigrated as inferior to whites, or find "KKK" and other intimidating graffiti on the walls at work.

Even office workers are not exempt. In May, 10 current and former black employees at Xerox Corp. offices in Houston filed harassment charges with the EEOC. One, Linda Johnson, says she has suffered racial slurs from a co-worker since 1999, when glaucoma forced her to quit the sales department and become a receptionist. Last year, a white colleague doctored a computer photo of her to make her look like a prostitute, she says. After she complained, her boss printed out the picture and hung it in his office, her charge says. "I tried to do what company procedures suggested and complain to my supervisor, then on up to human resources at headquarters," says Johnson, 47. "But they just sweep it under the rug." Xerox declined to comment on her case.

Worse yet are hangman's nooses, a potent symbol of mob lynchings in America's racial history. The EEOC has handled 25 noose cases in the past 18 months, "something that only came along every two or three years before," says Ida L. Castro, outgoing EEOC chairwoman. Management lawyers concur that racial harassment has jumped sharply. "I've seen more of these cases in the last few years than in the previous 10, and it's bad stuff," says Steve Poor, a partner at Seyfarth, Shaw, Fairweather & Geraldson, a law firm that helps companies defend harassment and discrimination suits.

Some lay the blame on blue-collar white men who think affirmative action has given minorities an unfair advantage. Their feelings may be fueled by the long-term slide in the wages of less-skilled men, which have lagged inflation since 1973. Since many whites see little evidence of discrimination anymore, the small number who harbor racist views feel more justified in lashing out at minorities, whom they perceive as getting ahead solely due to their race, says Carol M. Swain, a Vanderbilt University law professor who is writing a book about white nationalism.

SILENCE. Incidents of open racism at work occur below the national radar because all the parties have powerful incentives to keep it quiet. Plaintiffs' lawyers don't want employees to go public before a trial for fear of prejudicing their case in court. *BusinessWeek* spoke for more than a month with some lawyers before they agreed to let their clients talk. Even then, most workers refused to give their names, fearful of retaliation. Man-

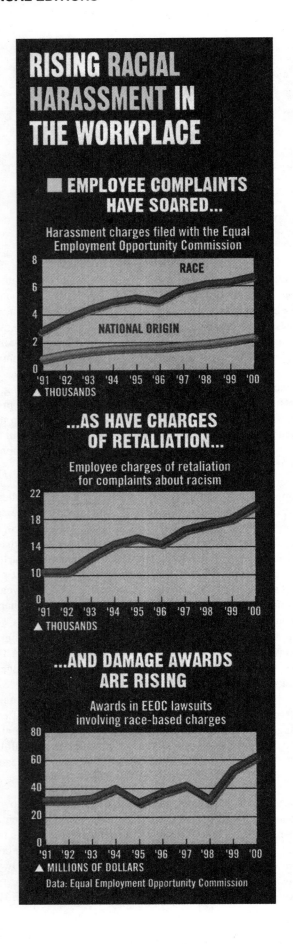

RISING RACIAL HARASSMENT IN THE WORKPLACE

■ **EMPLOYEE COMPLAINTS HAVE SOARED...**

Harassment charges filed with the Equal Employment Opportunity Commission

RACE

NATIONAL ORIGIN

'91 '92 '93 '94 '95 '96 '97 '98 '99 '00
▲ THOUSANDS

...AS HAVE CHARGES OF RETALIATION...

Employee charges of retaliation for complaints about racism

'91 '92 '93 '94 '95 '96 '97 '98 '99 '00
▲ THOUSANDS

...AND DAMAGE AWARDS ARE RISING

Awards in EEOC lawsuits involving race-based charges

'91 '92 '93 '94 '95 '96 '97 '98 '99 '00
▲ MILLIONS OF DOLLARS

Data: Equal Employment Opportunity Commission

agement and plaintiffs' lawyers alike say it takes tremendous nerve to file a suit or EEOC charges, given the likelihood that co-workers or bosses will strike back. Since 1990, the number of minorities filing charges of retaliation with the EEOC after they complained about racial mistreatment has doubled, to 20,000 a year.

Companies have an even greater desire to avoid bad publicity. Many suits end when employers settle. They routinely buy employees' silence with extra damage award money.

Because racial harassment allegations can be so embarrassing, they pose a difficult challenge for companies. Some quickly go on the offensive and take steps to change. Other employers hunker down for a fight, arguing that allegations are inaccurate or exaggerated. Northwest Airlines Corp., for example, is fighting charges made by black construction workers who found a noose last July at the airline's new terminal under construction at Detroit Metro Airport. Northwest also recently settled two noose-related suits, although it denied liability. Northwest spokeswoman Kathleen M. Peach says none of the noose incidents "rise to the level of harassment. You have to ask was it a joke at a construction site? Or was it in a cargo area where a lot of ropes are used? It's not as cut-and-dried as it seems."

When Ted Gignilliat told what he knew about two nooses at Lockheed, he too became a target, he says. One anonymous caller told him he would "wind up on a slab, dead."

Some employers dismiss nooses and slurs as harmless joking. This seems to be the view taken by Lakeside Imports Inc., New Orleans' largest Toyota Motor Corp. dealer. Last August, it signed a consent decree with the EEOC to settle charges brought by six black salesmen in its 50-person used-car department. The men said that their manager, Chris Mohrman, hit and poked them with two 3 1/2-foot-long sticks with derogatory words on them that he called his "n----- sticks."

Lakeside brushed aside the incident, according to case depositions. Mohrman's manager at the time, a white man named David Oseng, had hired the black salesmen. When he heard what was going on, Oseng said in his deposition, he told the dealership's top brass. Oseng said the top two managers "told me they were tired of all the problems with the n-----s. And if we hired another n-----, [I] would be terminated."

Lakeside lawyer Ralph Zatzkis says the dealer didn't admit any guilt and denies that anything serious happened. He says the sticks, which the EEOC obtained by subpoena, did have writing on them, but "those weren't racial remarks." Zatzkis dismissed the episode as "horseplay." Mohrman and the black salesmen left Lakeside and couldn't be reached. Zatzkis says Lakeside's top managers declined to comment.

Frivolous harassment charges do occur, say experts, but they're rare. "It takes a lot of energy to raise a complaint, and you can make major mistakes assuming what the employees' motives are," warns Haven E. Cockerham, head of human resources at R.R. Donnelley & Sons Co., which is fighting a class action for alleged racial discrimination and harassment that included claims of whites donning KKK robes.

Consider Adelphia Communications Corp., a $2.9 billion cable-TV company based in Coudersport, Pa. In February, the EEOC filed suit on behalf of Glenford S. James, a 12-year veteran, and other black employees in the company's Miami office. A manager there racially harassed minorities "on a daily basis" after he took over in August, 1999, the suit says. The manager twice put a noose over James's door, it says. Once, says the complaint, the manager told an employee to "order monkey meat or whatever they eat" for James.

In a suit filed in June, James says that Adelphia didn't stop the problem until he complained to the EEOC in May, 2000. Then, the manager was terminated or resigned. Adelphia declined to comment. However, its brief in the EEOC suit admits that the manager displayed a noose and "made inappropriate statements of a racial nature." The brief says Adelphia "promptly and severely disciplined" the manager "as a result of his actions." The manager couldn't be reached.

REVENGE. Whites who stand up for co-workers also can run into trouble. Ted W. Gignilliat, a worker at the Marietta facility of Lockheed since 1965, says he was harassed so badly for speaking up about two nooses that he had to take a leave of absence. He says he was threatened, his truck was broken into, and he got anonymous phone calls at work and at home—one telling him he would "wind up on a slab, dead." In March, 2000, a psychologist told Gignilliat to stop work; he went on disability leave until May of this year. He now works as an alarm-room operator in the plant's fire station. "It's in the middle of the security office, with guards, but I feel they will retaliate against me again for stepping forward," says Gignilliat.

Usually, of course, minorities bear the brunt of revenge. Roosevelt Lewis, who delivers Wonder bread for an Interstate Bakeries Corp. bakery in San Francisco, says his white superiors have been making his life miserable ever since he and other blacks filed a race suit in 1998. A jury awarded them $132 million last year (later reduced by a judge to $32 million). Lewis says this only exacerbated the behavior. "They're trying to make you insubordinate, to create an excuse to fire you," charges Lewis. He says he has complained to higher-ups, but the hassling continues.

Jack N. Wiltrakis, Interstate's head of human resources, says the company has a hotline to headquarters in Kansas City but has received no complaints. "If they have a problem, it's incumbent on them to tell us," he says. Interstate, which has 34,000 workers in 64 bakeries around the U.S., has been sued for race problems in New York, Orlando, Indianapolis, and Richmond, Va. It has settled the two cases, denying liability, and is still fighting the others, including Lewis'. Wiltrakis says the suits haven't prompted Interstate to launch new policies.

In the end, racist behavior by employees lands at the door of corporate executives. They face a dilemma: If they admit there's a problem, the company is exposed to lawsuits and negative publicity. But denial only makes matters worse. Until more employers confront the rise of ugly racism head on, Americans will continue to see behavior they thought belonged to a more ignominious age.

With Michael Arndt in Chicago and bureau reports

The Unifying Force of Diversity

by William A. Guillory

THE GREATEST challenge executives face today, while trying to retain balance in their own lives, is managing change. The world is shrinking, technology is escalating, business is unrestricted, and e-commerce has created a seamless world. We must deal with differences in people and in worldviews—and in how we conduct business locally and globally.

Constructively dealing with such issues, and leveraging them for competitive advantage, is broadly described as diversity. I define *diversity* as an environment wherein the most business-related differences are an integrated part of an organization. Diversity also encompasses appreciation for the richness and strengths brought by different perspectives, attitudes, and approaches. These differences include religion, life-styles, ethics, values, gender, workstyles, teamwork, work-life balance, personalities, customers, history, culture, language, and worldviews.

The first step in understanding how these differences affect your organization is identifying the business-related dimensions that prevent the performance desired. Identifying these dimensions not only establishes a business rationale, but also provides guidelines for addressing the issues that can have the greatest impact on the desired change.

For example, several years ago the Kellogg Company was dissatisfied with the number of women in decision-making and policy-making roles. In response, they established a formal mentoring program that paired selected women with seasoned professionals (both men and women). The focus was on preparing women for more influential roles within one year. Once the protégés critical learning experiences were defined, the mentor matching and relationship challenges were more clearly defined. The program has been a stunning success and has since been expanded to other population groups.

Formal mentoring programs are designed to establish a pattern of cross-gender, cross-cultural, and cross-ethnic mentoring relationships that occur as naturally as those involving individuals of the same gender with similar values.

For diversity to become a reality for each of us, it must become personal. In our workshops, we ask each individual to write at least five dimensions of diversity they personally experience and how each plays out. We use the phrase "work-life" to mean that work and personal activities are inseparable. An example of this exercise is shown in the chart above.

We discover that diversity expands beyond the issues of race and gender. Such experiences bring the definition of diversity to life in a meaningful way.

Given this personal commitment, we might ask, "What is the objective of diversity?" The bottom-line objective is to create a high-performance organization—to ensure the best use of employees. Most employees have similar aspirations: equal opportunity for recruitment, development, advancement, and success. These elements generate loyalty and pride. The problem is that some groups feel less included than others.

Inclusion is the sense of belonging or the feeling of being wanted and needed. The extent to which we are included also sends a message of how valued we are or our contribution. Inclusion involves transformation of fundamental beliefs, attitudes, and even values that promote the careers of some at the expense of others. If such mindsets prevent the professional development, performance, and profitability, then such perceptions serve no constructive purpose.

The most telling situations are in organizations where employees feel compelled to file class-action suits. Denny's, Texaco, and Coca Cola have since instituted dramatic cultural change programs involving external advisory groups to oversee programs. For example, using a 10-point plan, Denny's significantly increased its minority franchises. In 2001, Denny's was #1 in *Fortune's* 50 Best Companies for Minorities. The Texaco settlement included the following statement: "We are affirmatively committed to an environment of inclusion to eradicate all

Dimension	Workplace Applications
1. Managing diversity	*Using unique approaches to influence people to perform to their best abilities.*
2. Work-life	*Balancing my personal life, relationship with my children, and professional responsibilities.*
3. Family-friendly environment	*Having an environment to accommodate various family situations and responsibilities.*
4. Strategic awareness	*Learning how diversity is reshaping business by promoting new customers, new products and services, and independent contractors.*
5. Diversity champion	*Communicating the value of diversity, requiring and evaluating diversity performance.*

forms of prejudices within the company and to ensure tolerance, respect, and dignity for all people."

Any progressive organization could adopt and enforce such a policy.

Achieving inclusion involves a process: 1) Establish a baseline by conducting a performance-oriented cultural survey; 2) Select and prioritize the issues that allow the greatest breakthrough in performance and transforming the culture; 3) Create a five-year diversity strategic plan, linking action items to strategic business objectives; 4) Secure leadership's financial commitment, endorsement, and participation in the plan; 5) Establish a leadership support system with measurable accountability; 6) Implement the plan, recognizing that surprises and setbacks will occur; 7) Connect training to the competencies necessary to achieve the diversity action plan; 8) Conduct a follow-up survey 18 months later to measure performance.

The organization that put these steps into practice will be in a class alone. Mastering diversity is a very growth-producing process.

Nine Key Lessons

There are nine key lessons for ensuring a successful diversity process:

1. If a belief of "people are our most-valued resource" already exists, the diversity process moves faster. This is evident at Chevron, Texaco, HP, and Synoving Financial.

2. Leaders' vision, commitment, and participation is more powerful than any written statement. Examples are Carlos Guiterrez of Kellogg, Jack Lowe of TDIndustries, and Tom Cannell of Merck.

3. Sustaining diversity activities during hard times sends a clear message of commitment. Diversity is founded upon values that include freedom, equality, and fairness. Examples include Kellogg and Sempra Energy.

4. Involving middle managers is key to implementing a diversity plan. Examples are Texas Instruments and TDIndustries.

5. Integrating diversity into mainline processes ensures its long-term success. Strategic planning, succession planning, executive development, work processes, and business roles benefit from diversity.

6. Unless the diversity objectives are specific, definable, and measurable, there is no clear destination. "What gets measured, gets done!"

7. Diversity is a long-term commitment. Commitment must be sustained as the torch is passed from one leader to another. Examples are Eastman Kodak, Avon, and Texas Instrument.

8. Diversity actions will fail unless an existing infrastructure is used—or a new one is established.

9. In the mature stages, the diversity process becomes unique to each organization.

When these lessons become part of your unique process, the fears and resistance to diversity fall away.

Successful diversity programs have the potential for developing the human technology for constructively engaging radically different ways of thinking and doing. This process results in the creation of a new context that embraces such differences and overcomes the present cycle of "conflict and comprise." **EE**

William A. Guillory is CEO of Innovations International, an authority on diversity, empowerment, leadership, creativity, and spirituality. He is the author of The Living Organization *(Amazon.com).*

From *Executive Excellence*, June 2002, pp. 7-8. © 2002 by Executive Excellence.

Employee Rewards: Comp and Benefits

The Kindest Cut

With some sectors softening, make sure your organization has a policy for addressing the needs of laid-off workers before any announcements have to be made.

By Carolyn Hirschman

Have you looked at your severance policy lately? Chances are you haven't. But taking a fresh look at this important benefit may be a good idea, even if your organization does not anticipate any layoffs.

Most employers provide cash, medical benefits and outplacement services to employees who lose their jobs as a result of downsizing, mergers, acquisitions or other events. The idea is to help tide workers over until they find new jobs and to keep benefits competitive with those of other organizations.

"Even in this era of low unemployment, separation benefits continue to be an important concern for U.S. businesses," says outplacement firm Lee Hecht Harrison of Woodcliff Lake, N.J., in its 1998 triennial survey. Eighty-three percent of nearly 2,000 employers queried had severance policies. The company's next such survey is due out later this year.

Even if your company isn't at risk of laying off workers, revisiting your severance pay policy will help you keep up with changes in your workforce, industry and corporate culture, compensation experts say.

"Companies need to understand the job market isn't hot for everybody. It doesn't take into account your tenure and your family's goals. You have to look at the big picture," says Bernadette Kenny, executive vice president of Lee Hecht Harrison.

Downsizing is on the Upswing

As the days of tight labor fade, an increasing number of employers are letting people go. The pace of downsizing is picking up, with 142,208 job cuts announced during January, a 181 percent increase from January 2000, reports Challenger, Gray & Christmas, a Chicago-based outplacement firm. February saw 101,731 layoffs, almost triple that of the same period last year.

The dot-com sector in particular has taken a pounding at the hands of economic forces and Wall Street. Internet employers cut nearly 66,000 jobs during the past 15 months, according to Challenger, Gray & Christmas.

The continuing pace of mergers and acquisitions also is a factor. "With companies being bought and sold, severance is a frequent issue," notes Michael C. Lynch, an attorney in the Washington, D.C., office of the Pittsburgh law firm Reed, Smith, Shaw & McClay. One of the first questions merging companies face is whether and how to pay severance benefits to employees of the acquired firm, he says.

Although imminent layoffs are an obvious reason to re-examine severance policies, the best time to review or change your policy is when times are good. Kenny advises firms not to cut back on severance during bad times "unless you want to create an employee relations nightmare."

A better practice is to look at severance, as well as other benefits, periodically—perhaps every few years—to ensure that they match your workforce in such areas as age and seniority. You also want to make sure your severance is competitive with what's offered by peer companies and otherwise enhances your employer's public image.

However, Challenger cautions against changing severance policies to meet short-term ups and downs of the economy. "I don't think companies should alter their severance policies because of unemployment rates. It's going to be very difficult to manage if it swings up and down."

Going Out on a Waiver

Laid-off employees often are asked to sign a waiver stating that by accepting the employer's severance terms they agree not to sue for discrimination or make any other type of legal claim. Seventy percent of companies surveyed by outplacement firm Lee Hecht Harrison in 1998 required such releases.

Employers with standard, written severance policies that treat all employees the same can't require such a waiver, says Michael C. Lynch, a Washington, D.C., attorney with the Pittsburgh-based law firm Reed, Smith, Shaw & McClay. But employers with no severance plan and those that negotiate severance individually can require one in return for the severance arrangements that are made.

"To be legally binding, a release has to be given in exchange for consideration over and above what the employee is already entitled to by law or contract," Lynch says. This "additional consideration" can consist of extra severance pay, reimbursement for continued health insurance, job-search assistance or other help.

Companies with formal severance plans also can give workers a choice, Lynch says. Employees can take the standard severance package, not sign a release and reserve the right to sue or, in exchange for more generous terms, they can sign a release, thereby agreeing not to sue.

The Age Discrimination in Employment Act, which protects workers 40 and older, requires extra severance in return for signing a waiver. A 43-year-old employee who is laid off in a downsizing, for example, would sign a form agreeing not to sue the employer for age discrimination in return for a more generous severance package.

—Carolyn Hirschman

And Kenny warns that, "Whatever you do, severance must be consistent with corporate culture."

A Boost to Recruiting?

It's logical to think that a beefed-up severance package could help attract workers. But compensation experts agree that, other than a few exceptions, severance benefits alone won't help recruiting efforts much.

CEOs, whose tenures have become shorter and shakier than in past decades, could be lured by a generous severance, says Craig N. Clive, SPHR, a principal at Baylights Compensation Consulting LLC in Ellicott City, Md. "More and more executives are negotiating their severance package as part of their compensation package. They want to know what happens when the balloon bursts."

Similarly, because of the severe volatility and turnover at Internet firms, some applicants might be tempted by a guarantee of severance pay if they are laid off, experts say. But "the person who takes that kind of job is willing to take a risk," notes Bill Coleman, vice president of compensation for Salary.com, a web site based in Wellesley, Mass.

Even so, Alec Levenson, a labor economist at the Milken Institute, a

Santa Monica, Calif., think tank, says that severance would have to be "fairly expensive" to influence recruitment. He doesn't see it as "something that will attract people in high demand." For the rest of the workforce, severance won't be as important as salary and benefits, Levenson adds, so HR managers must think carefully about how they spend their compensation budgets.

Based on the latest available data, severance is generally a tiny part of the HR budget.

Based on the latest available data, severance is generally a tiny part of the HR budget. Civilian employers spent $5.80 per hour worked on all benefits, according to a March 2000 Bureau of Labor Statistics report, which notes that only 3 cents of that amount went for "other benefits," including severance.

Formal vs. Informal Policies

Severance policies and practices vary widely by employer size and industry, consultants say. Large established companies tend to have formal written policies with rela-

tively generous payments. Small and new firms are less formal, often negotiating severance on a case-by-case basis.

There are pros and cons to both approaches. A formal policy establishes what employees can expect if their jobs are eliminated. It also helps avoid claims of disparate treatment that can arise when severance is negotiated individually. "We strongly recommend that the company have a stated severance policy," says Kenny. "You open yourself up to a lot of different kinds of liability if you negotiate differently with Jane or Jack."

Another strategy, says Andrea Eisenberg, managing principal of the New York office of Right Management Consultants, a Philadelphia-based outplacement firm, is for employers to adopt temporary "event-driven" plans that typically last three to six months.

These plans typically offer terms not found in standard plans, including minimum payouts and early retirement, Eisenberg says, lasting only as long as it takes to arrange layoffs prompted by mergers or other short-term situations. "Usually, the company develops a policy or practice based on a philosophy of how they want to treat employees or

Calculator of Severance:
Manufacturing vs. Service Industries

MANUFACTURING INDUSTRIES
Percentage of companies paying indicated amount of severance:

	Key Execs	Senior Execs	Dept. Heads, Managers	Other Exempt	Non Exempt	Hourly
Less than 1 week per year:	8%	7%	7%	7%	8%	12%
1 week per year:	56	59	65	66	66	61
2 weeks per year:	19	20	19	19	19	23
3 weeks per year:	1	2	2	2	2	0
1 month per year:	9	8	6	3	2	1
Over one month:	6	4	2	2	2	3

SERVICE INDUSTRIES
Percentage of companies paying indicated amount of severance:

	Key Execs	Senior Execs	Dept. Heads, Managers	Other Exempt	Non Exempt	Hourly
Less than 1 week per year:	13%	12%	17%	19%	25%	24%
1 week per year:	46	45	56	58	58	56
2 weeks per year:	13	17	14	9	7	11
3 weeks per year:	0	0	2	0	0	0
1 month per year:	16	17	8	10	5	4
Over one month:	11	7	3	3	4	4

Column percentages in both charts may not equal 100 due to rounding.

Source: Right Management Consultants

[based on] what's going on in the market."

A standard severance plan doesn't mean that everyone must be treated exactly the same. Employers generally have a lot of discretion to set eligibility criteria. Certain employees can be excluded, and different formulas can apply to different job levels as long as employees in protected classes are not discriminated against, employment lawyers say.

KeyCorp, a Cleveland-based banking and financial services company of 23,000 workers, is using a severance policy established in 1994 as it eliminates 2,300 jobs through the end of 2002, says Katie Ladd, vice president of corporate employee relations and HR compliance. "We're very committed to making sure all employees are treated equitably."

Severance pay for laid-off Key-Corp workers ranges from two weeks' salary to one year, based on years of service, and the employee's job level in the company's hierarchy. Employees also receive continued health insurance and outplacement help, including the services of "transition centers" in Albany, N.Y.; Cleveland, Ohio; and Takoma, Wash., where KeyCorp has a large presence.

Severance payments end when employees find new jobs at Key-Corp, as have about 30 percent of those laid off so far, or if they refuse transfers to comparable jobs within the company, Ladd says. However, those who take jobs elsewhere continue to receive their full severance anyway.

Employers who prefer to negotiate severance packages individually retain the flexibility to change or eliminate severance, since no expectations have been established. However, there needs to be some degree of fairness, even if that means different terms based on the same general principles, experts say.

For example, an employer could create a general severance formula, decide whether or not to include medical benefits and set eligibility criteria, says Antoinette Pilzner, an attorney at the Detroit law firm Butzel Long PC. Workers who are laid off could receive more benefits on a negotiated basis.

Although case-by-case negotiations would seem to invite discrimination claims, they actually are rare, says Michael Richman, an attorney in the Washington, D.C., office of Reed, Smith, Shaw & McClay. "As long as a company has a rational business reason for distinguishing between two situations, there's a pretty good chance of being OK legally."

This individualized approach works well with top executives, small firms and companies with infrequent departures, Eisenberg says, adding that it doesn't make sense for companies with mass layoffs because it would be impractical to individually negotiate the severance terms of each employee.

The Dot-Coms Are Different

The issue of severance has become especially acute among dot-com firms, many of which have had to jettison employees in the storm of shake-ups and shake-outs that has hit the industry, and which are often too new or too small to think about it.

"The companies that are laying off don't have a ton of money," says Lori Zelman, vice president of HR at a New York-area Internet company, noting that severance plans aren't usually developed until layoffs occur. "It's hard to figure out what the criteria should be because most employees have been around only one or two years," Zelman adds. Policies based on seniority don't make sense, so any severance tends to be based on job level, with two weeks to three months the going amount—"significantly less" than at traditional employers, she says.

One Internet company based in the Southeast, which did not want to be further identified, had no formal severance policy but paid at least two weeks' salary to 17 employees

laid off last fall, says its HR manager. Although many workers got new jobs and job offers quickly, "We wanted to compensate them for the loss of their jobs," the manager says. The 150-person firm, begun in 1996, also brought in a recruiter and contacted potential employers.

This Internet company is more generous than most, HR experts say. The norm in this hard-driving, high-turnover industry is no severance pay—and no HR policies or managers at all.

The 'vast majority' of companies gave severance to all full-time employees who were laid off.

Many HR experts believe it's wrong for dot-com companies to terminate without severance workers who often have labored 60- and 70-hour weeks. "In a tight job market, people think they can get away with stuff that they shouldn't," Eisenberg says.

E. Lynne Pou of Human Resources Consulting in New York advises startups to offer at least some severance to employees in exchange for coming to a job with a potentially shaky future. According to Zelman, Internet companies make up in part for small or no severance payments with other types of outplacement help, such as contacting potential employers and holding resume-writing workshops.

Questions to Ask

Before adopting or changing a severance policy, a few key questions need to be answered. The answers will change, depending on your organization's corporate culture, workforce and employment needs, but the questions—whom to pay, how much and in what manner, and how to communicate changes in severance policy to the workforce—won't. Here are some options to consider:

Who should get severance. The best policies state clearly who is eligible. The "vast majority" of companies it surveyed in 1998 gave severance to all full-time employees who were laid off, says Lee Hecht Harrison. Forty-eight percent offered severance to part-time employees, while 7 percent offered it to temporary and contract staff.

A related issue is which conditions trigger severance. HR experts agree that workers who lose their jobs due to downsizing or other events beyond their control should receive severance, but they're split about someone who is fired for cause or forced to resign. While Lee Hecht Harrison found that only 13 percent of employers gave severance to workers terminated for cause in 1998, that was more than double the 5 percent figure in the 1995 survey.

How much to pay. Most employers use a formula based on years of service and some factor in the job level—one week's salary (base pay only) per year of service is typical. The higher the employee is in the organization, the less likely severance will be based only on tenure. Other factors can include employment agreements and the reason for the separation.

Severance covered an average of 21.8 weeks in 1999, compared with a record low of 12.8 weeks in 1996, according to Challenger, Gray & Christmas. Many employers set floors and some set ceilings on total payouts.

Today's norms are one to four weeks' severance per year of service for executives, with a minimum of six months to one year, Challenger says. For middle managers, the rate is one to two weeks per year of service, with a minimum of three to four months. For other workers, it's one week per year of service, with a minimum of one to two months (see charts).

While an employer has the option of stopping severance when a laid-off employee finds a new job, in most cases employers don't. Some firms even provide extra payments for workers who have trouble finding new jobs. The company's stock-option plan governs whether employees can get additional vesting as part of severance. Some employers speed it up to allow laid-off employees to exercise options within a certain time frame, says Clive of Baylight Corporation.

How severance is paid. There are three approaches: lump sum payments, continuation of salary and giving workers a choice between the two. Most employers select one method or the other. Fewer than 10 percent give workers a choice, according to the Lee Hecht Harrison survey.

Many employers prefer a lump sum payment because they don't have to continue medical benefits after workers leave. Conversely, many employees prefer regular payments because they continue to receive health insurance as long as the payments last.

Communicating changes in severance policy. Be straightforward but low-key, experts advise—the last thing you want is an anxious staff wondering when the ax will fall. HR should announce and explain—in memos, newsletters or meetings with managers—any changes in severance policy. Even better, announce changes in severance along with

changes in other benefits. If the change is for the better, employees may be reassured. If there will be layoffs, announce who is affected and when.

Extra Online Resources

For information on ensuring your severance pay program is legally safe, see the *HR Magazine* section of SHRM Online at www.shrm.org.

Carolyn Hirschman is a business writer based in Rockville, Md. She has written for a variety of business publications and has covered workplace issues since 1991.

Downsize with Dignity

by John Challenger

Employees in one firm returned from lunch only to discover they could not log on to their computers. A supervisor reported to work on New Year's Eve, having turned down three invitations to parties, only to be told he was no longer needed. At another company, employees were notified of their dismissal by e-mail.

Events like these suggest companies have much to learn about downsizing humanely and ethically. When facing a downsizing, leaders and managers need to ask five questions:

1. Who should do the planning? It should be a small group, for ease of scheduling meetings and control. The planning group should include people from such functions as finance, sales and marketing, human resources, operations, manufacturing, information technology, communications, security, and ethics managers. Its members should keep confidences. Nothing is worse than having details of a half-formed plan leak out, causing dissension and activating a rumor mill that distorts the plan's intent and facts, and is often driven by fear.

There is no good time to terminate a person's job.

Ideally, the planning group will have the trust and confidence of the workforce. Members should be capable of making difficult decisions compassionately, keeping the greatest good for the greatest number uppermost in their minds.

The best-handled downsizing comes from organizations that have ethical and supportive cultures. Recently an institution of higher learning made it known that staff cuts would be necessary, the approximate number, and why. Separate focus groups of administration, faculty, and staff were formed. When the recommendations were read from each, they were virtually identical. The college president said it was testimony to the sense of community that characterized the school. Workplaces that are split before a downsizing will splinter during the event and its aftermath in direct proportion to the degree of pre-existing acrimony in the workforce.

2. When should the timing be and what factors should affect it? The one day it should not be is Friday. If we want to be kind and helpful to those affected and those who survive a downsizing, we should avoid Friday layoffs and terminations. Losing your job on a Friday dumps the problem in your lap when you have little time to process the event, when you must face family and friends with the news, when you can't talk with others about what happened, when you can't access services or networks, when you can't start a job search, when little productive action can be taken until the new work week begins. Any other day of the week is better. Any significant job action will mean a relatively unproductive day. Rather than start a work week with a sizable hiccup midway, let that week get rolling and allow for good-byes and relaxed partings.

Don't delay terminations because of upcoming holidays. If you do, the criticism will likely just take another form: "Thanks a lot for letting me blithely go down the holiday shopping road in ignorance. Now I have all these bills coming in and no job."

The truth is there is no good time to terminate a person's job. What we can say is "do not leave people hanging." Anxiety and anger is proportionate to the degree people are kept in the dark and action is delayed. If action can be taken quickly after the decision to downsize is reached, do so. Delays allow leaks; the process gets out of control; people are hurt; and more infighting over "the list" occurs. At some point, you have to finalize the list, and that should be several days before implementation to allow for accurate exit packages to be prepared. Otherwise, supervisors may confuse who is on the list. False reassurances can result in people feeling betrayed. As job-specific decisions start to become person specific, feelings are hurt, tempers flare, and lawyers are consulted.

3. Who should know what, and when should they know it? All workers should be aware of business conditions. Those who are kept abreast of deteriorating business conditions, though disappointed their jobs are gone, are calmer, less hurt, more professional. People should know when the workload eases off. They will respect and work with managers who give clear information regularly, including the honesty to admit what they do not know or cannot say at the moment. The union that represented the workers at a firearms manufacturer supported its reduction in force. When asked why, the president of the local said, "We have been part of the process from the beginning. We have had a seat at the table. We know what the company is facing. We are trying to do our part to help. Ultimately, working together will save jobs in the long run."

4. How should those leaving and those staying be treated?

With respect! I am amazed when I see employers treating departing employees like criminals. These are the very people, often, who have given these employers the best years of their lives. Sometimes they have voluntarily taken pay cuts, weeks off without pay, to save jobs. Those left behind learn from what they see. They form opinions of the employer for whom they work. They act on those opinions. They assume they will be similarly treated. And so, even though they are still needed, they may quietly look for work with a new employer.

There is no harm in letting your humanity show.

Mistreatment breeds mistreatment. The person most at risk for violence in the workplace is the person who has been "disrespected," especially someone whose self-esteem is low. Make sure the people you are letting go leave with their dignity in tact. Do not have security escort people back to their offices or to the door. Have security ready to respond immediately to incidents or potential violence, yes, but let people say their good-byes, clean their desks without breathing down their necks, and leave under their own steam. In a recent downsizing, workers were so pleased they were treated with respect, they sought out the plant manager on the way out, to thank him personally.

Use common sense in turning off computers. Some employers point to the damage disgruntled employees might do if access were not taken from them immediately. These cases are rare. There is no harm in letting your humanity show. Nobody likes to let somebody go. The leader who makes a heart-felt statement to departing employees is ahead of the game. Tell people how difficult the situation is. Never promise the impossible. I cringe every time I hear a general manager or president say, "And this is the end of the layoffs." When, two months later, the company faces a second round of cuts, people will feel angry and betrayed. In contrast, one manager said, "I can't promise you that I won't be back here in a couple of months saying, 'Here we go again.' That will depend on business conditions. We will staff for what we need and, if anybody has to leave, we will take care of them." Those working under this manager applauded him and even said things like, "I am sure this was harder on you than on us. We know you fought for us. You told us the numbers all along. What could you do?"

Do your homework. Allow enough time to organize the handout material that clearly defines the safety net provided to each person being discharged. Have the staff available to answer benefit questions. Address the employees' highest anxiety. They will not hear much beyond, "We have to let you go," but be sure they hear that you will be available to answer questions in the days to come. Provide access numbers, and follow up promptly when an answer cannot be given, even if it is only to say there is nothing new to report.

Help people get on with their lives. The shorter the time between notification and last day worked, the better. Sometimes measures that seem kind are really cruel. For example, giving time off for interviews seems kind, but freeing them completely is much better. Time off for interviews focuses the employees's attention on the 20 percent of the job market that is visible, in which you apply for openings, but does not allow for the conversations with the 80 percent of the market where no position is listed. Rejected for jobs sought while still working, the employee enters the marketplace already depressed. Few people make headway in their searches while still employed.

It is common for employers to tell departing employees they will look internally for alternate jobs. In a downsizing, that is seldom realistic. It raises a false hope, which often delays the start of an effective job search. The employee waits to see what they come up with, only to be disappointed later.

Provide job search assistance and outplacement. Assure that it begins on the day people are notified. It will provide a safe haven for confidential discussions and frustrations. Quality outplacement counseling will help the entire organization come to terms with the loss. It will shorten the duration of unemployment and improve the quality of the job found for the former and still respected members of your community.

5. What public face should be put on the action? Keep the message short and to the point. The principles used to inform individuals should also govern the public release. Ethical companies keep their departing employees' dignity intact. One spokesman said, "We did not let any of our good employees go." That remark was on the front page of the regional newspaper. Support the people who have lost their jobs in their transitions. Make remarks like, "Their new employers will be fortunate to have them." Allude to the care and integrity that informed your process, noting specifics of planning and inclusion.

Such guidelines should be implemented through people who serve as the "conscience" of their companies. These people should have a place at the table from the beginning. Their input will prevent lawsuits and violence, reduce turnover among surviving employees, and retain the corporate image.

John A. Challenger is CEO of Challenger, Gray & Christmas, Inc. This article is adapted from his speech to the Ethics Officers Association Annual Conference and used with permission of Vital Speeches of the Day.

From *Executive Excellence*, March 2002, pp. 17-18. © 2002 by Executive Excellence.

THE WHISTLE-BLOWER

A HERO—AND A SMOKING-GUN LETTER

Watkins' memo spoke volumes about Enron's behavior. So did higher-ups' tepid response

At last, someone in the sordid Enron Corp. scandal seems to have done the right thing. Thanks to whistle-blower Sherron S. Watkins, a no-nonsense Enron vice-president, the scope and audacity of the accounting mess is becoming all too clear. Her blunt Aug. 15 letter to Enron CEO Kenneth L. Lay warns that the company might "implode in a wave of accounting scandals." And now that her worst fears have been realized, it is also clear that Watkins' letter went far beyond highlighting a few accounting problems in a handful of off-balance-sheet partnerships. Watkins' letter lays bare for all to see the underbelly of Enron's get-rich-quick culture.

Watkins, 42, a former Arthur Andersen accountant who remains Enron's vice-president for corporate development, put her finger on the rot: top execs who, at best, appeared to close their eyes to questionable accounting maneuvers; a leadership that had lost sight of ordinary investors and the basic principles of accounting; and watchdogs—the outside auditors and lawyers whose own involvement may have left them too conflicted to query the nature of the deals. Perhaps the question shouldn't be how Enron collapsed so quickly—but why it didn't implode sooner.

Lay's response to Watkins' complaints is nearly as damning as her letter itself. Yes, he talked to her for an hour. And, yes, he ordered an outside investigation. But contrary to Watkins' advice, he appointed the company's longtime Houston law firm, Vinson & Elkins, despite the obvious conflict: V&E had worked on some of the partnerships. And Enron and V&E agreed there would be no "second-guessing" of Andersen's ac-

counting and no "detailed analysis" of each and every transaction, according to V&E's Oct. 15 report. The inquiry was to consider only if there was new factual information that warranted a broader investigation. V&E declined comment.

Surprise: V&E concluded that a widespread investigation wasn't warranted. It simply warned that there was a "serious risk of adverse publicity and litigation." And Watkins' letter reveals the inadequacy of Lay's response in the months following CEO Jeffrey K. Skilling's sudden Aug. 14 resignation for "personal reasons." His departure triggered the letter. Lay never fully disclosed the partnerships or explained their impact to investors, even as he vowed there were no accounting issues and "no other shoe to fall." Even after Enron revealed on Oct. 16 a $1.2 billion hit to shareholder equity related to the partnerships, Lay continued to express ignorance about details of these deals and support for Chief Financial Officer Andrew S. Fastow, who managed and had stakes in certain partnerships. But on Oct. 24, Fastow was removed from his job and promptly left the company.

Watkins, an eight-year Enron veteran, is not some disgruntled naysayer who is easy to dismiss. Her lawyer, Philip H. Hilder, says she became familiar with some of the partnership dealings when she worked in June and July in Fastow's finance group. Her position allowed her to review the valuation of certain assets being sold into the partnerships, and that's when she saw "computations that just didn't jibe," says Hilder.

Former executives say the Tomball (Tex.) native was tenacious and competent. "She wasn't really an alarmist," says one

> Skilling's abrupt departure will raise suspicions of accounting improprieties and valuation issues.

> I am incredibly nervous that we will implode in a wave of accounting scandals. My 8 years of

> I realize that we have had a lot of smart people looking at this and a lot of accountants including AA&Co. have blessed the accounting treatment. None of that will protect Enron if these transactions are ever disclosed in the bright light of day. (Pl... ... problem of Waste Manag... ... paid $170...

former Enron employee. Her mother, Shirley Klein Harrington, a former high school accounting teacher, calls her daughter "a very independent, outspoken, good Christian girl, who's going to stand up for principle whenever she can." Watkins had previously worked at Andersen in Houston and New York and then for Germany's Metallgesellschaft AG.

At those companies, she befriended Jeffrey McMahon, whom she helped recruit. Now the CFO at Enron, McMahon "complained mightily" about the Fastow partnerships to Skilling, Watkins told Lay in the letter. "Employees question our accounting propriety consistently and constantly," she claimed. McMahon didn't return calls. Skilling has denied getting any warnings about accounting.

Watkins didn't stop there. Five days after she wrote to Lay, Watkins took her concerns directly to an Andersen audit partner, according to congressional investigators. He in turn relayed her questions to senior Andersen management on the Enron account. It's not known what, if any, action they took.

Of course, Skilling and Andersen execs shouldn't have needed a letter and a phone call from Watkins to figure out something was seriously amiss. Red flags abounded. And Wat-

kins, for one, had no trouble putting her finger on questionable accounting practices. She wondered if Enron was hiding losses in off-balance-sheet entities while booking large profits from the deals. At the same time, the outside partnerships were backed with Enron stock—a tactic sure to backfire when it was falling—and no outsiders seemed to have any capital at risk. Was Enron creating income essentially by doing deals with itself? "It sure looks to the layman on the street that we are hiding losses in a related company and will compensate that company with Enron stock in the future," she wrote.

In the end, Watkins grasped one thing that Enron's too-clever-by-half dealmakers didn't: Enron's maneuvering didn't pass the smell test. Even if Enron and its high-priced auditors and lawyers can ultimately show that they followed the letter of the law, it matters little. As Watkins herself wrote, if Enron collapses, "the business world will consider the past successes as nothing but an elaborate accounting hoax." And that seems destined to become Enron's epitaph.

By Wendy Zellner, with Stephanie Forest Anderson, in Dallas and with Laura Cohn in Washington

Speaking Out Has High Cost

Whistle-blowers often face retaliation by their employers in Japan, but a new push to protect insiders follows recent corporate scandals.

By MARK MAGNIER
TIMES STAFF WRITER

TOKYO—In 1973, salesman Hiroaki Kushioka discovered evidence linking his employer to price-fixing. He complained to his boss, a vice president of the package delivery company, but was told to keep quiet. He raised the issue with other company officials but was told not to rock the boat.

Frustrated, he turned to the media and government regulators. This, finally, created a stir. It also angered the company and landed Kushioka in employment hell, he says. As soon as the media attention died down, the company took its revenge.

In 1975, his employer, Tonami Transportation, transferred him to a tiny, remote subsidiary. For the next 27 years, Kushioka says, he was humiliated, badgered and bullied. The company stuck him in a room 9 feet square without a working telephone and made him weed lawns, shovel snow and arrange cushions. His pay remained virtually unchanged for more than two decades.

"I felt terrible humiliation," he says.

Tonami disputes Kushioka's version of events and blames his poor performance. But early this year, Kushioka filed a lawsuit against Tonami seeking an official apology and $415,000 in damages and forgone wages.

Kushioka's stubborn endurance and willingness to challenge Tonami legally have made him something of a model for a once-unthinkable movement: a growing push to protect whistle-blowers, in a country where loyalty and group harmony have long trumped notions of social justice.

Kushioka might still be languishing unnoticed in the corporate wilderness if a parade of recent scandals hadn't shocked many Japanese and undermined their faith in institutions that helped rebuild the nation after World War II.

Tainted-blood scandals in the early 1980s at the Health Ministry, wining and dining abuses in the 1990s at the Finance Ministry, and slush fund improprieties at the Foreign Ministry over the past two years have convinced Japanese that many elite bureaucrats were more interested in feathering their nests than safeguarding the public interest.

On other fronts, the auto industry, long a symbol of Japanese pride, was tarnished in 2000 after Mitsubishi Motors was discovered hiding customer complaints, thereby masking potentially deadly defects.

Especially shocking to many Japanese were revelations of crooked dealings in the food industry. This, after all, is a nation weaned on the belief that its farm products and inspection standards were among the world's best. Snow Brand, one of Japan's largest dairy producers, was accused of selling tainted milk after thousands of its consumers fell ill in 2000. And the meat-packing industry was caught this year mislabeling beef to boost profit margins and collect government handouts in the wake of a "mad cow" scandal.

A common theme in most of the cases was insiders speaking out. A telephone caller tipped regulators to look in a Mitsubishi Motors locker for thousands of long-hidden customer complaints. A supplier helped break the meat scandals. Other leakers laid bare the host of ministry scandals.

Still, activists remain concerned that Japan's cultural bias against those who speak out will undermine efforts to foster a vibrant whistle-blowing culture and secure greater legal protection against retaliation.

Most whistle-blowers don't stick around long enough to match the 27 years of exile and hounding that Kushioka says he endured. Even so, they face witch hunts, bullying and pariah treatment as long as they stay. The treatment here is arguably more devastating to people's sense of worth and self-esteem than in other countries, experts say, given Japan's long historical isolation and unique traditions.

Since its samurai days, Japan has stressed loyalty at almost any cost—whether to one's feudal lord, employer or ministry. Those who broke this code frequently were labeled traitors and sent away, a terrible fate in a group-oriented culture.

"Traditionally, betrayal is the biggest crime in Japan, almost worse than murder," says Tetsuo Yamaori, a religious scholar. "The price was *mura hachibu*, or exile from the village."

Group Harmony Prized

Closely related is a long-standing taboo against confrontation, challenging authority or disturbing the *wa*, or group harmony.

"Japanese don't like to be different from others. They also tend to hide unpleasant things from outsiders," says Etsuko Kawada, an independent lawmaker. "So whistle-blowing has met with suspicion on both counts."

Kawada should know. Her hemophiliac son, Ryuhei, is HIV-positive because the Health Ministry did not screen the nation's blood supply in the early 1980s, despite knowing the risks.

"If only someone in the ministry had spoken out, it would have saved so many people's lives," she says. "We need to change the system."

Another factor behind Japan's traditionally jaundiced eye toward whistle-blowers, analysts believe, is its view of right and wrong. Historically, Japan's concept of justice has been more malleable and dependent on situation and context, compared with the West's focus on objective rules.

"We're taught to respect those above us in the hierarchy, not to act on absolute standards," says Kazuko Miyamoto, a consumer advocate and author of the book "The Era of Whistle-Blowing."

That said, globalization, Japan's decade-long economic slide and growing suspicion of authority increasingly are spurring a far more sympathetic view toward those who disclose wrongdoing. A poll by the Consumer Research Institute in 2000 found that 45.1% of those surveyed supported whistle-blowing in the public interest, although 28% worried that it could spur betrayal.

In-house loyalty has also eroded in tandem with lifetime employment as middle-aged "salary men"—with extensive knowledge of corporate impropriety—are squeezed out of jobs and seek revenge.

"The Internet is also a growing force," says Iwao Taka, a professor with Tokyo's Reitaku University and a business ethics specialist. "Japan now has over 10,000 sites disclosing what's going on inside companies."

The social tussle over whether whistle-blowers are Benedict Arnolds or public saviors is frequently played out in a not-in-my-backyard approach.

For many Japanese, whistle-blowing is exemplary as long as it isn't in their company and doesn't jeopardize their jobs. Fresh in many minds is the food unit of Snow Brand, which went bankrupt after shoppers shunned the firm.

Business Lobby Vocal

The biggest opposition to whistle-blower protection laws—which might ensure, for instance, that people who speak out aren't denied promotions or forced out of their jobs—comes from Japan's mainstream business community—and many in the ruling Liberal Democratic Party. One company executive compared whistle-blowing to "telling on one's parents."

"Even if you create new laws, it doesn't solve the problem," says Mitsuru Shinozaki, a spokesman with the umbrella Federation of Economic Organizations. "Bullying isn't welcome, of course. But another law isn't going to stop it."

This view is tempered by other voices, however, arguing that whistle-blowing, when channeled through in-house hotlines and corporate compliance programs, provides indispensable alarm bells.

"Companies that change with the times have a better chance of competing and surviving," says Tadashi Kunihiro, a corporate attorney. "Just look at Snow Brand. It doesn't exist anymore."

Other opponents fear broader social damage. "Bringing Western ideas of whistle-blowing will accelerate the breakdown of Japanese society," religious scholar Yamaori says. "Japanese will lose their basic trust in one another, leading to chaos."

Working on Legislation

Lawmakers are now exchanging draft proposals and studying U.S. and British legal models. Some, such as members of the Democratic Party of Japan and the Social Democratic Party, favor a narrowly focused law initially covering only government workers, given industry's strong opposition.

Others, such as lawmaker Kawada, want as broad and comprehensive an approach as possible. Early betting is that Japan will see a civil service whistle-blower law passed within a year or two, followed later by a broader corporate law.

Japan already has one whistle-blower law on the books, covering the nuclear power industry, although it's never been tested. The statute was enacted in 2000 after an accident at a nuclear fuel-processing plant 80 miles northeast of Tokyo revealed that workers had for years transferred radioactive material using stainless steel buckets without speaking out.

A review of the 1968 Basic Consumer Protection Law now underway also is expected to strengthen whistle-blower safeguards in the food and medical areas.

Most Japanese seem to favor Britain's approach, which requires whistle-blowers to first exhaust internal complaint channels before going public. This contrasts with the more blanket protection afforded under the 1989 U.S. Whistleblower Protection Act—a law inspired by the 1986 space shuttle Challenger explosion, in which it turned out that an engineer had complained of defects and been fired.

Another legitimate Japanese concern is the greater difficulty that Japanese whistle-blowers face finding another job compared with their counterparts in the U.S. or Europe, where blacklisting is illegal and job-hopping more common.

"In Japan, people need to blow their whistles more quietly than in the U.S.," says Tetsuro Kuroda, director general of the Freedom of Information Citizens Center.

Whistle-blower Kushioka had a quarter-century in his tiny office to think about whether he'd done the right thing by going public.

"I was naive and didn't realize at first how much they'd retaliate against me," he says. "When I told the company I was going to the prosecutor's office, the pressure really got worse."

Asked about Kushioka's price-fixing allegations, Tonami officials would say only that "shortcuts were taken." Prosecutors launched an investigation at the time, but Japan was far more tolerant of monopolistic behavior in the mid-1970s than it is now, and the case was quietly dropped. Tonami denies any bullying and blames Kushioka's derailed career on his argumentative nature and poor leadership skills.

"His unique personality is the issue here, not whistle-blowing or human rights," says Noriaki Murata, a Tonami planning manager.

According to Kushioka, however, fellow employees would call his mother intimating that he had no pride and should quit his meaningless job.

Company officials also pressured his brother and father-in-law, who worked elsewhere, to persuade him to quit.

And a board member harassed Kushioka deep into the night hoping to exhaust him into leaving the company, he says.

Another Tonami board member asked colleagues to slip Kushioka some drinks and bait him into punching a co-worker, thereby giving the company cause for dismissal. The plot failed when the colleagues refused.

Perhaps the most heavy-handed effort involved phone calls and visits from someone identifying himself as part of the *yakuza*, or Japanese organized crime.

The man first tried to bribe Kushioka with $25,000 to quit, then sought to intimidate him, Kushioka says.

"If you don't resign, younger *yakuza* may stage a traffic accident, and the police would never know you were murdered," Kushioka recalls him saying.

Kushioka refused to give up, however, despite the enormous strain on those around him and on his mental health.

His entire family urged him to resign, and his mother even pleaded with his wife to divorce "my stupid son."

Early this year, faced with five more years until mandatory retirement, an increasingly sympathetic social environment and little to lose, he filed his suit against the company. The case is now working its way through the courts.

"Even though it won't help me now, Japan really needs a whistle-blower protection law," he says. "I'm determined to fight on, no matter how long it takes. I just hope I can win this case and create a good precedent for others."

Hisako Ueno in The Times' Tokyo Bureau contributed to this report.

Where Do You Draw
The Line?

**The shades of gray are many, and the number of right answers is infinite.
Consider these ethical dilemmas and their possible solutions.**

Ethics

Although most supply management organizations have some code of ethics, whether specific to supply management or to the organization as a whole, many situations still occur that don't have a prescribed right answer. The following are common scenarios containing questionable ethics issues. Possible approaches are offered as suggestions, but as you read, examine the situations and make your own decisions considering both cost- and value-based solutions to determine where you draw the line.

Supplier Relationship vs. Friendship

An on-site logistics supplier works alongside the supply management team, attends staff meetings, and naturally builds a relationship over time with some of the supply management staff including yourself. The supplier participates in after-hours activities and begins to be "one of the gang." It becomes nearly impossible for a newcomer to the office to distinguish between this person, as an employee of the supplier, and your organization's employees. Over the course of the year, you become close friends with this individual, your spouses become friends, and your families even vacation together.

1. After some competitive analysis, you feel certain that the current on-site supplier is no longer cost-competitive. You are not directly responsible for this supplier and have no quotes from alternate suppliers, but it's clear that your firm has been paying large premiums to maintain this long-term supplier relationship. So far, you have told nobody within your organization about these findings. What is your sequence of action in this scenario?

One Approach: Many supply managers may feel that such close personal relationships should not be cultivated with supplier on-site representatives. However, when considering this scenario, the business interests of your firm must take priority. How you handle this, as one who is not directly responsible for this supplier relationship, is open to some interpretation. Some may feel that since this supply management professional has no direct responsibility for this supplier, he or she has no business discussing the matter with the on-site representative or the supplier. Others may see it as appropriate

for the supply management professional to approach the supplier/friend privately, voice concerns that the supplier is noncompetitive, and push for significant voluntary cost reductions resulting in a win-win outcome.

If the supplier does nothing to alleviate these concerns, you may be forced to go to the responsible supply management team member to request a full competitive analysis and alternate quotes. The personal considerations should be set aside in this case.

In a properly structured long-term supplier partnership, the contract allows for periodic competitive bidding. A partner supplier must continue to maintain its cost advantage over competitors or risk being replaced.

2. In the course of business, your organization reassesses current costs and allows both the current on-site supplier and a competitor to bid the account. If the current provider loses the account, your good friend is out of a job. The competitor's bid comes in and is slightly lower than the current cost for the service, but your on-site provider has not yet submitted its bid. Your friend is facing a layoff if the on-site supplier does not underbid its competitor. This is not just a casual acquaintance, but a close friend, and you want to help in some way. What do you do?

One Approach: You do nothing. The minute you try to "help," you could be faced with ethical violations of preferential treatment and, in some organizations, legal repercussions if you divulge the competitor's quote or try to coach the friend in any way. Be a friend, but let the business take its course.

The Supplier Conference

A large supplier has scheduled a conference for 100 key customers. As part of this meeting, you have been invited to fly to the site on the supplier's airplane along with other customer representatives. The conference is to be held Wednesday through Sunday at a posh resort. Meals, accommodations, and entertainment are covered. Entertainment includes tickets to a sold-out college football game featuring a national championship contender.

Amid your polite protests, the supplier stresses that no single customer is being given special treatment. All are going to be treated alike, so you should not have an ethical issue with this. Besides, your attendance is expected at some meetings as the supplier will be unveiling the details of a new product/process to this select group. Your organization's competitors will certainly be attending. What is your response?

One Approach: Some organizations have policies in place regarding the payment of expenses for a representative of the organization to visit a supplier's conference or facility when it is deemed beneficial. If your organization has the budget to do so, attend the conference at your firm's expense. You should notify the supplier in writing that you will make your own travel and room reservations and pay for all meals. This will require that you obtain the approximate cost of banquets and reimburse the supplier accordingly.

Regarding entertainment, one good rule of thumb is to assess whether a strong business case can be made in favor of your attending. In the case of meals and light, inexpensive entertainment, one can make the argument that relationship building will ultimately benefit both the buying and the selling organization. In the ballgame example, attendance is not recommended. The key phrase is that the ballgame is sold out. By accepting tickets with high "street value," you are placing yourself in a position of indebtedness to the supplier. Furthermore, virtually no business purpose is gained by your attendance.

Some exceptions may be appropriate in the case of this scenario, such as accepting the supplier's hospitality based on past practice within your organization when there is evidence that no biases have affected purchasing decisions. However, in general, the best solution is to attend at your organization's expense.

A Token of Gratitude

Your supplier visits during the holidays and presents you with a token of her organization's gratitude—a luxury pen and pencil set. These are expensive but have no return value as they have been personalized with your name. Do you accept the gift?

One Approach: You do not accept the gift. Suppliers trying to gain influence have learned that most company ethics policies do not allow the buyer to receive token gifts of any kind. The very fact that a supplier would offer an expensive gift of this type means that he or she is trying to "beat the system" and perhaps gain undue influence.

Speaking at a Supplier's Conference

Every year, one of your key suppliers holds a large-scale national sales conference for its distributors. You have been asked to deliver a speech on perceived customer values relative to that supplier's product at this year's conference. The assignment carries with it travel and lodging expenses, as well as a modest $1,000 honorarium. You have experience delivering workshops and speeches on supply management topics, thus are qualified to perform the function, and you are aware that every year at this conference the supplier solicits such

customer feedback. In fact, this annual event has led to product and service improvements for your organization in the past. Do you participate?

One Approach: If indeed you are well qualified to speak and your organization's management sees a benefit, you could make a business case for attending. In fact, your organization may even view this as a part of your job responsibility. Given this logic, it is a potential conflict of interest to accept monetary compensation of any amount. In this case, it's best to perform the service pro bono, especially since you are the supply management professional responsible for this supplier's account. The question of who is responsible for the travel expenses is a tricky one. Some may deem it appropriate to accept the offer of the supplier to cover the expenses since the speech will be of benefit to the supplier. However, others may think it is inappropriate to accept the offer to pay for all travel expenses and consider it wise to have your organization cover the costs.

Upper Management Ethics

You work as a supply manager for a medium-sized, family-owned business in which the boss routinely accepts expensive vacations and other gratuities in the course of business, leading to questionable (and costly) supplier selections in some cases. This individual has a strong marketing background and has built a $100 million company from scratch. The boss believes that it's just "the way business is done." How do you approach this situation?

One Approach: Ethical behavior is rooted in the view that a supply manager must act in the best interest of the organization. In this scenario, you are responsible for the organization's purchase dollars, and yet are not allowed to make the best business decisions for the company. Depending on the relationship, you can remind the business owner, in a private meeting, that you have been hired to make the best business decisions for the company and using that logic, all supply decisions should come through you. If the business owner wants to continue receiving gratuities, that's fine, but you must be allowed to do your job. If the current behavior continues and suppliers learn that their gratuities are not influencing the sourcing decision, the floodgates of gifts and vacations will likely close to a trickle. Finally, if the business owner does not relinquish control of the sourcing function, you might be wise to look for another job.

For additional information regarding ethics in supply management, see *NAPM's Principles and Standards of Purchasing Practice*—a statement of ethics drafted by the NAPM Ethical Standards Committee.

*By **Mark A. Crowder, C.P.M.**, regional manager for Asia Pacific, International Supply Management Services for Deere & Company, Moline, Illinois.*

Reprinted with permission from the publisher, the Institute for Supply Management™, "Where Do You Draw the Line?" by Mark A. Crowder, C.P.M., *Purchasing Today*, Vol. 12, No. 1, January 2001, pp. 8-9.

Article 21

Was the Threat Real, or a Hoax?

If the editor ran the story, he might play into the terrorist's hands.

BY DOUG WALLACE

The Case

It was a cool Friday morning in September when a phone call set the North Star Press office buzzing. A poisoning threat had been made against American Meat Products—a major local employer—and that company's general counsel, Ny Charles, was on the line. He wanted to meet the editor.

Within an hour he was in the office of editor John Stenson, laying out the story. Someone claiming to have found poisoned AMP meat had called the Poison Control Center. But Ny thought it was a hoax, because the same caller had made a bomb threat against Liberty Bank, where AMP banked. Authorities had matched the voice prints.

As both Ny and the editor knew, AMP was involved in a serious labor dispute and hostility was rampant. Still the company had taken the threat seriously, Ny emphasized. AMP had pulled meat from the shelves of several stores and was running tests. Initial results revealed no poison.

"Why are you telling me this?" the editor asked Ny.

"One of your reporters got hold of the story," the attorney replied. "I'm not asking you to kill the story, John. But I'm hoping you'll wait to publish it until the Department of Agriculture tests are in."

It wasn't an outrageous request, John thought. But he wasn't ready to agree. After Ny left, John called several associate editors to an emergency meeting, where he heard arguments on both sides. On the one hand, the paper had the duty to alert the public to a potential health problem. Not to run the story would be pandering to corporate interests. On the other hand, running the story could make the newspaper a pawn in a terrorist's hands. But what if the paper held the story, and the threat was real?

After the meeting, John found himself alone in his office, which after the din of the previous hour felt eerily quiet. He leaned back in his chair and thought, what should he do?

James Houck, Managing Editor, Baltimore Sun

Our responsibility is to report the news accurately, fairly, and thoroughly. That's exactly what I would do. What's involved is information the public has a right to know. Potential damage to a company can't overshadow the possibility of danger to the public.

A basic rule applies here: when in doubt, print it. The company wants the story delayed, but the newspaper has no independent motive to do so. I wouldn't take sides.

Eugene Roberts, Editor, Philadelphia Inquirer

The paper has a two-part responsibility: there is an obligation to American Meat Products and a responsibility to the public. This could be a hoax, or it could be real.

My approach to this case is influenced by a situation I ran into 30 years ago, in my first newspaper job on a little hometown paper. Years earlier, a reporter had persuaded the city council to let him sit in on executive sessions, if he agreed not to report on stories they weren't prepared to give out. At one meeting, the city manager told of several abandoned gas mains into which gas had backed up. It was judged a containable situation, but there were no dollars to handle it immediately. The group thought the news would alarm the public, and the reporter agreed not to report it. Later a blast killed three people and left others hospitalized. That reporter had a hard time explaining his part in it all.

That incident had a big impact on me. When public safety is involved, it's a huge step to withhold information. The AMP case is about public safety, so my inclination is to run the story, including an account of the company's admirable action in removing the product. If the USDA could complete its tests in hours rather than days, my decision might be to wait. But otherwise I'd run it.

Doug Wallace's Comments

Both commentators focus on responsibility, a concept that first appeared in English and French dictionaries in 1787, concurrent with the advent of democratic governments. Responsibility is linked with power, for if the king unilaterally controls the course of events, we have no *response-ability*. Our choices don't matter. But once we have the power to act, our choices count. We become accountable for the consequences of our actions. To care and grieve with those hurt by our decisions is the challenge of managing responsibly.

What Actually Happened?

John Stenson decided that Friday to bet that the threats were a hoax. He held the story. And he was lucky, for on Monday USDA tests came back negative. Days later authorities arrested a man they believed had made the threats. The entire story appeared in the North Star Press.

This case—like all What Would You Do? cases—is a real one. In the real-life news story in the *St. Paul Pioneer Press Dispatch*, the editor wrote that his "primary concern was not whether a story would damage [AMP] sales, but whether the public interest would be served in publishing what amounted to rumors."

_____

This column originally appeared in Business Ethics *in Nov./Dec. 1989. Retired now, columnist Doug Wallace was formerly the vice president for social policy at Norwest Bank (today Wells Fargo) in Minneapolis.*

All cases in What Would You Do? are real, though disguised.

Leaders as Value Shapers

Leading through vivid, living, personal example is still the best, perhaps the only, way to lead. There is power in personal example.

KEVIN FREIBERG

GREAT LEADERS UNDERSTAND that their capacities to shape values and educate through vivid, living, personal example ultimately directs the course of a firm. The way people think about customers and coworkers, the way they behave, and their impressions of right and wrong are all influenced by watching their leaders live out their values.

Every firm builds its reputation on a set of values. The question is whether the values driving the business have been haphazardly acquired or purposefully instilled, protected, and promoted. This is why leaders must embrace their role as value shapers.

Values are the emotional rules that govern people's attitudes and behaviors. They establish boundaries that influence how an organization fulfills its mission. Values are deep-seated beliefs we have about the world and how it operates. They influence outcomes and ultimately determine quality. Values provide a framework for making choices and decisions. Values are the non-negotiables, the principles for which we stand.

I see two types of values—espoused values and the values people practice. When there is alignment, leaders operate out of personal integrity—doing what they say they're going to do.

Where there is a disconnect between our espoused values and the values we practice, we find hypocrisy. Professing a belief, philosophy, or standard to which you don't hold yourself accountable is an act of pretension and insincerity. Leaders who operate out of hypocrisy breed compliance because they lack influence and must lean on positional power.

Leadership functions on the basis of trust and credibility. That's why leaders must close the gap between their espoused values and the values they practice. Leaders who live their values inspire tremendous commitment and loyalty in others. As a result, they expand their influence and their ability to effect change.

Being Faithful to Our Values

When customers, suppliers, shareholders, and employees evaluate whether or not we are faithful to the values we profess, they use the following criteria.

1. How you spend your time. If you want to know what an executive values watch the way he or she allocates time. We spend time on those things that are most important to us. On the busiest days of the airline industry, you'll find Herb Kelleher, Southwest Airlines' indefatigable chairman and CEO, loading bags on the tarmac, working the galleys with the flight attendants, or helping mechanics in the maintenance hangar. The way he spends his time says, "We don't hide behind titles and job descriptions; we do whatever it takes to help each other out and serve the customer."

Make a list of the top five values driving your organization. Then look at your calendar and analyze the way you allocate your time. What does your schedule say to others about what you value?

2. How you spend your money. Take out your checkbook and audit your expenditures. Examine the last budget you prepared. Is it consistent with what you value? The way we spend money says a lot about our priorities. If you say people are your most important assets, is that reflected in your compensation structures and your policies?

3. Your reaction to critical incidents. Whether it is a customer complaint or commendation, how you handle the event sends a message. When a customer asks your team to go beyond the call of duty, how do you respond? When your people do something heroic, do you celebrate and publicize their actions?

At Southwest Airlines, they celebrate the courage and competence of individuals who rise to the occasion and protect the lives of the company's valued customers.

Critical incidents do not have to be monumental in nature. When Mike Snyder, CEO of Red Robin International, picks up a candy wrapper outside of one of his restaurants, he sends a message to his people that the details count.

4. What you reward and punish. Do your rewards specifically reinforce the values that are driving your business? Do your incentives promote internal competition or cooperation? When one of your people takes an intelligent risk with the intent to benefit the company and fails, do you reward or punish their effort? When someone who reports to you gives you constructive feedback, how do you respond? At Southwest Airlines, people are given awards for fun and humor, sensational service, telling it like it is, creativity, and risk-taking.

5. Questions you ask. Do the questions you ask demonstrate your concern for your employees? Do your questions encourage people to focus on the customer or on the numbers?

The questions you ask and answer reveal a lot about what you value. When asked about the money spent on reward and recognition Herb Kelleher said, "I could cut our budget substantially by cutting recognition events, but that would be like cutting out our heart."

6. Things you measure. If you believe your people are your major point of differentiation, are you as rigorous about measuring their satisfaction as you are about measuring their productivity or financial results? If you believe that part of leadership is serving your internal customers, do you give those customers a chance to evaluate the quality of the services you provide? Do your team leaders go through a 360-degree feedback process, and are the results tied to their compensation structure?

As leaders we also need to remember that *our walk talks.* Everything we do and everything we choose not to do says something about what we value.

The Power of a Strong Value System

Southwest Airlines, Disney, General Electric, Federal Express, Johnson & Johnson, TDI Industries, HewlettPackard, and Merck all rank among the most admired companies in the world. They find enormous strength in their core values because strong values:

1. Build trust and confidence. In organizations where a strong set of shared values exists, leaders have more confidence to let go of power and authority.

2. Foster accountability. A strong value system creates boundaries. When the boundaries are clear, employees have more freedom and authority to act. People willingly assume responsibility and accountability when you reduce the uncertainty that comes with ill-defined boundaries.

3. Establish a unified front. Strong values concentrate the efforts of a team. When people are drawn together by a common set of beliefs, the values holding them together suddenly become more important than the agenda or special interests of any one individual. The result is a spirit of cohesiveness that captures the diversity of gifts and talents people bring to the team.

4. Provide guidance in times of crisis. In a chaotic world where people feel pressured to compromise ethics and cut corners to get results or cover up mistakes, strong values serve as a moral compass. Where there are no easy answers to difficult challenges, a strong value system can help determine the rightness of your direction.

5. Create competitive advantage. People want to do business with leaders who have similar values. Customers want to do business with organizations they can count on. There is a strong sense of sincerity and authenticity in firms with clearly defined values. These companies are less likely to project a false image and make promises that they can't keep.

People who are not clear about those guiding principles for which they stand can never expect to lay a foundation for trust and credibility, let alone develop the capacity to exercise leadership. Great leaders understand that every moment of every day is a symbolic opportunity to communicate their values. They do not underestimate the power of personal example. Through their daily choices leaders carve out the character and reputation of the organization. And they provide the standard by which others calibrate their own behaviors.

Kevin Freiberg is a professional speaker and co-author of Nuts! *Southwest Airlines' Personal Success, 619-624-9691.*

From *Executive Excellence*, November 1998, pp. 7–8. © 1998 by Executive Excellence Publishing. Reprinted by permission.

The Parable of the Sadhu

After encountering a dying pilgrim on a climbing trip in the Himalayas, a businessman ponders the differences between individual and corporate ethics.

by Bowen H. McCoy

This article was originally published in the September–October 1983 issue of HBR. For its republication as an HBR Classic, Bowen H. McCoy has written the commentary "When Do We Take a Stand?" to update his observations.

Last year, as the first participant in the new six-month sabbatical program that Morgan Stanley has adopted, I enjoyed a rare opportunity to collect my thoughts as well as do some traveling. I spent the first three months in Nepal, walking 600 miles through 200 villages in the Himalayas and climbing some 120,000 vertical feet. My sole Western companion on the trip was an anthropologist who shed light on the cultural patterns of the villages that we passed through.

During the Nepal hike, something occurred that has had a powerful impact on my thinking about corporate ethics. Although some might argue that the experience has no relevance to business, it was a situation in which a basic ethical dilemma suddenly intruded into the lives of a group of individuals. How the group responded holds a lesson for all organizations, no matter how defined.

The Sadhu

The Nepal experience was more rugged than I had anticipated. Most commercial treks last two or three weeks and cover a quarter of the distance we traveled.

My friend Stephen, the anthropologist, and I were halfway through the 60-day Himalayan part of the trip when we reached the high point, an 18,000-foot pass over a crest that we'd have to traverse to reach the village of Muklinath, an ancient holy place for pilgrims.

Six years earlier, I had suffered pulmonary edema, an acute form of altitude sickness, at 16,500 feet in the vicinity of Everest base camp—so we were understandably concerned about what would happen at 18,000 feet. Moreover, the Himalayas were having their wettest spring in 20 years; hip-deep powder and ice had already driven us off one ridge. If we failed to cross the pass, I feared that the last half of our once-in-a-lifetime trip would be ruined.

The night before we would try the pass, we camped in a hut at 14,500 feet. In the photos taken at that camp, my face appears wan. The last village we'd passed through was a sturdy two-day walk below us, and I was tired.

During the late afternoon, four backpackers from New Zealand joined us, and we spent most of the night awake, anticipating the climb. Below, we could see the fires of two other parties, which turned out to be two Swiss couples and a Japanese hiking club.

To get over the steep part of the climb before the sun melted the steps cut in the ice, we departed at 3:30 A.M. The New Zealanders left first, followed by Stephen and myself, our porters and Sherpas, and then the Swiss. The Japanese lingered in their camp. The sky was clear, and we were confident that no spring storm would erupt that day to close the pass.

At 15,500 feet, it looked to me as if Stephen were shuffling and staggering a bit, which are symptoms of altitude sickness. (The initial stage of altitude sickness brings a headache and nausea. As the condition worsens, a climber may encounter difficult breathing, disorientation, aphasia, and paralysis.) I felt strong—my adrenaline was flowing—but I was very concerned about my ultimate ability to get across. A couple of our porters were also suffering from the height, and Pasang, our Sherpa sirdar (leader), was worried.

Just after daybreak, while we rested at 15,500 feet, one of the New Zealanders, who had gone ahead, came staggering down toward us with a body slung across his shoulders. He dumped the almost naked, barefoot body of an Indian holy man—a sadhu—at my feet. He had found the pilgrim lying on the ice, shivering and suffering from hypothermia. I cradled the sadhu's head and laid him out on the rocks. The New Zealander was angry. He wanted to get across the pass before the bright sun melted the snow. He said, "Look, I've done what I can. You have porters and Sherpa guides. You care for him. We're going on!" He turned and went back up the mountain to join his friends.

I took a carotid pulse and found that the sadhu was still alive. We figured he had probably visited the holy shrines at Muklinath and was on his way home. It was fruitless to question why he had chosen this desperately high route instead of the safe, heavily traveled caravan route through the Kali Gandaki gorge. Or why he was shoeless and almost naked, or how long he had been lying in the pass. The answers weren't going to solve our problem.

Stephen and the four Swiss began stripping off their outer clothing and opening their packs. The sadhu was soon clothed from head to foot. He was not able to walk, but he was very much alive. I looked down the mountain and spotted the Japanese climbers, marching up with a horse.

When I reached them, Stephen glared at me and said, "How do you feel about contributing to the death of a fellow man?"

Without a great deal of thought, I told Stephen and Pasang that I was concerned about withstanding the heights to come and wanted to get over the pass. I took off after several of our porters who had gone ahead.

On the steep part of the ascent where, if the ice steps had given way, I would have slid down about 3,000 feet, I felt vertigo. I stopped for a breather, allowing the Swiss to catch up with me. I inquired about the sadhu and Stephen. They said that the sadhu was fine and that Stephen was just behind them. I set off again for the summit.

Stephen arrived at the summit an hour after I did. Still exhilarated by victory, I ran down the slope to congratulate him. He was suffering from altitude sickness—walking 15 steps, then stopping, walking 15 steps, then stopping. Pasang accompanied him all the way up. When I reached them, Stephen glared at me and said: "How do you feel about contributing to the death of a fellow man?"

I did not completely comprehend what he meant. "Is the sadhu dead?" I inquired.

"No," replied Stephen, "but he surely will be!"

After I had gone, followed not long after by the Swiss, Stephen had remained with the sadhu. When the Japanese had arrived, Stephen had asked to use their horse to transport the sadhu down to the hut. They had refused. He had then asked Pasang to have a group of our porters carry the sadhu. Pasang had resisted the idea, saying that the porters would have to exert all their energy to get themselves over the pass. He believed they could not carry a man down 1,000 feet to the hut, reclimb the slope, and get across safely before the snow melted. Pasang had pressed Stephen not to delay any longer.

The Sherpas had carried the sadhu down to a rock in the sun at about 15,000 feet and pointed out the hut another 500 feet below. The Japanese had given him food and drink. When they had last seen him, he was listlessly throwing rocks at the Japanese party's dog, which had frightened him.

We do not know if the sadhu lived or died.

For many of the following days and evenings, Stephen and I discussed and debated our behavior toward the sadhu. Stephen is a committed Quaker with deep moral vision. He said, "I feel that what happened with the sadhu is a good example of the breakdown between the individual ethic and the corporate ethic. No one person was willing to assume ultimate responsibility for the sadhu. Each was willing to do his bit just so long as it was not too inconvenient. When it got to be a bother, everyone just passed the buck to someone else and took off. Jesus was relevant to a more individualistic stage of society, but how do we interpret his teaching today in a world filled with large, impersonal organizations and groups?"

I defended the larger group, saying, "Look, we all cared. We all gave aid and comfort. Everyone did his bit. The New Zealander carried him down below the snow line. I took his pulse and suggested we treat him for hypothermia. You and the Swiss gave him clothing and got him warmed up. The Japanese gave him food

and water. The Sherpas carried him down to the sun and pointed out the easy trail toward the hut. He was well enough to throw rocks at a dog. What more could we do?"

"You have just described the typical affluent Westerner's response to a problem. Throwing money—in this case, food and sweaters—at it, but not solving the fundamentals!" Stephen retorted.

I asked, "Where is the limit of our responsibility in a situation like this?"

"What would satisfy you?" I said. "Here we are, a group of New Zealanders, Swiss, Americans, and Japanese who have never met before and who are at the apex of one of the most powerful experiences of our lives. Some years the pass is so bad no one gets over it. What right does an almost naked pilgrim who chooses the wrong trail have to disrupt our lives? Even the Sherpas had no interest in risking the trip to help him beyond a certain point."

Stephen calmly rebutted, "I wonder what the Sherpas would have done if the sadhu had been a well-dressed Nepali, or what the Japanese would have done if the sadhu had been a well-dressed Asian, or what you would have done, Buzz, if the sadhu had been a well-dressed Western woman?"

"Where, in your opinion," I asked, "is the limit of our responsibility in a situation like this? We had our own well-being to worry about. Our Sherpa guides were unwilling to jeopardize us or the porters for the sadhu. No one else on the mountain was willing to commit himself beyond certain self-imposed limits."

Stephen said, "As individual Christians or people with a Western ethical tradition, we can fulfill our obligations in such a situation only if one, the sadhu dies in our care; two, the sadhu demonstrates to us that he can undertake the two-day walk down to the village; or three, we carry the sadhu for two days down to the village and persuade someone there to care for him."

"Leaving the sadhu in the sun with food and clothing—where he demonstrated hand-eye coordination by throwing a rock at a dog—comes close to fulfilling items one and two," I answered. "And it wouldn't have made sense to take him to the village where the people appeared to be far less caring than the Sherpas, so the third condition is impractical. Are you really saying that, no matter what the implications, we should, at the drop of a hat, have changed our entire plan?"

The Individual Versus the Group Ethic

Despite my arguments, I felt and continue to feel guilt about the sadhu. I had literally walked through a classic moral dilemma without fully thinking through the consequences. My excuses for my actions include a high adrenaline flow, a superordinate goal, and a once-in-a-lifetime opportunity—common factors in corporate situations, especially stressful ones.

Real moral dilemmas are ambiguous, and many of us hike right through them, unaware that they exist. When, usually after the fact, someone makes an issue of one, we tend to resent his or her bringing it up. Often, when the full import of what we have done (or not done) hits us, we dig into a defensive position from which it is very difficult to emerge. In rare circumstances, we may contemplate what we have done from inside a prison.

Had we mountaineers been free of stress caused by the effort and the high altitude, we might have treated the sadhu differently. Yet isn't stress the real test of personal and corporate values? The instant decisions that executives make under pressure reveal the most about personal and corporate character.

As a group, we had no process for developing a consensus. We had no sense of purpose or plan.

Among the many questions that occur to me when I ponder my experience with the sadhu are: What are the practical limits of moral imagination and vision? Is there a collective or institutional ethic that differs from the ethics of the individual? At what level of effort or commitment can one discharge one's ethical responsibilities?

Not every ethical dilemma has a right solution. Reasonable people often disagree; otherwise there would be no dilemma. In a business context, however, it is essential that managers agree on a process for dealing with dilemmas.

Our experience with the sadhu offers an interesting parallel to business situations. An immediate response was mandatory. Failure to act was a decision in itself. Up on the mountain we could not resign and submit our résumés to a headhunter. In contrast to philosophy, business involves action and implementation—getting things done. Managers must come up with answers based on what they see and what they allow to influence their decision-making processes. On the mountain, none of us but Stephen realized the true dimensions of the situation we were facing.

One of our problems was that as a group we had no process for developing a consensus. We had no sense of purpose or plan. The difficulties of dealing with the sadhu were so complex that no one person could handle them. Because the group did not have a set of preconditions that could guide its action to an acceptable resolution, we reacted instinctively as individuals. The cross-cultural nature of the group added a further layer of complexity. We had no leader with whom we could all identify and in whose purpose we believed. Only Stephen was willing to take charge, but he could not gain adequate support from the group to care for the sadhu.

Some organizations do have values that transcend the personal values of their managers. Such values, which go beyond profitability, are usually revealed when the organization is under stress. People throughout the organization generally accept its values, which, because they are not presented as a rigid list of commandments, may be somewhat ambiguous. The stories people tell, rather than printed materials, transmit the organization's conceptions of what is proper behavior.

For 20 years, I have been exposed at senior levels to a variety of corporations and organizations. It is amazing how quickly an outsider can sense the tone and style of an organization and, with that, the degree of tolerated openness and freedom to challenge management.

Organizations that do not have a heritage of mutually accepted, shared values tend to become unhinged during stress, with each individual bailing out for himself or herself. In the great takeover battles we have witnessed during past years, companies that had strong cultures drew the wagons around them and fought it out, while other companies saw executives—supported by golden parachutes—bail out of the struggles.

Because corporations and their members are interdependent, for the corporation to be strong the members need to share a preconceived notion of correct behavior, a "business ethic," and think of it as a positive force, not a constraint.

As an investment banker, I am continually warned by well-meaning lawyers, clients, and associates to be wary of conflicts of interest. Yet if I were to run away from every difficult situation, I wouldn't be an effective investment banker. I have to feel my way through conflicts. An effective manager can't run from risk either; he or she has to confront risk. To feel "safe" in doing that, managers need the guidelines of an agreed-upon process and set of values within the organization.

After my three months in Nepal, I spent three months as an executive-in-residence at both the Stanford Business School and the University of California at Berkeley's Center for Ethics and Social Policy of the Graduate Theological Union. Those six months away from my job gave me time to assimilate 20 years of business experience. My thoughts turned often to the meaning of the leadership role in any large organization. Students at the seminary thought of themselves as antibusiness. But when I questioned them, they agreed that they distrusted all large organizations, including the church. They perceived all large organizations as impersonal and opposed to individual values and needs. Yet we all know of organizations in which people's values and beliefs are respected and their expressions encouraged. What makes the difference? Can we identify the difference and, as a result, manage more effectively?

WHEN DO WE TAKE A STAND?

by Bowen H. McCoy

I wrote about my experiences purposely to present an ambiguous situation. I never found out if the sadhu lived or died. I can attest, though, that the sadhu lives on in his story. He lives in the ethics classes I teach each year at business schools and churches. He lives in the classrooms of numerous business schools, where professors have taught the case to tens of thousands of students. He lives in several casebooks on ethics and on an educational video. And he lives in organizations such as the American Red Cross and AT&T, which use his story in their ethics training.

As I reflect on the sadhu now, 15 years after the fact, I first have to wonder, What actually happened on that Himalayan slope? When I first wrote about the event, I reported the experience in as much detail as I could remember, but I shaped it to the needs of a good classroom discussion. After years of reading my story, viewing it on video, and hearing others discuss it, I'm not sure I myself know what actually occurred on the mountainside that day!

I've also heard a wide variety of responses to the story. The sadhu, for example, may not have wanted our help at all—he may have been intentionally bringing on his own death as a way to holiness. Why had he taken the dangerous way over the pass instead of the caravan route through the gorge? Hindu businesspeople have told me that in trying to assist the sadhu, we were being typically arrogant Westerners imposing our cultural values on the world.

I've learned that each year along the pass, a few Nepali porters are left to freeze to death outside the tents of the unthinking tourists who hired them. A few years ago, a French group even left one of their own, a young French woman, to die there. The difficult pass seems to demonstrate a perverse version of Gresham's law of currency: The bad practices of previous travelers have driven out the values that new travelers might have followed if they were at home. Perhaps that helps to explain why our porters behaved as they did and why it was so difficult for Stephen or anyone else to establish a different approach on the spot.

Our Sherpa sirdar, Pasang, was focused on his responsibility for bringing us up the mountain safe and sound. (His livelihood and status in the Sherpa ethnic group depended on our safe return.) We were weak, our party was split, the porters were well on their way to the top with all our gear and food, and a storm would have separated us irrevocably from our logistical base.

The fact was, we had no plan for dealing with the contingency of the sadhu. There was nothing we could do to unite our multicultural group in the little time we had. An ethical dilemma had come upon us unexpectedly, an element of drama that may explain why the sadhu's story has continued to attract students.

I am often asked for help in teaching the story. I usually advise keeping the details as ambiguous as possible. A true ethical dilemma requires a decision between two hard choices. In the case of the sadhu, we had to decide how much to sacrifice ourselves to take care of a stranger. And given the constraints of our trek, we had to make a group decision, not an individual one. If a large majority of students in a class ends up thinking I'm a bad person because of my decision on the mountain, the instructor may not have given the case its due. The same is true if the majority sees no problem with the choices we made.

Any class's response depends on its setting, whether it's a business school, a church, or a corporation. I've found that younger students are more likely to see the issue as black-and-white, whereas older ones tend to see shades of gray. Some have seen a conflict between the different ethical approaches that we followed at the time. Stephen felt he had to do everything he could to save the sadhu's life, in accordance with his Christian ethic of compassion. I had a utilitarian response: do the greatest good for the greatest number. Give a burst of aid to minimize the sadhu's exposure, then continue on our way.

The basic question of the case remains, When do we take a stand? When do we allow a "sadhu" to intrude into our daily lives? Few of us can afford the time or effort to take care of every needy person we encounter. How much must we give of ourselves? And how do we prepare our organizations and institutions so they will respond appropriately in a crisis? How do we influence them if we do not agree with their points of view?

We cannot quit our jobs over every ethical dilemma, but if we continually ignore our sense of values, who do we become? As a journalist asked at a recent conference on ethics, "Which ditch are we willing to die in?" For each of us, the answer is a bit different. How we act in response to that question defines better than anything else who we are, just as, in a collective sense, our acts define our institutions. In effect, the sadhu is always there, ready to remind us of the tensions between our own goals and the claims of strangers.

The word *ethics* turns off many and confuses more. Yet the notions of shared values and an agreed-upon process for dealing with adversity and change— what many people mean when they talk about corporate culture—seem to be at the heart of the ethical issue. People who are in touch with their own core beliefs and the beliefs of others and who are sustained by them can be more comfortable living on the cutting edge. At times, taking a tough line or a decisive stand in a muddle of ambiguity is the only ethical thing to do. If a manager is indecisive about a problem and spends time trying to figure out the "good" thing to do, the enterprise may be lost.

Business ethics, then, has to do with the authenticity and integrity of the enterprise. To be ethical is to follow the business as well as the cultural goals of the corporation, its owners, its employees, and its customers. Those who cannot serve the corporate vision are not authentic businesspeople and, therefore, are not ethical in the business sense.

At this stage of my own business experience, I have a strong interest in organizational behavior. Sociologists are keenly studying what they call corporate stories, legends, and heroes as a way organizations have of transmitting value systems. Corporations such as Arco have even hired consultants to perform an audit of their corporate culture. In a company, a leader is a person who understands, interprets, and manages the corporate value system. Effective managers, therefore, are action-oriented people who resolve conflict, are tolerant of ambiguity, stress, and change, and have a strong sense of purpose for themselves and their organizations.

If all this is true, I wonder about the role of the professional manager who moves from company to company. How can he or she quickly absorb the values and culture of different organizations? Or is there, indeed, an art of management that is totally transportable? Assuming that such fungible managers do exist, is it proper for them to manipulate the values of others?

What would have happened had Stephen and I carried the sadhu for two days back to the village and become involved with the villagers in his care? In four trips to Nepal, my most interesting experience occurred in 1975 when I lived in a Sherpa home in the Khumbu for five days while recovering from altitude sickness. The high point of Stephen's trip was an invitation to participate in a family funeral ceremony in Manang. Neither experience had to do with climbing the high passes of the Himalayas. Why were we so reluctant to try the lower path, the ambiguous trail? Perhaps because we did not have a leader who could reveal the greater purpose of the trip to us.

Why didn't Stephen, with his moral vision, opt to take the sadhu under his personal care? The answer is partly because Stephen was hard-stressed physically himself and partly because, without some support system that encompassed our involuntary and episodic community on the mountain, it was beyond his individual capacity to do so.

I see the current interest in corporate culture and corporate value systems as a positive response to pessimism such as Stephen's about the decline of the role of the individual in large organizations. Individuals who operate from a thoughtful set of personal values provide the foundation for a corporate culture. A corporate tradition that encourages freedom of inquiry, supports personal values, and reinforces a focused sense of direction can fulfill the need to combine individuality with the prosperity and success of the group. Without such corporate support, the individual is lost.

That is the lesson of the sadhu. In a complex corporate situation, the individual requires and deserves the support of the group. When people cannot find such support in their organizations, they don't know how to act. If such support is forthcoming, a person has a stake in the success of the group and can add much to the process of establishing and maintaining a corporate culture. Management's challenge is to be sensitive to individual needs, to shape them, and to direct and focus them for the benefit of the group as a whole.

For each of us the sadhu lives. Should we stop what we are doing and comfort him; or should we keep trudging up toward the high pass? Should I pause to help the derelict I pass on the street each night as I walk by the Yale Club en route to Grand Central Station? Am I his brother? What is the nature of our responsibility if we consider ourselves to be ethical persons? Perhaps it is to change the values of the group so that it can, with all its resources, take the other road.

Bowen H. McCoy retired from Morgan Stanley in 1990 after 28 years of service. He is now a real estate and business counselor, a teacher and a philanthropist.

UNIT 3

Business and Society: Contemporary Ethical, Social, and Environmental Issues

Unit Selections

Key Points to Consider

- How well are organizations responding to issues of work and family schedules, day care, and telecommuting?

- Should corporations and executives face criminal charges for unsafe products or pollution? Why or why not?

- What ethical dilemmas is management likely to face when conducting business in foreign environments?

 **Links: www.dushkin.com/online/**
These sites are annotated in the World Wide Web pages.

CIBERWeb
http://ciber.centers.purdue.edu

Communications for a Sustainable Future
http://csf.colorado.edu

National Immigrant Forum
http://www.immigrationforum.org

Stockholm University
http://www.psychology.su.se/units/ao/ao.html

Sympatico: Workplace
http://sympatico.workopolis.com

United Nations Environment Programme (UNEP)
http://www.unep.ch

United States Trade Representative (USTR)
http://www.ustr.gov

Both at home and abroad, there are social and environmental issues that have potential ethical consequences for management. Incidents of insider trading, deaths resulting from unsafe products or work environments, AIDS in the workplace, and the adoption of policies for involvement in the global market are a few of the issues that need to be seriously addressed by management.

This unit investigates the nature and ramifications of prominent ethical, social, and environmental issues facing management today. The unit articles are grouped into three sections. The first article scrutinizes the importance of companies gaining and maintaining trust in the marketplace. "Ethics in Cyberspace" reveals that when it comes to business ethics, old values still hold true in the "new economy." The next article examines the growth of corporate ethics programs. The last article in this subsection reflects why the corporate social audit is receiving renewed interest.

The first two articles in the second subsection address some of the salient contemporary ethical issues that are related to recent corporate misdeeds that crushed stock prices and eviscerated pension plans. The next article points out that workplace diversity is an issue extending beyond ethnicity and gender. The last article in this subsection examines ethical issues related to the spread of technology in the workplace.

The subsection *Global Ethics* concludes this unit with two readings that provide helpful insight into ethical issues and dilemmas inherent in multinational operations. They describe adapting ethical decisions to a global marketplace and offer guidelines for helping management deal with ethical issues in international markets.

TRUST
IN THE
MARKETPLACE

**John E. Richardson and
Linnea Bernard McCord**

Traditionally, ethics is defined as a set of moral values or principles or a code of conduct.

> ... Ethics, as an expression of reality, is predicated upon the assumption that there are right and wrong motives, attitudes, traits of character, and actions that are exhibited in interpersonal relationships. Respectful social interaction is considered a norm by almost everyone.
>
> ... the overwhelming majority of people perceive others to be ethical when they observe what is considered to be their genuine kindness, consideration, politeness, empathy, and fairness in their interpersonal relationships. When these are absent, and unkindness, inconsideration, rudeness, hardness, and injustice are present, the people exhibiting such conduct are considered unethical. A genuine consideration of others is essential to an ethical life. (Chewning, pp. 175–176).

An essential concomitant of ethics is of trust. Webster's Dictionary defines trust as "assured reliance on the character, ability, strength or truth of someone or something." Businesses are built on a foundation of trust in our free-enterprise system. When there are violations of this trust between competitors, between employer and employees, or between businesses and

consumers, our economic system ceases to run smoothly. From a moral viewpoint, ethical behavior should not exist because of economic pragmatism, governmental edict, or contemporary fashionability—it should exist because it is morally appropriate and right. From an economic point of view, ethical behavior should exist because it just makes good business sense to be ethical and operate in a manner that demonstrates trustworthiness.

Robert Bruce Shaw, in *Trust in the Balance*, makes some thoughtful observations about trust within an organization. Paraphrasing his observations and applying his ideas to the marketplace as a whole:

1. Trust requires consumers have confidence in organizational promises or claims made to them. This means that a consumer should be able to believe that a commitment made will be met.

2. Trust requires integrity and consistency in following a known set of values, beliefs, and practices.

3. Trust requires concern for the well-being of others. This does not mean that organizational needs are not given appropriate emphasis—but it suggests the importance of understanding the impact of decisions and actions on others—i.e. consumers. (Shaw, pp. 39–40)

Companies can lose the trust of their customers by portraying their products in a deceptive or inaccurate manner. In one recent example, a Nike advertisement exhorted golfers to buy the same golf balls used by Tiger Woods. However, since Tiger Woods was using custom-made Nike golf balls not yet available to the general golfing public, the ad was, in fact, deceptive. In one of its ads, Volvo represented that Volvo cars could withstand a physical impact that, in fact, was not possible. Once a company is "caught" giving inaccurate information, even if done innocently, trust in that company is eroded.

Companies can also lose the trust of their customers when they fail to act promptly and notify their customers of problems that the company has discovered, especially where deaths may be involved. This occurred when Chrysler dragged its feet in replacing a safety latch on its Minivan (Geyelin, pp. A1, A10). More recently, Firestone and Ford had been publicly brought to task for failing to expeditiously notify American consumers of tire defects in SUVs even though the problem had occurred years earlier in other countries. In cases like these, trust might not just be eroded, it might be destroyed. It could take years of painstaking effort to rebuild trust under these circumstances, and some companies might not have the economic ability to withstand such a rebuilding process with their consumers.

A *20/20* and *New York Times* investigation on a recent *ABC 20/20* program, entitled "The Car Dealer's Secret" revealed a sad example of the violation of trust in the marketplace. The investigation divulged that many unsuspecting consumers have had hidden charges tacked on by some car dealers when purchasing a new car. According to consumer attorney Gary Klein, "It's a dirty little secret that the auto lending industry has not owned up to." (*ABC News 20/20*)

The scheme worked in the following manner. Car dealers would send a prospective buyer's application to a number of lenders, who would report to the car dealer what interest rate the lender would give to the buyer for his or her car loan. This interest rate is referred to as the "buy rate." Legally a car dealer is not required to tell the buyer what the "buy rate" is or how much the dealer is marking up the loan. If dealers did most of the loans at the buy rate, they only get a small fee. However, if they were able to convince the buyer to pay a higher rate, they made considerably more money. Lenders encouraged car dealers to charge the buyer a higher rate than the "buy rate" by agreeing to split the extra income with the dealer.

David Robertson, head of the Association of Finance and Insurance Professionals—a trade group representing finance managers—defended the practice, reflecting that it was akin to a retail markup on loans. "The dealership provides a valuable service on behalf of the customer in negotiating these loans," he said. "Because of that, the dealership should be compensated for that work." (*ABC News 20/20*)

Careful examination of the entire report, however, makes one seriously question this apologetic. Even if this practice is deemed to be legal, the critical issue is what happens to trust when the buyers discover that they have been charged an additional 1–3% of the loan without their knowledge? In some cases, consumers were led to believe that they were getting the dealer's bank rate, and in other cases, they were told that the dealer had shopped around at several banks to secure the best loan rate they could get for the buyer. While this practice may be questionable from a legal standpoint, it is clearly in ethical breach of trust with the consumer. Once discovered, the companies doing this will have the same credibility and trustworthiness problems as the other examples mentioned above.

The untrustworthiness problems of the car companies was compounded by the fact that the investigation appeared to reveal statistics showing that black customers were twice as likely as whites to have their rate marked up—and at a higher level. That evidence—included in thousands of pages of confidential documents which *20/20* and *The New York Times* obtained from a Tennessee court—revealed that some Nissan and GM dealers in Tennessee routinely marked up rates for blacks, forcing them to pay between $300 and $400 more than whites. (*ABC News 20/20*)

This is a tragic example for everyone who was affected by this markup and was the victim of this secret policy. Not only is trust destroyed, there is a huge economic cost to the general public. It is estimated that in the last four years or so, Texas car dealers have received approximately $9 billion of kickbacks from lenders, affecting 5.2 million consumers. (*ABC News 20/20*)

Let's compare these unfortunate examples of untrustworthy corporate behavior with the landmark example of Johnson & Johnson which ultimately increased its trustworthiness with consumers by the way it handled the Tylenol incident. After seven individuals, who had consumed Tylenol capsules contaminated by a third party died, Johnson & Johnson instituted a total product recall within a week costing an estimated $50 million after taxes. The company did this, not because it was responsible for causing the problem, but because it was the right thing to do. In addition, Johnson & Johnson spearheaded the development of more effective tamper-proof containers for their industry. Because of the company's swift response, consumers once again were able to trust in the Johnson & Johnson name. Although Johnson & Johnson suffered a decrease in market share at the time because of the scare, over the long term it has maintained its profitability in a highly competitive market. Certainly part of this profit success is attributable to consumers believing that Johnson & Johnson is a trustworthy company. (Robin and Reidenbach)

The e-commerce arena presents another example of the importance of marketers building a mutually valuable relationship with customers through a trust-based collaboration process. Recent research with 50 e-businesses reflects that companies which create and nurture trust find customers return to their sites repeatedly. (Dayal.... p. 64)

In the e-commerce world, six components of trust were found to be critical in developing trusting, satisfied customers:

- State-of-art reliable security measures on one's site
- Merchant legitimacy (e.g., ally one's product or service with an established brand)
- Order fulfillment (i.e. placing orders and getting merchandise efficiently and with minimal hassles)
- Tone and ambiance—handling consumers' personal information with sensitivity and iron-clad confidentiality
- Customers feeling that they are in control of the buying process
- Consumer collaboration—e.g., having chat groups to let consumers query each other about their purchases and experiences (Dayal…, pp. 64–67)

Additionally, one author noted recently that in the e-commerce world we've moved beyond brands and trademarks to "trustmarks." This author defined a trustmark as a

… (D)istinctive name or symbol that emotionally binds a company with the desires and aspirations of its customers. It's an emotional connection—and it's much bigger and more powerful than the uses that we traditionally associate with a trademark…. (Webber, p. 214)

Certainly if this is the case, trust—being an emotional link—is of supreme importance for a company that wants to succeed in doing business on the Internet.

It's unfortunate that while a plethora of examples of violation of trust easily come to mind, a paucity of examples "pop up" as noteworthy paradigms of organizational courage and trust in their relationship with consumers.

In conclusion, some key areas for companies to scrutinize and practice with regard to decisions that may affect trustworthiness in the marketplace might include:

- Does a company practice the Golden Rule with its customers? As a company insider, knowing what you know about the product, how willing would you be to purchase it for yourself or for a family member?
- How proud would you be if your marketing practices were made public…. shared with your friends….

or family? (Blanchard and Peale, p. 27)

- Are bottom-line concerns the sole component of your organizational decision-making process? What about human rights, the ecological/environmental impact, and other areas of social responsibility?
- Can a firm which engages in unethical business practices with customers be trusted to deal with its employees any differently? Unfortunately, frequently a willingness to violate standards of ethics is not an isolated phenomenon but permeates the culture. The result is erosion of integrity throughout a company. In such cases, trust is elusive at best. (Shaw, p. 75)
- Is your organization not only market driven, but also value-oriented? (Peters and Levering, Moskowitz, and Katz)
- Is there a strong commitment to a positive corporate culture and a clearly defined mission which is frequently and unambiguously voiced by upper-management?
- Does your organization exemplify trust by practicing a genuine relationship partnership with your customers—*before, during, and after* the initial purchase? (Strout, p. 69)

Companies which exemplify treating customers ethically are founded on a covenant of trust. There is a shared belief, confidence, and faith that the company and its people will be fair, reliable, and ethical in all its dealings. *Total trust is the belief that a company and its people will never take opportunistic advantage of customer vulnerabilities*. (Hart and Johnson, pp. 11–13)

References

ABC News 20/20, "The Car Dealer's Secret," October 27, 2000.

Blanchard, Kenneth, and Norman Vincent Peale, *The Power of Ethical Management*, New York: William Morrow and Company, Inc., 1988.

Chewning, Richard C., *Business Ethics in a Changing Culture* (Reston, Virginia: Reston Publishing, 1984).

Dayal, Sandeep, Landesberg, Helen, and Michael Zeissner, "How to Build Trust Online," *Marketing Management*, Fall 1999, pp. 64–69.

Geyelin, Milo, "Why One Jury Dealt a Big Blow to Chrysler in Minivan-Latch Case," *Wall Street Journal*, November 19, 1997, pp. A1, A10.

Hart, Christopher W. and Michael D. Johnson, "Growing the Trust Relationship," *Marketing Management*, Spring 1999, pp. 9–19.

Hosmer, La Rue Tone, *The Ethics of Management*, second edition (Homewood, Illinois: Irwin, 1991).

Kaydo, Chad, "A Position of Power," *Sales & Marketing Management*, June 2000, pp. 104–106, 108ff.

Levering, Robert; Moskowitz, Milton; and Michael Katz, *The 100 Best Companies to Work for in America* (Reading, Mass.: Addison-Wesley, 1984).

Magnet, Myron, "Meet the New Revolutionaries," *Fortune*, February 24, 1992, pp. 94–101.

Muoio, Anna, "The Experienced Customer," *Net Company*, Fall 1999, pp. 025–027.

Peters, Thomas J. and Robert H. Waterman Jr., *In Search of Excellence* (New York: Harper & Row, 1982).

Richardson, John (ed.), *Annual Editions: Business Ethics 00/01* (Guilford, CT: McGraw-Hill/Dushkin, 2000).

_____, *Annual Editions: Marketing 00/01* (Guilford, CT: McGraw-Hill/Dushkin, 2000).

Robin, Donald P., and Erich Reidenbach, "Social Responsibility, Ethics, and Marketing Strategy: Closing the Gap Between Concept and Application," *Journal of Marketing*, Vol. 51 (January 1987), pp. 44–58.

Shaw, Robert Bruce, *Trust in the Balance*, (San Francisco: Jossey-Bass Publishers, 1997).

Strout, Erin, "Tough Customers," *Sales Marketing Management*, January 2000, pp. 63–69.

Webber, Alan M., "Trust in the Future," *Fast Company*, September 2000, pp. 209–212ff.

Dr. John E. Richardson is Professor of Marketing in the Graziadio School of Business and Management at Pepperdine University, Malibu, California

Dr. Linnea Bernard McCord is Associate Professor of Business Law in the Graziadio School of Business and Management at Pepperdine University, Malibu, California

ethics
in CYBERSPACE

WHEN IT COMES TO BUSINESS ETHICS, THERE'S NOTHING NEW UNDER THE SUN. THE OLD-FASHIONED LESSONS OF FAIR-DEALING AND FORTHRIGHTNESS STILL HOLD TRUE IN THE NEW ECONOMY.

by Marianne M. Jennings

In the so-called "new economy," it may seem that the rules of business have changed to suit the faster pace of the technological times. Certainly, the landscape for business is different from what it was ten years ago. But as we examine the conduct and consequence of the new companies that rode the tidal wave of the new economy, one thing becomes increasingly clear: There is nothing new under the sun. There is no such thing as "cyberethics" or "ethics in e-commerce." There is simply the practice of business ethics.

I have found that this idea is not always an easy sell, especially to new-economy converts. For example, early in 2000 I gave a speech on the importance of ethics in business to an audience of very young and successful e-commerce entrepreneurs. They offered a chilly reception for my discussion on the importance of honesty and keeping one's word in business. When I had finished, one young man approached me and said, "You're just going to have to face the fact that with new ways of doing business, these old rules don't work. You can't expect us to live by them."

The discipline of business ethics ha(s) provided very little to managers because of its focus on theory and the impractical.

I left the speech with significantly increased self-doubt. I questioned whether my expectations about ethics in business were unrealistic or old-fashioned. I feared I had become one of those stodgy professors who fails to grasp business trends and simply continues teaching the irrelevant.

However, over the next year increasing revelations about the practices of companies in the "new economy" and the market's downturn renewed my commitment to teaching traditional ethical values and principles in business, no matter what trends surround it. Those basic principles I discussed nearly two years ago with that somewhat hostile crowd still hold true today.

And judging from the ethical missteps of companies in the new economy, as noted in the discussion and lessons that follow, we have not done as much in academia as we should have to help future business leaders understand the whats, whys, and hows of business ethics.

A look at these ethical missteps offers a perfect teaching opportunity for lessons in business ethics. Students can see for themselves the consequences when these basic principles are violated—the same principles that have been labeled by too many as outmoded or inapplicable to new forms of business.

Lesson 1:
Honesty Is the Best Policy

In 1993, Andrew Stark published his seminal piece, "What's the Matter with Business Ethics?" in *Harvard Business Review*. Professor Stark concluded that the discipline of business ethics had provided very little to managers because of its focus on theory and the impractical. Further, he indicted members of the discipline for their unrealistic expectations for business behavior. Unfortunately, Professor Stark was simply part of the discipline's majority who believe that ethics and business are mutually exclusive terms: It must be all or nothing at all.

Likewise, theorists in business ethics frequently condemn a business for being in business. These theorists might advise a company to go out of business rather than violate their self-defined ethical principles. Professor Stark understandably chastised this group for being impractical. But he then went on to take the position at the opposite extreme—that sometimes a business has to be unethical to survive.

One of the clear lessons of the new economy is that neither approach is realistic, practical, or even frequent in running a business. Just because a business is "soft," in the sense that it has no factories or produces no pollutants—as nearly all new economy companies were in the late 1990s—does not mean that it is ethical. And very often it is the decision to behave in an unethical fashion that prompts the demise of a business rather than assures its survival.

The underlying "social responsibility" arguments about business—particularly the pro-environment focus—have not served as accurate predictors of honesty-in-fact in terms of business behavior, especially among the "new economy" companies. These leaders possessed an odd sense of immunity, a sense of ethical invincibility perhaps born of years of business ethics instruction centered on topics of social responsibility. So long as the company employees were engaged in volunteer work, there seemed little cause to worry about undisclosed risk, postponed write-downs, and conflicts of interest. Who can blame them?

For the past decade, ethics instruction has focused on topics such as global warming, sweatshops, environmentalism, and diversity. While those are important topics in the field, few scholars were doing research or teaching the

ethics of earnings management. And, as examples below will indicate, earnings management became an art form in new economy companies, bordering on cooking the books.

But a look at the lack of transparency in the financial statements of many of the new economy companies tells us that perhaps, as a matter of business ethics, we should begin with disclosure of expenses. Only then should we work our way up to saving the planet.

> While we may think that the recent evolution in business has presented us with new rules, some fundamental principles do not change.

As we teach ethics, one of the foremost lessons is perhaps that no one business ethics principle provides a free pass from accountability in other areas. Virtue does not result from obscuring financial activities. An ethical company has a multifaceted approach to creating its culture. Our responsibility is to be certain students understand all aspects of business ethics so that they can create, and work within, that culture effectively.

Lesson 2:
History Repeats Itself

Consider a scenario with the following characteristics:

- High-price earnings multipliers
- Economic disturbances abroad
- High levels of optimism
- Insiders selling their shares
- Insider trading
- An abundance of options
- Speculation
- A false security and a feeling of invincibility

This list seems to be a description of market conditions before the bubble began to burst in April 2000. However, those factors actually were taken from readings on the climate that preceded the 1929 stock market crash *and* the Holland Tulip Market of the 1600s (from *The Causes of the 1929 Stock Market Crash* by Harold Bierman Jr., and *Tulipmania: The Story of the World's Most Coveted Flower and the Extraordinary Passions It Aroused* by Michael Dash). Historical perspective is crucial to understanding the present. Our role as academicians surely includes providing students with that perspective so that they can understand that their experiences are not unique, and that history does have its lessons.

The Holland Tulip market was one that evolved from the love of a new flower. As the price for the flower increased, investors began to purchase tulip bulbs. As bulb prices increased and supplies decreased, investors sought bulb futures, an investment in air! At one point, one tulip bulb future was selling for $10,000 in today's dollars. When everyone realized that there was nothing to their investments, save the hope of a bulb sometime in the future, the market collapsed. Investors and companies wanted it all as quickly as possible and discarded the basics of sound investment to be part of a wild scheme.

Sound familiar? As students examine the investments in dot-coms that had no record of earnings—just expenses and hope for the future—the Holland tulip market becomes incredibly relevant. During the height of the dot-com mania in which IPOs were creating billionaires overnight, it was as if the financial statements of these companies were reading, "Well, if it hadn't been for all of our expenses, we would have made money."

While we may think that the recent evolution in business has presented us with new rules, some fundamental principles do not change. Expenses in excess of earnings, no matter how sound the model for predicting future earnings, are still expenses that reduce earnings.

Establishing the ground rules for business and business ethics still remains a critical part of a solid business education. A simple look at even the California gold rush provides students with a historical foundation. At the time, many individuals and businesses purchased land, options, and investments in mines. Their risk was high and not always undertaken with complete or honest information. Quick returns, frauds, and schemes were the downfall of nearly all involved.

Their dreams turned to dust, but the true winners from the gold rush economy were those very staid businesses that supplied the materials for the expanded mining industry there. For example, Levi Strauss, the company that sold the miners their pants, remains an established company today, just as the companies that sold the dot-coms their furniture, supplies, and services survive.

There is an element of patience and virtue in the long term that should be taught as part of the study of ethics. Double-digit growth is not sustainable for extended periods of time, but steadily increasing growth is. With that knowledge base, students can understand how often ethical shortcuts interfere with that long-term goal of increasing success.

Lesson 3:
What Goes Around Comes Around

Two examples of new economy companies and their financial statements illustrate the ease with which business ethics can be incorporated into discussion. A look at MicroStrategy Inc. and Dell Computers offers students a challenging example of why transparent financial statements matter.

A related ethical issue surrounding financial reporting choices is the absence of independent boards among the dot-com companies.

When MicroStrategy issued its IPO, its share price was $6. By March 2000, that price had climbed to $333. However, when MicroStrategy announced in December 2000 that the Securities Exchange Commission was investigating it for "accounting improprieties," its share price dropped 62 percent in one day.

As the investigation unfolded, we learned the following:

- PricewaterhouseCoopers certified its financials for 1999 (profit figure).
- PricewaterhouseCoopers then forced MicroStrategy to correct the 1999 financials—they showed a loss.
- PricewaterhouseCoopers settled a lawsuit with shareholders for $51 million (plus interest from September 2000 on May 10, 2001).
- Share price on May 10, 2001, was $4.95, and on October 11, $1.61, up from $1.40.

MicroStrategy then offered the following explanation in its annual reports filed with the SEC:

> The Company has concluded that certain of its software sales that include service relationships will be accounted for using contract accounting, which spreads the recognition of revenue over the entire contract period as opposed to separating it between the software and services components. The effect of these revisions is to defer the time when revenue is recognized for large, complex contracts that combine both products and services.

> The Company, with the concurrence of PricewaterhouseCoopers, LLP, its auditors, will reduce its 1999 reported revenue from $205.3 million to between approximately $150.0 million and $155.0 million, and its results of operations from diluted net income per share of $0.15 to a diluted loss per share between approximately ($0.43) and ($0.51).

MicroStrategy broke no laws in its interpretation of accounting principles with regard to booking revenues. But a change, insisted upon by its auditors, took the company financials from a position of net income per share to a net loss of some $0.58 per share lower. Here, the moment for teaching business ethics comes when we ask not simply whether MicroStrategy *could* report its earnings this way, but whether it *should*.

Students are able to see the long-term impact of that choice, or that interpretation of an accounting rule, on the company and all of its stakeholders. More than the restatement of earnings and its impact is the psychological impact on the market as the company loses reputational capital in terms of the reliability of its financial reports.

A related ethical issue surrounding financial reporting choices is the absence of independent boards among the dot-com companies. That false sense of invincibility was evident as the majority of the dot-coms opted not to have outsiders on their boards. There are reasons and historical foundations for independence on boards, particularly in audit committees.

However, the dot-coms seemed particularly hostile to the very suggestion of such outside input. When asked in 1999 about the lack of outsiders on board, Jeff Dachis, the former CEO of Razorfish, said, "I control 10 percent of the company. What's good for me is good for all shareholders. Management isn't screwing up. We've created enormous shareholder value." Razorfish's IPO sold at $56 per share; it was at $1.11 in May 2001. Dachis was replaced as CEO in 2000. The stock price in October 2001 was $0.21, up from $0.14 per share.

Dell Computer provides another example of ethical issues in financial reporting and how earnings are obtained. During the late 1990s, a sizable percentage of Dell's earnings was the result of the company's rather complex stock purchase program that employed puts and calls. Dell was using its own stock to hedge earnings, and doing a darn good job of it, so long as the company's stock price was increasing and Dell was on the correct side in terms of its balance of puts and calls. But when the market took its downturn, Dell experienced reductions in earnings.

This type of accounting practice resulted in increased SEC oversight and disclosure rules in which companies must be specific in disclosing their OCI (Other Comprehensive Income). Further, the SEC has new rules in place on puts and calls by companies in their own stock because of the potential for manipulation of stock prices.

Warren Buffett has commented on the new liberties in financial reporting and referred to some of the creative accounting methods used to report earnings as the "distortion *du jour*." Mr. Buffett offers the ethical perspective on these issues as he raises the issue of whether the United States is losing its longstanding position of candor, or transparency, in its companies' financial statements.

While these financial reporting issues are not new, the new economy seemed to provide the incentives for pushing the envelope on managing earnings practices, resulting in new regulations for those abuses of transparency. Interestingly, 66 percent of all of the SEC investigations for accounting fraud now involve dot-com companies.

While many investors have lost significant amounts, study of these experiences is valuable to students. Students must explore the basic ethical questions: Are these disclosures complete and honest? What are the implications for this decision on how to report revenue? If I were

an investor, is this information I would want disclosed? And would I want more discussion of the risk involved in this approach to financial reporting?

Trust Must Be Earned

The May 14, 2001, cover of *Fortune* magazine has a photo of Mary Meeker, the new economy analyst from Morgan Stanley, and the question, "Can we ever trust again?" Inside the magazine, the stories raise two basic concerns in business ethics: conflicts of interest and insider trading.

The conflicts of interest in the new economy centered on the role of analysts. While many investors assumed that analysts such as Meeker were offering their candid assessments of companies, the analysts very often stood to benefit personally, or through their companies, if they endorsed an IPO. Many became cheerleaders for the companies they were supposed to be evaluating independently.

Other players also had conflicts of interest in the new economy stock offerings. Lawyers who were offering their professional opinions as part of the disclosures in the IPO registration materials often were to be paid in shares of the new company. Their opinions on the legal issues facing the company were in conflict with their economic interest in the IPO not only going forward, but going well.

In addition, insider trading occurred in the form of the so-called "pump and dump" stock sales. In this money-making venture, even television analysts got in on the game of purchasing a particular stock and then taking to the airways, the Internet, and the print media to pump the stock to investors. When the investors took the bait and bought, increasing the value of the shares, the pumper would then dump the shares at a significant profit. Even a teenager, 15-year-old Jonathan Lebed, managed to turn an investment of $8,000 into a handsome $800,000 profits. He used different screen names to pump shares he had purchased, and then sold them after intrigued investors caused the prices to climb. And he did all this without missing a day of school.

These conflicts and self-dealing stock-trading scenarios are teaching moments to show what happens to markets when investors lose trust in the fundamental fairness that they assumed existed. Beyond the ethical principles is that exploration of the underlying reasons they exist— that markets function because of certain assumptions about values and behaviors. Investors hold back when they perceive that they cannot get a fair shake in a market that has no level playing field. An examination of economic volatility differences across nations can show students what happens when there is a perception of corruption in markets. In this respect, stock market investments are no more sophisticated than money kept in a jar or under a mattress.

THE VERY NATURE OF E-COMMERCE DEMANDS MORE TRUST THAN HAS EVER EXISTED IN OUR BUSINESS TRANSACTIONS. WE TRUST THAT EVERYONE WILL HONOR PLEDGES MADE WITH SIMPLY A **CLICK**.

The very nature of e-commerce demands more trust than has ever existed in our business transactions. We trust that those responding via electronic means are indeed who they purport to be. We trust that companies will not misuse the credit information we provide to them to pay for merchandise ordered electronically. And we trust that everyone will honor pledges made with simply a click.

Go Back to the Basics

As I think back to the young man's skepticism about the role of ethics in the new economy, my mindset has changed. It is *because* of the nature of the new economy and e-commerce, not in spite of it, that we need basic ethics more than ever.

As teachers and scholars, we and our students can benefit from the experiences of the fallen dot-com companies in the now not-so-new new economy. They serve as the perfect examples to demonstrate how the basic principles of ethics, such as honesty, fairness, and the avoidance of conflicts of interest, are a cornerstone to success, even when the means for doing business changes.

Marianne Jennings is a professor of legal and ethical studies at the College of Business at Arizona State University in Tempe, Arizona.

From *Biz Ed*, January/February 2002, pp. 18-23. © 2002 by AACSB International, The Association to Advance Collegiate Schools of Business. Reprinted by permission.

Business and society

Adding corporate ethics to the bottom line

Thomas Donaldson examines the logic behind the growth of corporate ethics programmes and seeks evidence for their success or failure

Corporate ethics programmes were like hummingbirds in the 1950s. You didn't see one often and when you did it seemed too delicate to survive. Now, these curiosities have proved their sturdiness, flourishing and migrating steadily from their historical home in Europe and the US to Asia, Africa and Latin America. Most of the 500 largest corporations in the US now boast a code of ethics, and the proportion among a broader collection of US companies has risen to 80 percent. Similarly, a recent study of FTSE 350 companies and non-quoted companies of equivalent size undertaken by the London Business School and Arthur Andersen showed that 78 percent of the responding companies had a code of conduct, compared with 57 percent three years ago.

In the 1950s, ethics programmes were the personal creations of charismatic leaders, such as General Johnson who fashioned Johnson & Johnson's Credo statement; today they are produced by a wide variety of organisations. They encompass not only written standards of conduct, but internal education schemes, formal agreements on industry standards, ethics offices, social accounting techniques and social projects.

The popularity of ethics programmes raises several questions. Do they deliver what they promise in making companies more ethical? Do they aid companies in achieving traditional performance measures such as return on investment or customer satisfaction? And, should companies institute new programmes, or perhaps change the ones they have?

The vogue for ethics programmes does not resolve the most common theoretical question asked of business ethics, namely, what counts as ethical? Even the socially screened investment movement that specialises in assessing stocks for ethical characteristics often seems confused. Consider the tendency of such funds to screen out the "sin" stocks of tobacco, alcohol and firearms. As a result, high-tech stocks, ones unlikely to produce sinning products, have become darlings of such funds. But while Microsoft, for example, will probably never produce wine and so almost always finds itself on the screened funds' lists, it has been found in violation of US anti-trust laws, a sin greater in some people's eyes than fermenting grapes.

Ethics programmes, however, offer a solution to the question of what is ethical by simply decreeing an answer. It makes little difference to Motorola whether other companies agree or disagree that its principle of "uncompromising integrity" prohibits even small payments in countries where bribery is common. Motorola is content to set the standard for itself.

Similarly, programmes created by industries or international organisations decree their own rules, although they often make use of existing standards as templates. The Organisation for Economic Co-operation and Development's (OECD) recent prohibitions on companies based in member countries from engaging in foreign bribery were developed through extensive discussion among participating countries, although they contain precepts seen earlier in the US Foreign Corrupt Practices Act.

"Ethics schemes have spread, yet no evidence suggests this is the result of a fall in standards

Corporate ethics programmes have spread widely, yet no evidence suggests this growth is the result of a decline in standards. Studies indicate that between 25 and 60 percent of employees in any given year admit to having seen ethical misbehaviour, depending upon the context in which the question is asked.

What, then, has driven the ethics boom? Likely factors include the stronger focus by the media on corporate conduct, increased government pressure and growing maturity of business institutions. Recently, media exposure of labour standards in

Asia prompted a cascade of initiatives by companies such as Nike in the US and Puma in Germany.

Moreover, people have seen that companies reeling from media and legal pressures suffer heavy losses. Names in the financial services industry such as Prudential Group, Daiwa Bank, Salomon Brothers, and Kidder, Peabody are sobering reminders that these problems can damage both a company's brand and its financial prospects. According to Roy C. Smith and Ingo Walter, financial experts who have analysed these cases, Prudential Group's fraud at Prudential Securities and Prudential Insurance cost it $1.8bn in fines and settlements; Daiwa Bank's concealment of its trading losses cost it fines and the loss of its US licence; Salomon Brothers' government bond auction scandal cost it $500m in fines and settlements and $1bn in market capitalisation; and Kidder Peabody's insider trading scandals and falsification of government bond trades cost it its viability—it was sold by General Electric in 1994 and is now defunct.

Often fines and court judgments take a back seat to the cost in damaged reputations. In the US, the 1994 legal dispute involving the Bankers Trust Company and its sale of derivatives cost it tens of millions in an out-of-court settlement. But more significant was the company's damaged reputation: in a matter of months, its share price halved. And while Royal Dutch/Shell avoided significant legal action for its alleged passivity during the trial and execution of Nigerian environmentalists, the effect on its reputation in the late 1990s was substantial.

Governments, too, have applied increasing pressure on companies, prompting new designs for ethics programmes. In 1991, US Federal Sentencing Guidelines offered companies a dramatic incentive to develop formal schemes. The guidelines promise reduced penalties for companies found guilty of criminal conduct as long as they meet requirements for compliance and ethics programmes. In turn, compliance-oriented ethics programmes, usually with designated ethics officers, have boomed. Both the Ethics Officers Association and the Defense Industry Ethics Initiative have hundreds of members and share best practice for establishing ethics offices, hot lines, code design, web pages and training programmes. Most of the largest 200 companies in the US belong to one or both of these groups.

Finally, many experts argue that the ethics boom stems partly from the maturing of democratic capitalism. With Marxism dead, capitalism must nonetheless face the moral expectations of market participants. Consumers acknowledge the capacity of markets to generate wealth, but interpret the social contract between business and society as involving more than unmitigated profit-mongering.

The limits of law and regulation to cope with corporate ethics became obvious in the past century when consumers saw that regulation inevitably lags behind knowledge inside an industry. For example, governments were powerless to regulate successfully the use of asbestos because knowledge about its carcinogenic effects was held not by regulators outside the industry, but by employees inside it. By the time the law caught up, it was too late. Society expects companies to use their knowledge in a responsible way.

Most economists agree that externally imposed regulation can be invasive and inefficient. Companies, in turn, reason that if they can substitute moral persuasion for inefficient regulation, then they will benefit.

If the ethics programmes of 50 years ago resembled a rare bird, today they resemble a Brazilian aviary. They fall into three types:

- code and compliance;
- identity and values;
- social outreach.

Each programme has a different goal. Code and compliance programmes are the most common and focus on regulating the behaviour of employees. These formal documents specify employee behaviour in detail and are often written by lawyers. Such codes govern conflict of interest, accepting gifts, anti-competitive behaviour, entertaining customers and so on. Some industries have slowly developed highly specialised compliance programmes. For example, the financial services industry has raised compliance nearly on a par with other aspects of corporate management such as human resources, finance and marketing.

Employees are often asked to sign a document each year indicating that they have read and understood the code. Thus, if the code is broken, it becomes easier to identify and penalise offenders. Motives for such codes are usually starkly self-interested: companies hope to avoid legal and reputational harm by specifying and monitoring behaviour.

A variant of compliance programmes is the trend towards third-party sponsored codes. The ISO 9000 code (regulated in conjunction with The Council for Economic Priorities), the Japanese ESC 2000 Code, the Caux Roundtable Principles, the Sullivan Corporate Responsible Principles, OECD directives on foreign bribery and Kofi Annan's recent Global Compact from the United Nations are a few examples. Many such codes attempt to regulate labour standards in factories that supply global companies, as well as to specify standards for other aspects of behaviour.

Companies such as Mattel, Levi Strauss and Royal Dutch/Shell have developed their own codes. However, increasingly companies find it convenient, if not more efficient, to use third-party resources for monitoring. One example is the work done by the non-profit, anti-corruption group Transparency International. This group not only publishes yearly rankings of bribe-paying and bribe-taking countries, but has worked with corporations and governments to clean up institutions in host countries.

Identity and values programmes, which sometimes exist alongside compliance variants, differ starkly from their counterparts in tone and motivation. They usually draw inspiration from a list of the company's values that emphasises positive concepts such as integrity, respect for others, teamwork and service to stakeholders. Not unlike mission statements, values programmes aim to express what the corporation stands for, to specify an "identity". Royal Dutch/Shell's "principles" and Johnson & Johnson's Credo are examples. Most very large US corporations possess such programmes and companies in other countries are following suit.

Nonetheless, many corporations launch values programmes only to see them wither. In contrast, companies that have been successful in maintaining schemes tend to renew them from time to time and managers use language from values statements to justify business decisions. The tone of values programmes is markedly different from compliance codes. They emphasise positive against negative concepts and self-motivation rather than external sanction. The phrasing tends to be in plain language and sometimes even emotional, in contrast to legalistic compliance codes.

Finally, "social outreach" programmes, the least common type, emphasise the company's role as a social citizen. Two trends dominate such programmes. The first is the "social accounting" movement with its roots in Europe and the second is the "competency-based" responsibility movement from Europe and the US. Social accounting programmes rest on the premise that companies should account for social activities in much the same way as they account for their financial activities.

Recently a group of 300 global companies called the Global Reporting Initiative (GRI) began formulating standards to improve social reporting. European companies including BP and the social accounting pioneer Norsk Hydro of Norway, have adopted such programmes. To date, social accounting is a legal requirement only in France, where companies with over 300 employees are expected to produce a *bilan social*.

The second form of social outreach emphasises a corporation's core competency in its attempt to contribute to society. Increasingly, such programmes are adopted by companies which want to move beyond writing cheques for good causes.

One of the first to use a competency-based programme was US pharmaceutical company, Merck. Merck startled the world in 1980s when it moved to develop a drug, Mectizan, that would treat the tropical disease river blindness. Because potential users of the drug constituted some of the world's poorest people, no one, including Merck, expected the drug to make a profit. Merck also knew that developing such a drug would cost hundreds of millions of dollars. But relying upon its identity/values tradition of emphasising the health of the customer as the best means to achieve profit, Merck pushed ahead.

The result was remarkable. Merck reaped a public relations windfall and even more significant, the World Health Organisation last year announced that river blindness was on the short list of diseases officially eradicated. Following Merck's success, peer pressure on other pharmaceutical companies proved intense. Since then, Pfizer has announced a $60m project to eliminate the eye disease trachoma and SmithKline Beecham has agreed to give away its drug to cure lymphatic filariasis.

Competency-based initiatives have spread. Ericsson developed a project on magnetic pollution; with help from UNICEF, Procter & Gamble is developing Nutri-Delight, a new product that addresses malnutrition in poorer countries; and BP in 1998 agreed to give solar-powered refrigerators to doctors in Zambia for storing malaria vaccines. Danone sponsors employees in Hungary to work with local groups to raise health standards for children.

Such efforts are not without risk. Monsanto applied its scientific expertise in an initiative with the International Rice Institute, groups from Thailand and the Thai government to educate poor farmers about how to improve crop yields using scientifically engineered seeds and modern chemicals. But Monsanto has since been the target of vigorous criticism in the media, much of it alleging that Monsanto's technology is a hazard to the environment.

Ethics and profits

The motives behind the three kinds of ethics programmes vary markedly. A 1999 study by the Conference Board demonstrated that the reasons behind ethics codes are markedly different in different cultures. Codes dominated by considerations of bottom-line success turn out to be far more popular in the US than elsewhere. The study showed that 64 percent of all US codes are dominated by self-interested or "instrumental" motives, while 60 percent of European codes were dominated by "values" concerns.

Despite geographic differences, the Conference Board study demonstrated that increasing numbers of senior managers are involved. About 95 percent of companies formulating ethics codes include contributions from the chief executive, in contrast to 80 percent in 1987; and 78 percent of company boards of directors in contrast to 21 percent in 1987.

Do better corporate ethics fuel higher profits? This question has been studied for decades with no resolution. A 1999 academic study by Roman, Hayibor and Agle summarised 52 research projects devoted to corporate ethics and profit. At first sight, the results appear encouraging for corporate ethics programme defenders. The authors concluded that 33 studies showed a positive link between corporate ethics and profit, 14 showed no effect or were inconclusive and only five suggested a negative relationship. Nonetheless, the problems of grappling with the relationship between ethics and profit are huge. They include determining not only what "counts" as a more "ethical" company, but also excluding reputational effects that can follow financial success. It is difficult to know what to conclude. Even if better ethics is good business, the question of whether programmes make better ethics remains.

The 2000 National Business Ethics Survey in the US confirmed earlier studies showing that merely having a code of ethics does nothing to improve corporate ethics. Indeed, this most recent study confirmed the trend of earlier pessimistic studies in showing a slight positive correlation between merely having formal ethical standards and poorer ethics—in this instance poorer ethics being reflected in the percentage of employees who feel pressure to compromise ethics. The picture, however, is different for companies being restructured.

The study showed that when organisations are not in transition, the presence of ethics programme elements (such as formal standards, training and an advice line) is not statistically related to the pressure employees feel to compromise on ethical standards. But when organisations are in transition, pressure to lower ethical standards is significantly higher if formal initiatives are missing.

"Ethics programmes are successful when they are seen by employees as being about values

Evidence is accumulating that ethics programmes are more successful when they are seen by employees not as being about compliance, but about values. A 1999 study undertaken by academics Weaver and Trevino showed that when employees construed companies' ethics programmes as being oriented towards "values" rather than "compliance", they displayed far more commitment to the organisation, more willingness to deliver bad news and more willingness to seek advice.

Another study by the same authors strongly suggests that programmes fare better when they are "integrated" rather than "decoupled"; in other words ethics policies fare better when they are integrated with other corporate structures and policies, such as reward policies, and where people who occupy corporate structures are held accountable. In contrast, less successful "decoupled" ethical policies appear to conform to external expectations while making it easy to insulate much of the organisation from those expectations. Hence, companies that attempt to manage ethics without co-operation of senior managers and without adjusting structures and policies are less likely to succeed.

"The forces that have propelled ethics programmes into being are showing no signs of abating

In line with this finding, a 1992 US study by the Institute of Chartered Financial Analysts of 5,000 people in the financial services industry showed that only 11 percent of financial services managers who witnessed unethical behaviour reported their concerns. Clearly, financial services companies need more than a well-constructed compliance mechanism.

Studies support the connection between employee evaluation of their company's ethical behaviour and important indicators such as loyalty. The 2000 National Business Ethics Survey undertaken by the Ethics Resource Center in the US indicated that 43 percent of employees who disagree that the head of their organisation "sets a good example of ethical business behaviour" also feel pressure to compromise ethics standards. But only 8 percent of employees who agree that he or she sets a good example feel ethical pressure.

In a recent KPMG integrity survey, four out of five employees who felt that managers would uphold ethical standards said they would recommend their company to potential recruits; whereas only one in five employees who did not believe managers supported ethical standards would do so. The study also found that four out of five employees who felt management would uphold ethical standards also believed customers would recommend the company to others, while the figure halved for employees who did not have faith in managers' ethical standards.

Conclusion

First, we should get used to ethics programmes. The forces that propelled them into being show no signs of abating. Yet not all ethics programmes are created equal. Corporate ethics programmes can either fit with or conflict with the interests and aims of the corporations that create them.

Companies that wish to define their identity and communicate their values to employees, stockholders and customers, should adopt different programmes from ones who simply want to limit legal and public relations problems. Even in the latter case, however, evidence suggests that compliance programmes will be more successful when connected to positive values with which employees can empathise. For any ethics programmes, furthermore, the evidence is strong that merely having a formal code is not enough. Any such statement must be synchronised with the company's organisational structures, its culture and its leadership.

Finally, companies aiming for high standards of social citizenship, or aiding society by doing more than just giving money away, require a different kind of programme. Current trends for such programmes are towards social accounting systems and making creative social use of a company's core competencies.

Thomas Donaldson is Mark O. Winkelman Professor at the Wharton School, University of Pennsylvania.

Corporate Social Audits— This Time Around

Homer H. Johnson

One of the more exciting new ideas emerging from the social activism of the 1960s and '70s was the concept of the corporate social audit. If companies were to be held responsible for their societal and environmental impact, then an annual social audit, similar to the annual financial audit, would seem to be an ideal mechanism to assess corporate responsibility in this area.

First seriously proposed in the mid-1950s, the social audit had a very rapid increase in interest and discussion. One prediction claimed that by 1980 all companies would be required to submit to an annual social audit. However, even the wisest of prophets are sometimes wrong, and contrary to prediction, discussion of the corporate social audit was practically nonexistent by 1980. In fact, its history appeared to be a textbook example of the S curve, with a 20-year history of rise and demise.

The collapse of the social audit was probably triggered by several factors. A major factor was a lack of enthusiasm for voluntary auditing by the business community itself. Much of the drive for the audits was coming from social activists, academics, and others, with the business community being dragged reluctantly into the discussion. The idea was new and quite radical. Viable models and measurements were lacking. And managers feared that exposing their firms to a social audit could open the doors to public criticism and possible government intervention.

To some extent, the business community's lack of interest in voluntary social auditing led to what was probably the most significant business-related social legislation in the country's history. Between 1969 and 1972, four regulatory agencies were established that greatly affected American business: the Occupational Safety and Health Administration (OSHA), the Equal Employment Opportunity Commission (EEOC), the Consumer Product Safety Commission (CPSC), and the Environmental Protection Agency (EPA).

In some sense, the federal government had begun its own form of social auditing, with the power to discipline companies that were not in compliance with social standards. For the activists, who never really trusted businesses to audit themselves anyway, this was the direction to go. And in the business community, whatever limited interest there had been for voluntary social audits was pretty much gone; by virtue of the new federal legislation, companies were already, if reluctantly, submitting to a social audit.

No longer at a dead end, the corporate social audit has received renewed interest. Why is it going to work now?

Finally, the dramatic shift in America's political mood in the late 1970s, away from the social agenda of the '50s and '60s, ended the discussion of voluntary social audits. The election of Ronald Reagan in late 1980 was a seminal event in signaling the pendulum swing toward a more conservative agenda. A dominant theme that emerged was the contention that government had become too big and too intrusive in the affairs of American business. Social audits in general, and federal regulation in particular, fell out of favor, and numerous attempts were made to repeal the social legislation of the previous decade.

However, interest in social auditing had not totally disappeared. With the renewed interest in corporate social responsibility that emerged in the 1990s, the social audit has also been given new life. And this time it appears to be here to stay. In its current state, and with the various types and processes being used, the future of social auditing seems set, and the business community will be facing several of its issues in the coming decade.

THE CURRENT STATE OF SOCIAL AUDITING

A social audit is a standard process for identifying, measuring and reporting the ethical, social and environmental impact of an organization. This definition is broad enough to cover both general and specific audit processes. Of interest here are social audits that focus on the U.S. for-profit sector, toward which the original concept was targeted. If one applies the general definition of a social audit to the current for-profit scene, one finds three broad areas in which social audits are being applied (ignoring the documentation required by regulatory agencies):

1. social "screens," which are used for socially responsible investing;

2. social assessments used by public interest groups to evaluate the degree of corporate compliance to standards advocated by the group; and

3. internal audits initiated by companies, which may or may not be released to the public.

In all three areas, models have been developed based on standardized criteria, as well as measurement, scoring, and reporting. A major difference among the three is that the audits in the first two areas are conducted by an external agency, often without the cooperation of the firm being audited. In the third area, the audit is conducted by the firm itself, or by its invitation, often with independent and external attestation.

Examples of audits can demonstrate the processes evolving in each of these three areas. The Domini Social Equity Fund was chosen for its social screen. The process used by the Council on Economic Priorities was chosen as an example of ratings by a public interest group. Two examples were chosen from the category of internal audits: SA8000 as an example of an audit of a more narrow focus, and the 1995 audit of The Body Shop as an example of a comprehensive audit. These four models in themselves help define the current state of social auditing. Moreover, they will provide the basis of social auditing efforts in the near future.

Socially Responsible Investing: Domini Social Index/KLD

Socially responsible investing (SRI) is a process by which publicly held companies are screened for their social and environmental activities and investments are made (through stock or bond purchases) only in those companies that meet the standards set by the investing group. Social investing has grown considerably in the last decade, evolving to the level of sophistication at which it is as profitable for investors as other types of mutual funds. The audit process for SRI serves two ends. First, it assures the individual or institutional investor that the

investment is supporting companies that engage in socially responsible activities. Second, it exerts some degree of pressure on companies to conform to the standards set by the investment group.

A key component in the SRI process is the social screen, which is the application of social criteria to investment decisions on conventional investments, such as stocks, bonds, and mutual funds. Social screens can be exclusionary or qualitative. If an investment fund wishes not to invest in companies that manufacture alcoholic beverages or tobacco products, the fund can set up an exclusionary or "negative" screen to eliminate them from its list of investment possibilities. However, for many issues a company's performance is rarely of the either/or variety that lends itself to an exclusionary screen. Qualitative screens look at both the positive and negative aspects of a company's performance on a given area of interest, such as the environment or diversity, and evaluate—or let the investor evaluate—whether the company has sufficiently met the investment standard.

Domini Social Investments is one of the better known organizations using social screening. Its Domini Social Equity Fund (DSEF) was the first socially responsible index fund in the United States. To select companies for the portfolio, the social research firm of Kinder, Lydenberg, Domini & Co. (KLD) created the Domini 400 Social Index (DSI 400), which monitors the performance of 400 U.S. corporations that pass multiple, broad-based social screens. The data used for these ratings are derived from a variety of sources, including corporate public documents, trade publications, news sources, court records, and government data. In addition, KLD conducts an annual survey that is completed by the company, and interviews company officers. These data are used to generate a profile of the company organized around several major criteria. A final step in verifying the data is the submission of a draft of KLD's profile to the company for a response.

The Domini Index uses five exclusionary screens, eliminating any firm that engages in the manufacture or selling of alcohol, gambling, tobacco, military items, or nuclear power. The Index also assesses each company through seven qualitative screens: community, diversity, employee relations, environment, product(s), non-U.S. operations, and other. This last category includes such areas as top management pay and tax disputes. The criteria for this assessment are presented, in part, in **Figure 1**. The research data for each company are summarized in a rating for each of the criteria, as well as in a written report that justifies the ratings. The rating system scores the company on both strengths and concerns, so a company may pick up positive as well as negative scores on the same criterion.

The KLD profiles are publicly available for both investment firms and individual investors. One of the advantages of the KLD database is that it can be customized to meet the interests of an investment or

Figure 1
Domini Social Index Screening Criteria

Qualitative Screens

1. **Community**—housing support, charitable giving, election support, etc.

2. **Diversity**—women and minority preparation, family benefits, gay/lesbian policies, etc.

3. **Employee Relations**—union relations, employee involvement, retirement benefits, etc.

4. **Environment**—beneficial products and services, pollution prevention, alternative fuels, etc.

5. **Product**—quality, benefits to the disadvantaged, safety, etc.

6. **Non-U.S. Operations**—charitable giving outside the U.S., labor relations, and operations in Burma.

7. **Other**—compensation of top management, ownership, tax disputes.

Exclusionary Screens

1. **Alcohol**—derives revenue from the manufacture of alcohol.

2. **Tobacco**—derives revenue from the manufacture of tobacco products.

3. **Gambling**—derives revenue from gambling enterprises.

4. **Military**—more than 2% of gross revenues from sale of weapons.

5. **Nuclear Power**—ownership or operation of nuclear power plants, or related to nuclear fuel.

Source: KLD Web site

public interest group. Thus one could select a specific set of criteria (given that they are within the bounds of KLD research) on which a company is to be assessed, and the KLD database will provide customized ratings, or rank-order companies, based on those criteria.

Public Interest Groups: Council on Economic Priorities

Another major category of social audits comprises those conducted by public watchdog groups such as the

Coalition for Environmentally Responsible Businesses (CERES), the Council on Economic Priorities (CEP), Consumer Alert, and numerous state-sponsored public interest research groups (PIRGs). This form of social assessment may be particularly relevant as the economy becomes more global and the activities of American companies expand well beyond the boundaries of U.S. regulatory control. As with SRI, some watchdog groups are very specific in the issues they monitor, whereas others observe several areas. Accuracy in Media monitors fairness, balance and accuracy in news reporting, while Corporate Watch monitors and researches such issues as corporate agriculture, social change, the environment, globalization, and human rights.

The CEP is probably the best-known organization in the corporate social responsibility arena. It has been rating firms on social and environmental issues since 1975. The information is made available to millions of consumers, investors, policymakers, and businesses so that more informed choices can be made about products and investments. As noted on its Web site, CEP strives to "empower consumers, investors, managers, employees, and activists to cast their economic vote as conscientiously as their political vote."

A primary tool for CEP's data collection is its own 15-page questionnaire, which has a section on each of ten evaluation categories and is completed by designated company representatives. Secondary information is also gathered from the Dow Jones News Retrieval, *Business Week*, the *Economist*, the *Wall Street Journal*, product data from *Consumer Reports*, and company reports. CEP's most popular rating method is its Corporate Report Card (see **Figure 2**), which is used to rate publicly traded companies across 11 categories: environment, women's advancement, minority advancement, charitable giving, community outreach, family benefits, social disclosure, workplace issues, military contracts, animal testing, and gay/lesbian issues. CEP gathers information about companies on these topics, analyzes the data, and awards a letter grade (A, B, C, D, or F) based on each firm's performance in that area (except weapons, animal testing, and gay/lesbian issues, which are rated on a yes/no basis).

CEP distributes its research through numerous publications, products, and services: *Shopping for a Better World* is a shopping guide for socially conscious consumers; *Corporate Citizenship*, issued by *Financial Times*, discusses both the ethical and practical dimensions of corporate responsibility; *Research Report*, published ten times a year, notifies members of the latest results from CEP research programs; SCREEN Research Service provides social and environmental performance data on more than 600 publicly owned U.S. corporations; and CEP's Corporate Services Program is a comprehensive program designed to assist any company in becoming more socially responsible. A database containing

---

Figure 2
Council on Economic Priorities: Areas Covered by Audit

1. **Environment**—environmental management program, impact on environment, voluntary reporting, etc.

2. **Women**—treatment and compensation of women, women's advancement, use of female-owned suppliers.

3. **Minorities**—treatment and compensation of minorities, integration into work force, support of minorities' purchasing programs.

4. **Charitable Giving**—extent of corporate giving, long-term vs. short-term investments, program focus.

5. **Community Outreach**—volunteer efforts, programs sponsored and organized, internal mechanisms to promote community improvement.

6. **Family Benefits/Worklife**—family medical coverage, family leave, flexible work arrangements, etc.

7. **Workplace Issues**—financial compensation, training and education, safety conditions, etc.

8. **Social Disclosure**—willingness to provide information to public on practices.

Ungraded Areas

Animal Welfare—use of animals for medical or nonmedical purposes.

Weapons Contracts—production and/or sale of civilian or noncivilian goods and services to Department of Defense, as well as handguns.

Gay/Lesbian Issues—existence and evaluation of programs and policies for homosexual employees.

---

company report cards can be accessed at www.cepnyc.org.

Company-sponsored Self-Audits

External agencies like KID and CEP conduct standardized audits without the permission of the target companies, although the companies may cooperate by providing information. But a company can also voluntarily sponsor an audit itself. Two quite different examples are described here: (1) The Body Shop and its attempt to develop a comprehensive stakeholder social audit process; and (2) the SA8000, a social audit tool focusing on labor practices.

The Body Shop. The 1995 Values Audit of The Body Shop is an excellent example of a "stakeholder audit." Whereas the three other audits described here focus on specific issues of concern to the sponsoring organization, a stakeholder audit begins by identifying a company's major stakeholders (customers, employees, suppliers, and so on) and assessing how well the company has performed in relation to its goals and values relative to that group and/or the expectations of each group of stakeholders.

Many firms assess select groups of stakeholders on a regular basis, such as through customer or employee surveys. However, these differ from stakeholder audits in that, with the latter, (1) the various stakeholder assessments are integrated in a single document, (2) the audit is conducted by an independent, outside auditor rather than by the company itself, (3) company performance is evaluated according to its goals and stakeholder expectations and perhaps compared to the performance of other companies, and (4) at least in the case of The Body Shop, the audit report becomes a public document.

According to Sillanpää (1998), the 1995 audit of The Body Shop, designed and conducted by Professor Kirk Hanson of Stanford University, assessed 39 areas of audits grouped into the 11 categories shown in **Figure 3**. Note that the audit covers the major categories one would expect in a stakeholder-based audit—shareholders, customers, employees, franchisees, suppliers, environment, and community. The Body Shop has made commitments in the areas of human rights, animal welfare, and purchasing goods from indigenous peoples and the economically deprived. Thus the auditor thought it important to assess its progress in these areas in the categories related to social change and communities in need. Although the company leadership had been committed to honest and open communication in promotional claims and public statements, this honesty and openness had been questioned, and the company had a tendency to react defensively to criticism. The audit category of public relations was an attempt to assess and address these issues.

The method used in the audit included a review of internal company documents, the company's audit data, public records, and some 300 interviews with employees, managers, suppliers, franchisees, critics, journalists, and outside experts. There were several visits to the corporate and manufacturing facilities in the U.K. and the U.S., and unannounced visits to stores in both countries, as well as to competitors' outlets. The auditors also attended U.K., U.S., and international franchisee conferences.

The audit report consists of a brief summary of The Body Shop's performance in each of the 39 areas, highlighting positive and negative aspects alike. In addition, the company was assigned a one- to five-star

Figure 3
Audit Categories: 1995 Values Report—
The Body Shop

1. **Company Values and Mission**—company purpose, advocacy of responsible business.

2. **Shareholder Relations**—financial performance, timely and accurate information, etc.

3. **Customer Relations**—social usefulness of product, product quality, promotional claims, etc.

4. **Employee Relations**—wages and benefits, HR policies, opportunities for women.

5. **Franchisee Relations**—terms of agreement, handling franchise complaints, disclosure, etc.

6. **Supplier Relations**—terms and conditions, prompt payment, achieving goals through suppliers.

7. **Trading with Communities in Need**—program concepts, goals, results.

8. **Environment**—pollution abatement, energy conservation, etc.

9. **Community Relations**—relations with local community, corporate philanthropy, etc.

10. **Public Relations**—accuracy of communication, openness, reaction to criticism.

11. **Contributions to Social Change**—animal welfare, environmental and human rights, etc.

rating for each of the areas, based on how its performance measured up to comparable companies and comparing it against its own values and goals, its performance claims, and the performance of best-practice companies. A three-star rating was considered average, with ratings of more than three indicating better than average performance and less than three indicating worse than average. No overall rating was given for the company. The auditor's (unedited) report was made public on The Body Shop Web site.

There is always a question as to what happens with social audit data. In the case of The Body Shop, the company developed a follow-up process that targeted the areas of concern and developed action plans to correct them. The 1997 Values Report, which was also available on the Web site, is an assessment of the progress made in correcting those problems.

SA8000. The only "true" social audit, as defined by financial audit standards, is Social Accountability 8000. Using standard categories and procedures, it is conducted by an independent auditor who certifies that a firm is in compliance with the standards the audit sets forth. The models for SA8000 are the quality audit ISO 9000 and the environmental audit ISO 14000. However, a major difference between SA8000 and the ISO audits is that this new standard includes performance requirements as well as system requirements. For example, a company cannot engage in or support the use of child labor, and must establish, maintain, and communicate policies and procedures to eliminate its use.

SA8000 arose out of concerns about the labor practices and conditions of many major U.S. corporations' overseas suppliers—suppliers that are beyond the regulatory boundaries of the United States. Human rights organizations and the popular press had publicized numerous cases of forced labor, unsafe working conditions, insufficient wages, use of physical punishment, and the like. In an attempt to redress these worldwide problems, a voluntary labor standard was proposed that would be used by both U.S. corporations and their suppliers. The development of the standard was spearheaded by the Council on Economic Priorities Accreditation Agency (CEPAA), an affiliate of CEP, with the involvement of such organizations as Amnesty International, The National Child Labor Committee, Avon Products, Reebok, International Textile Workers, and others.

Using ISO 9000 and ISO 14000 as assessment models, the SA8000 system takes into account the regulations of the International Labor Organization (ILO), the Universal Declaration of Human Rights, and the United Nations Convention on the Rights of the Child. To be SA8000-certified, a company must meet the measurable, verifiable standards in nine areas (see **Figure 4**). Most of these standards are enforced by laws in the U.S., but may not be upheld in countries that do not support basic human rights.

Compliance with SA8000 standards is verified through third-party audits conducted by individuals and firms accredited by CEPAA. Several major auditing firms have passed the accreditation process. CEPAA will regularly monitor the auditors' performance, and evaluate complaints from workers' groups or other parties about any auditor's behavior or judgment.

Originally, SA8000 applied only to the manufacturing industry. However, in late 1998, after reviewing the results of pilot audits conducted in agricultural settings, the CEPAA Advisory Board authorized the use of SA8000 in agriculture. Currently, the system does not apply to firms engaged in extractive industries, such as mining or forestry.

THE FUTURE OF SOCIAL AUDITING

This discussion in no way attempts to present a comprehensive review of the numerous ethical, social, and environmental audits that have been developed in the

---

Figure 4
Social Accountability 8000 Standards

1. **Child Labor**—no child labor, education availability for young workers, safe working conditions, etc.

2. **Forced Labor**—no forced labor, no deposit of identity papers, etc.

3. **Health and Safety**—safe conditions, health and safety training, sanitary conditions, etc.

4. **Freedom of Association and Right to Collective Behavior**—right to collective bargaining and trade unions.

5. **Discrimination**—no discrimination based on race, creed, caste, religion, gender, or union membership in hiring, promotion, etc.

6. **Disciplinary Practices**—no corporal punishment, no mental or physical coercion, no verbal abuse.

7. **Working Hours**—restrictions on working hours, overtime, etc.

8. **Compensation**—wages meet minimum standards in check or cash, no reduction for discipline purposes.

9. **Management Systems**—ensure that standards are met by company, suppliers, etc.

---

sometimes dramatic change—is the rule. Organizations have become more difficult to manage. And our everyday lives have been altered significantly, whether in banking, shopping, or communicating.

"The result of these concerns is a neopopulism in which the public is demanding greater social responsibility and accountability from the business community."

Business Week notes further that although the public has given credit to corporations for the new prosperity, it also has some serious concerns about the role corporations play in people's lives. A major concern is whether HMOs are being controlled by big insurance companies for whom health care is determined by cost rather than patient need. Deregulation in many areas has increased costs and decreased service, which is the opposite of what the public was promised. Privacy has emerged as a major issue now that cookies track our every move on the Web, the dot-coms sell our personal data, and employers demand blood tests. Add to the list the huge corporate campaign contributions, the slowness to act on product safety problems, the support of sweatshops—the list could go on for several pages. The result of these concerns is a neopopulism in which the public is demanding greater social responsibility and accountability from the business community.

What differs from the 1960s, when the public also demanded greater social accountability, is that the business community is now on board. Consider that most major corporations now have a section in their annual reports devoted to their social and civic activities. Still others issue separate reports detailing their community and environmental commitments. Time Warner recently issued a corporate social responsibility report entitled "Community Connections," which covered its activism in several key areas, such as its extensive support of education and literacy, its support of the arts, its promotion of diversity, volunteer activities by its employees, and its support of local institutions.

So a major task of the business leader today is deciding how to satisfy the new social contract. What activities should be given top priority? How will these be monitored and measured? And how will the information be presented to the different publics served by the company? Certainly a related issue is: How should the company respond to the data from external audits by SRI funds and public interest groups, or from government concerns? (Consider the response of Bridgestone/Firestone to the recent furor over its tires.)

last decade. Rather, it attempts to highlight four of the better-known examples of social audits as applied to the for-profit sector, and to use them as examples of both the current and future state of social auditing. The central question, of course, is whether social audits are here to stay this time around or whether they will suffer the same fate as before, fading into the background after a short burst of interest. Certainly the climate today is favorable. As a recent *Business Week* editorial argues, the new economy has produced a new social contract, whereby the general public expects business to adhere to a much higher social standard ("New Economy… " 2000).

The "new economy" is not easily defined, though several key elements seem to be dominant. Globalization and free markets are certainly major factors. Innovation, production, and investment are not restricted by national boundaries. In fact, boundaries have all but collapsed in many areas of business. Technology is a major driver, as information can be exchanged anywhere in the world, almost instantaneously, at very little cost. This is a knowledge- and idea-based economy that has created a vast array of new jobs and new wealth. It is an economy in which risk and uncertainty are a given. Change—

Given the social audit categories highlighted here, one would predict a reasonably bright future for Socially Responsible Investing. Most major families of funds now have an SRI fund, and the fact that these are performing as well as, and sometimes better than, the average mutual fund indicates that being a "responsible investor" does not put one at a disadvantage. Corporate boards and leaders need to pay particular attention to this area because, as of 1999, some $2.16 trillion had been invested in socially screened portfolios and mutual funds. Of this amount, approximately $1 trillion is in the hands of institutions or funds that have used their ownership to sponsor proxy resolutions on social issues.

Audits by public interest groups should also remain strong. The reason is quite simple—in many cases, these groups provide the only public and systematic monitoring of businesses (and governments) on social issues. However, most public interest groups are focused on single issues, or at least a narrow band of issues, such as protection of natural resources, animal rights, international labor practices, or fairness in the media. Thus, it is expected that the narrow "audits" will remain popular, while the more comprehensive auditing processes, as conducted by the CEP, will probably show little growth because of the extensive resources needed.

In the category of company-sponsored social audits there is a great deal of fragmented monitoring of the social and environmental areas, primarily for regulatory purposes or for presentation in annual reports. However, these efforts rarely reach the level of the formal social auditing process described in the examples cited here. There may be some (very positive) motivation for companies to begin limited auditing in the future, based on recent evidence linking social responsibility with financial performance. If these results hold, companies may begin conducting audits of select stakeholder areas in the near future.

There is, however, one audit area that should show dramatic growth—and considerable controversy—in the next decade: social audits, both self-sponsored and generated by public interest groups, that focus on the foreign operations of U.S. and European companies, particularly in underdeveloped countries, well beyond the jurisdiction of U.S. regulatory control. Pressure is growing from the United Nations, the U.S. Congress, labor unions, and social activists for some form of monitoring and auditing of both U.S. and non-U.S. firms abroad. Concerns cover a wide range of topics, including the use of child labor, unsafe working conditions, ecological destruction, and the support of oppressive governments.

Many companies seem receptive to the idea of some sort of supervision in these areas, and have taken steps to monitor operations and correct abuses. For example, under the auspices of the UN, 50 of the world's largest corporations recently signed a "global compact" that commits them to supporting free trade unions, abolishing child labor, and upholding other social standards, as well as reporting on their progress annually.

> "Given the absence of any international regulatory authority, who decides the criteria and standards for the social audit?"

Most U.S. corporations, then, will likely be conducting some type of annual monitoring or auditing of their operations, both at home and abroad, in at least the next decade. However, this activity has brought to the surface what is probably the central issue in social auditing: Given the absence of any international regulatory authority, who decides the criteria and standards for the social audit? Note that this issue could also be raised with SRI or any other group conducting social audits. As the examples cited here indicate, the criteria used in social auditing vary widely and reflect the interests of the audit sponsors. Thus, the screens of the Domini Social Equity Fund define what the principals in that organization think is socially responsible behavior, as do the screens employed by CEP in developing its company ratings for social responsibility. An important question is whether these groups should be the final arbitrators of what constitutes socially responsible behavior by American business. And if not these groups, then who?

Consider the apparel industry, which has been under attack because of issues related to overseas facilities and suppliers. In an apparent move to correct these issues (or at least blunt the criticism), the industry has developed the Worldwide Responsible Apparel Production (WRAP) certification program. Member companies will voluntarily submit to an audit of their facilities, and ask their suppliers to do likewise. The audit is subjected to attestation by an independent auditing agency, and those facilities that pass the audit will be certified as having met international social standards.

However, the WRAP audit categories and process are very similar to SA8000. (Possibly the standards as well, though the processes are too new to allow comparison.) So why the need for the two audits? The issue here appears to be one of control over audit categories and standards. The apparel industry seems to be saying that it is capable of monitoring itself, with the help of independent auditors. And certainly some members of the industry are probably quite apprehensive about having a public interest group—which they may see as having a political agenda—decide whether or not their facilities and suppliers meet social standards.

As a counter argument, public interest groups would probably maintain that the apparel industry has done a poor job of monitoring itself in the past. Moreover, they would argue, only through an auditing process developed and supervised by a truly independent organization can the public really have confidence that basic social and environmental standards are being met.

Adding to the controversy is the issue of "transparency." Should the audit data for a facility or company be made public, as was The Body Shop's? Or is it sufficient to indicate simply that the facility has passed an audit and is certified? Again, there seems to be a difference of opinion, with most public interest groups arguing for transparency and most corporations seeming to be against it.

Thus, business leaders with overseas operations and suppliers face a rather serious dilemma. Many companies will have to adopt a social auditing process, but which one? Should they use the industry model, or SA8000, or one of the processes being developed in Europe? Or should they develop their own process, as did Reebok in Malaysia? Note that this issue is now one of significance to retailers, such as Wal-Mart and Nordstrom, that face boycotts as well as civil suits because of where, and by whom, the goods they sell are manufactured. It is doubtful that this issue will be resolved in the near future, and we can probably expect continuing debate over auditing processes—and social standards—for the next several years.

One could raise the final question of whether all this corporate social audit activity is the function of a robust U.S. economy. And in a weakening economy, will much of the interest in corporate social responsibility also fade? There is probably some truth to the belief that in slower economic times attention turns to other issues, such as job creation. However, although interest in social responsibility may wane a bit as the economy slows, it is expected to remain strong in the long term. One reason is that the new economy has brought with it new social standards. Moreover, a new set of social issues has emerged, such as genetically modified food products and Internet privacy

issues, that are arousing public notice. And in the global labor arena, a slower U.S. economy should increase the pressure for auditing operations outside the country because of concern for the loss of American jobs to (substandard) foreign sources.

The question asked at the beginning of this article was whether the social audit was here to stay this time around. And the answer, it appears, is "yes."

References

Edward Alden, "Trade Liberalization Voluntary Plan Will Hold Companies to Account," *Financial Times*, July 28, 2000, p. 22.

Georgia Lee, "AAMA to Launch Anti-Sweatshop Plan," *Women's Wear Daily*, October 1, 1999, p. 2.

The Body Shop Values Report (Littlehampton, Eng.: The Body Shop International, 1995).

Victoria Colliver, "More Retailers Added to Sweatshop Allegation," *San Francisco Examiner*, March 4, 2000, p. C-2.

Council on Economic Priorities Accreditation Agency, *Social Accountability 8000, An International Standard*, New York, October 1997.

Domini Social Investments, LLC, www.domini.com (1997–1999).

Homer H. Johnson, "Does It Pay to Be Good? Corporate Social Responsibility and Financial Performance," working paper, Loyola University, Chicago, 2000.

Kinder, Lydenberg, Domini & Co., www.kld.com (1999).

National Green Pages™, www.coopamerica.org (1999).

"New Economy, New Social Contract," *Business Week*, September 11, 2000, p. 182.

Maria Sillanpää, "The Body Shop Values Report—Towards Integrated Stakeholder Auditing," *Journal of Business Ethics*, October 1998, pp. 1,443–1,456.

Social Investment Forum & Co-op America, www.socialinvest.org/default.html (1999).

Sandra A. Waddock and Samuel B. Graves, "The Corporate Social Performance—Financial Performance Link," *Strategic Management Journal*, April 1997, pp. 303–319.

Homer H. Johnson is a professor of organizational development and psychology and director of the Center for Organization Development at Loyola University, Chicago, Illinois. The author wishes to express his thanks to Julie Dunkle Zipperer and Beverly Spangler for their assistance in collecting data on the various audit instruments.

Reprinted with permission from *Business Horizons*, May/June 2001, pp. 29-36. © 2001 by the Trustees at Indiana University, Kelley School of Business.

Scandals shred investors' faith

Because of Enron, Andersen and rising gas prices, the public is more wary than ever of Corporate America

John Waggoner and Thomas A. Fogarty

USA TODAY

A drumbeat of corporate misdeeds has helped crush stock prices and eviscerate pension plans. But the biggest victim may be trust—investors' trust in financial advisers, stock analysts and Corporate America.

During the bull market, corporations and those who ran them seemingly could do no wrong. Now they're feeling the backlash, in the form of congressional hearings, bankruptcy trials and investor outrage.

Unless Corporate America moves quickly to regain public confidence, Wall Street could languish for years.

"The guy in Georgia who stored dead bodies instead of cremating them went to jail," says Maggie Green, a marketing analyst in Oklahoma City. "But these guys steal billions, and have any of them gone to jail yet?"

Trust keeps the financial system together. Once lost, it can take years for Wall Street to regain it. Signs of how badly trust has eroded are everywhere. Investors are starting to give up on the stock market and are plowing money into their homes instead. And Congress is warming up to write new business regulations.

Unless Corporate America moves quickly to regain public confidence, Wall Street could languish for years.

Examples of corporate misdeeds bombard investors nearly every day. On Tuesday and again today, Congress is flaying oil executives on charges of keeping gasoline prices artificially high by manipulating supply. Industry representatives deny

Market distrust

Business scandals have helped slow the flow of money into stock mutual funds since the high in 2000: (dollars in billions)

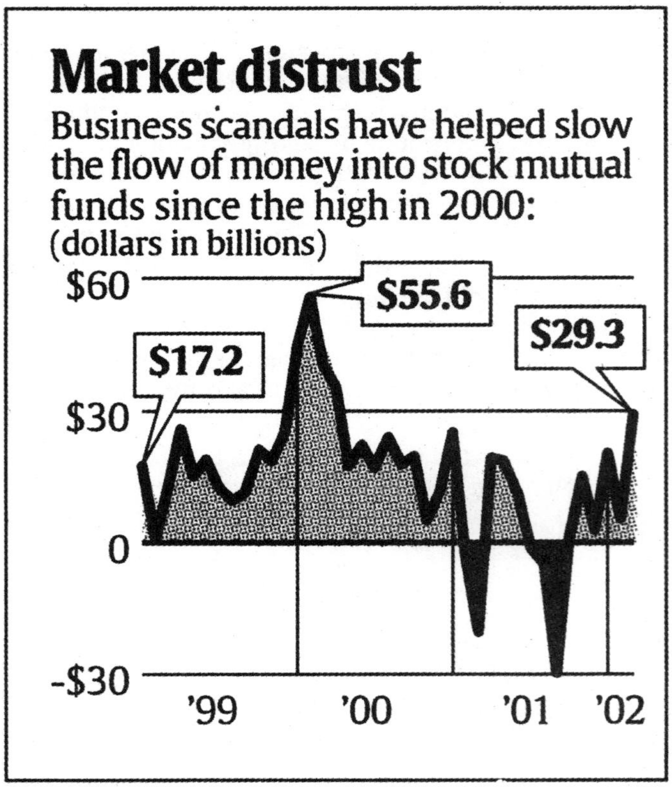

Source: Investment Company Institute
By Julie Snider, USA TODAY

wrongdoing. But that's just the most recent development. In the past few months:

• Enron, the Houston-based energy trading company, collapsed into bankruptcy protection amid allegations of fraudulent accounting.

• The New York attorney general has accused Merrill Lynch, the nation's largest brokerage firm, of publicly hyping stocks to secure investment banking business. Merrill Lynch's CEO apologized to investors for internal e-mails in which analysts disparaged stocks they publicly touted.

"Investors may not have done their homework for the companies whose stocks they bought, but until Enron they always assumed the financial numbers companies provided were correct."

• Arthur Andersen, a Big Five accounting firm, faces a criminal trial Monday on charges of obstruction of justice in the Enron scandal. The government charges Andersen with shredding key documents.

The list seems endless: Firestone sued for knowingly selling defective tires. Communications giants WorldCom and Qwest—as well as conglomerate Tyco— investigated for their accounting practices.

Investors may not have done their homework for the companies whose stocks they bought, but until Enron they always assumed the financial numbers companies provided were correct, says John Markese, president of the American Association of Individual Investors.

"My trust has become somewhat jaded," says Anthony Breault, an American investor working in Sydney. "It's difficult to put hard-earned money into companies we believe in based on the figures provided."

Stoking the outrage: The public doesn't believe CEOs and other top executives have shared the pain of this bear market. Some people point to Kmart, which gave former CEO Chuck Conaway a severance package of $9.5 million after filing for bankruptcy protection in January. The package included forgiveness of a $5 million loan.

Others can't get Enron executives off their mind. "I just can't believe they're out there walking free," Green says.

Investors haven't staged a mass exodus from the stock market, but the flow of money has slowed dramatically since 2000. Mutual fund investors have put $55 billion into stock funds through March, according to the Investment Company Institute. That's up from 2001 but a far cry from 2000, when they flooded stock funds with $168 billion in new money.

Clearly, fear of the bear market has kept some away. Worries about corporate integrity haven't helped. "People aren't jumping back in," Markese says. Given a choice between putting money into stocks or real estate, many choose the red-hot real estate market.

Restoring trust

Financial scandals have spawned proposals to restore public trust. Under scrutiny:

• **Insider partnerships.** The Financial Accounting Standards Board is considering tighter limits on Enron-style partnerships, which hid debt from the company's books and boosted the appearance of profitability. The goal: assuring the so-called special purpose entities are used as intended—mainly to reduce borrowing costs.

• **Overly ambitious earnings projections.** The Securities and Exchange Commission may require fuller disclosure in corporate financial reports. Companies would have to tell investors how they arrived at some profit estimates.

• **Accounting firms doubling as auditors and strategists.** SEC Chairman Harvey Pitt has called for a governing board for the accounting profession that would be controlled by non-accountants. President Bush has a separate proposal for a new board. Some in Congress favor forced separation of auditing and consulting.

• **Retirement.** In Congress, several bills would protect workers from the risks of holding too much company stock in 401(k) plans. In general, workers could diversify out of company stock received as a matching contribution after three years. The bills also would require 30-day notice to workers who might be barred from moving money in their retirement accounts during an administrative change in the plan.

• **Executive compensation.** Bush favors requiring CEOs to return stock option awards and bonuses if their firms' earnings statements must be revised downward because of fraud or mismanagement.

• **Self-serving stock touts.** The National Association of Securities Dealers may limit Wall Street analysts' ability to trade stocks of companies they cover. Investment banks would be prohibited from issuing research on a company for 40 days after an initial public offering of stock.

Polls show declining trust

Polls show trust in business, though never very high, is plummeting. Just 16% of Americans say they have a great deal of confidence in major companies, down from a pre-Enron high of 28%, a Harris poll says. Executives have taken a beating, too. Just 16% of Americans rate their ethics as high, down from 25% before Enron, says a USA TODAY/CNN/Gallup Poll.

The recent scandals have refocused the public's skepticism about American business, says John Richardson, a Pepperdine University business professor. "Before Enron, most of the heat was on marketing as the most corrupt element of American business, but this has put accounting and finance on the front burner," Richardson says.

As a result, Richardson says, classroom discussions on ethics this year have shifted to Enron, Andersen and Merrill Lynch from, say, Nike, which once misled golfers by promoting a type of mass-produced balls as those used by Tiger Woods. He uses a different, custom-made ball. The new lessons seem more profound. Students "see these as something that's not going to go away," Richardson says.

Ritu Gupta, one of Richardson's part-time MBA students, says the business scandals validate her decision a year ago to go to work at her family's small manufacturing business in Santa Fe Springs, Calif. Classmates have become deeply skeptical of big corporations, she says. That may not be all bad if it makes them self-reliant rather than "trusting 110% the big bosses," she says.

Bear market reveals excesses

The lessons Enron and Andersen have left for business students have yet to sort themselves out, says finance professor Keith Brown at the University of Texas. But if problems fester to the point that the average little guy starts to believe that stock investing is a sucker's game, he says, "We'll have a serious problem."

New regulations one way to repair public trust in Corporate America

Peter Kendall, co-editor of newsletter *The Elliott Wave Financial Forecast*, says a bear market often reveals the worst excesses of a bull market. "Everything that was revered on the upside is a target in a bear market." Those excesses have to be corrected before the public regains its confidence.

Typical features of the so-called recrimination phase:

• **Reviled CEOs.** "Those who had Teflon in the bull market have Velcro in the bear market," Kendall says. In 1929, the chief target was Richard Whitney, president of the New York Stock Exchange. Kenneth Lay, former CEO of Enron, may be the current target.

• **Tarnished icons.** You don't have to be a CEO to incur a sudden loss of status in a bear market. James Cramer, co-founder of TheStreet.com, became famous enough to be part of ad campaigns for Rockport shoes. Now he's the subject of an unflattering book by a former associate.

• **Increased interest in regulation.** The Securities Act of 1934, the groundwork for most of today's securities law, was a result of abuses during the roaring '20s—as was the Investment Company Act of 1940, the foundation of mutual fund regulation.

The Securities and Exchange Commission is considering rules for corporate disclosure. The National Association of Se-

curities Dealers (NASD) has proposed rules to limit conflicts of interest with stock analysts. Several pension reform bills are in front of Congress, which is holding hearings nearly every day on business abuses. This week was the oil industry's turn in the hot seat.

"Gasoline companies have not been forthcoming as government has sought to understand how competitive the industry truly is," said Sen. Joe Lieberman, D-Conn., at a hearing Tuesday on gas pricing. "That further erodes the confidence of the American people—who have a right, through their government, to ensure that companies are behaving fairly."

Reform and regulation are one step to regaining the public's confidence. But that often happens well after much of the damage is done to investors' trust.

"The government takes steps after the horses have left the barn," Kendall says.

Painful as it is to watch, the public floggings of corporate wrongdoers by congressional committees and the press are beneficial.

The SEC took wide-ranging steps to reform the financial system after the bear market of 1973–74. But investors continued to yank money from mutual funds for nearly a decade. It took a generation to get over the excesses of the 1920s, despite the government's overhaul of the financial system.

Louis Thompson, head of the National Investor Relations Institute, says the problems uncovered at Enron and among financial analysts are every bit as serious as those of the past.

"The collapse of (railroad company) Penn Central in the 1970s, the fall of (junk-bond dealer) Drexel Burnham Lambert in the 1980s—none of these touched the magnitude of Enron," Thompson says. "Now we see it's beyond Enron. It's an ethical problem, and it has touched nearly every nerve—shareholders, employees and employers."

He says he'd like to see analysts banned from owning stocks they cover. And he says he'd like to see companies that underwrite stocks be banned from issuing research reports on those companies for six months.

Is the system broken beyond repair? Bill Nygren, manager of the Oakmark mutual fund, doesn't think so. "The U.S. has the best financial disclosure in the world," Nygren says.

But, he adds, the bull market made investors sloppy. A diligent investor should look at several years' worth of annual reports, not just earnings per share. "The rules were never written so that one line gave a clear picture of a business."

It would be wrong to think that only corporations made mistakes that need to be corrected. Investors should bear part of the blame, too, says Jeffrey Seglin, a professor who teaches ethics at Emerson College in Boston and author of *The Good, the Bad, and Your Business*. "When things get tough, we look for people to blame," Seglin says. "Fraud and Ponzi schemes are wrong, but if Vanguard isn't returning 20% a year, that's not wrong."

Painful as it is to watch, the public floggings of corporate wrongdoers by congressional committees and the press are beneficial.

"The market is largely self-correcting," says former SEC commissioner Arthur Levitt. "Humiliation and embarrassment have already begun to change behavior."

One example: Corporate earnings reports are getting longer as companies disclose more. IBM's recent financial discussion of its earnings grew by 10 pages from the previous year.

And, ultimately, the corporate scandals will lead to a better system. "This is a healthy cleansing of weak and unscrupulous companies," says Phil Reeder, an investor in Rancho Bernardo, Calif. "All of this is positive for the long-term investor."

Of course, in the long term, as late economist John Maynard Keynes noted, we're all dead.

Thompson says action has to start now: "If we all show an interest in reform, we can help restore investor confidence. But we have a lot of work to do."

From *USA Today Newspaper*, May 2, 2002, pp. 1A, 2A. © 2002 by USA Today Newspaper. Reprinted by permission.

HOW TO FIX CORPORATE GOVERNANCE

Excessive pay, corrupt analysts, auditing games:
It all adds up to capitalism's biggest crisis since the trustbuster era.
What will it take to restore the public's faith in the system?

A disenchanted investor vows to vote in favor of every shareholder resolution he can find. An angry employee says she feels betrayed by bosses who have grown rich on stock options while putting the squeeze on health benefits and salaries. A dealmaker, trying to close a sale, hears yet another buyer grouse: "Who's to say this guy isn't lying about the numbers like everyone else?"

Faith in Corporate America hasn't been so strained since the early 1900s, when the public's furor over the monopoly powers of big business led to years of trustbusting by Theodore Roosevelt. The latest wave of skepticism may have started with Enron Corp.'s ugly demise, but with each revelation of corporate excess or wrongdoing, the goodwill built up by business during the boom of the past decade has eroded a little more, giving way to widespread suspicion and mistrust. An unrelenting barrage of headlines that tell of Securities & Exchange Commission investigations, indictments, guilty pleas, government settlements, financial restatements, and fines has only lent greater credence to the belief that the system is inherently unfair.

Some corporate chieftains claim that the backlash is overblown, a form of "corporate McCarthyism," in the words of Joseph P. Nacchio, head of Qwest Communications, which is one of dozens of companies under investigation by the SEC for questionable accounting. But increasingly, the public perception is that too many corporate executives have committed egregious breaches of trust by cooking the books, shading the truth, and enriching themselves with huge stock-option profits while shareholders suffered breathtaking losses. Meanwhile, despite a decade or more of boardroom reforms, many directors seem to have become either passive or conflicted players in this morality play, unwilling to question or follow up on even the most routine issues. If the governance of the modern corporation isn't completely broken, it is going through a severe crisis of confidence.

The sight of Enron employees tearfully testifying before Congress was a watershed moment in American capitalism. They painted a picture of betrayal by company leaders that left them holding huge losses in their pension plans. Enron added to the sense that no matter how serious their failure or how imperiled the corporation, those in charge always seem to walk away vastly enriched, while employees and shareholders are left to suffer the consequences of the top managers' ineptitude or malfeasance.

In many ways, Enron and its dealings with Arthur Andersen are an anomaly, a perfect storm where greed, lax oversight, and outright fraud combined to unravel two of the nation's largest companies. But a certain moral laxity has come to pervade even the bluest of the blue chips. When IBM used $290 million from the sale of a business three days before the end of its fourth quarter last year to help it beat Wall Street's profit forecast, it did what was perfectly legal—and yet entirely misleading. That one-time undisclosed gain, used to lower operating costs, had nothing to do with the company's underlying operating performance. Such distortions have become commonplace, as companies strive to hit a target even at the cost of clarity and fairness.

ERODING CONFIDENCE

		JAN. 29, 2002 Tyco International discloses that it paid a director $10 million in cash and gave a further $10 million to his favorite charity in exchange for his help on an acquisition.
JAN. 10, 2000 AOL buys Time Warner in a deal worth $183 billion—which later results in a $54 billion write-off, the largest ever.	**AUGUST, 2001** Harvey Pitt, a Washington lawyer who had represented auditors auditors and corporations, often in front of the SEC, succeeds Levitt.	**FEB. 7, 2002** Enron Audit Committee Chairman Robert Jaedicke claims that management failed to disclose critical information to the board.
MAR. 10, 2000 The NASDAQ reaches 5048.6, the height of the high-tech bubble. It is now 1713.	**DEC. 2, 2001** Enron files for the largest corporate bankruptcy in U.S. history. In doing so, it becomes a national symbol of business corruption and greed.	**MAR. 14, 2002** A federal grand jury indicts auditor Arthur Andersen on charges of obstruction of justice.
JANUARY, 2001 Oracle CEO Larry Ellison exercises 23 million stock options for a record gain of more than $706 million—weeks before lowering earnings forecasts.	**JAN. 11, 2002** Al Dunlap agrees to pay $15 million to settle a lawsuit from Sunbeam shareholders and bondholders alleging that he cooked the books at the maker of small appliances.	**APR. 1, 2002** Xerox agrees to pay a $10 million SEC fine to settle charges that it engaged in fraudulent accounting practices.
FEBRUARY, 2001 Arthur Levitt Jr. leaves as head of the SEC after business lobbyists kill his plan to prohibit auditing firms from consulting for clients.	**JAN. 22, 2002** Credit Suisse First Boston agrees to pay $100 million in fines to settle charges that brokers allotted shares in initial public offerings to certain investors in exchange for outsize commissions on other trades.	**APR. 8, 2002** The New York State Attorney General charges that Merrill Lynch analysts were privately referring to certain stocks as "crap" and "junk" while publicly recommending them to investors.
MAY, 2001 Arthur Andersen agrees to pay $110 million to settle a shareholders suit alleging fraud in its audit of Sunbeam.	**JAN. 28, 2002** Global Crossing, once a high-flying telecom-service provider, files for Chapter 11. In the preceding three years, the company's insiders had cashed in $1.3 billion in stock.	**APR. 9, 2002** Arthur Andersen partner David Duncan pleads guilty to charges of obstructing justice in the Enron case.

The inevitable result is growing outrage among corporate stakeholders. "I feel thoroughly disillusioned and disgusted," complains Eugene J. Becker, a small investor living near Baltimore. "These people cannot police themselves. Greed is their driver. It's time for stockholders to start showing their disillusionment in tangible ways." This year, for the first time, Becker is casting "no" votes against management at the eight public companies in which he is a shareholder.

Unchecked, that rising bitterness and distrust could prove costly to business and to society. At risk is the very integrity of capitalism. If investors continue to lose faith in corporations, they could choke off access to capital, the fuel that has powered America's record of innovation and economic leadership. The loss of trust threatens our ability to create new jobs and reignite the economy. It also leaves a taint on the majority of executives and corporations who act with integrity. Directors who fail to direct and CEOs who fail at moral leadership are arguably the most serious challenge facing Corporate America today.

More than a half-century ago, Columbia University professors Adolf A. Berle and Gardiner C. Means made clear the divergence between the owners of the corporation and the professional managers hired to run it. They warned that widely dispersed ownership "released management from the overriding requirement that it serve stockholders." A great irony of the boom era is that after years of lavish stock-option rewards meant to remedy the problem, this divergence is more extreme than ever. The senior executives of public corporations today are often among the largest individual owners of those enterprises, and board members are far more likely to have major equity stakes as well.

In theory, this ownership was supposed to align the interests of management and directors with those of shareholders. The law of unintended consequences, however, took hold. Whether through actual stock ownership or option grants, many executives and directors realized that their personal wealth was so closely tied to the price of the company stock that maintaining the share price became the highest corporate value. Investors rode the boom along with management, leading to the "irrational exuberance" of the late 1990s.

But there was a dark side to runaway stock prices. As the market overheated, it became less and less tolerant of even the slightest whiff of bad news—rumors of which could wipe out hundreds of millions of dollars of market value at a stroke. "Through the 1980s and 1990s, we constructed an architecture that emphasized reporting good news, to the point where CEOs and CFOs could not be frank with the investment community," says Anita M. McGahan, a Boston University business professor. "Many of these companies needed a course correction. But the stakes in admitting problems were very high, both because the market overvalued their stock and because of executive pay."

The tyranny of the daily stock price has led to borderline accounting and in some cases, outright fraud. And why not, when every upward tick of the stock means massive gains for option-rich executives? "Excessive CEO pay is the mad-cow disease of American boardrooms," says J. Richard Finlay, chairman of Canada's Center for Corporate & Public Governance. "It moves from company to company, rendering directors incapable of applying common sense."

A study by Finlay shows that many boards devote far more time and energy to compensation than to assuring the integrity of the company's financial reporting systems. At Oracle Corp., where CEO Laurence J. Ellison's exercise of stock options just before the company issued an earnings warning led to a record $706.1 million payout last year, the full board met on only five occasions and acted by written consent three times. The compensation committee, by contrast, acted 24 times in formal session or by written consent. "Too many boards are composed of current and former CEOs who have a vested interest in maintaining a system that is beneficial to them," says Finlay. "If you look at the disconnect between audit and compensation committees, you begin to understand how misplaced the priorities of many boards are."

Enron's implosion is the most visible manifestation of a system in crisis. Self-interested executives gorged with stock-option wealth, conflicted outside advisers, and a shockingly uninvolved board: Rarely has a total breakdown in corporate governance been so clearly documented—and oddly enough, by other directors, in a report filed by William C. Powers Jr., an Enron board member. He and his colleagues found an almost total collapse in board oversight. The Powers report concluded that the board's controls were inadequate, that its committees carried out reviews "only in a cursory way," and that the board failed to appreciate "the significance of some of the specific information that came before it." That is as complete a definition of "asleep at the wheel" as you'll ever find.

With many directors lulled into complacency by climbing stock prices and their own increasing wealth, all too often the last vestige of internal control was lost. "There was this convergence of self-interest," says Edward E. Lawler III, director of the Center for Effective Organizations at the University of Southern California. "They were all doing well, and nobody wanted to rock the boat. With the escalation in board compen-

sation through stock options, directors were the last people to the feeding trough. Once they got tied in, there was really no restraining force."

It's not just the corporation that is at fault. Many of the corporation's outside professionals fell prey to greed and self-interest as well, from Wall Street analysts and investment bankers to auditors and lawyers and even regulators and lawmakers. These players, who are supposed to provide the crucial checks and balances in a system that favors unfettered capitalism, have in many cases been compromised.

Many analysts urged investors to buy shares in companies solely because their investment banker colleagues could reap big fees for handling underwriting and merger business. Far too many auditors responsible for certifying the accuracy of a company's accounts looked the other way so their firms could rake in millions from audit fees and millions more from higher-margin consulting work. Some outside lawyers invented justifications for less-than-pristine practices to win a bigger cut of the legal fees. Far too often, CEOs found they could buy all the influence they wanted or needed. Enron managed to help write energy policy in the Bush Administration, while the Business Roundtable and Silicon Valley combined to derail efforts to change the accounting treatment for stock options.

Ending the crisis in Corporate America will take more than a single initiative or two. The breakdown has been so systemic and far-reaching that it will require major reforms in a number of critical areas. Here's where to start:

EXECUTIVE PAY

As a matter of basic fairness, Plato posited that no one in a community should earn more than five times the wages of the ordinary worker. Management guru Peter F. Drucker has long warned that the growing pay gap between CEOs and workers could threaten the very credibility of leadership. He argued in the mid-1980s that no leader should earn more than 20 times the company's lowest-paid employee. His reasoning: If the CEO took too large a share of the rewards, it would make a mockery of the contributions of all the other employees in a successful organization.

CEO PAY
During the past two years, as the market cratered, executives went right on raking in the dough—as nearly 200 companies swapped or repriced their stock options

After massive increases in compensation, Drucker's suggested standard looks quaint. CEOs of large corporations last year made 411 times as much as the average factory worker. In the past decade, as rank-and-file wages increased 36%, CEO pay climbed 340%, to $11 million. "It's just way off the charts," says Jennifer Ladd, a shareholder who is fighting for lower executive pay at companies in her portfolio. "A certain amount of wealth is ridiculous after a while."

Oddly enough, CEOs came to command such vast wealth through the abuse of a financial instrument once viewed as a symbol of enlightened governance: the humble stock option. Throughout the 1990s, governance experts applauded the use of options, maintaining that they would give executives a big payday only when shareholders profited. And for a while, as the bull market ran its course, that's the way it worked. But as the market cratered during the past two years, a funny thing happened: Shareholders lost their shirts, but executives went right on raking in the dough.

In recent months, especially, shareholder anger has boiled over, as company proxies disclosed the many ways compensation committees subverted pay for performance. There is, of course, a fundamental difference between investors who have their own money at risk in the market and option holders, who do not. But companies have gone even further to shield top executives from losses in a falling market. Some awarded huge option grants despite poor performance, while others made performance goals easier to reach. Nearly 200 companies swapped or repriced options—all to enrich members of a corporate elite who already were among the world's wealthiest people.

When CEOs can clear $1 billion during their tenures, executive pay is clearly too high. Worse still, the system is not providing an incentive for outstanding performance. It should be a basic tenet of corporate governance never to reprice or swap a stock option that is under water. After all, no company would hand out free shares to stockholders to make them whole in a falling market.

To really fix the problem, Congress needs to require companies to expense options. If every option represented a direct hit to the bottom line, boards would be less inclined to dole them out by the millions. Determining the value of an option for accounting purposes is no slam-dunk. It may be that companies should mark-to-market all or a portion of the actual gains or losses in vested stock options every year. At the very least, Congress should provide preferential tax treatment to encourage boards to replace their plain-vanilla option grants, which reward CEOs if the stock rises, with indexed options, which provide a payday only when the stock appreciation outstrips that of peer companies.

THE BOARD

When Enron collapsed, many pointed an accusing finger at the board, and rightly so. Rarely has there been a management team so intent on deception or a group of directors so sound asleep. But accountability is a two-way street. It's not enough that the board keep a watchful eye on management. Just as important, the shareholders must keep an eye on the board.

That's difficult to do. Shareholders aren't invited to board meetings, individual board members rarely speak out, and when they do it's usually to trumpet the company line. The fact is investors know practically nothing of what goes on behind the closed doors of the boardroom. They must instead rely on directors to represent their interests vigorously. To make sure that happens, changes are badly needed.

In recent weeks, Congress, the White House, federal regulators, and the stock exchanges have all proposed reforms, including some that would require CEOs to vouch for the accuracy of company disclosures and disgorge personal profits from corporate wrongdoing. But the reforms would not guarantee the thing in greatest demand and shortest supply: accountability of all directors. "They're not going far enough," says Peter C. Clapman, chief counsel for TIAA-CREF, the world's largest pension system. "They're underestimating the total needs of a better corporate governance system.

To ensure accountability, shareholder resolutions that pass by a majority of the shares voted for three consecutive years should be binding. Today when a resolution passes, it is frequently ignored. At Bristol-Meyers Squibb Co., for example, a proposal to hold annual elections for directors has won a majority of votes cast for five straight years. But the company has never acted on it, claiming that it failed to get a majority of all the shares outstanding. Making resolutions binding would make companies profoundly answerable to shareholders.

In addition, the stock exchanges, which set many of the governance rules companies must follow, should come up with meaningful regulations and enforce them. At a minimum, the exchanges should limit every board to no more than two insiders, require every board to appoint a lead director who can convene the board without the CEO, assign only independent outsiders to the audit, compensation, and nominating committees, and restrict directors from serving on more than three boards. Companies such as Disney have begun making such changes.

THE BOARD
A ban on stock sales by directors for the duration of their terms would encourage them to blow the whistle on management when necessary

Other reforms could help to make boards more inclined to act ahead of a crisis. A ban on stock sales by directors for the duration of their terms would encourage them to blow the whistle on management when necessary without fear of the short-term price declines that may follow. Mandatory term limits—requiring directors to resign after 10 years or at age 70, whichever comes first—would prevent board members from becoming entrenched.

Even more important, the exchanges should require every board to conduct an extensive annual self-evaluation, involving both a review of board policies and an anonymous appraisal of individual directors. Some boards—including Kmart, Campbell Soup, and Occidental Petroleum—already do a version of this, but they need to go further. The findings need to be made public, and every three years the board member with the lowest ratings should be required to resign. Tough medicine, but a bruised ego is a small price to pay for better governance.

ACCOUNTING

The past few months have pointed up so many weak spots in corporate accounting that it's hard to prioritize what needs fixing the most. Clearly, auditors are not always skeptical enough. Obviously, board audit committees need a kick in the pants. Everyone agrees that rule-making needs to become a lot faster and a lot more effective.

But the deepest problem uncovered by the spate of recent accounting scandals is how easy it has been for all the players involved to pass the buck. The board fingers management, management blames the auditor, the auditor blames the rules. Why isn't it clear who's responsible for what and what the penalties are for doing a bad job?

There are steps that would help restore investor confidence. First, there should be limits put on consulting work done by a company's auditing firm. The audit panel should review all nonaudit engagements to ensure that they don't jeopardize the audit. Auditors should rotate every few years to ensure a "fresh look" by a new firm. There should be more forensic auditing to dig behind the journal entries.

Finally, the proxy statement should clearly delineate which responsibilities fall to the board and which to management. At Enron, the audit committee was charged with reviewing related party transactions. In fact, the committee carried out only cursory reviews. But shareholders had no way of knowing it was even part of their duties. By contrast, Cendant Corp., in the wake of an accounting fraud in a predecessor company, takes extra care to spell out board responsibilities. For example, it makes clear that the board has reviewed and approved the non-audit work provided by auditors. But Cendant is the exception.

An expanded auditor statement in the annual report would also help. Instead of just asserting that the financials meet generally accepted accounting principles, the auditors' statement should illuminate just where in the wide range of acceptable practices a particular company falls. As an up-close reviewer of the numbers, the auditor is in a unique position to judge how dependent the financial statements are on assumptions that could prove faulty. They already share this information with the audit committee. Including it in the auditors' statement would give investors access to the same insight.

ACCOUNTING
"When the SEC and the Justice Dept. get their act together and start sending some CFOs and CEOs to jail, you'll see a real wake-up call"

Finally, a price must be exacted for failure to do the right thing. "We had Sunbeam, Waste Management and Cendant—and I don't think anybody has gone to jail yet, and I don't know why," says Philip B. Livingston, president of Financial Executives International, a professional group of finance managers. "When the SEC and the Justice Dept. get their act together and start sending some CFOs and CEOs to jail, you'll see a real wake-up call."

ANALYSTS

If investors have learned anything from this crisis, it's that Wall Street's analysts are often loath to put a bad spin on a stock. Historically, "sell" ratings have constituted fewer than 1% of analysts' recommendations, according to Thomson Financial/First Call. It's not that analysts have had "an ethical bypass at birth," as was said of Gordon Gekko in the movie *Wall Street*. It's more a case of an inherently conflicted system, that is now the focus of a Justice Department investigation.

Analysts are often rewarded for their ability to attract and maintain investment banking business. They're often under pressure from the companies they cover, big institutional investors, and their own employers to maintain positive ratings. These are conflicts that may never be resolved. But there are some steps that could alleviate the pressures that prevent analysts from telling the truth.

First, education is paramount. "Investors need to realize that the free research they're getting is often just a marketing tool," says Kent Womack, a professor at Dartmouth College's Amos Tuck School of Business. Better disclosure also could help. It should be mandatory that reports prominently disclose a firm's specific investment banking relationship with the company it's covering.

THE ANALYSTS
Most stock-rating terms are part of an elaborate web of euphemisms. "Neutral," for example, means "dump this loser, and run for your life"

And an overhaul of the language of ratings would be helpful as well. In normal English, most ratings sound like variations on "we think this is a decent stock that you should own." In ratings land, terms such as "accumulate" and "hold" are part of an elaborate web of euphemisms in which "neutral" means "dump this loser, and run for your life." And it would make sense if all analysts used the same terms.

To help restore analysts' integrity, their compensation should not be dependent on investment banking fees earned from the companies they cover. At the least, that conflict should be disclosed. Two prominent securities-industry trade groups have recommended that analysts be paid on stock-picking and earnings-estimate prowess, a practice some firms are adopting. Some groups have already barred analysts from owning stocks that they cover.

The SEC may soon approve some of these changes. Still, even the best regulation can't make analysts completely unbiased. A healthy skepticism and a willingness to look beyond retail analysis when choosing stocks may be the best bet of all. Says James Grant, publisher of *Grant's Interest Rate Observer*: "These days, the newsstands are thick with publications that are more inclined to search rather than cheer." Otherwise, to quote Gekko, "you're walking around blind without a cane, pal."

REGULATORS

Business abuses have raised fresh concerns about the power and influence of Corporate America over elected officials and policymakers in Washington. From Enron's cozy ties to energy policy mandarins to the ease with which the accounting industry defeated a proposal to sever their consulting operations from audit in 2000, there's plenty of evidence that regulators often are outgunned or co-opted by special interests. It's not surprising, then, that a mid-February Harris Poll found that 87% of American adults thought big companies wielded too much clout in the nation's capital.

Since politicians depend on money from private interests to fund their campaigns, there's not much that can be done to reduce radically the influence industry holds over regulators. But some small steps could make a difference. For starters: more transparency in regulatory decision-making. At the SEC, for example, some key decisions are deliberately relegated to staff, which can meet in private, unlike the commissioners. More of the agency's business should be out in the open.

SEC Chairman Harvey L. Pitt's "two strikes and you're out" proposal for corporate bigwigs is also on the right track. He wants the power to ban corporate miscreants from serving as officers and directors. But the proposal's effectiveness hinges on the fine print. If it applies only to those convicted of financial crimes, it could be meaningless, since the SEC settles most cases.

Without adequate funding, though, the financial cops won't be able to police their beat. The SEC's workload has soared even as staffing has remained stagnant. Congress should approve a hefty increase in the agency's budget, including Pitt's request for pay parity to retain top lawyers and accountants. Likewise, lawmakers should require accounting firms to pony up annually to fund the Financial Accounting Standards Board instead of forcing the rulemakers to go hat-in-hand to the firms they joust with.

LEADERSHIP

As the 1990s unfolded, Enron came to represent the triumph of New Economy thinking over Old Economy principles. It was fast, adaptive, innovative, and profitable—a corporate culture perfectly suited to what it did: creating and exploiting new markets. Everyone envied and emulated Enron.

THE CULTURE
In the future, a CEO must set the company's moral tone—by being forthright, for starters, and by taking responsibility for any shortcomings

While Enron's culture emphasized risk-taking and entrepreneurial thinking, it also valued personal ambition over teamwork, youth over wisdom, and earnings growth at any cost. What's more, the very ideas Enron embraced were corrupted in their execution. Risk-taking without oversight resulted in failures. Youth without supervision resulted in chaos. And an almost unrelenting emphasis on earnings, without a system of checks and balances, resulted in ethical lapses that ultimately led to the company's downfall. While Enron is the extreme case, many other companies show the same symptoms.

If the challenge for executives in the 1990s was to transform corporate behemoths into nimble competitors, the challenge in coming years will be to create corporate cultures that encourage and reward integrity as much as creativity and entrepreneurship. To do that, executives need to start at the top, becoming not only exemplary managers but also the moral compass for the company. CEOs must set the tone by publicly embracing the organization's values. How? They need to be forthright in taking responsibility for shortcomings, whether an earnings shortfall, product failure, or a flawed strategy and show zero tolerance for those who fail to do the same.

The best insurance against crossing the ethical divide is a roomful of skeptics. CEOs must actively encourage dissent among senior managers by creating decision-making processes, reporting relationships, and incentives that encourage opposing viewpoints. At too many companies, the performance review system encourages a "yes-man culture" that subverts the organization's checks and balances. By advocating dissent, top executives can create a climate where wrongdoing will not go unchallenged.

None of these proposals can guarantee that another Enron, Cendant, or Sunbeam will never surface. No one can legislate or mandate ethical behavior. But leadership must create an environment where honesty and fairness is paramount. If integrity is to be the foundation for competitiveness, it has to begin at the top.

By John A. Byrne, with Louis Lavelle, Nanette Byrnes, and Marcia Vickers in New York and Amy Borrus in Washington

America addresses work force diversity

Judy C. Nixon
Judy F. West

Progressive companies understand that they must create a work force as diverse as the customer base that they serve. Recent U.S. Census Bureau data shows that America is more diverse than ever. Therefore, the appropriate management of today's diverse work force is critical to a company's success.

Workplace diversity is an increasingly important issue and it extends beyond ethnicity and gender. In the past, affirmative action programs were seen as a fairness issue. Today, diversity is a strategic business issue. Diversity management is the process through which each individual's contributions are valued and used in achieving organizational goals.[1] The challenges of working through diversity issues are multifaceted and require that the topics of availability, fairness, and synergy be addressed.[2] In a survey of 131 U.S. companies by The Conference Board, 42 percent of companies reported that they viewed diversity as a competitive opportunity, and 24 percent called it "part of good manage-

ment." Only 4 percent said it would have no serious impact on their business.[3] Although effective integration of diversity can result in a competitive edge, lack of the utilization of diversity potential is likely to breed tension, conflict, and misunderstanding. Today, many organizations are developing cultures that support, honor, and value differences.[4]

A study funded by the Center for Innovative Management Studies examined the work environment of 2,000 employees in research and development departments of 18 U.S. corporations. The results show that managers consistently rate women lower than men in the area of innovation and rate foreign-born contributors lower than U.S.-born on scales of promotability. Although this study covered only one small area, experts agree that one would find similar results throughout American business.[5] Diversity should not only play a role in the hiring process, but also in the promotion and employee development processes. Because people of different genders and cultures have different experiences in an organization, many are unable to see or understand the experience of others. Although

corporate culture is different for each organization, traditionally, the business world has reflected values, behaviors, and assumptions based on the experiences of a rather homogeneous, white, middle-class, male work force.[6] This reflects ethnocentrism—the belief that one's own group or subculture is inherently superior to other cultures.[7] So what is diversity and why is it important?

> *"Diversity should not only play a role in the hiring process, but also in the promotion and employee development processes."*

Diversity

Multicultural diversity is a concept about which many people are unaware. It includes such differences as age, economic status, education, family type, gender, personality type, race, religion, geographic origin, and sexual orientation.[8] In addition, by defining diversity broadly as being everything that makes us different from others, including communication styles and work styles, all employees can "buy into" the value of building a culture that supports diversity.[9]

Managing diversity relates to a company's efforts to minimize tensions resulting from ethnicity, gender, or other differences among workers, while getting supervisors to understand and appreciate those differences. Perhaps, increased understanding can be gained through communicating synergistically. This means each must open their mind and heart to new possibilities, alternatives, and options. Valuing differences is the essence of synergy, and the key to the realization that all humans see the world, not as *it is*, but as *they are*.[10] What is reflected by past research?

Background

The number of people who enter the U.S. work force each year is steadily declining—a reflection of the declining birthrate. However, the proportions of women, Latinos, Asians, African-Americans, and the foreign-born entering the work force are increasing. According to a report by the Hudson Institute, *Work Force 2000: Work and Workers for the 21st Century*, only 15 percent of new entrants to the U.S. work force for the years 1988–2000 were native white males. White women made up 42 percent of new job entrants, with the remaining 43 percent from native non-white and immigrant populations. In fact, the latest U.S. Census figures show fully one-third of the American population is composed of ethnic minorities and these groups will represent a majority by the year 2010. In addition, new immigrants are now largely Asian (34 percent) and Latino (34 percent) who will make up many of the new entrants into the work force.[11]

Today, companies and industries that are progressive in their approaches to human resource development are using the phrase "managing diversity," instead of the term "affirmative action." As a result of demographic changes, the concept of managing diversity becomes a much more proactive force.[12] The new corporate attitude differs strongly from earlier policies of equal opportunity and affirmative action. Industry must recognize diverse groups of employees, in addition to the white men who formed the basis for the traditional work force. Women and minorities who obtain high-tech skill and high levels of language, math, and reasoning skills should be afforded commensurate career opportunities.

> *"As a result of demographic changes, the concept of managing diversity becomes a much more proactive force."*

The Society for Human Resource Management with Fortune magazine in 2001 undertook a diversity study of *Fortune* 1000 companies and Top 100 Companies to Work For. The results revealed diversity initiatives' positive impact on the organizations' bottom line and identified training as a critical component of diversity initiatives. Most firms reported that they provided diversity training to all employee groups from the highest ranked executives to part-time workers. Forty percent of the organizations said they increased diversity training initiatives over the last three years (1998–2000) and 66 percent said they planned to increase diversity training in 2001. The SHRM/Fortune study identified these bottom-line results from diversity initiatives: improved corporate culture (79 percent), improved recruitment (77 percent), improved client relations (52 percent), and higher employee retention (41 percent).[13]

> *"Diversity policies can be developed to nurture and develop all employees as exemplified by many successful companies."*

Diversity policies can be developed to nurture and develop all employees as exemplified by many successful companies. Presented below are several companies and their efforts to promote diversity. These are provided to share more ideas of the importance of diversity and to show that costs are minimal when compared with the benefits.

Successful Companies

Some companies have devised their own programs and others have joined outside efforts. One of the first independent corporate diversity councils specifically designed to help member firms manage diversity issues through cooperative efforts included companies such as US Airways, NationsBank, Duke Power, and IBM.[14]

Avon Products Inc. established a network. It began a Managing Diversity Program as an effort to move away from assimilation as a corporate value and to raise the awareness of negative stereotypes and how they affect the workplace. One of the ways that Avon raised awareness was by sending groups of 25 managers from different racial and ethnic backgrounds to work in the American Institute for Managing Diversity, Atlanta Headquarters.[15] Avon's success is evident in the number of women who have advanced to management positions.[16]

Other entities making significant strides are: Corning, Apple, DuPont, Hewlett-Packard, Honeywell, Procter & Gamble, Hughes, Mobil, Digital, Ernst & Young, the

Internal Revenue Service, and Verizon.

Corning provides minority job rotation for expanded job experience and better promotion opportunities. Apple Computer appointed a multicultural and affirmative action manager. DuPont and Hewlett-Packard provide diversity awareness workshops, seminars, and training; and Honeywell and Procter & Gamble established mentoring programs, advisory counsels, and minority networks.[17] Hughes Aircraft set up a program of planned mentoring to encourage development of women and minorities for positions of greater responsibility. Hughes also sponsors a Youth Motivation Task Force to encourage minority high school students to consider a technical education and created the Hughes Galaxy Institute for Education that designs curricula for kindergarten through fifth-grade by using communication satellites, television, and interactive technology.[18]

Mobil Oil established a program for increasing diversity; Digital Equipment Corporation actively recruits candidates from all countries, and works actively to promote those employees once hired. Digital also has a Core Group consisting of eight to ten employees that come together to confront their prejudices. It has one of the leading diversity training programs in the United States.[19]

Ernst & Young was the first in its industry to assign a full-time partner to oversee minority recruiting and retention. The firm has strong ties with organizations that support development of ethnic minorities as well as colleges and universities with diverse enrollment.[20]

The Criminal Investigation division at the Internal Revenue Service has an aggressive program to build and maintain a diverse work force. This division has a Diversity Council to provide a voice for employees to address diversity-related concerns, and improve the quality of their work life.[21]

Verizon says its large and diverse customer base demands that it also employ individuals who interact effectively with people of different backgrounds. The company works with diversity recruitment channels and forms strategic partnerships with professional and community-based organizations as well as with colleges with diverse student populations.[22]

KFC uses a Designate Program to attract "seasoned" executives from other companies. Special attention is given to attracting and keeping female and minority-group members.[23]

> ## "Managing diversity presents major challenges for human resource professionals in many U.S. corporations."

Kinney Shoes uses an educational program that enables women and minorities to enter the corporation in numbers that reflect the customer base. It implemented a training program to ensure that the work force, through the hiring practices of store managers, mirrors that of the diverse customer base. The program includes educational seminars on valuing diversity that focuses on managing people in the workplace who are from different cultural backgrounds. Through seminars, participants explore how a common situation is viewed by persons from different cultural backgrounds and how communication patterns affect different groups of people in different ways.[24]

Managing diversity presents major challenges for human resource professionals in many U.S. corporations. One challenge is the debate about treatment of gay and lesbian employees. Managers and employees from companies such as DEC, U.S. West, Inc., Levi-Strauss, & Co., Coors, AT&T, and Sun Microsystems formed groups to lobby top management on issues important to employees—one was sexual orientation.[25] Also, some of the above companies participated in "Invisible Diversity," the first national conference that addressed gay and lesbian issues in the workplace. Panels discussed why sexual orientation should be included in corporate diversity programs and if it is included, how a company can implement such programs.

Although the challenges of working through diversity issues are multifaceted, Eastman Kodak, through its Diversity Framework program, addresses six areas: external relations, communications, representation, career development, education, and work force-support systems to address needs of diverse employees. They also include: dependent care, more flexible schedules, and family-leave policies. Work force-support systems encompasses five employee networks: women, working parents, African-Americans, Latinos(as), and other minority groups.[26]

In response to employee complaints that management was insensitive to diversity issues, the Prudential's CEO asked the human resources department to devise a managing diversity program that would reach organizational objectives by maximizing the contribution of every segment of the employee population. The company's diversity effort has gone beyond a mere program and is now institutionalized.[27]

Diversity efforts follow a three-part strategy model at the Chemical Group of Monsanto. The strategy includes:

- raising awareness
- establishing accountability as a measure of performance, and

- changing the processes that support the ways in which people are managed

The model presumes that as diversity increases in the workplace, perceived homogeneity decreases. Therefore, barriers to effective relationships and reduced productivity are decreased. The program features formalized discussions between bosses and employees. During the 2-hour discussion session, trainers help a boss and an employee discuss job responsibilities, organizational norms, expectations, and the mission of the work group. Also, part of Monsanto's diversity strategy targets barriers that prevent people from understanding diversity. These barriers include:

- denial of issues,
- lack of awareness,
- lack of trust, and
- compulsion to "fix" others

One of the goals of the program is to prevent women and minorities from leaving.[28] One of the more celebrated diversity programs in American companies is at Inland Steel Industries, a 100-year-old Chicago-based producer of cold-rolled steel. Inland instituted a five-year career planning program for all employees to shift their expectations from who they are to who they can become. Their philosophy changed from diversity seen strictly as a moral issue (and perhaps a legal issue) to one that diversity is increasingly becoming an important business strategy issue.[29] Their short-term and long-term responses to diversity challenges are yielding advantageous synergy. The healthcare arena is succeeding with diversity programs, also. Many hospitals and health care systems use Lewis Griggs' videotape series on the management of diversity in the workplace. Hospital managers are learning through experience to rec-

ognize and cope with cross-cultural clashes among employees. Kaiser Permanente has taken diversity training system-wide. Kaiser views managing diversity as a separate issue from compliance with the Equal Employment Opportunity Commission.[30]

The Ford Motor Company increased its focus on employee awareness of ethnic and minority issues in the wake of the September 11, 2001 tragedy at the World Trade Center in New York and elsewhere. Planned and impromptu "Islam 101" meetings are held at the Dearborn, MI plant where non-Muslim and Muslim workers gain a better understanding of Islam. Dearborn is home to the country's most concentrated Arab-American community and Ford employs hundreds of these workers.[31] Ford now has ten different employee resource groups representing African-Americans, Latinos, Middle Easterners, gays, lesbians, bisexuals, Chinese, Asian-Indians, parents, and professional women of all backgrounds. Ford's competitors have organized similar groups.[32]

To summarize how most of the programs view diversity, nine elements characterize most organizational culture initiatives:

1. Define diversity areas. Age, ethnicity, socioeconomic status, educational level, regional origins, and other differentiating characteristics are included. Corporate norms of dress, speech, and behavior may be relaxed to account for differences

2. Survey organization. One-on-one interviews and questionnaires can be used to identify values, norms, and other cultural characteristics of the organization

3. View diversity as "business asset"

4. Create separate diversity department. Separate and dis-

tinct offices, staff, and budgetary allocations as well as easy access to top management are provided

5. Separate from HR department. View as a way to enhance productivity, rather than staff function

6. Establish top-level initiative and support that is visible to all in the organization

7. Integrate with reward structure. Develop and maintain a diverse staff. Promote harmonious, productive working relation ships as partial criteria for pay increases, bonuses, and promotion

8. Monitor program results.

9. Integrate with TQM.[33]

Progress made by these companies results from coping with and overcoming several problems.

Problems

The increasing diversity of the labor force is bringing to the workplace new problems for human resource professionals. The responses to a survey of more than 400 Society for Human Resource Management members provide insights into problems and opportunities associated with diversity. The most frequently cited negative consequences of diversity are communication problems and increased training costs.[34] In contrast, benefits are numerous and overshadow many of the problems.

"To meet the challenges of the 21st century, corporations need to develop a diversity of talent that enables them to be innovative, responsive, and flexible."

Benefits

To meet the challenges of the 21st century, corporations need to develop a diversity of talent that enables them to be innovative, responsive, and flexible. This calls for personal development plans, self-development, experimentation, and the tolerance of mistakes.[35] Nearly half of the responses reported in a recent survey revealed that diversity contributes to creating a corporate culture more tolerant of different behaviors. The vast majority of respondents argue that gains from a diverse work force far outweigh the costs. Seven advantages of addressing diversity include:

- developing greater understanding of diverse customer needs to better serve diverse markets
- gaining advantage by being a leader among competitors who are not capitalizing on the benefits of diversity
- attracting and retaining the best talent in the labor pool
- effectively using the talent of diverse associates for increased innovation and productivity by enhancing teamwork and reducing interpersonal conflicts
- increasing employee satisfaction, morale, and commitment of organizational goals
- enhancing communication and coordination
- eliminating or reducing lawsuits and penalties related to discrimination[36]

These findings substantiate claims made ten years ago in pioneer work by Benson, Rosen and Lovelace that greater diversity leads to new organizational opportunities. It contributes to creating a corporate culture more tolerant of many different behavioral styles. This opportunity results when more views come together and greater responsiveness occurs among diverse groups of customers.[37]

Another recent study showed that business senior management teams comprising culturally diverse and women members had significantly higher sales growth rates than firms with all white male management teams.[38]

An added benefit to diversifying the ethnicity of a sales unit, for example, is spreading the market risk. When agents can continually work within and among a variety of target markets, it opens new doors and enables an agency to benefit from individual market strengths and minimize weaknesses.

In addition, as appropriate strategies and programs are developed to cope with issues, companies may avoid expensive lawsuits and administrative agency charges. For example, a Chicago federal court ruled that Quasar Co., an American division of Japan's Matsushita Electric Corporation, discriminated against American employees by reserving certain managerial positions for employees of Japanese national origin. Evidence indicated that they were evaluated and paid on a different basis from that used for American workers. Also, they were exempted from layoffs. The verdict: $2.4 million to the claimants. Lesson learned: diversity is important for international firms as well as American firms.[39]

Finally, concepts like competitiveness, leadership, and maximization of human resources caused companies like Apple, Digital, Hewlett-Packard, Avon, and others cited, to adopt diversity programs. Their programs are not just concepts, business school words, or affirmative action and EEO attempts. They help develop cultures that embrace diversity that go beyond organizational and personal self-interest to a more loyal, productive work force.

Suggestions

When asked about successful managing diversity programs, the largest number of companies focus on efforts to open communication channels and increase sensitivity to cultural and gender differences.

As more foreign companies enter the U.S., foreign employers should:

- maintain a solid human resource department
- establish a commitment between foreign management and the work force
- educate and train international managers working in the U. S. about U.S. labor and employment laws
- audit company policies and practices regularly[40]

Also, cross-cultural training can be a part of the diversity training program for those managers who may be sent on expatriate assignments. Briefly, seven rules are:

1. select and screen managers who have effective interpersonal skills
2. provide formal language training
3. develop understanding of host country management styles, communication, and decision-making styles
4. provide an introduction program upon arrival
5. structure job appropriately
6. require support of superiors; and
7. encourage support for families. A part of success, however, will depend upon outcomes desired after the training.

An appropriate set of desired outcomes include:

- increased awareness of others
- increased understanding of customs
- gained awareness of one's own prejudices
- knowledge of each other

- recognition of when to use particular skills
- awareness of the implications of one's behavior[41]

Implementing a Diversity Program

Around the world, diversity training is still in the infancy stage, and companies are learning important lessons from their early efforts. There are seven key guidelines for implementing a diversity training program:

1. Distinguish between education and training, and incorporate both into the long-term employee training and development program.
2. Position training as part of an overall strategy for managing diversity, not as the end itself as many companies have done. Once the training is over, it is viewed as having accomplished what was intended.
3. Wait until employees and management are ready—that is, when the need presents itself and not just to do "something".
4. Conduct a needs analysis to determine number 3.
5. Include diverse employees in the design of the training program.
6. Test the program on a sample before implementing the entire structured long-term plan.
7. Use both in-house and outside consultants for training in order to add credibility and acceptance.[42]

Also, an external source is to use diversity training games. Perhaps many games can be adapted; however, one specific game called, "The Diversity Game," is offered by Quality Educational Development, Inc. (QED). The purpose of the game is to raise awareness about diversity topics in a non-threatening manner and to stimulate conversations about appropriate issues.[43]

Because the U.S. work force is becoming more culturally diverse, methods should be developed to encourage all staff to value benefits that can be realized through a diverse work force. One way to accomplish this is to implement a continuous training program. Before beginning the program, determination must be made about:

- senior management support
- employee participation
- goals that are realistic
- an instructor who understands different learning styles

"A successful training program promotes understanding cultural diversity among all workers."

A successful training program promotes understanding cultural diversity among all workers. Top executives must demonstrate commitment and leadership. Managers must exercise fairness and value all employees regardless of their varying viewpoints and backgrounds. Employees must recognize that productivity can be increased through harmonious cooperation as synergy increases.

As diversity awareness becomes a primary focus of organizational training, many companies are re-evaluating their policies and programs. Many recognize the potential synergy and untapped contribution that are possible through "pooling" ideas and talents. All employers should evaluate their corporate cultures before attempting to implement a diversity program; this includes every function, from recruiting to serving customers. Of special importance is an ideal diversity expert who would have human resource, equal employment opportunity, and specialized training expertise.

Diversity is an important business strategy issue. Although the challenges of working through diversity issues are multifaceted, short-term and long-term responses to diversity must address three challenges: availability of qualified trainers, fairness to all employees by management, and an expectation that resulting synergy will yield higher benefits for all.

Notes

1. Karsten, Margaret, *Management and Gender*, Quorum Books, 1994, Westport, CT, 73.
2. Jackson, Susan E., and Alvarez, Eden B., "Working Through Diversity as a Strategic Imperative," *Diversity in the Workplace Human Resources Initiatives*, The Guilford Press, NY, 1993, 25.
3. Makower, Joel, "Managing Diversity in the Workplace," *Business and Society Review*, 1995, 48–54.
4. Eron, Ann M. Van, "Ways to Assess Diversity Success," *HR Magazine*, August 1995, 51–52.
5. Makower, loc. cit.
6. Songer, N., "Workforce Diversity," *Business and Employee Review* April–June, 1991, 3–6.
7. Daft, Richard L., *Understanding Management*, 1995, Dryden Press, Fort Worth, 341.
8. Snyder, Alice, "How to Sell to a Culturally Diverse Market," *American Salesman*, 1991, vol. 36, No. 9, 16–22.
9. Eron, Ann, loc. cit.
10. Covey, Stephen R., *The Seven Habits of Highly Effective People*, 1989, Simon and Schuster, NY, NY, 264–277.
11. Neukrug, Edward S., *The Journal of Intergroup Relations*, vol. XXI, No. 2, Summer 1994, 3–11.
12. Turner, Robert M., "Managing Diversity in the Accounting Profession," *Massachusetts CPA Review*, Vol. 66, No. 3, Summer 1992, 17–19.
13. Management Training and Development, "Five Hours of Diversity Training Has A Positive Bottom-Line Impact," Institute of

Management and Administration, July 2001, NY, NY, 1, 10–12.

14. Reynolds, Larry, "Companies Will Work Together on Workforce Diversity," *HR Focus*, December 1992, 17.

15. Boone and Kurtz, *Contemporary Business Communication*, 1994, Prentice Hall, Englewood Cliffs, NY, 658.

16. Caudron, Shari, "Successful Companies Realize that Diversity is a Long Term Process, Not a Program," *Personnel Journal*, Vol. 72, No. 4, April 1993, 54–55.

17. Laporte, Suzanne B., "12 Companies That Do the Right Thing," *Working Woman*, January 1991, 157–159.

18. Barclay, David, "Commitment from the Top Makes it Work," *IEEE Spectrum*, June 1992, Vol. 29, No. 6, 24–27.

19. Boone and Kurtz, 657.

20. "Managing a Multicultural Work force," *Black Enterprise*, July, 2001, 121.

21. "Managing a Multicultural Work force," loc. cit.

22. "Managing a Multicultural Work force," loc. cit.

23. Daft, Richard L., 336.

24. Santora, Joyce E., "Kinney Shoe Steps into Diversity," *Personnel Journal*, Vol. 70, No. 9, 1991, 72–77.

25. Steward, Thomas A., "Gay in Corporate America," *Fortune*, December 16, 1991, 44–56.

26. Allerton, Haidee, "Navigating the Differences," *Training & Development*, April 1993, 31.

27. Caudron, Shari, loc. cit.

28. Galagan, Patricia A., "Trading Places at Monsanto," *Training & Development*, Vol. 47, No. 4, April 1993, 44–49.

29. Makower, loc. cit.

30. Wagner, Mary, *Modern Health-care*, vol. 22, No. 39, September 30, 1991, 24–29.

31. Hakim, Danny, "Ford Motor Workers Get on the Job Training in Religious Tolerance," *The New York Times*, November 19, 2001, (B)6.

32. Garsten, Ed, "Ford Groups Shine Light on Diversity," The Associated Press, *The Sun*, December 12, 2001, (D)8.

33. Laudicina, Eleanor v., "Diversity and Productivity: Lessons from the Corporate Sector," *Public Productivity & Management Review*, Vol. 16, No. 4, 457–463.

34. Rosen, Benson, and Lovelace, "Piecing Together the Diversity Puzzle," *HR Magazine*, Vol. 36, No. 6, June 1991, 78–84.

35. Bennett, Roger, "Developing People for Real: Some Issues and Approaches," *Journal of European Industrial Training*, Vol. 16, No. 5, 1992, 5.

36. Enron, Ann, loc. cit.

37. Weaver, Vanessa, "What These CEOs and Their Companies Know About Diversity", *Business Week*, September 10, 2001.

38. Rosen, Benson and Lovelace, loc. cit.

39. Payson, Martin F. and Rosen, Philip B., "Playing By Fair Rules," *HR Magazine*, Vol. 36, No. 4, April 1991, 42–43.

40. Payson and Rosen, loc. cit., 42, 43.

41. Phillips, Nicola, "Cross Cultural Training," *Journal of European Industrial Training*, Vol. 17, No. 2, 1993, i–iii.

42. Delatte, Ann P. and Baytos, Larry, "Guidelines for Successful Diversity Training," *Training the Human Side of Business*, January 1993, 55–60.

43. Gunsch, Dawn, "Games Augment Diversity Training," *Personnel Journal*, June 1993, 78.

JUDY C. NIXON, Ph.D., is the Hart Professor of Business Administration in the Department of Management, School of Business Administration, at the University of Tennessee at Chattanooga. She has had many articles published about ethics in organizations, intercultural preparation for managers, cultural diversity, customer satisfaction, and corporate child care programs. Her article, "Principles for Infusing Ethics in Your Company" appeared in the fall 1993 issue of Business Forum.

JUDY F. WEST, Ph.D., has recently retired as a professor in the School of Business Administration at The University of Tennessee at Chattanooga. She has published numerous articles, three books, and has traveled throughout 58 countries. Her career includes roles as a business owner-manager, consultant, and CEO.

From *Business Forum*, Vol. 25, Nos. 1 and 2, 2002, pp. 4–9. © 2002 by Business Forum, School of Business, California St. University, Los Angeles, CA 90032.

Virtual Morality:
A New Workplace Quandary

By Michael J. McCarthy
Staff reporter of The Wall Street Journal

WHERE DO YOU DRAW THE LINE.COM? The explosion of the Internet into the workplace has empowered millions of employees, in a matter of keystrokes, to quietly commandeer company property for personal use. And ethical questions are mushrooming well beyond the propriety of workers frittering away a morning shopping online or secretly viewing pornographic Web sites.

Cautionary tales are piling up—from United Parcel Service of America Inc., which caught one employee using a UPS computer to run a personal business, to Lockheed Martin Corp., where a single e-mail heralding a religious holiday that was sent to 60,000 employees disabled company networks for more than six hours. The flood of e-mail traffic cost Lockheed Martin hundreds of thousands of dollars in lost productivity, and the employee lost his job.

Every day, companies face unexpected twists in the world of virtual morality. With the surge in day trading, is it OK for employees to log on to make a quick stock deal? How about sending out e-mails from work supporting a politician? Or using office computers to hunt for a new job? And if any of this is permissible occasionally, just when does it cross into excess?

This is a new spin on the old nuisance of employees making personal phone calls at work, but with greatly magnified possibilities. For one thing, the Web can be extremely seductive, lulling users to click screen after screen for hours at a time. Productivity can indeed suffer when dozens or hundreds of workers succumb to the temptation. What's more, unlike phone calls, electronic messages are often retrievable months or years later, and can be used as evidence in litigation against companies or individual employees.

In addition, though many workers don't realize it, when they surf the Web from work they are literally dragging their company's name along with them. Most Web sites can, and often do, trace the Internet hookups their visitors are using and identify the companies behind them. That leaves a serious potential for embarrassment if employees are visiting any number of places, from job-search sites to racist chat rooms. Caught off guard by the geometric growth of such issues, many companies have lost all hope of handling matters case by case. Some are using sophisticated software that monitors when, how and why workers are using the Internet (See "Now the Boss Knows Where You're Clicking"). Others are taking first stabs at setting boundaries.

Boeing Co., for one, seems to accept the inevitable with a policy specifically allowing employees to use faxes, e-mail and the Internet for personal reasons. But the aerospace and aircraft company also sets guidelines. Use has to be of "reasonable duration and frequency" and can't cause "embarrassment to the company." And chain letters, obscenity and political and religious solicitation are strictly barred.

Other companies are more permissive, but make it abundantly clear that employees can't expect privacy. Saying it recognizes that employees may occasionally need to use the Web or e-mail for personal reasons, Columbia/HCA Healthcare Corp. issues this warning in its "electronic communication" policy: "It is sometimes necessary for authorized personnel to access and monitor their contents." And, it adds, "in some situations, the company may be required to publicly disclose e-mail messages, even those marked private."

Attorneys have been advising companies to write such policies and alert employees that online activities will be monitored and that they can be disciplined. Such

The Wall Street Journal Workplace-Ethics Quiz

The spread of technology into the workplace has raised a variety of new ethical questions, and many old ones still linger. Compare your answers with those of other Americans. See answers at end of article.

Office Technology

1. Is is wrong to use company e-mail for personal reasons?
   ❑ Yes ❑ No

2. Is is wrong to use office equipment to help your children or spouse do schoolwork?
   ❑ Yes ❑ No

3. Is it wrong to play computer games on office equipment during the workday?
   ❑ Yes ❑ No

4. Is it wrong to use office equipment to do Internet shopping?
   ❑ Yes ❑ No

5. Is is unethical to blame an error you made on a technological glitch?
   ❑ Yes ❑ No

6. Is it unethical to visit pornographic Web sites using office equipment?
   ❑ Yes ❑ No

Gifts and Entertainment

7. What's the value at which a gift from a supplier or client becomes troubling?
   ❑ $25 ❑ $50 ❑ $100

8. Is a $50 gift to a boss unacceptable?
   ❑ Yes ❑ No

9. Is a $50 gift FROM the boss unacceptable?
   ❑ Yes ❑ No

10. Of gifts from suppliers: Is it OK to take a $200 pair of football tickets?
    ❑ Yes ❑ No

11. Is it OK to take a $120 pair of theater tickets?
    ❑ Yes ❑ No

12. Is it OK to take a $100 holiday food basket?
    ❑ Yes ❑ No

13. Is it OK to take a $25 gift certificate?
    ❑ Yes ❑ No

14. Can you accept a $75 prize won at a raffle at a supplier's conference?
    ❑ Yes ❑ No

Truth and Lies

15. Due to on-the-job pressure, have you ever abused or lied about sick days?
    ❑ Yes ❑ No

16. Due to on-the-job pressure, have you ever taken credit for someone else's work or idea?
    ❑ Yes ❑ No

Sources: Ethics Officer Association, Belmont, Mass: Ethical Leadership Group, Wilmette, Ill.; surveys sampled a cross-section of workers at large companies and nationwide

warnings make it difficult for employees to win any suit asserting that they expected their communications to be private—already an uphill claim given that the equipment belongs to the company in the first place.

Some 27% of large U.S. firms have begun checking employee e-mail, a huge jump from 15% in 1997, the American Management Association recently found. Some routinely do this to search for obscene language or images. Passed along employee to employee, those could constitute grounds for a sexual-harassment suit.

But the practice has generated controversy, particularly when workers are not forewarned. Earlier this month, California Gov. Gray Davis vetoed a measure that would have barred employers from secretly monitoring e-mail and computer files. Under the bill, companies would be allowed to do so only after they established monitoring policies and notified employees of them. Asserting that employers have a legitimate need to monitor company property, Gov. Davis said, "Every employee also understands that expense reports submitted for reimbursement are subject to employer verification as to their legitimacy and accuracy."

But even if a manager is within legal rights to peek at employee e-mail, does that make any kind of digital fishing expedition ethical? What's an employer to do, for example, if such a search of an employee's e-mail reveals that he has an undisclosed drug problem or is looking for another job?

To balance employee rights and a company's legal interests, some privacy advocates say, employers should check e-mail only after a worker is suspected of misconduct. "Just because companies own bathrooms doesn't mean they have the right to install cameras and monitor whatever goes on in there," says Marc Rotenberg, executive director of the Electronic Privacy Information Center, an advocacy group in Washington.

Against the tide, some companies and government agencies are trying to cling to "zero tolerance" policies, prohibiting any personal use of company equipment. One is Ameritech Corp., whose business code of conduct specifically states that computers and other company equipment "are to be used only to provide service to customers and for other business purposes," says a spokeswoman for the telecommunications company. The "policy ensures our employees are focused on serving customers," she adds. Reminders about the policy are sent periodically.

BellSouth was a similar hard-liner until the summer of 1998, when it caved. "We got a lot of questions from people saying they were afraid to give someone their company e-mail address for things like weekend soccer clubs," says Jerry Guthrie, the company's ethics officer. "We work long hours—we wanted to offer it as a benefit to employees."

Before BellSouth employees can log on to their computers, however, they now must click "OK" to a message warning them against misuse of e-mail and the

Internet, and alerting them that their actions can be monitored. Since the company changed the policy to allow for personal use, its security department has conducted more than 60 investigations of abuse. Some employees were suspended or fired for violations including accessing pornographic sites and spending too much time on non-business Web pages, including sports sites.

BellSouth, like many other companies, uses filtering technology to block certain sites, but even that is a chore. Since each division currently filters different sites, the company is in the process of standardizing which sites will be blocked company-wide. "Some [other] companies block sports and financial sites," says Mr. Guthrie, though BellSouth doesn't intend to. But, he says, BellSouth will probably block access to "sex sites, hate sites and gambling sites."

In May, Zona Research Inc., an Internet market researcher in Redwood City, Calif., found that fully one-third of companies screen out any sites not on an approved list. In its survey of more than 300 companies, Zona also found that 20% of companies filter sites based on the user's job and another 13% based on the time of day.

But companies trying to construct such dams are discovering leaks all the time. Gambling, adult and other controversial sites are sanitizing or disguising their address names to operate under the radar of firms monitoring and blocking Internet content. One site remained undetected to cyber-smut police until it made headlines recently. Not to be confused with 1600 Pennsylvania Avenue, www.whitehouse.com offers X-rated content.

Now the Boss Knows Where You're Clicking

By Michael J. McCarthy
Staff Reporter of The Wall Street Journal

When labor laws changed recently in England, Turner Broadcasting System Inc. worried about a pileup of overtime claims from employees in its CNN London bureau. Then the Turner computer-security group sprang into action.

The department decided to order software that could monitor every Web page every worker visits—and help pinpoint anyone wasting company time online. "If we see people were surfing the Web all day, then they don't have to be paid for that overtime," says Darren Valiance, a Turner network-security specialist, referring to the British operation. "In a perfect world, people would realize they're at work to work."

Get ready for a combustible new office issue. Advancing technology is rapidly extending electronic-eavesdropping capability to every office that uses the Internet. There is a new set of Internet-surveillance systems, with names like WEBsweeper, Disk Tracy and SecureVIEW. Some can conduct desktop-to-laptop sweeps, monitoring Web use from the mailroom to the executive suite.

Turner, a unit of Time Warner Inc., says it is planning to install software called Telemate.Net, which plumbs a company's network and churns out reports identifying and ranking its heaviest individual Internet users. It details the top sites visited across the whole company, and can do the same for particular departments, like sales or accounting.

Telemate.Net can also report Web site visits by individual employees and rank them by roughly two dozen categories, including some that most employers wouldn't be to happy about—from games, humor and pornography to cults, shopping and job-hunting. And it

can instantly generate logs naming precisely who went to what sites at what times.

Telemate.Net Software Inc., an Atlanta company that went public last month, lists some blue-chip corporate clients: Arthur Andersen & Co., Maytag Corp., Philip Morris Cos. and Sears, Roebuck & Co.

Right after installing Telemate.Net in February, says Douglas Dahlberg, the information-technology manager for Wolverton & Associates Inc., he unearthed some disturbing results. Something called broadcast. com was the company's third-most-visited site. People were downloading music from the site, it turns out, using up 4% of the company's bandwidth, or Internet capacity. "When I saw that, I yanked it," says Mr. Dahlberg, who removed the so-called RealAudio capability from Wolverton's system.

Before starting Telemate.Net up, Wolverton, a civil-engineering company in Norcross, Ga., notified its three dozen employees that it would be monitoring their computer usage. "It just mustn't sink in," says Mr. Dahlberg. "I can see every little Web page you read—and still there were problems."

Indeed in April, E*Trade Group Inc., the online investment service, showed up as Wolverton's eighth-most-visited site, using up nearly 3% of overall bandwidth. That transmission capacity is a precious resource, since Wolverton's engineers routinely have to send data-heavy computer-aided-design files to clients through e-mail during the workday. In June, Mr. Dahlberg was irritated to find cnnsi.com pop up as Wolverton's No. 8 site. "Our clients should be in [the top 10], not CNN Sports," he says.

This type of electronic-file analysis hasn't been available until very recently, computer-network specialists say. The raw data have always been there, but in a form that was virtually impenetrable. From his cramped cubicle at CNN Center in Atlanta, network security specialist Mr. Vallance, a 27-year-old in black Converse high-tops, taps away at his keyboard to demonstrate one recent afternoon.

Pulling up data logs, he reveals screen after screen of enigmatic coding, individuals identified by numbers like 123.43.87.99 and other gobbledygook. A former Air Force information-security expert, Mr. Vallance knows how hard it is to scan these logs to separate routine Web site visits and e-mails from suspicious transactions. There are some easy tip-offs, though: late-night log-ons, and any lines marked "rejected" by Turner's firewalls, or devices that protect computer networks from hackers and other outsiders.

It's only 1 p.m. and Mr. Valiance guesses that these logs, just since that morning, would fill about 2,000 screens. "Trying to look through all this is impossible," he says, but scrolling through them manually is the only way he can do surveillance on employee Web usage right now.

At many companies, information technicians are called upon only after a supervisor suspects an employee is burning up hours online or visiting pornographic or other offensive pages. The computer department can quickly generate a report on an individual's transactions, and the suspicion can be rapidly borne out or disproved.

New software like Telemate.Net completely reverses that process, allowing the computer department to tip off the manager. The software systematically sorts through all employee Web site visits every day, and sorts them into categories. Any visits to amazon.com, for instance, would show up on a company report under "shopping." Visits to jobhunt.com go under "employment." By clicking on a category, a company manager can pull up "drill down" reports revealing the name of each visitor to each site, as well as what times he or she logged on to it.

Certainly there are privacy issues here. Though the company says it isn't aware of any legal challenges to its system, some overseas laws restrict what it can do. In Germany, for instance, laws forbid Telemate.Net to generate reports on Internet usage by individual employees. Mindful of privacy issues in the U.S., Telemate.Net has designed a special "VIP" function that will automatically erase the specific Web pages of anyone the computer department programs it to—the CEO, for example.

Telemate.Net's founding business 13 years ago was selling systems to help companies monitor phone usage, checking for such things as excessive personal calls. Two years ago, the company developed a sister system for the Internet. It sells Telemate.Net for $995 to $4,995 for each system a company requires. The price depends on the number of reports generated and other factors.

Several companies listed as clients in a Telemate.Net filing with the Securities and Exchange Commission had little to say on the subject. "I don't have time to run this down," said a spokesman for Maytag, the appliance maker. A Sears spokeswoman said the retailer couldn't confirm if it was a client and "didn't want to participate" in a story about monitoring employee Web use.

By policy, Philip Morris said, it won't discuss anything that might jeopardize its computer-network security. An Arthur Andersen spokeswoman said, "Our IT [information technology] folks say we don't use it much."

While marketing itself as "network intelligence for the Internet economy, Telemate.Net says it hopes its software will also be used as a tool to use the Web more productively. "Lots of companies gave employees Internet access as a perk, and now they're realizing it's an asset that has to be managed," says Vijay Balakrishnan, senior vice president, marketing.

When asked, Telemate.Net said it does indeed turn the system on itself, conducting surveillance on its 170 employees. And it has turned up some surprises. "We have a guy here—one of our top salespeople—who surfs a lot, spends an hour to an hour and a half a day working on his stock portfolio—but he's a top performer," says Morten Jensen, Telemate.Net's director, product management. "Does Jim, our VP for sales, care?" asks Mr. Jensen. "No."

How One Firm Tracks Ethics Electronically

BY MICHAEL J. MCCARTHY
Staff Reporter of THE WALL STREET JOURNAL

BETHESDA, Md.—Lockheed Martin Corp. is turning business ethics into rocket science.

While some companies worry about workers wasting time on the Web, the aerospace giant is aggressively steering them into cyberspace as part of a broad program—born of a bribery scandal—to audit, record and perfect the measurement of employee morals.

Using internal computer programs with names like Merlin and Qwizard, many of Lockheed Martin's 160,000 employees go online these days for step-by-step training on ethics and legal compliance. The system records each time an employee completes one of the sessions, which range from sexual harassment and insider trading to kickbacks and gratuities. Last month, it began alerting managers to employees who haven't yet taken required sessions.

Lockheed Martin's electronic ethics program also closely tracks alleged wrongdoing inside the company. It

Rocket Science

Lockheed keeps close tabs on how employees are disciplined for ethics violations.

	1995	1999*
Discharge		
	56	25
Suspension		
	47	14
Written reprimand		
	59	51
Oral reprimand		
	164	146
Other		
	60	66
Total sanctions		
	386	302

*Figures to June 30.

Source: Lockheed Martin

knows, for example, that it takes 30.4 days on average to complete an internal investigation of ethics violations, and that the company has fired 217 people for them since 1995. In the first six months of this year, 4.8% of its ethics allegations involved conflicts of interest, while 8.9% involved security and misuse of assets.

In short, Lockheed Martin is tackling ethical matters with a scientific precision usually associated with its F-16 fighter jets.

One big reason for these complex ethics metrics: legal defense in case the company faces charges again.

Lockheed Corp. did not have such a sophisticated program in place in 1995, when, on the eve of its merger with Martin Marietta Corp., it agreed to pay a $24.8 million fine and plead guilty to conspiring to violate U.S. antibribery laws. Lockheed admitted that it illegally paid $1 million to an Egyptian lawmaker in 1990 for helping sell its C-130 aircraft in that country.

To keep from losing government contracts, Lockheed Martin submitted to a 60-page administrative agreement that amounted to a three-year probationary period. Like clockwork, it was required to turn over to the U.S. Air

Force periodic ethics reports, including details of ethical complaints made to its employee hotline and other misconduct allegations.

In its leafy, suburban office park here in the shadow of the federal government, Lockheed Martin hardly wants to jeopardize its contractor status. Fully 70% of its $26.3 billion in sales comes solely from the U.S. government. "If they debar the corporation, that's death for this company," says David T. Clous, vice president for ethics and business conduct.

What's more, the electronic ethics program could win the company lenient treatment should it be indicted in a future case. The decade-old Federal Sentencing Guidelines, which codified fines and penalties for corporate wrongdoing, also established that fines for criminal conduct could be reduced by as much as 95% if a company had concrete internal programs to detect and prevent illegal acts. But if a company couldn't produce a paper trail of proof that it had tried to prevent wrongdoing, fines and penalties could be ratcheted up by 400%.

As part of its drive to stay on the straight and narrow, Lockheed Martin also developed an ethics game, which every single employee, up to Chairman Vance D. Coffman, must play once a year. With cards and tokens, workers spend one-hour sessions packed around tables, considering how to handle ethical quandaries drawn from actual Lockheed Martin cases—from harassment to padded work schedules.

The Ethics Challenge, as it is called, has been a hit—except for one year, when the ethics department revised the game so that it no longer indicated which answers were right or wrong. The idea was to let players debate. But the indecision drove the company's exacting engineers nuts. "They had a hard time with it," says Brian Sears, an ethics officer for the aeronautics division. The game was revised again, to offer "preferred answers."

Meanwhile, the ethics department went to work developing numerous "interactive" training sessions, on security, software-license compliance and labor charging. The courses, with actors playing out hypothetical cases, were originally produced for CD-ROMs, at a cost of about $150,000 apiece.

Clicking along at a workstation, an employee usually takes about 45 minutes to complete a session. A sample question from the kickback-and-gratuity clinic:

A kickback may be in the form of:

> *A. Cash*
> *B. Gift to a family member*
> *C. Donation to a charity at your request*
> *D. All of these* (The correct answer is D.)

From the sexual-harassment segment:

Which is the best means of addressing harassment when it first occurs?

> A. Ignore the harasser
> B. Be direct and tell the harasser his or her behavior is unwelcome and offensive
> C. Report the harasser to your manager or Human Resources
>
> (The correct answer is B.)

To provide proof that it has been systematically teaching employees the laws appropriate to their divisions and positions, Lockheed Martin also wanted an up-to-the-minute auditing system, which would track who had taken what training session and when. Last year, turning to the power of the Web, it began using its automated Merlin system to instantly track the number of courses taken and by whom.

The company says employees have warmed up to the program, particularly since it went online and workers no longer have to check out CD-ROMs or visit special workstations to meet their training requirements. But Lockheed is realistic. "We never envision people lining up and saying, 'Rah-rah, it's time for compliance training,'" says Tracy Carter Dougherty, director of ethics communication and training.

"Computer-based training can't completely replace personalized training," says Joseph E. Murphy, an ethics and compliance specialist with Compliance Systems Legal Group in Warwick, R.I. But having a system with mandatory clinics and quizzes will help "convince a prosecutor or regulator that the company is trying to prevent and detect problems," he adds.

Indeed, Steven Shaw, the U.S. Air Force deputy general counsel who held a debarment ax over Lockheed Martin until the probationary period ended last year, says he is pleased the company is still keeping close statistical tabs on ethical conduct and compliance training. And

Ethics-Quiz Answers

1. 34% said personal e-mail on company computers is wrong
2. 37% said using office equipment for schoolwork is wrong
3. 49% said playing copmuter games at work is wrong
4. 54% said Internet shopping at work is wrong
5. 61% said it's unethical to blame your error on technology
6. 87% said it's unethical to visit pornographic sites at work
7. 33% said $25 is the amount at which a gift from a supplier or client becomes troubling, while 33% said $50, and 33% said $100
8. 35% said a $50 gift to the boss is unacceptable
9. 12% said a $50 gift *from* the boss is unacceptable
10. 70% said it's unacceptable to take the $200 football tickets
11. 70% said it's unacceptable to take the $120 theater tickets
12. 35% said it's unacceptable to take the $100 food basket
13. 45% said it's unacceptable to take the $25 gift certificate
14. 40% said it's unacceptable to take the $75 raffle prize
15. 11% reported they lie about sick days
16. 4% reported they take credit for the work or ideas of others

noting that the company hasn't been indicted since the Egypt case, he adds, "To me, that says a lot about a company that large. You'll always have people who will make mistakes."

Values in Tension: Ethics Away from Home

When is different just different, and when is different wrong?

by Thomas Donaldson

When we leave home and cross our nation's boundaries, moral clarity often blurs. Without a backdrop of shared attitudes, and without familiar laws and judicial procedures that define standards of ethical conduct, certainty is elusive. Should a company invest in a foreign country where civil and political rights are violated? Should a company go along with a host country's discriminatory employment practices? If companies in developed countries shift facilities to developing nations that lack strict environmental and health regulations, or if those companies choose to fill management and other top-level positions in a host nation with people from the home country, whose standards should prevail?

Even the best-informed, best-intentioned executives must rethink their assumptions about business practice in foreign settings. What works in a company's home country can fail in a country with different standards of ethical conduct. Such difficulties are unavoidable for businesspeople who live and work abroad.

But how can managers resolve the problems? What are the principles that can help them work through the maze of cultural differences and establish codes of conduct for globally ethical business practice? How can companies answer the toughest question in global business ethics: What happens when a host country's ethical standards seem lower than the home country's?

Competing Answers

One answer is as old as philosophical discourse. According to cultural relativism, no culture's ethics are better than any other's; therefore there are no international rights and wrongs. If the people of Indonesia tolerate the bribery of their public officials, so what? Their attitude is no better

or worse than that of people in Denmark or Singapore who refuse to offer or accept bribes. Likewise, if Belgians fail to find insider trading morally repugnant, who cares? Not enforcing insider-trading laws is no more or less ethical than enforcing such laws.

The cultural relativist's creed—When in Rome, do as the Romans do—is tempting, especially when failing to do as the locals do means forfeiting business opportunities. The inadequacy of cultural relativism, however, becomes apparent when the practices in question are more damaging than petty bribery or insider trading.

In the late 1980s, some European tanneries and pharmaceutical companies were looking for cheap waste-dumping sites. They approached virtually every country on Africa's west coast from Morocco to the Congo. Nigeria agreed to take highly toxic polychlorinated biphenyls. Unprotected local workers, wearing thongs and shorts, unloaded barrels of PCBs and placed them near a residential area. Neither the residents nor the workers knew that the barrels contained toxic waste.

We may denounce governments that permit such abuses, but many countries are unable to police transnational corporations adequately even if they want to. And in many countries, the combination of ineffective enforcement and inadequate regulations leads to behavior by unscrupulous companies that is clearly wrong. A few years ago, for example, a group of investors became interested in restoring the SS *United States*, once a luxurious ocean liner. Before the actual restoration could begin, the ship had to be stripped of its asbestos lining. A bid from a U.S. company, based on U.S. standards for asbestos removal, priced the job at more than $100 million. A company in the Ukranian city of Sevastopol offered to do the work for less than $2 million. In October 1993, the ship was towed to Sevastopol.

The Culture and Ethics of Software Piracy

Before jumping on the cultural relativism bandwagon, stop and consider the potential economic consequences of a when-in-Rome attitude toward business ethics. Take a look at the current statistics on software piracy: In the United States, pirated software is estimated to be 35% of the total software market, and industry losses are estimated at $2.3 billion per year. The piracy rate is 57% in Germany and 80% in Italy and Japan; the rates in most Asian countries are estimated to be nearly 100%.

There are similar laws against software piracy in those countries. What, then, accounts for the differences? Although a country's level of economic development plays a large part, culture, including ethical attitudes, may be a more crucial factor. The 1995 annual report of the Software Publishers Association connects software piracy directly to culture and attitude. It describes Italy and Hong Kong as having "'first world' per capita incomes, along with 'third world' rates of piracy." When asked whether one should use software without paying for it, most people, including people in Italy and Hong Kong, say no. But people in some countries regard the practice as *less* unethical than people in other countries do. Confucian culture, for example, stresses that individuals should share what they create with society. That may be, in part, what prompts the Chinese and other Asians to view the concept of intellectual property as a means for the West to monopolize its technological superiority.

What happens if ethical attitudes around the world permit large-scale software piracy? Software companies won't want to invest as much in developing new products, because they cannot expect any return on their investment in certain parts of the world. When ethics fail to support technological creativity, there are consequences that go beyond statistics—jobs are lost and livelihoods jeopardized.

Companies must do more than lobby foreign governments for tougher enforcement of piracy laws. They must cooperate with other companies and with local organizations to help citizens understand the consequences of piracy and to encourage the evolution of a different ethic toward the practice.

A cultural relativist would have no problem with that outcome, but I do. A country has the right to establish its own health and safety regulations, but in the case described above, the standards and the terms of the contract could not possibly have protected workers in Sevastopol from known health risks. Even if the contract met Ukranian standards, ethical businesspeople must object. Cultural relativism is morally blind. There are fundamental values that cross cultures, and companies must uphold them. (For an economic argument against cultural relativism, see the insert "The Culture and Ethics of Software Piracy.")

At the other end of the spectrum from cultural relativism is ethical imperialism, which directs people to do everywhere exactly as they do at home. Again, an understandably appealing approach but one that is clearly inadequate. Consider the large U.S. computer-products company that in 1993 introduced a course on sexual harassment in its Saudi Arabian facility. Under the banner of global consistency, instructors used the same approach to train Saudi Arabian managers that they had used with U.S. managers: the participants were asked to discuss a case in which a manager makes sexually explicit remarks to a new female employee over drinks in a bar. The instructors failed to consider how the exercise would work in a culture with strict conventions governing relationships between men and women. As a result, the training sessions were ludicrous. They baffled and offended the Saudi participants, and the message to avoid coercion and sexual discrimination was lost.

The theory behind ethical imperialism is absolutism, which is based on three problematic principles. Absolutists believe that there is a single list of truths, that they can be expressed only with one set of concepts, and that they call for exactly the same behavior around the world.

The first claim clashes with many people's belief that different cultural traditions must be respected. In some cultures, loyalty to a community—family, organization, or society—is the foundation of all ethical behavior. The Japanese, for example, define business ethics in terms of loyalty to their companies, their business networks, and their nation. Americans place a higher value on liberty than on loyalty; the U.S. tradition of rights emphasizes equality, fairness, and individual freedom. It is hard to conclude that truth lies on one side or the other, but an absolutist would have us select just one.

The second problem with absolutism is the presumption that people must express moral truth using only one set of concepts. For instance, some absolutists insist that the language of basic rights provide the framework for any discussion of ethics. That means, though, that entire cultural traditions must be ignored. The notion of a right evolved with the rise of democracy in post-Renaissance Europe and the United States, but the term is not found in either Confucian or Buddhist traditions. We all learn ethics in the context of our particular cultures, and the power in the principles is deeply tied to the way in which they are expressed. Internationally accepted lists of moral principles, such as the United Nations' Universal Declaration of Human Rights, draw on many cultural and religious traditions. As philosopher Michael Walzer has noted, "There is no Esperanto of global ethics."

The third problem with absolutism is the belief in a global standard of ethical behavior. Context must shape ethical practice. Very low wages, for example, may be considered unethical in rich, advanced countries, but developing nations may be acting ethically if they encourage investment and improve living standards by accepting low wages. Likewise, when people are malnourished or starving, a government may be wise to use more fertilizer in order to improve crop yields, even though that means settling for relatively high levels of thermal water pollution.

When cultures have different standards of ethical behavior—and different ways of handling unethical behavior—a company that takes an absolutist approach may find itself making a disastrous mistake. When a manager at a large U.S. specialty-products company in China caught an employee stealing, she followed the company's practice and turned the employee over to the provincial authorities, who executed him. Managers cannot operate in another culture without being aware of that culture's attitudes toward ethics.

If companies can neither adopt a host country's ethics nor extend the home country's standards, what is the answer? Even the traditional litmus test—What would people think of your actions if they were written up on the front page of the newspaper?—is an unreliable guide, for there is no international consensus on standards of business conduct.

What Do These Values Have in Common?

Non-Western	Western
Kyosei (Japanese): Living and working together for the common good.	Individual liberty
Dharma (Hindu): The fulfillment of inherited duty.	Egalitarianism
Santutthi (Buddhist): The importance of limited desires.	Political participation
Zakat (Muslim): The duty to give alms to the Muslim poor.	Human rights

Balancing the Extremes: Three Guiding Principles

Companies must help managers distinguish between practices that are merely different and those that are wrong. For relativists, nothing is sacred and nothing is wrong. For absolutists, many things that are different are wrong. Neither extreme illuminates the real world of business decision making. The answer lies somewhere in between.

When it comes to shaping ethical behavior, companies must be guided by three principles.

• Respect for core human values, which determine the absolute moral threshold for all business activities.
• Respect for local traditions.
• The belief that context matters when deciding what is right and what is wrong.

Consider those principles in action. In Japan, people doing business together often exchange gifts—sometimes expensive ones—in keeping with long-standing Japanese tradition. When U.S. and European companies started doing a lot of business in Japan, many Western businesspeople thought that the practice of gift giving might be wrong rather than simply different. To them, accepting a gift felt like accepting a bribe. As Western companies have become more familiar with Japanese traditions, however, most have come to tolerate the practice and to set different limits on gift giving in Japan than they do elsewhere.

Respecting differences is a crucial ethical practice. Research shows that management ethics differ among cultures; respecting those differences means recognizing that some cultures have obvious weaknesses—as well as hidden strengths. Managers in Hong Kong, for example, have a higher tolerance for some forms of bribery than their Western counterparts, but they have a much lower tolerance for the failure to acknowledge a subordinate's work. In some parts of the Far East, stealing credit from a subordinate is nearly an unpardonable sin.

People often equate respect for local traditions with cultural relativism. That is incorrect. Some practices are clearly wrong. Union Carbide's tragic experience in Bhopal, India, provides one example. The company's executives seriously underestimated how much on-site management involvement was needed at the Bhopal plant to compensate for the country's poor infrastructure and regulatory capabilities. In the aftermath of the disastrous gas leak, the lesson is clear: companies using sophisticated technology in a developing country must evaluate that country's ability to oversee its safe use. Since the incident at Bhopal, Union Carbide has become a leader in advising companies on using hazardous technologies safely in developing countries.

Some activities are wrong no matter where they take place. But some practices that are unethical in one setting may be acceptable in another. For instance, the chemical EDB, a soil fungicide, is banned for use in the United States. In hot climates, however, it quickly becomes harmless through exposure to intense solar radiation and high soil temperatures. As long as the chemical is monitored, companies may be able to use EDB ethically in certain parts of the world.

Defining the Ethical Threshold: Core Values

Few ethical questions are easy for managers to answer. But there are some hard truths that must guide managers' actions, a set of what I call *core human values*, which define minimum ethical standards for all companies.[1] The right to good health and the right to economic advancement and an improved standard of living are two core human values. Another is what Westerners call the Golden Rule, which is recognizable in every major religious and ethical tradition around the world. In Book 15 of his *Analects*, for instance, Confucius counsels people to maintain reciprocity, or not to do to others what they do not want done to themselves.

Although no single list would satisfy every scholar, I believe it is possible to articulate three core values that incorporate the work of scores of theologians and philosophers around the world. To be broadly relevant, these values must include elements found in both Western and non-Western cultural and religious traditions. Consider the examples of values in the insert "What Do These Values Have in Common?"

At first glance, the values expressed in the two lists seem quite different. Nonetheless, in the spirit of what philosopher John Rawls calls *overlapping consensus*, one can see that the seemingly divergent values converge at key points. Despite important differences between Western and non-Western cultural and religious traditions, both express shared attitudes about what it means to be human. First, individuals must not treat others simply as tools; in other words, they must recognize a person's value as a human being. Next, individuals and communities must treat people in ways that respect people's basic rights. Finally, members of a community must work together to support and improve the institutions on which the community depends. I call those three values *respect for human dignity, respect for basic rights*, and *good citizenship*.

Those values must be the starting point for all companies as they formulate and evaluate standards of ethical conduct at home and abroad. But they are only a starting point. Companies need much more specific guidelines, and the first step to developing those is to translate the core human values into core values for business. What does it mean, for example, for a company to respect human dignity? How can a company be a good citizen?

I believe that companies can respect human dignity by creating and sustaining a corporate culture in which employees, customers, and suppliers are treated not as means to an end but as people whose intrinsic value must be acknowledged, and by producing safe products and services in a safe workplace. Companies can respect basic rights by acting in ways that support and protect the individual rights of employees, customers, and surrounding communities, and by avoiding relationships that violate human beings' rights to health, education, safety, and an adequate standard of living. And companies can be good citizens by supporting essential social institutions, such as the economic system and the education system, and by working with host governments and other organizations to protect the environment.

The core values establish a moral compass for business practice. They can help companies identify practices that are acceptable and those that are intolerable—even if the practices are compatible with a host country's norms and laws. Dumping pollutants near people's homes and accepting inadequate standards for handling hazardous materials are two examples of actions that violate core values.

Similarly, if employing children prevents them from receiving a basic education, the practice is intolerable. Lying about product specifications in the act of selling may not affect human lives directly, but it too is intolerable because it violates the trust that is needed to sustain a corporate culture in which customers are respected.

Sometimes it is not a company's actions but those of a supplier or customer that pose problems. Take the case of the Tan family, a large supplier for Levi Strauss. The Tans were allegedly forcing 1,200 Chinese and Filipino women to work 74 hours per week in guarded compounds on the Mariana Islands. In 1992, after repeated warnings to the Tans, Levi Strauss broke off business relations with them.

Creating an Ethical Corporate Culture

The core values for business that I have enumerated can help companies begin to exercise ethical judgment and think about how to operate ethically in foreign cultures, but they are not specific enough to guide managers through actual ethical dilemmas. Levi Strauss relied on a written code of conduct when figuring out how to deal with the Tan family. The company's Global Sourcing and Operating Guidelines, formerly called the Business Partner Terms of Engagement, state that Levi Strauss will "seek to identify and utilize business partners who aspire as individuals and in the conduct of all their businesses to a set of ethical standards not incompatible with our own." Whenever intolerable business situations arise, managers should be guided by precise statements that spell out the behavior and operating practices that the company demands.

Many companies don't do anything with their codes of conduct; they simply paste them on the wall.

Ninety percent of all *Fortune* 500 companies have codes of conduct, and 70% have statements of vision and values. In Europe and the Far East, the percentages are lower but are increasing rapidly. Does that mean that most companies have what they need? Hardly. Even though most large U.S. companies have both statements of values and codes of conduct, many might be better off if they didn't. Too many companies don't do anything with the documents; they simply paste them on the wall to impress employees, customers, suppliers, and the public. As a result, the senior managers who drafted the statements lose credibility by proclaiming values and not living up to them. Companies such as Johnson & Johnson, Levi Strauss, Motorola, Texas Instruments, and Lockheed Martin, however, do a great deal to make the words meaningful. Johnson & Johnson, for example, has become well known for its Credo Challenge sessions, in which managers discuss ethics in the context of their current business problems and are invited to criticize the company's credo and make suggestions for changes. The participants' ideas are passed on to the company's senior managers. Lockheed Martin has created an innovative site on the World Wide Web and on its local network that gives employees, customers, and suppliers access to the company's ethical code and the chance to voice complaints.

If a company declared all gift giving unethical, it wouldn't be able to do business in Japan.

Codes of conduct must provide clear direction about ethical behavior when the temptation to behave unethically is strongest. The pronouncement in a code of conduct that bribery is unacceptable is useless unless accompanied by guidelines for gift giving, payments to get goods through customs, and "requests" from intermediaries who are hired to ask for bribes.

Motorola's values are stated very simply as "How we will always act: [with] constant respect for people [and] uncompromising integrity." The company's code of conduct, however, is explicit about actual business practice. With respect to bribery, for example, the code states that the "funds and assets of Motorola shall not be used, directly or indirectly, for illegal payments of any kind." It is unambiguous about what sort of payment is illegal: "the payment of a bribe to a public official or the kickback of funds to an employee of a customer...." The code goes on to prescribe specific procedures for handling commissions to intermediaries, issuing sales invoices, and disclosing confidential information in a sales transaction—all situations in which employees might have an opportunity to accept or offer bribes.

Codes of conduct must be explicit to be useful, but they must also leave room for a manager to use his or her judgment in situations requiring cultural sensitivity. Host-country employees shouldn't be forced to adopt all home-country values and renounce their own. Again, Motorola's code is exemplary. First, it gives clear direction: "Employees of Motorola will respect the laws, customs, and traditions of each country in which they operate, but will, at the same time, engage in no course of conduct which, even if legal, customary, and accepted in any such country, could be deemed to be in violation of the accepted business ethics of Motorola or the laws of the United States relating to business ethics." After laying down such absolutes, Motorola's code then makes clear when individual judgment will be necessary. For example, employees may sometimes accept certain kinds of small gifts "in rare circumstances, where the refusal to accept a gift" would injure Motorola's "legitimate business interests." Under certain circumstances, such gifts "may be accepted so long as the gift inures to the benefit of Motorola" and not "to the benefit of the Motorola employee."

Striking the appropriate balance between providing clear direction and leaving room for individual judgment makes crafting corporate values statements and ethics codes one of the hardest tasks that executives confront. The words are only a start. A company's leaders need to refer often to their organization's credo and code and must themselves be credible, committed, and consistent. If senior managers act as though ethics don't matter, the rest of the company's employees won't think they do, either.

Conflicts of Development and Conflicts of Tradition

Managers living and working abroad who are not prepared to grapple with moral ambiguity and tension should pack their bags and come home. The view that all business practices can be categorized as either ethical or unethical is too simple. As Einstein is reported to have said, "Things should be as simple as possible—but no simpler." Many business practices that are considered unethical in one setting may be ethical in another. Such activities are neither black nor white but exist in what Thomas Dunfee and I have called *moral free space*.[2] In this gray zone, there are no tight prescriptions for a company's behavior. Managers must chart their own courses—as long as they do not violate core human values.

Many activities are neither good nor bad but exist in *moral free space*.

Consider the following example. Some successful Indian companies offer employees the opportunity for one of their children to gain a job with the company once the child has completed a certain level in school. The companies honor this commitment even when other applicants are more qualified than an employee's child. The perk is extremely valuable in a country where jobs are hard to find, and it reflects the Indian culture's belief that the West has gone too far in allowing economic opportunities to break up families. Not surprisingly, the perk is among the most cherished by employees, but in most Western countries, it would be branded unacceptable nepotism. In the United States, for example, the ethical principle of equal opportunity holds that jobs should go to the applicants with the best qualifications. If a U.S. company made such promises to its employees, it would violate regulations established by the Equal Employment Opportunity Commission. Given this difference in ethical attitudes, how should U.S. managers react to Indian nepotism? Should they condemn the Indian companies, refusing to accept them as partners or suppliers until they agree to clean up their act?

Despite the obvious tension between nepotism and principles of equal opportunity, I cannot condemn the practice for Indians. In a country, such as India, that emphasizes clan and family relationships and has catastrophic levels of

The Problem with Bribery

Bribery is widespread and insidious. Managers in transnational companies routinely confront bribery even though most countries have laws against it. The fact is that officials in many developing countries wink at the practice, and the salaries of local bureaucrats are so low that many consider bribes a form of remuneration. The U.S. Foreign Corrupt Practices Act defines allowable limits on petty bribery in the form of routine payments required to move goods through customs. But demands for bribes often exceed those limits, and there is seldom a good solution.

Bribery disrupts distribution channels when goods languish on docks until local handlers are paid off, and it destroys incentives to compete on quality and cost when purchasing decisions are based on who pays what under the table. Refusing to acquiesce is often tantamount to giving business to unscrupulous companies.

I believe that even routine bribery is intolerable. Bribery undermines market efficiency and predictability, thus ultimately denying people their right to a minimal standard of living. Some degree of ethical commitment—some sense that everyone will play by the rules—is necessary for a sound economy. Without an ability to predict outcomes, who would be willing to invest?

There was a U.S. company whose shipping crates were regularly pilfered by handlers on the docks of Rio de Janeiro. The handlers would take about 10% of the contents of the crates, but the company was never sure which 10% it would be. In a partial solution, the company began sending two crates—the first with 90% of the merchandise, the second with 10%. The handlers learned to take the second crate and leave the first untouched. From the company's perspective, at least knowing which goods it would lose was an improvement.

Bribery does more than destroy predictability; it undermines essential social and economic systems. That truth is not lost on businesspeople in countries where the practice is woven into the social fabric. CEOs in India admit that their companies engage constantly in bribery, and they say that they have considerable disgust for the practice. They blame government policies in part, but Indian executives also know that their country's business practices perpetuate corrupt behavior. Anyone walking the streets of Calcutta, where it is clear that even a dramatic redistribution of wealth would still leave most of India's inhabitants in dire poverty, comes face-to-face with the devastating effects of corruption.

unemployment, the practice must be viewed in moral free space. The decision to allow a special perk for employees and their children is not necessarily wrong—at least for members of that country.

How can managers discover the limits of moral free space? That is, how can they learn to distinguish a value in tension with their own from one that is intolerable? Helping managers develop good ethical judgment requires companies to be clear about their core values and codes of conduct. But even the most explicit set of guidelines cannot always provide answers. That is especially true in the thorniest ethical dilemmas, in which the host country's ethical standards not only are different but also seem lower than the home country's. Managers must recognize that when countries have different ethical standards, there are two types of conflict that commonly arise. Each type requires its own line of reasoning.

In the first type of conflict, which I call a *conflict of relative development*, ethical standards conflict because of the countries' different levels of economic development. As mentioned before, developing countries may accept wage rates that seem inhumane to more advanced countries in order to attract investment. As economic conditions in a developing country improve, the incidence of that sort of conflict usually decreases. The second type of conflict is a *conflict of cultural tradition*. For example, Saudi Arabia, unlike most other countries, does not allow women to serve as corporate managers. Instead, women may work in only a few professions, such as education and health care. The prohibition stems from strongly held religious and cultural beliefs; any increase in the country's level of economic development, which is already quite high, is not likely to change the rules.

To resolve a conflict of relative development, a manager must ask the following question: Would the practice be acceptable at home if my country were in a similar stage of economic development? Consider the difference between wage and safety standards in the United States and in Angola, where citizens accept lower standards on both counts. If a U.S. oil company is hiring Angolans to work on an offshore Angolan oil rig, can the company pay them lower wages than it pays U.S. workers in the Gulf of Mexico? Reasonable people have to answer yes if the alternative for Angola is the loss of both the foreign investment and the jobs.

Consider, too, differences in regulatory environments. In the 1980s, the government of India fought hard to be able to import Ciba-Geigy's Entero Vioform, a drug known to be enormously effective in fighting dysentery but one that had been banned in the United States because some users experienced side effects. Although dysentery was not a big problem in the United States, in India, poor public sanitation was contributing to epidemic levels of the disease. Was it unethical to make the drug available in India after it had been banned in the United States? On the contrary, rational people should consider it unethical not to do so. Apply our test: Would the United States, at an earlier stage of development, have used this drug despite its side effects? The answer is clearly yes.

But there are many instances when the answer to similar questions is no. Sometimes a host country's standards are inadequate at any level of economic development. If a country's pollution standards are so low that working on an oil rig would considerably increase a person's risk of developing cancer, foreign oil companies must refuse to do business there. Likewise, if the dangerous side effects of a drug treatment outweigh its benefits, managers should not accept health standards that ignore the risks.

When relative economic conditions do not drive tensions, there is a more objective test for resolving ethical problems. Managers should deem a practice permissible only if they can answer no to both of the following questions: Is it possible to conduct business successfully in the host country without undertaking the practice? And Is the practice a violation of a core human value? Japanese gift giving is a perfect example of a conflict of cultural tradition. Most experienced businesspeople, Japanese and non-Japanese alike, would agree that doing business in Japan would be virtually impossible without adopting the practice. Does gift giving violate a core human value? I cannot identify one that it violates. As a result, gift giving may be permissible for foreign companies in Japan even if it conflicts with ethical attitudes at home. In fact, that conclusion is widely accepted, even by companies such as Texas Instruments and IBM, which are outspoken against bribery.

Does it follow that all nonmonetary gifts are acceptable or that bribes are generally acceptable in countries where they are common? Not at all. (See the insert "The Problem with Bribery.") What makes the routine practice of gift giving acceptable in Japan are the limits in its scope and intention. When gift giving moves outside those limits, it soon collides with core human values. For example, when Carl Kotchian, president of Lockheed in the 1970s, carried suitcases full of cash to Japanese politicians, he went beyond the norms established by Japanese tradition. That incident galvanized opinion in the United States Congress and helped lead to passage of the Foreign Corrupt Practices Act. Likewise, Roh Tae Woo went beyond the norms established by Korean cultural tradition when he accepted $635.4 million in bribes as president of the Republic of Korea between 1988 and 1993.

Guidelines for Ethical Leadership

Learning to spot intolerable practices and to exercise good judgment when ethical conflicts arise requires practice. Creating a company culture that rewards ethical behavior is essential. The following guidelines for developing a global ethical perspective among managers can help.

Treat corporate values and formal standards of conduct as absolutes. Whatever ethical standards a company chooses, it cannot waver on its principles either at home or abroad. Consider what has become part of company lore at Motorola. Around 1950, a senior executive was negotiating with officials of a South American government on a $10 million sale that would have increased the company's annual net profits by nearly 25%. As the negotiations neared completion, however, the executive walked away from the deal because the officials were asking for $1 million for "fees." CEO Robert Galvin not only supported the executive's decision but also made it clear that Motorola would neither accept the sale on any terms nor do business with those government officials again. Retold over the decades, this story demonstrating Galvin's resolve has helped cement a culture of ethics for thousands of employees at Motorola.

Design and implement conditions of engagement for suppliers and customers. Will your company do business with any customer or supplier? What if a customer or supplier uses child labor? What if it has strong links with organized crime? What if it pressures your company to break a host country's laws? Such issues are best not left for spur-of-the-moment decisions. Some companies have realized that. Sears, for instance, has developed a policy of not contracting production to companies that use prison labor or infringe on workers' rights to health and safety. And BankAmerica has specified as a condition for many of its loans to developing countries that environmental standards and human rights must be observed.

Allow foreign business units to help formulate ethical standards and interpret ethical issues. The French pharmaceutical company Rhône-Poulenc Rorer has allowed foreign subsidiaries to augment lists of corporate ethical principles with their own suggestions. Texas Instruments has paid special attention to issues of international business ethics by creating the Global Business Practices Council, which is made up of managers from countries in which the company operates. With the overarching intent to create a "global ethics strategy, locally deployed," the council's mandate is to provide ethics education and create local processes that will help managers in the company's foreign business units resolve ethical conflicts.

In host countries, support efforts to decrease institutional corruption. Individual managers will not be able to wipe out corruption in a host country, no matter how many bribes they turn down. When a host country's tax system, import and export procedures, and procurement practices favor unethical players, companies must take action.

Many companies have begun to participate in reforming host-country institutions. General Electric, for example, has taken a strong stand in India, using the media to make repeated condemnations of bribery in business and government. General Electric and others have found, however, that a single company usually cannot drive out entrenched corruption. Transparency International, an organization based in Germany, has been effective in helping coalitions of companies, government officials, and others work to reform bribery-ridden bureaucracies in Russia, Bangladesh, and elsewhere.

Exercise moral imagination. Using moral imagination means resolving tensions responsibly and creatively. Coca-Cola, for instance, has consistently turned down requests for bribes from Egyptian officials but has managed to gain political support and public trust by sponsoring a project to plant fruit trees. And take the example of Levi Strauss, which discovered in the early 1990s that two of its suppliers in Bangladesh were employing children under the age of 14—a practice that violated the company's principles but was tolerated in Bangladesh. Forcing the suppliers to fire the children would not have ensured that the children received an education, and it would have caused serious hardship for the families depending on the children's wages. In a creative arrangement, the suppliers agreed to pay the children's regular wages while they attended school and to offer each child a job at age 14. Levi Strauss, in turn, agreed to pay the children's tuition and provide books and uniforms. That arrangement allowed Levi Strauss to uphold its principles and provide long-term benefits to its host country.

Many people think of values as soft; to some they are usually unspoken. A South Seas island society uses the word *mokita*, which means, "the truth that everybody knows but nobody speaks." However difficult they are to articulate, values affect how we all behave. In a global business environment, values in tension are the rule rather than the exception. Without a company's commitment, statements of values and codes of ethics end up as empty plati-tudes that provide managers with no foundation for behaving ethically. Employees need and deserve more, and responsible members of the global business community can set examples for others to follow. The dark consequences of incidents such as Union Carbide's disaster in Bhopal remind us how high the stakes can be.

Notes

1. In other writings, Thomas W. Dunfee and I have used the term *hypernorm* instead of *core human value*.
2. Thomas Donaldson and Thomas W. Dunfee, "Toward a Unified Conception of Business Ethics: Integrative Social Contracts Theory," *Academy of Management Review*, April 1994; and "Integrative Social Contracts Theory: A Communitarian Conception of Economic Ethics," *Economics and Philosophy*, spring 1995.

GLOBAL STANDARDS, LOCAL PROBLEMS

"When in Rome" doesn't work anymore. More and more global firms are finding a correlation between ethical standards and economic success.

Meryl Davids

AH, THE GOOD OLD DAYS. BACK 30, 20, EVEN 10, years ago, companies could run their overseas business pretty much however they wanted. What happened in a land far away bore little consequence to the main operations. If a factory employed underage workers in Third World countries, well, that's just the way things were done over there. Giving and accepting elaborate gifts? Part of the culture. And if your subsidiary didn't adhere to the same pollution control standards as its American counterparts, it was easily justified on the grounds that environmental laws overseas weren't as strict.

But if the world shrinking to a marble has been good for American companies profiting from international operations and trade, it has also added brutal new pressures for principled behavior on a global scale. Global business ethics has now become "the ultimate dilemma for many U.S. businesses," as one business publication stated.

"The world is highly interconnected now, so American consumers increasingly know and care if a company is, say, dumping chemical waste in a river in China," says Robert MacGregor, a leader of the Caux Round Table, a group of international business leaders aiming to focus attention on global corporate responsibility. "Companies that are concerned with their reputations, and that's nearly all companies, recognize they have to focus on their global principles."

Ignoring global ethical issues can even cost you customers at home. "We have evidence that if consumers know that a company is unethical anywhere in the world, they will exercise their disapproval at the cash register," MacGregor says, not to mention the impact it has on employees and investors.

Brother, Can You Spare a Thousand?

While the heightened focus on international ethics—led by a growing charge by nonprofit organizations including Caux, the U.N., the World Bank, and others—does make it riskier to operate overseas, in many ways it is also a welcome relief to many U.S. firms. Companies here have long decried the uneven playing field created by our Foreign Corrupt Practices Act. Passed in 1977, among other things it prohibits American countries from paying bribes for expedited services. Companies from other countries, including several in Europe, however, can not only legally make those payments, but they can also deduct the money from their taxes.

With this disparity, trying to open factories or get products unloaded in countries where such payoffs are the norm has proven difficult, if not impossible, for American companies in many locales. Which areas are the most rife with problems? According to a Corruption Perception Index developed by nonprofit group Transparency International, Cameroon, Paraguay, Honduras, Tanzania, and Nigeria are seen as most corrupt (see table). While Frank Vogl, vice president of the group and a former World Bank official, says the survey measures only perceptions (of ordinary citizens, business leaders, and experts), "countries that are seen to have high levels of corruption almost certainly do have them." Russia, too, falls near the bottom of the scale, as does China, a situation many believe has contributed to these countries' current economic woes.

"The rogue capitalism in Russia, and the cronyism and lack of transparency in Asia, aren't good for business there—or here," MacGregor says. "Principled business is not just a theoretical notion; it has pragmatic implica-

The Transparency International 1998 Corruption Perceptions Index

Country Rank	Country	1998 CPI Score	Standard Deviation	Surveys Used	Country Rank	Country	1998 CPI Score	Standard Deviation	Surveys Used
1	Denmark	10.0	0.7	9	44	Zimbabwe	4.2	2.2	6
2	Finland	9.6	0.5	9	45	Malawi	4.1	0.6	4
3	Sweden	9.5	0.5	9	46	Brazil	4.0	0.4	9
4	New Zealand	9.4	0.7	8	47	Belarus	3.9	1.9	3
5	Iceland	9.3	0.9	6	48	Slovak Republic	3.9	1.6	5
6	Canada	9.2	0.5	9	49	Jamaica	3.8	0.4	3
7	Singapore	9.1	1.0	10	50	Morocco	3.7	1.8	3
8	Netherlands	9.0	0.7	9	51	El Salvador	3.6	2.3	3
9	Norway	9.0	0.7	9	52	China	3.5	0.7	10
10	Switzerland	8.9	0.6	10	53	Zambia	3.5	1.6	4
11	Australia	8.7	0.7	8	54	Turkey	3.4	1.0	10
12	Luxembourg	8.7	0.9	7	55	Ghana	3.3	1.0	4
13	United Kingdom	8.7	0.5	10	56	Mexico	3.3	0.6	9
14	Ireland	8.2	1.4	10	57	Philippines	3.3	1.1	10
15	Germany	7.9	0.4	10	58	Senegal	3.3	0.8	3
16	Hong Kong	7.8	1.1	12	59	Ivory Coast	3.1	1.7	4
17	Austria	7.5	0.8	9	60	Guatemala	3.1	2.5	3
18	United States	7.5	0.9	8	61	Argentina	3.0	0.6	9
19	Israel	7.1	1.4	9	62	Nicaragua	3.0	2.5	3
20	Chile	6.8	0.9	9	63	Romania	3.0	1.5	3
21	France	6.7	0.6	9	64	Thailand	3.0	0.7	11
22	Portugal	6.5	1.0	10	65	Yugoslavia	3.0	1.5	3
23	Botswana	6.1	2.2	3	66	Bulgaria	2.9	2.3	4
24	Spain	6.1	1.3	10	67	Egypt	2.9	0.6	3
25	Japan	5.8	1.6	11	68	India	2.9	0.6	12
26	Estonia	5.7	0.5	3	69	Bolivia	2.8	1.2	4
27	Costa Rica	5.6	1.6	5	70	Ukraine	2.8	1.6	6
28	Belgium	5.4	1.4	9	71	Latvia	2.7	1.9	3
29	Malaysia	5.3	0.4	11	72	Pakistan	2.7	1.4	3
30	Namibia	5.3	1.0	3	73	Uganda	2.6	0.8	4
31	Taiwan	5.3	0.7	11	74	Kenya	2.5	0.6	4
32	South Africa	5.2	0.8	10	75	Vietnam	2.5	0.5	6
33	Hungary	5.0	1.2	9	76	Russia	2.4	0.9	10
34	Mauritius	5.0	0.8	3	77	Ecuador	2.3	1.5	3
35	Tunisia	5.0	2.1	3	78	Venezuela	2.3	0.8	9
36	Greece	4.9	1.7	9	79	Colombia	2.2	0.8	9
37	Czech Republic	4.8	0.8	9	80	Indonesia	2.0	0.9	10
38	Jordan	4.7	1.1	6	81	Nigeria	1.9	0.5	5
39	Italy	4.6	0.8	10	82	Tanzania	1.9	1.1	4
40	Poland	4.6	1.6	8	83	Honduras	1.7	0.5	3
41	Peru	4.5	0.8	6	84	Paraguay	1.5	0.5	3
42	Uruguay	4.3	0.9	3	85	Cameroon	1.4	0.5	4
43	South Korea	4.2	1.2	12					

The column 1998 CPI Score relates perceptions of the degree of which corruption is seen by business people—a perfect 10.00 would be a totally corruption-free country. Standard Deviation indicates differences in the values of the sources for the 1998 index: the greater the variance, the greater the differences of perceptions of a country among the sources. The number of surveys used had to be at least 3 for a country to be included in the CPI.

Copyright 1998 Transparency International and Gottingen University.

tions." The belief that moral values such as openness and trust are such an integral part of successful capitalism was even held by capitalism's proud papa, Adam Smith, MacGregor says. Before writing his *Wealth of Nations*, Smith penned a treatise arguing that for capitalism to work it must be based on shared rules and common values. "When you violate those rules, the system doesn't work the way it should," MacGregor warns.

Larry Smeltzer, an ethics professor at the College of Business at Arizona State University, also sees a correlation between ethical standards and economic success. "If you look at the more progressive industrialized countries in the world—Canada, Western Europe, parts of Asia—you find a higher sense of ethics there. It goes hand in hand," Smeltzer says. By contrast, countries with low ethical gauges, such as Mexico and many African countries, have equally scant business norms. "The lack of openness and predictable business standards drives companies away," Smeltzer says. "Why would you want to do business in, say Libya, where you don't know the rules?"

Smeltzer uses the analogy of a pickup football game by some guys in a park. If you just start playing without discussing guidelines, he says, conflict is likely to result. If rules are clearly established beforehand, however, the game will run smoothly. "The need for grease payments in China tells me I'm not clear what the rules there are, so someone has to help me navigate," he says. And, Smeltzer recently wrote in an ethics paper, bribes in China given to establish connections in the government add an estimated 3% to 5% to companies' operating costs.

It was China's troubling ethics climate, in fact, that persuaded Levi Strauss & Co. to exit the market there in 1993, despite the lure of a billion potential denim-clad pairs of legs. Levi's elaborate "principled reasoning approach" demanded a thorough ethical analysis and, says, spokesperson Gavin Power, ethical issues, especially regarding workers rights, were too troubling to permit continued operations. (Having closely followed the situation there since, Levi now says it has identified several trustworthy contractors and it may soon reenter the market.) While the 1993 decision might seem financially irrational, Smeltzer believes that a close analysis shows it made good economic sense. "If the rules for business play are uncertain with respect to its citizens, how can the Chinese government provide assurances of fairness to its potential business citizens?" he reasoned in the ethics paper.

People and Pollution Woes

In addition to the issue of bribes, two other areas are increasingly coming under the hot glare of ethics-watchers: human rights and the environment. American consumers may not get too worked up over "gifts" to foreign partners or government officials, but they will quickly show their displeasure at the thought of mistreated—especially underage—workers, and toxic waste polluting pristine waters and wildernesses around the world.

Even an ethically sensitive company like Levi Strauss can find that navigating international human rights offers tough sailing. The company won great praise for its 1993 China decision, and for its handling of an incident at its Bangladesh plants in 1992. (In the latter incident, the company discovered soon after it had stepped up its campaign to monitor foreign plants that two sewing subcontractors employed young children—a norm in a country where kids without jobs frequently beg or prostitute themselves for money. Levi's cleverly solved the problem by having the contractors remove the children from the factory but continue to pay their wages on condition that they attend school full time. When they reached the local maturity age of 14, they were guaranteed back their jobs.) But even this company's ethics record has rough spots. "They treat most of their workers decently, but go to the Philippines and you will see people working 90 hours a week making Dockers," charges Charles Kernaghan, director of the nonprofit watchdog group the National Labor Committee.

Kernaghan and his group are determined to ensure that American consumers know what companies are doing overseas. His group was behind the Kathie Lee Gifford/Wal-Mart incident of 1996, when Gifford cried on air over accusations that her line was produced in sweatshops around the world employing underaged kids.

Gifford may have thought the issue would disappear when she announced that she had hired independent monitors to check conditions in factories where her line is produced, but the National Labor Committee is bent on assuring that it doesn't. The New York-based group claims some of Gifford's items are still made in sweatshops in China, where women work 84-hour weeks in unsafe factories and live 12 to a room in dirty, watched dorms. "There is a Kathie Lee and Wal-Mart Corporate Code of Conduct, but these workers have never heard of them," Kernaghan says. He also claims that Wal-Mart's campaign to assure Americans that many of its garments are made right here "is very much misleading." The NLC physically counted 105,000 private-label items in 14 stores last year and found that 83% of the items were made offshore, compared to an industry norm of 50% to 60%—a disparity Kernaghan continually points out in his numerous speeches, media contacts, and Web site.

Treating the Earth responsibly has become the third leg of the tripod on which a solid international ethics reputation now rests.

Meanwhile, treating the Earth responsibly has become the third leg of the tripod on which a solid international ethics reputation now rests. "The environment is an area of concern for companies involved with global ethics plans," says Bob Echols, manager of international

CAUX ROUND TABLE GENERAL PRINCIPLES

1. The Responsibilities of Businesses: Beyond Shareholders Toward Stakeholders. Businesses have a role to play in improving the lives of all their customers, employees, and shareholders by sharing with them the wealth they have created. Suppliers and competitors as well should expect businesses to honor their obligations in a spirit of honesty and fairness.

2. The Economic and Social Impact of Business: Toward Innovation, Justice, and World Community. Businesses established in foreign countries to develop, produce, or sell should also contribute to the social advancement of those countries by creating productive employment and helping to raise the purchasing power of their citizens. Businesses also should contribute to human rights, education, welfare, and vitalization of the countries in which they operate.

Businesses should contribute to economic and social development not only in the countries in which they operate, but also in the world community at large, through effective and prudent use of resources, free and fair competition, and emphasis upon innovation in technology, production methods, marketing, and communications.

3. Business Behavior: Beyond the Letter of Law Toward a Spirit of Trust. While accepting the legitimacy of trade secrets, businesses should recognize that sincerity, candor, truthfulness, the keeping of promises, and transparency contribute not only to their own credibility and stability but also to the smoothness and efficiency of business transactions, particularly on the international level.

4. Respect for Rules. To avoid trade frictions and to promote freer trade, equal conditions for competition, and fair and equitable treatment for all participants, businesses should respect international and domestic rules. In addition, they should recognize that some behavior, although legal, may still have adverse consequences.

5. Support for Multilateral Trade. Businesses should support the multilateral trade systems of the GATT/ World Trade Organization and similar international agreements. They should cooperate in efforts to promote the progressive and judicious liberalization of trade and to relax those domestic measures that unreasonably hinder global commerce, while giving due respect to national policy objectives.

6. Respect for the Environment. A business should protect and, where possible, improve, the environment, promote sustainable development, and prevent the wasteful use of natural resources.

7. Avoidance of Illicit Operations. A business should not participate in or condone bribery, money laundering, or other corrupt practices: Indeed, it should seek cooperation with others to eliminate them. It should not trade in arms or other materials used for terrorist activities, drug traffic, or other organized crime.

---

compliance at Raytheon Company, in Lexington, Mass., which is currently rolling out an ambitious worldwide plan in the 80 countries in which it does business.

Caux's MacGregor cites three reasons for the increased interest. First, American and international reporters are now likely to write about the chemical waste a company dumps far away in a river in China. Second, he says, the increasing recognition that environmental actions in one part of the world affect all others is leading business people to consider their own children and neighbors, though they live thousands of miles away from the pollution. And third, MacGregor says, there is cost. "If you are dumping waste out the back door [even in an undeveloped country], eventually you will have to spend the money cleaning it up," he says.

What To Do—And Not Do

How does a company doing business internationally navigate these ethical storm waters? According to the experts, by implementing a true ethics program with teeth, not by merely trotting out a piece of paper. And by recognizing that, despite cultural differences, certain core ethical values are held by all people around the globe.

Writing a code of ethics that clearly states what's expected of employees is a typical first step. Then you need to get input on the proposed code from foreign nationals, perhaps via committees made up of people from the various affected cultures. "Often, this is where companies begin to do it wrong," says W. Michael Hoffman, executive director of the Center for Business Ethics at Bentley College in Waltham, Massachusetts. "They take their code of ethics and translate it into foreign languages, and Joe sends it over to Juan and Hans overseas with instructions to roll it out to their divisions. But because it doesn't mesh with their culture and they don't understand why they should care, these guys don't support it." For example, Hoffman says, without a firm rationale, Japanese will not readily follow a rule that says they should not accept expensive gifts, because presents are an integral part of that society and to refuse such a gift often humiliates the giver.

How to report ethical violations is also sometimes culture-specific. "In France, Germany, and other European countries, it has been my experience that employees are very reluctant to raise an issue regarding a fellow employee," Raytheon's Echols says. Raytheon's solution is to provide numerous reporting mechanisms—ranging from phoning or faxing the corporate headquarters to speaking face-to-face with a local ethics contact, to mailing in an anonymous, postage-paid card—so the staffer can choose the one most comfortable to him. Echols is also investigating incorporating an ethics section in his company's Web site, and allowing staffers to send confidential information that way.

Once signed off on by all the affected cultures, the ethical code must then become a living document for employees. Each worker must be clear how to apply that code to everyday actions. At Minneapolis-based Honeywell Inc., which has nearly half its employees outside the U.S., senior management regularly emphasizes ethics in its regional newsletters. One such publication for the Asia-Pacific, for example, carried a message from the president that the company would prefer to lose business rather than succumb to paying a bribe. An ethics advice line encourages employees to discuss ethical decisions they are unclear about. The company, which recently rewrote its code to be less focused on the U.S. and more applicable globally, also conducts training around the world. The codes various aspects, from child labor issues to gifts and gratuities, are enumerated specifically in its code of ethics handbook.

Businesses that employ factory workers around the globe are turning to independent monitors to watch out for employee rights overseas.

More and more businesses that employ factory workers around the globe are also turning to independent monitors to watch out for employees rights overseas. The National Labor Committee favors using local religious and human-rights groups to do that job, but companies largely seem to be favoring monitoring by such auditing groups as Pricewaterhouse Coopers and Ernst & Young. Once abuses are discovered, they must be swiftly resolved. "We either work with our subcontractor to correct the problems, or if that can't be done we will and have terminated our relationship with them," Levi's Power says.

Honeywell has put teeth into its ethical principles by making adherence to the company's code a condition of employment. "Sometimes the situation is clear enough that termination is the appropriate response, and we have fired people for violating the code," says Lisa Dercks, vice president and ethics officer at Honeywell. Such consequences are important for telling employees that top management takes this topic seriously, Bentley's Hoffman says. Other companies take the opposite approach, basing employee compensation in part on adherence to ethical codes.

When drafting its code of ethics, companies must strike a balance between being sensitive to foreign cultures and their own internal sense of right and wrong. "The two extremes are ethical fanaticism, which says my way is always right, and ethical relativism, which says there are no absolutes," Hoffman says. However, there are several absolute ethical standards that everyone in the world agrees with, "and these become your core values," he says, pointing to the Caux General Principles as a good starting point for corporate discussion (see box, "Caux Round Table General Principles").

"The process that you set up to ensure that you're making solid ethical decisions is key," Hoffman says. "If you follow the process, you can be comfortable with your decision, even if other ethical companies might come to a different conclusion."

Meryl Davids, a business journalist based in Coral Springs, Fla., frequently writes for JBS.

From *Journal of Business Strategy*, January/February 1999, pp. 38–43. © 1999 by Faulkner & Gray. Reprinted by permission.

UNIT 4

Ethics and Social Responsibility in the Marketplace

Unit Selections

Key Points to Consider

- What responsibility does an organization have to reveal product defects to consumers?

- Given the competitivesness of the business arena, is it possible for marketing personnel to behave ethically and both survive and prosper? Explain. Give suggestions that could be incorporated into the marketing strategy for firms that want to be both ethical and successful.

- Name some organizations that make you feel genuinely valued as a customer. What are the characteristics of these organizations that distinguish them from their competitors? Explain.

- Which area of marketing strategy is most subject to public scrutiny in regard to ethics--product, pricing, place, or promotion? Why? Give some examples of unethical techniques or strategies involving each of these four areas.

 **Links: www.dushkin.com/online/**
These sites are annotated in the World Wide Web pages.

Business for Social Responsibility (BSR)
http://www.bsr.org/

Total Quality Management Sites
http://www.nku.edu/~lindsay/qualhttp.html

U.S. Navy
http://www.navy.mil

From a consumer viewpoint, the marketplace is the "proof of the pudding" or the place where the "rubber meets the road" for business ethics. In other words, what the company has promulgated about the virtues of its product or service has little meaning if the company's actual marketing practices and its treatment of the consumer contradict its claims.

At its core, marketing has a very noble and moral purpose: to satisfy human needs and wants and to help people through the exchange process. Marketing involves the coordination of the variables of product, price, place, and promotion to address effectively and efficiently the needs of consumers. Unfortunately, at times the unethical marketing practices of some firms have cast a shadow of suspicion over marketing in general. Since marketing is the aspect of business that is most visible to the public, it has perhaps taken a disproportionate share of the criticism directed toward the free-enterprise system.

This unit takes a careful look at the strategic process and practice of incorporating ethics into the marketplace. The first subsection, *Marketing Strategy and Ethics,* contains three articles describing how marketing strategy and ethics can be integrated in the marketplace. The first article, "The Perils of Doing the Right Thing," describes the difficulties some companies have encountered when attempting to do the right thing. The last two articles in this subsection scrutinize ways of improving marketing practices on the Internet.

In the next subsection, *Ethical Practices in the Marketplace,* the first article delineates the importance of having an organizational culture that encourages and supports sound ethical behavior and socially responsible business practices. The next selection reflects a creative approach that has helped companies grow bigger and stronger by going green. The "100 Best Corporate Citizens" reflects a ranking of some of America's most profitable and socially responsible public companies.

147

The Perils of Doing the Right Thing

By Andrew W. Singer

At a May 11 press conference, Ford Motor Co. released its first-ever "corporate citizenship" report. In the 98-page document, titled "Connecting With Society," the company acknowledged serious concerns about its highly profitable sport utility vehicles. Not only do SUVs pollute the air and guzzle gas at rates far higher than conventional automobiles, the report conceded, they may be hazardous to other drivers.

Ford's was an unusual announcement. SUVs, after all, contribute about half of the company's earnings. The public's taste for these vehicles has shown no sign of waning. And even though they're three times as likely as cars to kill the other driver in a crash, the government has yet to declare these vehicles inherently unsafe.

What, then, was the company doing announcing that it had problems with these immensely popular, high-margin vehicles?

The front page of the next day's *New York Times* noted that Ford scion and chairman William Clay Ford Jr., whose family controls 40 percent of the company's voting shares, "has been active in environmental causes since his days at prep school and at Princeton" and was now worried "that car makers could get reputations like those of tobacco companies" if they ignored these problems. (The company did *not* pledge to stop producing SUVs, however.)

The company has been lauded for its candor. Veteran automobile-industry analyst Mary Ann Keller, now an executive with Priceline.com Inc., calls the announcement a "welcome instance of leadership." Norman Bowie, Dixons Professor of Business Ethics and Social Responsibility at London Business School, describes Ford's decision as "significant and courageous."

What makes the company's action noteworthy is that it carries real risks. According to Bowie, the biggest danger is a "backlash" among current and prospective SUV owners, who could begin to think the cars dangerous.

"Public tastes are fickle," says Brock Yates, editor-at-large of *Car and Driver*. "No one anticipated the surge in interest in SUVs, and like all fads it could disappear." And credit agency Standard & Poor's has warned that "[t]he automaker's stability could be affected if the sport-utility market slumped."

Before one proclaims a new era of social responsibility, then—as some did in the wake of the Ford press conference—one would do well to pause. Good corporate citizenship is praiseworthy, of course. But it isn't always easy. Indeed, if one looks at the experiences of other companies once acclaimed as "leaders," it is a decidedly mixed history. For all their high promise and initial acclaim, many firms later emerged scarred and chastened, victims of public derision, consumer boycotts, shareholder rebellion, and even bankruptcy.

If Ford does follow through on its exemplary course, it might do well to consider some of the lessons learned by other companies—often the hard way:

Lesson No. 1: Make sure what you are doing is really leadership— and not just self-adulation.

When asked about Ford's quandary—financial dependence on a product that carries potential environmental and safety problems—Bentley College business ethicist W. Michael Hoffman responds, "You can be ethical, and smart too."

Hoffman recalls a story recounted at a 1977 Bentley ethics conference, about a small paper company located on a polluted

New England stream. At a celebration of the first Earth Day, the mill's owner "got religion." He spent $2.5 million in an effort to clean up the company's effluent and, several months later, went broke, since he couldn't compete with other paper companies that didn't follow his example. He was unrepentant, though, "encased in a kind of angelic halo as he spoke of the necessity of clean water and sacrificing material things for spiritual ends." When it was pointed out that the water was no cleaner overall, he said, "Well, that's those other 17 fellows upstream."

"He went out of business, and he put 500 people out of work," Hoffman says. "But he felt ethically pure. That's just crazy." He describes the mill owner's attempt to "do it on his own" as a typically individualistic, American response.

Ford Motor could behave like the mill owner—act alone—and simply stop making SUVs. But that could be financially disastrous. "Ford's executives can do other things," Hoffman continues. "If they are truly concerned about a product but know they can't disarm unilaterally, then they have to work diligently within their industry and with government."

Cornell University economist Robert H. Frank says that the fact that Ford is concerned "is a positive thing." But this is "a collective-action problem," he says. "It's not a matter of Ford breaking any law." The solution Frank suggests: William Clay Ford should sit down with the U.S. secretary of transportation and work something out; a possible solution might involve instituting new passenger-vehicle taxes based on weight, emission levels, and fuel economy.

In late July, Ford took another step, announcing that it had decided to increase the fuel economy of its SUVs by 25 percent over the next five years. Its main competitor, General Motors, bristled: Vice chairman Harry Pearce expressed annoyance at Ford's claim of being "somehow the environmental leader." GM, he insisted, is and will be far superior to Ford in the area of fuel economy. On the other hand, the company is proceeding with full production of the 7,000-plus-pound Hummer, a version of the Humvee, a military transport made famous in the Gulf War.

Lesson No. 2: Be prepared to be attacked by virtue of your virtue.

H.B. Fuller Co., a Minneapolis-based adhesives manufacturer, enjoyed a reputation as one of America's most socially responsible companies. It endowed a chair in the study of business ethics at the University of Minnesota and established a charitable foundation dedicated to the environment, the arts, and social programs. Minnesotans regarded longtime president Elmer L. Andersen so highly that they elected him governor in 1960.

But beginning in the late 1980s, the company was dogged by reports that one of its adhesives, Resistol, had become the drug of choice for glue-sniffing street kids in Central America.

H.B. Fuller seemed unprepared for the furor that arose over the abuse of one of its products. "It's a social problem. It's not a product problem," the company argued. Still, it pulled the product off retail shelves in Guatemala and Honduras.

That didn't stop activists from protesting Fuller's continued marketing of Resistol to industrial customers, and to retailers in neighboring countries. Activists picketed annual shareholder meetings and brought wrongful-death suits against the company. "At risk are millions of dollars and the reputations of the company's top leaders," noted the Minneapolis *Star Tribune*.

How could such a well-regarded company become ensnared in such a circumstance? After all, Fuller's competitors were manufacturing and marketing glue in Latin America at the time, and impoverished street kids were abusing their products too. "But no one expected much of those companies," says Bowie. Social critics mostly gave them a free pass.

Unfortunately, "If you do something ethical, and then market it, and there's a little failure, you get hammered," says Bowie, who adds that company leaders were perhaps not as "proactive as they should have been."

Michael G. Daigneault, president of the nonprofit Ethics Resource Center in Washington, D.C., observes, "There are risks inherent in being perceived as, or fostering the perception of being, an exceptionally ethical or socially responsible organization. People will hold you to that standard."

This isn't to say that such a reputation is not positive. But it can backfire, particularly if a company is "overzealous" in promoting itself in this area. Daigneault says that companies that have made absolute statements—like Wal-Mart Stores Inc. claiming that all of its products are made in the United States, or Tom's of Maine Inc. insisting that all of its products are "natural"—have sometimes invited criticism. "The irony," he says, "is that a lot of these organizations have the best intentions, and many actually walk the talk—99 percent of the time." But the 1 percent of the time that they slip up, someone will be waiting for them.

Lesson No. 3: Expect to have your motives questioned and your leadership credentials challenged.

"The only thing good without qualification is a good will," wrote Immanuel Kant. In business, however, it's often difficult to distinguish goodwill from economic self-interest.

Consider the case of Smith & Wesson, the nation's largest handgun manufacturer. In March, the company entered into an agreement with federal, state, and local governments to restrict the sale of handguns. The company agreed to sell only to "authorized dealers and distributors" that would conform to a code of conduct. Among other things, this required dealers to conduct background checks on buyers at gun shows, and it put some restrictions on multiple gun sales. No other gun manufacturer signed the agreement.

On some fronts, Smith & Wesson was celebrated for its commitment. President Clinton observed that "it took a lot of courage" for the company to sign the agreement in the face of industry resistance. Housing and Urban Development secretary Andrew Cuomo described the settlement as "the most important announcement" during his tenure at HUD, and added, "The principles of the agreement will provide a framework for a new, enlightened gun policy for this nation."

Target of Criticism

"No loaded firearms or live ammunition beyond this point," reads the sign on the front door of Smith & Wesson's headquarters in Springfield, Mass.—a reminder that this is not your average business. Nor was there anything quite ordinary about the industry reaction to the firearms manufacturer's decision to accept some restrictions on its handgun sales.

Smith & Wesson CEO Edward Shultz says he wasn't surprised by the response to the firm's March 17 settlement announcement. "When you take this sort of step, you don't do it without a lot of thought. Certainly, it would have been easier to go with the crowd."

The National Rifle Association denounced Smith & Wesson, the nation's largest gun maker, for surrendering to the Clinton administration. NRA president Charlton Heston asserted that Smith & Wesson's British owner, Tomkins PLC, places less value on the Second Amendment right to bear arms than Americans do. The attorney general of Connecticut warned of "extreme elements that want to punish [Smith & Wesson] or retaliate against it for doing the right thing."

Why such a strong reaction? "We're dealing with the most anti-gun administration in recent history," says Shultz. The fact that S&W is even talking to the Clinton administration "irritates folks."

Still, Shultz says, he hadn't counted on the breadth of the detractors. The majority of S&W customers agree with the company's actions, he asserts. But its move seems to have "had an impact on anyone who owns a firearm." It's as if an automaker had installed safety air bags before any of its competitors and "it angered not just its customers but anyone who owned a car."

Shultz says he understands the emotions of the critics. As a boy in eastern Iowa, he "grew up with guns as a part of [his] daily life. But my head says that the world is changing and we will have to get in harmony with it."

Lawsuits against gun makers—who are being held partly responsible for bloodshed like that which rocked Columbine High School last year—will continue for the next five to 10 years, he predicts. "When you have the federal government after you, and the states, and lots of the cities, it's hard to say that all these people are wrong and you're right."

Will the company be stronger in the long run for signing the agreement? "Our belief was that if we didn't make this decision, we would go out of business," due to ceaseless, costly litigation. "This way, we can still prosper."

Significantly, perhaps, when New York became the first state to take the firearms-manufacturing industry to court in late June, Smith & Wesson was not named in the lawsuit. Local governments have since dropped S&W from lawsuits, too. Meanwhile, though, "The rest of the industry has held fast," noted *The New York Times*. No other gun maker signed the agreement, which requires manufacturers to take steps such as installing safety locks on guns.

Shultz has been working in the consumer-goods sector for 37 years, the last nine of which he has spent in the firearms industry. "I came from the outside to make a change here" because the company was in some financial trouble in 1992. At that time, "I never dreamed of the things that we face today in the legal and political arena."

He says that what S&W is doing is viewed as a huge compromise because it's voluntary, rather than mandated by laws and regulations. Inevitably, though, the firearms industry has to go through change. "Change is expensive, it's painful, and it involves some risk," he says.

"I've spent most of my career dealing with conflicts relating to change," Shultz says. "If I retire, it will probably be from one change too many."

—A.W.S.

Reaction was somewhat less approving in other quarters, however. The National Rifle Association and the National Shooting Sports Foundation (NSSF) denounced Smith & Wesson for "selling out" the industry and called for an immediate boycott of the company's products. (See "Target of Criticism.")

Still, Smith & Wesson CEO Edward Shultz says he's comfortable with his decision. Standards of social responsibility change, he says: "We can't operate as we did in 1935 or 1955 or 1975 and still be described as responsible." In 1955, a customer could order a gun out of a catalog, and the weapon would be delivered to that person's house. "Today, that would be viewed as totally irresponsible," he says.

"From a pure business standpoint, it makes sense to find a solution," Shultz continues. "To understand what's going on, you have to get in a conversation with the people trying to put you out of business," like anti-handgun groups. It also made sense to "settle," given the numbers of lawsuits being brought against the firearms industry in the wake of the Columbine shooting and other acts of carnage. "Rather than go out of business paying for lawsuits, if we go out of business, it will be because customers refuse to buy our products," he says.

Opposition to the company's position proved more lasting and damaging than anticipated. Some dealers refused to sell S&W products, incensed by the code of conduct that the manufacturer imposed on them. In June, Smith & Wesson announced that it was suspending firearms manufacturing at two New England factories for three weeks. It acknowledged that a contributing factor was "the reaction of some consumers to the agreement Smith & Wesson signed with federal, state and local government entities."

"I don't think they anticipated the severity of the response," says Robert Delfay, president and CEO of the NSSF, the largest firearms-industry trade group. Many members saw it as an infringement of their Second Amendment right to bear arms.

Also, inevitably, some critics saw the firm's actions as a matter of sheer expediency. "I don't view what Smith & Wesson did as leadership," Delfay says. "We think it was capitulation to strong-arm tactics by government officials." As he sees it, the gun makers showing real leadership are those that haven't "capitulated to government blackmail."

"Was that a decision of conscience?" asks ethicist Mark Pastin, president of the Council of Ethics Organizations in Alexandria, Va., of the S&W action. "Or a response to what the market demands of the company?"

Consultant Eileen Shapiro, author of *The Seven Deadly Sins of Business*, insists that Smith & Wesson's decision *did* represent a leadership position, because it involved real action: "They did something that matched their rhetoric."

It's not exceptional that some ambiguity attends the gun maker's action. Few business actions, after all, are ethically "pure." Most are a kind of double helix: one strand virtue, the other economic self-interest. It is almost impossible to disentangle the two.

Shapiro, for one, disputes that Ford Motor took any leadership position with its May announcement. Ford isn't redeploying any of its assets. It will still build SUVs. Moreover, she says, "This guy [William Ford] actually drives an SUV!"

A week after the Ford press conference, automobile-industry watcher Brock Yates said, "Internally, we're hearing a lot of concern and confusion. It's seen as a hollow gesture. The grandest gesture would have been to cancel the Excursion, which has become a paradigm for SUV evil."

In sum, even when a company takes a socially responsible stance, it should still expect to have its moral bona fides questioned. Ed Shultz speaks from experience: "Leadership is never very popular, particularly if decisions are made to change and to move forward."

Lesson No. 4: Circumstances beyond your control—including public hysteria—can undermine your position.

In the early 1990s, chemicals manufacturer Monsanto Co. placed a big bet on an exciting new business: sustainable agriculture. It committed its resources to developing seemingly miraculous genetically altered crops—cotton that could be grown without pesticides, tomatoes altered to ripen slowly, potatoes that were insect-resistant.

"Monsanto is in a unique position to contribute to the global future," gushed prominent biodiversity advocate Peter Raven at

a "global forum" in 1995. "Because of your skills, your dedication, and your understanding, you are equal to the challenge."

The first breakthrough had come two years earlier, in November 1993. After nine years of investigation, the FDA approved the use of Monsanto's bovine growth hormone (marketed under the name of Posilac), which when injected into a cow's pituitary gland increased milk output by 25 percent.

Monsanto spent $1 billion to develop Posilac, with Wall Street's approval. Posilac, after all, was the first of perhaps dozens of genetically altered agricultural products to be introduced in years ahead. The profits anticipated would fill company coffers.

The company's CEO, Robert B. Shapiro, was acclaimed as a visionary. "Bob Shapiro displayed enormous vision in committing the company to sustainable business practices" that neither deplete the world of resources nor damage the environment, noted Robert H. Dunn, president of Business for Social Responsibility, a San Francisco-based membership organization.

Only a few years later, however, things had gone terribly wrong with Monsanto's new direction. A wave of protesters had arisen to campaign against Posilac, and foreign governments were beginning to pay attention. In 1998, a British researcher declared on television that eating genetically modified (GM) potatoes could stunt rats' growth. A Cornell University study contended that pollen from GM corn harmed butterflies.

Europe resisted the U.S.-dominated GM crop business; supermarket chains rejected foods containing GM ingredients. France, citing the precautionary principle, ordered the destruction of hundreds of hectares of rapeseed that had been accidentally planted with seeds containing GM material. Brazil sent out police to burn GM crops. U.S. food processors, such as Archer Daniels Midland Co., advised suppliers to segregate GM from non-GM crops.

Environmentalists turned on Monsanto. Greenpeace told the European Union that it "cannot continue to let GMOs [genetically modified organisms] contaminate our food and environment."

All of this battered the company's share price. Early this year, one analyst noted that "investors have valued Monsanto's $5 billion-a-year agricultural-business unit at less than zero dollars during the past week."

What happened? "In ethics, some stands look appropriate at the time," Bowie observes. But then circumstances change, or science changes, "or people get hysterical—so what looked like a good decision at one time no longer looks like a good decision."

When Bowie asked his London students this past summer why the reaction against GM foods was so severe—why the "hysteria"—they answered: "We don't trust the government." In part, this was because of the British government's belated response to the dangers of "mad cow" disease, which it long downplayed. Asks Bowie: "How could Monsanto anticipate that students wouldn't trust their government because of mad cow disease?"—and by extension, that they wouldn't believe the government when it insisted that GM foods were safe?

"You can't rationalize emotions," says one analyst who follows the company but asked not to be identified in this article.

151

"[Robert] Shapiro felt that the Green Movement didn't have a rational case," and so the company was reluctant to modify its position. "They should have been more sensitive to the perception of these bold moves. They didn't lay the groundwork."

Ironically, in June, the Paris-based Organization for Economic Cooperation and Development—once at the heart of the GM opposition—announced that genetically modified crops approved for human consumption are as safe as other foods. The announcement may have come a bit late, however, for Robert Shapiro and Monsanto. The company was acquired by Pharmacia & Upjohn Inc. last December—for a price considerably lower than what it could have fetched a few years earlier. Robert Shapiro was slated to be "non-executive" chairman of the merged company for 18 months, and then give way to a successor.

"In the end, Shapiro was a trailblazer," concludes the analyst. One day, the world may view positively the company's technological achievement, the medical applications, the improved yields from these crops. "There is a future, but perhaps the market wasn't ready for them."

Given the costs that some of the companies mentioned here—H.B. Fuller, Monsanto, Smith & Wesson, the New England mill owner—have paid, one might well ask: Does social responsibility pay? Does it make economic sense to take a leadership position where the environment or corporate citizenship is involved?

For years, many have asserted that good ethics is good business, Pastin observes. "But there were no examples. Now there are examples, but they are hard to interpret." There has never been systemic, credible evidence that good ethics indeed leads to good financial results, he notes.

That said, some view Ford Motor's May announcement as evidence of a new era of social responsibility. "Ford has definitely demonstrated leadership as one of the first large, global companies to file a social report as a companion to its financial report," says Dunn of Business for Social Responsibility. The company "instilled in the report a spirit of candor, acknowledging the issues it must address."

Ford has "obviously learned the lesson" of the last 20 years regarding such matters—namely, "that companies that are honest and forthright are forgiven by the public, but those that stonewall earn the public's enmity," says Booz-Allen & Hamilton leadership consultant James O'Toole, whose guess is

that Ford has enough data to conclude that the safety and environmental problems regarding SUVs are real. Moreover, the automaker might have a similar problem to that of the tobacco industry: By sitting on the data, it risks lawsuits later.

By acting in an honest, straightforward manner, the companies expect to be treated accordingly by the public. "Ford is trying to establish its credentials, give itself credibility," O'Toole says. "Young William Ford is laying the foundation of trust."

"I think we're entering a new age of corporate citizenship in which candor will be rewarded," says veteran PR executive Robert Dilenschneider. "Younger people—young CEOs—are willing to stick their necks out farther than the older generation. Bill Ford is a perfect example."

Others note a certain irony here. "It's interesting that it's the Ford Motor Co. that has seen fit to come forward to talk about some safety and environmental problems with SUVs," says Bentley College's Hoffman. "Maybe it has something to do with the lessons learned from the business-ethics movement."

One of the landmark cases in that movement, after all, was the 1979 Ford Pinto case, in which the state of Indiana indicted Ford on charges of criminal homicide after a rear-ended Pinto burst into flames, killing a passenger. "It made world headlines and sent reverberations through Corporate America," Hoffman says.

Even though Ford was eventually acquitted, it "was found guilty in the court of public opinion, as well as in civil cases," particularly when it was disclosed that the company had conducted a cost-benefit analysis to determine whether it should improve safety by adding a $5.08 bladder to fuel tanks—and opted not to do so. The negative public reaction "sent a message to Corporate America," Hoffman says, "that the American public would be watching corporations more carefully in terms of their social responsibility and ethical commitment."

Given the history of other companies that took a lead in "doing the right thing," though, Ford shouldn't expect an unhindered path toward an enlightened future. There are real risks with tampering with the SUV business model: risks to the company's profits, its share price, and its reputation.

ANDREW W. SINGER is publisher and co-editor of Ethikos, *a Mamaroneck, N.Y.-based publication that examines ethical and compliance issues in business. He is writing a book on the perils of corporate leadership. His last article was a review of* When Pride Still Mattered *in the February issue.*

Ethical Marketing for Competitive Advantage on the Internet

Claire Gauzente

LARGO University of Angers

Ashok Ranchhod

Southampton Business School

Executive Summary

Marketing practice is now busy integrating the potential of information and communication technologies through the utilization of databases and Internet marketing. Billions of potential consumers can now be reached this way. Nevertheless, a brief observation of the practices of marketing on the Internet show that some firms implement aggressive actions such as pop-ups, deceiving banners and hyperlinks and other forms of intrusive mechanisms which impinge on personal privacy. As technology moves from desk based PC applications to mobile communications, there is potential to become even more intrusive, with the possibility of local tracking (within a 50 metre radius of a food or retail outlet).

Given the fact that such powerful devices will become the norm within two to five years, we advocate that firms that wish to differentiate themselves from their competitors will have to turn to marketing ethics in order to gain and keep consumers. Short-term thinking will push firms towards ever shorter campaigns and advertising plans, pushing companies towards an unethical stance. This danger can be averted by firms adopting a proactive ethical attitude towards consumers within their e-marketing strategies. In order to adopt such a proactive stance, companies need to develop a model of ethical interactivity with consumers. The model of ethical interactivity that is introduced and discussed in the paper, develops seven types of practice (notice, choice, access, contact, security, horizon, and intrusiveness). Correct interpretation of these practices leads to empowered consumers creating greater benefits for the firm and for the consumers themselves.

Keywords: Online privacy, Internet, Ethical behavior, Long-term competitiveness

"The function within business firms most often charged with ethical abuse is Marketing"
Murphy and Laczniak, 1981 (p. 251)

The development of internet-based technologies opens endless possibilities for Marketers. Marketing research can be carried out subtly by actively archiving the procedures that each individual undertakes on the Web, through Web tracking software. Thus making a whole new set of variables available to the marketer. The technological opportunities are obviously highly appealing for Marketers to explore and use extensively and intensively. However, we suggest that exploiting all these opportunities can be a threat to marketing performance in the long run. Technology has no inherent morality and the way in which it is utilized is what really matters. In this matter, both the deontological as well as the utilitarian view of ethics (Bergman, 1997) apply. Paying close attention to the ethical aspects of the use of web-based technologies in marketing might constitute a differentiating force for proactive firms.

In a first section, we will discuss current marketing practices on the Internet and propose 7 criteria for judging the ethicalness of marketing practices. In the second section, we develop the potential advantages of ethical marketing on the Internet.

Delineating Ethical Marketing Practices

The observation of marketing practice on the Internet can give an idea of the types of unethical practices that are either already in place or recommended by certain marketing consultancy sites. A simple analysis of many sites highlights two important issues. The first one is concerned with the gathering of consumer information and the second one is concerned with the utilization of various marketing techniques. These are many and varied ranging from banners to fixed spot advertisements and flash advertisements and the selling or exchange of consumer information.

Gathering Information—The Issue of Consumer Information Privacy

As Kelly (2000) notes, Internet technology provides opportunities to gather consumer information "on an unprecedented scale"". However some aspects of information gathering are visible (such as self-divulgence of information for purchase, self-divulgence of information in accessing a web-site, self-divulgence of information for free merchandise) and some are less visible (such as anonymous profile data, IP, cookies). Owing to these possible uses and abuses of information, many consumers remain hesitant about Internet purchasing. The development of software allowing "private Internet experience" and 'completely undetected surfing' is an indication of consumer concern regarding the invasion of privacy. A survey of the top 100 commercial web sites shows that only 20 per cent apply a full ethical policy. This shows that there is room for the development of competitive advantage (Culnan, 1999a and b). Culnan's reports on Internet privacy policy show that five aspects can used to describe a web site's position concerning privacy:

1. Notice, that is an indication to the consumer about what information is collected, how it will be used; whether is will be disclosed to third parties and whether cookies are used or not.
2. Choice: is the consumer given the choice to agree with aspects of information gathering?
3. Access: does the consumer have access to the information gathered? Is the consumer given the possibility to review and correct the information?
4. Security concerns the protection of information transfer and subsequent storage.
5. Contact: are consumers given a contact person or address for asking questions or registering complaints regarding privacy?

Using Information—The Issue of Marketing Tools

Advertising is an important marketing tool on the Internet with a range of possibilities for customer interactivity and involvement (Ranchhod, 1998). Banner advertising has been an important vehicle for many Internet based advertisements with much research dedicated to its design elements. At the same time, marketing professionals try to understand how individuals surf through websites and consequently attempt to increase the CTR (click-through ratio). In this respect, researchers as well as practitioners try to identify key variables: type and size of ad banners, animation, use of color, sounds, images, incen-

tives, etc (see http://www.bannertips.com/). Certain practices can be observed and are recommended as efficient ones: pop-ups, deceiving banners (computer-like messages, with "ok" button). Here are some excerpts from the advice given for designing an efficient banner:

- Feature a Call To Action,
- Create Urgency,
- Use the Word "FREE,"
- Certain truisms remain true—intrigue and sex sell

Parallel to Internet advertising, the development of e-mail marketing and spam are features of aggressive e-marketing.

Judging Marketing Practices

In the field of advertising, Nwachukwu et al. (1997) found that three variables are important for judging the ethical nature of an ad: individual autonomy, consumer sovereignty and harmfulness of product. These ideas are utilized to assess specific ads and to assess sovereignty in terms of consumer awareness of a product's use and availability. Individual autonomy refers to the ability of the individual to recognize the manipulative power of advertising. Consumer sovereignty refers to the level of knowledge and sophistication of the target audience (e.g. the marketing of infant formula in less developed countries illustrates low consumer sovereignty). Lastly, harmfulness of product refers to the nature of the product (advertising for cigarettes can be deemed unethical as the product is detrimental to people's health). On the Internet, harmfulness could be defined by the advertising of pornography or harmful visual imagery.

Other aspects that surely need to be considered in Internet advertising are the levels of ad intrusiveness and personal privacy. Figure 1 illustrates how some areas of Internet advertising compare with general advertising tactics. (see figure 1).

The model shows how individual autonomy, consumer sovereignty and harmfulness of product interact with the seven factors that are shown. The composite of seven factors in addition to Culnan's (op. cit.) factors of notice, choice, contact, security and access, include horizon (time element) and intrusiveness. We feel that the time element, in terms of how long companies can access customer information is important as is the degree of intrusiveness as shown in Figure 1.

These seven factors could be used to evaluate the overall degree of ethical interactivity of a company on the Internet. A zero level (or minimum) ethical stance corresponds to an offer of notice and security (see table 1) However, as noted by Culnan (op. cit), the level of disclosure can range from a comprehensive privacy policy notice (PPN) to a discrete statement. This might be difficult

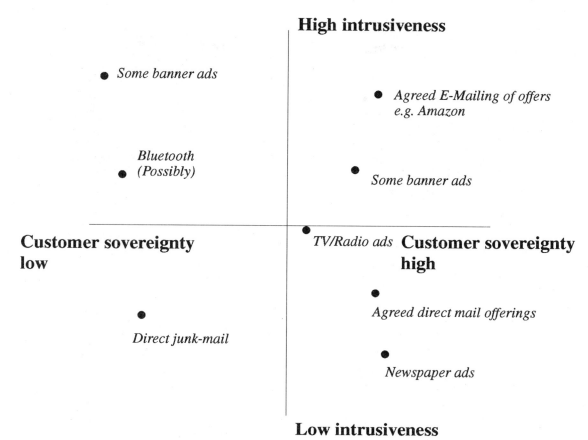

High intrusiveness

● *Some banner ads*

● *Agreed E-Mailing of offers e.g. Amazon*

Bluetooth (Possibly) ●

● *Some banner ads*

Customer sovereignty low

● *TV/Radio ads* **Customer sovereignty high**

● *Agreed direct mail offerings*

● *Direct junk-mail*

● *Newspaper ads*

Low intrusiveness

FIGURE 1 throws some light on how advertising on the Internet can impinge on customer autonomy and sovereignty by being intrusive and disrespectful of personal privacy. If we consider the key factors pointed out by Nwachukwu et al., take into account Culnan's (op.cit.) criteria of online privacy and add intrusiveness to the mix, it is possible to create a model for understanding and judging ethical marketing practices on the Internet. This model is illustrated in FIGURE 2.

to provide as customer details can be either gathered from the home page or through hyperlinks to the home page. Nonetheless, paying attention to these two factors show the degree of ethical concern afforded to the consumer by a company.

We would consider that a comprehensive PPN linked from the homepage and the highest level of security are the minimal level that firms should aspire to in order to exhibit a reasonable degree of ethical behavior on the Internet. However, this may not be entirely sufficient and a higher levels of ethical interactivity should also be considered by most firms. Higher levels of ethical interactivity can be offered by a serious consideration of the five other criteria, which are choice, contact, access, horizon, intrusiveness. Each of these in its own right helps to improve the levels of ethical interactivity undertaken by a firm as depicted in Table 1.

All these factors help to create *consumer empowerment*. Not only should consumers be given the chance to self disclose private information, they should also be given the opportunity to clearly and precisely agree on the manner in which it will be used. In particular, the level of intrusive-

ness of marketing techniques could be agreed upon, as some consumers are open to a variety of techniques, looking at them as sources of information. However in some cases, intrusions may simply be considered to be fun, such as the viral marketing strategy adopted for a computer game (http://www.missingsheep.com/). For others an official letter of introduction may be the only way forward. Consumers should also be made aware of the frequency of contact, choosing their own level frequency. The horizon criterion relates to the time frame in which the information will be utilized. Here again, consumers could choose to receive marketing incentives for either a short or a long period of time. Finally, the possibility of anonymous visits to a website, free of any tracking could also be offered.

Leveraging the degree of ethical interactivity will help to tailor marketing actions according to *consumer ethical flexibility*. The ethical sensitivity of a consumer could even become a *segmentation criterion*. This is all the more important than ethical sensitivity is likely to differ from one sector to another, just as Nwachukwu et al. (op. cit.) noted about certain products like cigarettes. Also, for instance,

FIGURE 2
Delineating Ethical Internet Marketing

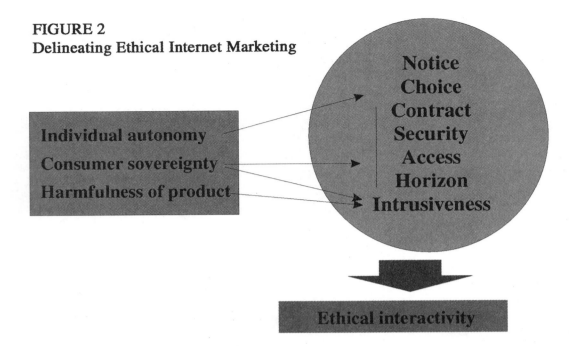

consumers could be less ethically sensitive when buying a book and far more ethically sensitive when using online banking.

Gains from using Ethics in E-Marketing

Singhapakdi (1999) showed that marketing managers who perceive an ethical problem in a situation are more likely to have an ethical intention. Hence, we suggest that marketing professionals engage in more thought and reflect on their marketing practices on the Internet. This could lead to a greater consciousness and hence to the development of more ethical intentions and practices. The question of adopting an ethical marketing behavior does not only boil down to providing a firm's policy concerning information privacy, it should also be demonstrated in marketing actions. The seven criteria presented above can serve as a guideline for firms wanting to implement an ethical e-marketing strategy. Survey of other web sites practices can also help. For instance, in France, the site Voilà.fr decided to ban the use of "pop-ups", as this was deemed too aggressive for Internet users.

The comfort of secure navigation is a key to internet-user satisfaction (Szymanski and Hise, 2000), the absence of intrusive techniques can be part of this comfort and hence lead to consumer satisfaction and loyalty. The design of the web site is often mainly evaluated in terms of pleasure and interactivity (Eighmey, 1997; Ghose and Dou, 1998 Chen and Wells, 1999; Boulaire and Mathieu, 2000). We argue that it should integrate ethical considerations. Avoiding misleading, deceiving signs, controlling the ad banners that appears and preventing other intrusive advertising will be important in the future.

It will also be important to inform consumers that a particular firm takes an ethical stance through the creation and diffusion of Internet ethical charts. Chonko and Hunt (2000) deplore the lack of ethical guidelines in marketing practices, however such a development and its diffusion to consumers will be critical in the future.

Both the deontological and utilitarian views of ethics can be used to design ethical web-sites. Whether any practices should be banned on the Internet, within a free society is a moot point. However, it is possible for firms to exercise self-restraint and also develop personalized sites that depend on each individual's tolerance levels.

As Internet software becomes more sophisticated, it will be increasingly possible to tailor sites for individual ethical preferences. The seven criteria mentioned above could form the basis of creating and sustaining competitive advantages (Table 1).

This table clearly illustrates that ethical marketing is critically associated with a firm's long term orientation. Advantages like image, trust, relationship quality, database reliability and database update are typically representative of the goals of long-term, market oriented firms. A firm that has a short term orientation will lose its competitive advantages in the long run against firms that develop ethics as a marketing weapon for the consumer's benefit.

Conclusions

While the potentialities of ICT are endless, the very interactiveness of the Internet creates new and serious ethical problems reflected by the use of short-term aggressive actions. Firms that follow ethical marketing stances are likely to be more competitively advantaged in the future.

TABLE 1
Ethical Marketing Criteria and Competitive Advantage

Notice	Choice	Contact	Security	Access	Horizon	Intrusiveness
First level of ethics ↗ Institutional image	Choice about disclosure: ↗ reliable data Choice about use: ↗ target marketing actions ↗ Overall: ↗ trust	↗ interactivity ↗ opportunities to communicate with consumers ↗ development of consumers knowledge	↗ increased trust ↗ image	↗ trust ↗ accurate information ↗ reliable database	↗ update reliable database ↗ possibility to identify long term relationships opportunities	Agreed marketing actions leading to ↗ targeted marketing action ↗ profitable marketing actions

↗ Better value for consumers
↗ better relationship quality
↗ increase of lifetime value for customers
↗ differentiating advantage

Ethical marketing can be judged against seven criteria: notice, choice, contact, security, access, horizon and intrusiveness. The importance paid to each criterion can reflect the degree of ethical interactivity that the firm is willing to exhibit. At the same time firms need to understand the impact on individual autonomy and safeguard customer sovereignty. In the long run, increasing ethical interactivity is likely to produce consumers who feel empowered, creating competitive advantage for a firm and satisfaction for the consumers.

REFERENCES

Bergman, Alexander. 1997. "Ethique et gestion." in *Encyclopédie de Gestion*, Economica Paris.

Boulaire, Christelle and A. Mathieu. 2000. "La fidélité à un site web : proposition d'un cadre préliminaire." *Actes du XVIème Congrès International de l'Association Française du Marketing* (Montréal): 303–312.

Chen, Q. and W. D. Wells. 1999. "Attitude toward the Site." *Journal of Advertising Research* 39 (5): 27–37

Chonko, Lawrence B. and Shelby D. Hunt. 2000. "Ethics and Marketing Management -A Retrospective and Prospective Commentary." *Journal of Business Research* 50: 235–244

Culnan, Mary J. 1999a. Privacy and the Top 100 Web Sites : Report to the Federal Trade Commission [Online] Available: http://www.msb.edu/faculty/culnanm/gippshome.html

Culnan, Mary J. 1999b. Georgetown Internet Privacy Policy Survey : Report to the Federal Trade Commission [Online]

Available: http://www.msb.edu/faculty/culnanm/gippshome.html

Eighmey, J. 1997. "Profiling User Responses to Commercial Web Sites" *Journal of Advertising Research* 37 (3): 59–66

Ghose, S. and W. Dou. 1998. "Interactive Functions and Their Impacts on The Appeal of Internet Presence Sites." *Journal of Advertising Research* 38 (2): 29–43

Kelly, Eileen P. 2000. "Ethical and Online Privacy in Electronic Commerce." *Business Horizons* May/June 43(3): 3

Murphy, Patrick E. and Gene R. Laczniak. 1981. "Marketing Ethics: A Review with Implications for Managers, Educators and Researchers." in *Review of Marketing*. Eds B.M. Enis and K.J. Roehring, AMA, 251–266.

Nwachukwu Saviour L.S., Scott. J. Vitell, Faye W. Gilbert and James H. Barnes. 1997. "Ethics and Social Responsibility in Marketing: An Examination of Ethical Evaluation of Advertising Strategies." *Journal of Business Research* 39: 107–118

Ranchhod, Ashok. 1998. "Advertising into the Next Millennium." *International Journal of Advertising* 17 (4): 427–446.

Singhapakdi, Anusorn. 1999. "Perceived Importance of Ethics and Ethical Decision in Marketing." *Journal of Business Research*, 45(1): 89–99

Szymanski, D.M. and Hise, R.T. 2000. "E-Satisfaction: An Initial Examination." *Journal of Retailing* 73 (3): 309–322.

Dr. Claire Gauzente is Assistant Professor of Marketing and Organization at the University of Angers, UFR de Droit, Economie et Gestion, 13 allée F. Mitterrand, 49036 Angers cx 01, France. (33)241-962 235. claire.gauzente@univ-angers.fr Ashok Ranchhod is Professor of Marketing at the Southampton Business School, Southampton Institute, East Park Terrace Southampton, SO14 0RH, UK. (44) (0)23 8031 9541. ashok.ranchhod@solent.ac.uk

From *Academy of Marketing Science Review*, 2001. © 2001 by Academy of Marketing Science, http://www.amsreview.org/amsrev/forum/gauzente10-01.html.

designing a trust-based e-business strategy

trust will make or break an e-business.

EXECUTIVE briefing

Trust determines the success or failure of many companies. Unless they feel a sense of trust, buyers will not return to a business, and this situation holds true whether the business is offline or online. To enjoy sustained success in e-business, companies need to understand how trust is defined and then incorporate the factors that influence perceptions of trust in their online strategies.

By Fareena Sultan and Hussain A. Mooraj

IN RECENT YEARS, NO OTHER TECHNOLOGY HAS affected marketing and business activities as significantly as the Internet. While the popular press has focused on the demise of many dot-coms, online B2B activity has continued to grow. The Gartner Group predicts that B2B e-commerce will hit $8.5 trillion by 2005. Of this, 42% or $3.6 trillion will be North America's share. At the same time, dot-coms that were promising to overthrow age-old established players have lost their sting or are no more. E-business is awash with change.

We contend that the development of trust between all the stakeholders is crucial for fueling the expansion of e-business. A December 2000 Jupiter Media Metrix survey found that trust issues were the number one priority for firms seeking new partners. Trust is especially critical for developing and sustaining new relationships. So it stands to reason that trust is going to be a key differentiator in determining the success or failure of many e-business companies.

Conventionally, companies have preferred to interact with parties that they know. However, in today's business environment, interaction with new entrants is inevitable. Many companies are interacting with unfamiliar players, particularly with small- to medium-sized firms. Using trust as the foundation for new relationships is a way to retain value in a business.

We interviewed managers to try to determine how trust is defined and examined factors that influence perceptions of trust in B2B interactions. (See Exhibit 1.)

Defining Trust in E-Business

We know from the offline world that a business can't have liquidity without returning buyers and there will be no returning buyers without trust. This rule holds true for the Internet as well. Trust is imperative for success in e-business and to ensure repeat customers. According to the TRUST-EC project, which was conducted in 2000 on behalf of the European Commission, e-business can be defined in a broad sense as the carrying out of business activities that lead to an exchange of value, where the parties interact electronically, using network or telecommunications technology. The question arises: How do various players engaged in e-business define trust? Trust is an elusive concept and has varied definitions depending on the discipline and the stakeholders investigating trust relationships.

We found that managers distinguish between two types of trust environments they encounter: (1) trust in the relationship among businesses, consumers, and other stakeholders; and (2) trust in the B2B Web site and its functionality.

In each of these two cases, respondents in our study articulated a variety of definitions of trust. For example, Mamoon Yunus, global systems architect at webMethods, a B2B integration firm, states that trust in e-business can be defined as "the ability to do business reliably, in a repeated fashion and securely with non-repudiation." In his opinion, trust is all about fulfilling the promise to the customer and is a fundamental aspect of any successful Internet strategy.

EXHIBIT 1 The study

- Thirteen one-on-one interviews with senior managers and executives
- Seven companies with a high level of involvement with the Internet in various capacities
- Interviewees included senior management, technology managers, sales and marketing executives, and Internet consultants

Company	Sample Business Focus	Respondent
1. ZEFER	Internet consulting	1. Managing director
		2. Director business consulting
		3. Principal business consulting
2. webMethods	B2B integration software provider	4. Global accounts architect
		5. Regional Sales Manager
3. KeyCommerce Inc.	E-marketplace solutions provider	6. CEO
4. Anchorsilk Inc.	B2B platform provider and ASP	7. President and CEO
5. State Street Corp.	Global financial services	8. Sr VP e-business incubator
		9. VP mkt. communication
		10. VP technology acquisition and corporate procurement
		11. Senior purchasing officer
6. Compaq	Computer hardware	12. Director Internet and e-business
7. NetNumina	E-business systems integrator	13. CTO

Definitions of trust are contingent on the nature of e-business being conducted. Much of e-business between firms starts first with online procurement. According to Albert Hofeldt, a principal at ZEFER, an Internet strategy consulting firm, the definition of trust varies depending on whether we are dealing with direct or indirect procurement. He is of the view that in indirect procurement, the factor that matters most is the price, whereas in direct procurement the more critical factors are availability and order fulfillment. Thus, dimensions of trust can include such elements as offering a good price, having products available, and fulfilling orders in a timely manner.

Todd Alcock, regional sales manager at webMethods, says that "trust is defined by the brand and promise to the customer, and how you back your promise." He also states that trust in technology vendors is defined by the perception of confidence that their people, processes, and technology are going to be capable in driving the success of your company. Peter DeBruin,

senior purchasing officer at State Street Corp., has yet another definition. He defines trust as "the ability to deliver on implicit or explicit statements and to execute the activity in a manner that the client wants it to be and is promised."

What Influences Trust?

Understanding the factors that influence customer perceptions of trust can help managers make better decisions. Our study unveiled seven factors that influence trust. (See Exhibit 2.) These factors, explained below, form a "circle of trust" that is necessary for success in e-business. To establish trust you need to have a good brand and good ratings. To operationalize and maintain trust, you need management domain knowledge, good security and clear privacy policies, current and functional technology, good order fulfillment, and responsive customer service.

Brand. We found that trust in the brand name is one of the most important factors when buying online. Brand recognition and reputation play important roles in instilling trust and helping businesses succeed online. For new entrants, it's important to leverage other known brands and associate with them in some form to create a sense of stability and longevity. This can be done through partnerships. For example, ZEFER leveraged the Sun Microsystems brand by forging a close working partnership.

According to Mansoor Khan, CEO of Key Commerce, "Trust will be created only if there is a pre-existing business relationship. However, if there is no prior business relationship, then brand becomes the single most important trust cue. This is especially true for small- and medium-sized firms."

EXHIBIT 2 The circle of trust

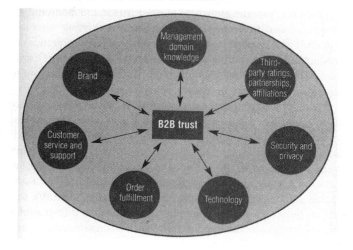

Management domain knowledge. Our study shows that building a trusting B2B relationship is predicated on having a dedicated management team. Anne Bowen, senior executive vice president of State Street Corp., explains that "Clients want to integrate their back-end systems with State Street because they perceive us to be experts in our domain."

Relatively new entrants such as e-marketplaces have to cross a hurdle stemming from the lack of any track record of suc-

Questions to Help Establish Trust With Unknown Parties

1 Who are the backers and participants? Are they large corporations or a VC?
2 Do they have the resources to ensure the transaction and aid in troubleshooting?
3 Do they have a dedicated management team?
4 How technically savvy are they?
5 Do they have the infrastructure to support the transactions?
6 Will the company survive in the long term?

cessful business relationships. They have to encourage participants by displaying the management team's domain expertise. In such cases, executive bios and "about us" buttons on Web sites are important trust cues.

Third-party ratings, partnerships, and affiliations. Our study indicates that new firms that have no proven track record to fall back on would be wise to incorporate certification by third parties and include customer testimonials on a Web site. Investors should be clearly identified and brands of partners and affiliates should be leveraged.

One trust cue that has been proposed for e-marketplaces is supplier performance ratings. Open Ratings and Dun and Bradstreet offer supplier performance ratings to e-marketplaces like the "Buyer Insight" ratings program. While this product may help build B2B trust, Forrester Research reports that widespread adoption will require several years.

However, in some industries like aerospace and medicine, no amount of certification will compensate for existing tried and tested relationships to invoke trust because the consequences of product failure are immense. In these instances, working first on establishing a personal relationship offline and then moving to the online world may be necessary.

Security and privacy. Successful B2B transactions can only take place in a secure environment that also protects customer privacy. To increase the level of trust, our study recommends that companies incorporate security in software such as firewalls. This would typically have functionality like Secure Socket Layer (SSL), which prevents interception of data and packet sniffing, authentication (to conform your identity), and authorization (to prevent unauthorized access to information). Digital certificates and repudiation logs also ensure security and can act as trust indicators.

Omar Hussain, CEO of Anchorsilk, a B2B platform provider, says, "Whereas in B2C e-commerce consumers worry about putting their credit card information on the Web, in B2B e-commerce one of the biggest fears is that sellers' prices will become available to competition." Today, technological security is taken for granted. However, privacy policies and the level of security still need to be clearly specified on the Web site.

Technology. In an e-marketplace, being technology agnostic depicts neutrality, which in turn creates trust. The level of IT so-

phistication within a company and personalization options also contribute to the overall trust environment.

Max Grasso, chief technology officer at NetNumina, a system integration company, is of the opinion that "Internet technology itself does not change the nature of trust relationships. However, a repeated failure of technology does affect this relationship." Successful companies must not only have current technology on a Web site, but also one that functions as expected.

Order fulfillment. We believe that making a commitment to deliver flawless execution and fulfillment helps engender trust. This commitment should be communicated clearly on Web sites. The site should also clearly articulate the intention to measure customer service and rectify mistakes. The technology on a Web site, at the very least, should allow the buyer to control the time of delivery of orders. In addition, Web sites should have the capability to check the status of an order with tracking functionality. Toffer Winslow, former director of business consulting at ZEFER, states, "Without flawless execution and order fulfillment there can be no trust."

Customer service and support. Our study found that poor online customer service is holding back the growth of B2B e-business and preventing companies from building trust on the Web. In the next generation of online commerce, companies must provide a high quality, consistent level of service across all channels (e-mail, wireless, call centers). This would entail personalized marketing, service, sales and support to win the trust of the customer. According to Ed Jay, former managing director of the Boston office at ZEFER, trust is eroded if you have different service levels across different channels.

Studies at the E-business Center at MIT have established the role of "virtual advisors" in establishing trust on the Internet. These are software programs that offer support to customers in complex buying decisions.

Private vs. Public E-Marketplaces

Is there a difference between trust in private and public e-marketplaces? Our study found that in private e-marketplaces the trust issue is solved to a large degree because you know the suppliers and membership is usually restricted. Michael Podavano, director of Internet and e-business at Compaq, says, "When a customer is part of a community, there is even more reason to build trust; in private e-marketplaces you have to have absolute trust or risk banishment." Having a sense of community leads companies to further integrate their business processes. This in turn enhances trust between parties.

Large corporations that have their own private marketplace need a single interface that's integrated with the various divisions. Stephen Dill, vice president of marketing at State Street Corp., states, "Trust implications are that all Web initiatives should be under one umbrella, which gives an impression of being customer-centric (e.g., having a single sign on)."

One aspect of public e-marketplaces that encourages trust is the sharing of perfect information. Here, participants are looking for price and order fulfillment and e-marketplaces

Steps to Create B2B Trust

In relationships with unknown parties
- Check with companies the unknown party has dealt with
- Use authenticated processes for checking financial backgrounds and confirm ability to pay bills
- Have conceptual discussions about the technology before entering into transactions
- Meet top executives and sales engineers
- Examine whether you can 'identify' with the individual or firms
- Ask for proof of concepts, trial installations, and conduct usability testing
- Develop an explicit contract that has recourse for eventualities
- Evaluate the level of effort being put into maintaining the relationship
- Keep feelers out in industry to find out what is going on

On Your Web site
- Ensure there are no "trustbusters"
- Leverage other brands by displaying partnerships and affiliations
- Exhibit management teams, explains domain expertise, and display job listings
- Have third parties rate your site
- State clearly privacy/security policies and specify security level
- State commitment to measure customer service and rectify mistakes
- Display customer testimonials
- Provide tools to allow control of time of delivery and order tracking
- Allow product comparisons of competitors' products on own Web site
- Establish a multi-layer process; buyer can contact many parties in one firm

might have contracts and SLAs (Service Level Agreements) to enforce compliance with agreements. Public e-marketplaces give a price advantage and guarantee fulfillment. What they do not always give are operational and relationship benefits.

Create Trust

There's usually a learning period before two entities start transacting with each other online. We recommend checking references in order to establish trust with unknown parties. It's important to identify companies that the unknown party has dealt with and to examine their experience with goods and services. Authenticated processes should be used for checking financial backgrounds. Given the state of affairs in the technology sector these days, the ability to pay bills is one of the main criteria for screening companies.

Industry feelers play an important role in identifying trustworthy B2B firms that you would want to do business with. It's best to validate any vendor claims with current users. Before transacting with the firm, have conceptual discussions with their team, meet their sales engineers, ask for demos and trial products, carry out extensive usability testing, and meet their executive team. Finally, develop an explicit contract with recourse for any eventualities.

Assisting the customer in the buying process can create trust. According to Gary Beaudreau, vice president corporate procurement at State Street Corp., "There is a need to enforce that the customer's B2B decision is the right one. Suppliers can help accomplish this in a number of ways, including initially guiding

customers through the transaction process in order to establish trust and confidence and providing detailed information on the products and services in order to simplify the overall experience."

To enhance customer service and support, e-business firms need to form multi-layer processes whereby customers can contact many parties in one firm. Allowing input from customers on a B2B Web site through the free flow of information in chat rooms and forums can also create trust. Even if it hurts, a democratic aspect instills trust. Live advisers, text chat, audio, and 1-800 numbers all help create an environment conducive to building trust.

Another way to create trust is to take a customer perspective and allow product comparisons. To maintain true neutrality, it's a good idea to allow the customer to compare competitors' products on the Web site.

In our study nearly all the participants indicated the need to establish *relationship trust* before trust in the B2B Web site can be achieved. To do this, examine whether you can "identify" with the individuals within the other firm. If so, you're more likely to build trust. Review the level of effort put in by the parties to maintain the relationship, such as responsiveness to e-mail and level of preparation for meetings.

Consistency Is Key

Trust generally is built over time and with experience. However, with more and more businesses going online, the need to work with new and unfamiliar entities is coming to the fore-

Trustbusters

We identified 10 "trustbusters" that can make or break a company in the B2B space. Firms need to take a proactive stance to avoid these trustbusters.

- Inferior quality of the product
- Poor Web site content
- Complex Web site navigation and outdated links
- Slow response time of Web pages (i.e., more than three to seven seconds per page)
- Repeated failures of technology
- Lack of customization/personalization
- Lack of advisers (live chat, text chat, audio, 1-800 numbers)
- Inferior customer service
- Different service levels over different channels (in person vs. online)
- Poor order fulfillment

front. Companies need these new customers to enable growth in e-business transactions. However, buyers and sellers still need to establish an element of trust before any B2B transactions can take place.

Online trust is hard to establish because people have trouble assessing intentions over the Internet. Customers who have been through a similar online transaction might come away with different notions as to whether an experience was trustworthy. Firms need to ensure that a maximum number of trust cues are presented online.

To create trust, a company must have the seven elements from the circle of trust in place. To maintain trust, a company must eradicate "trustbusters." Many of the trust factors are not easily carried over from the bricks-and-mortar environment and

need to be established anew in the electronic environment. Just because a company is successful at gaining customers' trust in offline transactions doesn't mean this trust will automatically be translated online. However, existing offline trust can facilitate the process. While the Internet as a new technology may not influence existing B2B relationships, B2B transactional relationships are affected.

In today's business environment, companies have to acquire, retain, and service customers in a multi-channel environment. Consistent interactions and service in a multi-channel environment are critical factors in building trust. The ability to provide products and services in a trustworthy manner, across multi-channels, is a new challenge for customer-oriented firms in e-business. Only through trust-based strategies can a firm be successful in e-business.

Additional Reading

Jones, Sara, Marc Wilkens, Phillip Morris, Marcelo Masera (2000), "Trust Requirements in E-Business," *Communications of the ACM,* 43(12), 81–87.

Urban, Glen L., Fareena Sultan, and William Qualls (2000), "Placing Trust at the Center of Your Internet Strategy," *Sloan Management Review,* 42(1), 39–48.

About the Authors

Fareena Sultan is an associate professor in the College of Business Administration at Northeastern University and consults on technology issues. She may be reached at f.sultan@neu.edu.

Hussain A. Mooraj is an MBA candidate at Northeastern University. Mooraj was formerly an Engagement Leader with ZEFER Corp. in Boston. He may be reached at h.mooraj@neu.edu

From *Marketing Management,* November/December 2001, pp. 40-45. © 2001 by the American Marketing Association. Reprinted by permission.

Managing for Organizational Integrity

By supporting ethically sound behavior, managers can strengthen the relationships and reputations their companies depend on.

Lynn Sharp Paine

Many managers think of ethics as a question of personal scruples, a confidential matter between individuals and their consciences. These executives are quick to describe any wrongdoing as an isolated incident, the work of a rogue employee. The thought that the company could bear any responsibility for an individual's misdeeds never enters their minds. Ethics, after all, has nothing to do with management.

In fact, ethics has *everything* to do with management. Rarely do the character flaws of a lone actor fully explain corporate misconduct. More typically, unethical business practice involves the tacit, if not explicit, cooperation of others and reflects the values, attitudes, beliefs, language, and behavioral patterns that define an organization's operating culture. Ethics, then, is as much an organizational as a personal issue. Managers who fail to provide proper leadership and to institute systems that facilitate ethical conduct share responsibility with those who conceive, execute, and knowingly benefit from corporate misdeeds.

Managers must acknowledge their role in shaping organizational ethics and seize this opportunity to create a climate that can strengthen the relationships and reputations on which their companies' success depends. Executives who ignore ethics run the risk of personal and corporate liability in today's increasingly tough legal environment. In addition, they deprive their organizations of the benefits available under new federal guidelines for sentencing organizations convicted of wrongdoing. These sentencing guidelines recognize for the first time the organizational and managerial roots of unlawful conduct and base fines partly on the extent to which companies have taken steps to prevent that misconduct.

Prompted by the prospect of leniency, many companies are rushing to implement compliance-based ethics programs. Designed by corporate counsel, the goal of these programs is to prevent, detect, and punish legal violations. But organizational ethics means more than avoiding illegal practice; and providing employees with a rule book will do little to address the problems underlying unlawful conduct. To foster a climate that encourages exemplary behavior, corporations need a comprehensive approach that goes beyond the often punitive legal compliance stance.

An integrity-based approach to ethics management combines a concern for the law with an emphasis on managerial responsibility for ethical behavior. Though integrity strategies may vary in design and scope, all strive to define companies' guiding values, aspirations, and patterns of thought and conduct. When integrated into the day-to-day operations of an organization, such strategies can help prevent damaging ethical lapses while tapping into powerful human impulses for moral thought and action. Then an ethical framework becomes no longer a burdensome constraint within which companies must operate, but the governing ethos of an organization.

How Organizations Shape Individuals' Behavior

The once familiar picture of ethics as individualistic, unchanging, and impervious to organizational influences has not stood up to scrutiny in recent years. Sears Auto Centers' and Beech-Nut Nutrition Corporation's experiences illustrate the role organizations play in shaping individuals' behavior—and how even sound moral fiber can fray when stretched too thin.

In 1992, Sears, Roebuck & Company was inundated with complaints about its automotive service business. Consumers and attorneys general in more than 40 states had accused the company of misleading customers and selling them unnecessary parts and services, from brake jobs to front-end alignments. It would be a mistake, however, to see this situation exclusively in terms of any one individual's moral failings. Nor did management set out to defraud Sears customers. Instead, a number of organizational factors contributed to the problematic sales practices.

In the face of declining revenues, shrinking market share, and an increasingly competitive market for undercar services, Sears management attempted to spur the performance of its auto centers by introducing new goals and incentives for employees. The company increased minimum work quotas and introduced productivity incentives for mechanics. The automotive service advisers were given product-specific sales quotas—sell so many springs, shock absorbers, alignments, or brake jobs per shift—and paid a commission based on sales. According to advisers, failure to meet quotas could lead to a transfer or a reduction in work hours. Some employees spoke of the "pressure, pressure, pressure" to bring in sales.

Under this new set of organizational pressures and incentives, with few options for meeting their sales goals legitimately, some employees' judgment understandably suffered. Management's failure to clarify the line between unnecessary service and legitimate preventive maintenance, coupled with consumer ignorance, left employees to chart their own courses through a vast gray area, subject to a wide range of interpretations. Without active management support for ethical practice and mechanisms to detect and check questionable sales methods and poor work, it is not surprising that some employees may have reacted to contextual forces by resorting to exaggeration, carelessness, or even misrepresentation.

Shortly after the allegations against Sears became public, CEO Edward Brennan acknowledged management's responsibility for putting in place compensation and goal-setting systems that "created an environment in which mistakes did occur." Although the company denied any intent to deceive consumers, senior executives eliminated commissions for service advisers and discontinued sales quotas for specific parts. They also instituted a system of unannounced shopping audits and made plans to expand the internal monitoring of service. In settling the pending lawsuits, Sears offered coupons to customers who had bought certain auto services between 1990 and 1992. The total cost of the settlement, including potential customer refunds, was an estimated $60 million.

Contextual forces can also influence the behavior of top management, as a former CEO of Beech-Nut Nutrition Corporation discovered. In the early 1980s, only two years after joining the company, the CEO found evidence suggesting that the apple juice concentrate, supplied by the company's vendors for use in Beech-Nut's "100% pure" apple juice, contained nothing more than sugar water and chemicals. The CEO could have destroyed the bogus inventory and withdrawn the juice from grocers' shelves, but he was under extraordinary pressure to turn the ailing company around. Eliminating the inventory would have killed any hope of turning even the meager $700,000 profit promised to Beech-Nut's then parent, Nestlé.

A number of people in the corporation, it turned out, had doubted the purity of the juice for several years before the CEO arrived. But the 25% price advantage offered by the supplier of the bogus concentrate allowed the operations head to meet cost-control goals. Furthermore, the company lacked an effective quality control system, and a conclusive lab test for juice purity did not yet exist. When a member of the research department voiced concerns about the juice to operating management, he was accused of not being a team player and of acting like "Chicken Little." His judgment, his supervisor wrote in an annual performance review, was "colored by naïveté and impractical ideals." No one else seemed to have considered the company's obligations to its customers or to have thought about the potential harm of disclosure. No one considered the fact that the sale of adulterated or misbranded juice is a legal offense, putting the company and its top management at risk of criminal liability.

An FDA investigation taught Beech-Nut the hard way. In 1987, the company pleaded guilty to selling adulterated and misbranded juice. Two years and two criminal trials later, the CEO pleaded guilty to ten counts of mislabeling. The total cost to the company—including fines, legal expenses, and lost sales—was an estimated $25 million.

Acknowledging the importance of organizational context in ethics does not imply forgiving individual wrongdoers.

Such errors of judgment rarely reflect an organizational culture and management philosophy that sets out to harm or deceive. More often, they reveal a culture that is insensitive or indifferent to ethical considerations or one that lacks effective organizational systems. By the same token, exemplary conduct usually reflects an organizational culture and philosophy that is infused with a sense of responsibility.

For example, Johnson & Johnson's handling of the Tylenol crisis is sometimes attributed to the singular personality of then-CEO James Burke. However the decision to do a nationwide recall of Tylenol capsules in order to avoid further loss of life from product tampering was in reality not one decision but thousands of decisions made by individuals at all levels of the organization. The "Tylenol decision," then, is best understood not as an isolated incident, the achievement of a lone individual, but as the reflection of an organization's culture. Without a shared set of values and guiding principles deeply ingrained throughout the organi-

Corporate Fines Under the Federal Sentencing Guidelines

What size fine is a corporation likely to pay if convicted of a crime? It depends on a number of factors, some of which are beyond a CEO's control, such as the existence of a prior record of similar misconduct. But it also depends on more controllable factors. The most important of these are reporting and accepting responsibility for the crime, cooperating with authorities, and having an effective program in place to prevent and detect unlawful behavior.

The following example, based on a case studied by the United States Sentencing Commission, shows how the 1991 Federal Sentencing Guidelines have affected overall fine levels and how managers' actions influence organizational fines.

Acme Corporation was charged and convicted of mail fraud. The company systematically charged customers who damaged rented automobiles more than the actual cost of repairs. Acme also billed some customers for the cost of repairs to vehicles for which they were not responsible. Prior to the criminal adjudication, Acme paid $13.7 million in restitution to the customers who had been overcharged.

Deciding before the enactment of the sentencing guidelines, the judge in the criminal case imposed a fine of $6.85 million, roughly half the pecuniary loss suffered by Acme's customers. Under the sentencing guidelines, however, the results could have been dramatically different. Acme could have been fined anywhere from 5% to 200% the loss suffered by customers, depending on whether or not it had an effective program to prevent and detect violations of law and on whether or not it reported the crime, cooperated with authorities, and accepted responsibility for the unlawful conduct. If a high ranking official at Acme were found to have been involved, the maximum fine could have been as large as $54,800,000 or four times the loss to Acme customers. The following chart shows a possible range of fines for each situation:

What Fine Can Acme Expect?

	Maximum	Minimum
Program, reporting, cooperation, responsibility	$2,740,000	$685,000
Program only	10,960,000	5,480,000
No program, no reporting, no cooperation, no responsibility	27,400,000	13,700,000
No program, no reporting, no cooperation, no responsibility, involvement of high-level personnel	54,800,000	27,400,000

Based on Case No.: 88-266, United States Sentencing Commission, *Supplementary Report on Sentencing Guidelines for Organizations.*

zation, it is doubtful that Johnson & Johnson's response would have been as rapid, cohesive and ethically sound.

Many people resist acknowledging the influence of organizational factors on individual behavior—especially on misconduct—for fear of diluting people's sense of personal moral responsibility. But this fear is based on a false dichotomy between holding individual transgressors accountable and holding "the system" accountable. Acknowledging the importance of organizational context need not imply exculpating individual wrongdoers. To understand all is not to forgive all.

The Limits of a Legal Compliance Program

The consequences of an ethical lapse can be serious and far-reaching. Organizations can quickly become entangled in an all-consuming web of legal proceedings. The risk of litigation and liability has increased in the past decade as lawmakers have legislated new civil and criminal offenses, stepped up penalties, and improved support for law enforcement. Equally—if not more—important is the damage an ethical lapse can do to an organization's reputation and relationships. Both Sears and Beech-Nut, for instance, struggled to regain consumer trust and market share long after legal proceedings had ended.

As more managers have become alerted to the importance of organizational ethics, many have asked their lawyers to develop corporate ethics programs to detect and prevent violations of the law. The 1991 Federal Sentencing Guidelines offer a compelling rationale. Sanctions such as fines and probation for organizations convicted of wrongdoing can vary dramatically depending both on the degree of management cooperation in reporting and investigating corporate misdeeds and on whether or not the company has implemented a legal compliance program. (See the insert "Corporate Fines Under the Federal Sentencing Guidelines.")

Such programs tend to emphasize the prevention of unlawful conduct, primarily by increasing surveillance and control and by imposing penalties for wrongdoers. While plans vary, the basic framework is outlined in the sentencing guidelines. Managers must establish compliance standards and procedures; designate high-level personnel to oversee compliance; avoid delegating discretionary authority to those likely to act unlawfully; effectively communicate the company's standards and procedures through training or publications; take reasonable steps to achieve compliance through audits, monitoring processes, and a system for employees to report criminal misconduct without fear of retribution; consistently enforce standards through appropriate disciplinary measures; respond appropriately when offenses are detected; and, finally, take reasonable steps to prevent the occurrence of similar offenses in the future.

There is no question of the necessity of a sound, well-articulated strategy for legal compliance in an organization. After all, employees can be frustrated and frightened by the complexity of today's legal environment. And even managers who claim to use the law as a guide to ethical behavior often lack more than a rudimentary understanding of complex legal issues.

Managers would be mistaken, however, to regard legal compliance as an adequate means for addressing the full range of ethical issues that arise every day. "If it's legal, it's ethical," is a frequently heard slogan. But conduct that is lawful may be highly problematic from an ethical point of view. Consider the sale in some countries of hazardous products without appropriate warnings or the purchase of goods from suppliers who operate inhumane sweatshops in developing countries. Companies engaged in international business often discover that conduct that infringes on recognized standards of human rights and decency is legally permissible in some jurisdictions.

Legal clearance does not certify the absence of ethical problems in the United States either, as a 1991 case at Salomon Brothers illustrates. Four top-level executives failed to take appropriate action when learning of unlawful activities on the government trading desk. Company lawyers found no law obligating the executives to disclose the improprieties. Nevertheless, the executives' delay in disclosing and failure to reveal their prior knowledge prompted a serious crisis of confidence among employees, creditors, shareholders, and customers. The executives were forced to resign, having lost the moral authority to lead. Their ethical lapse compounded the trading desk's legal offenses, and the company ended up suffering losses—including legal costs, increased funding costs, and lost business—estimated at nearly $1 billion.

A compliance approach to ethics also overemphasizes the threat of detection and punishment in order to channel behavior in lawful directions. The underlying model for this approach is deterrence theory, which envisions people as rational maximizers of self-interest, responsive to the personal costs and benefits of their choices, yet indifferent to the moral legitimacy of those choices. But a recent study reported in *Why People Obey the Law* by Tom R. Tyler shows that obedience to the law is strongly influenced by a belief in its legitimacy and its moral correctness. People generally feel that they have a strong obligation to obey the law. Education about the legal standards and a supportive environment may be all that's required to insure compliance.

Discipline is, of course, a necessary part of any ethical system. Justified penalties for the infringement of legitimate norms are fair and appropriate. Some people do need the threat of sanctions. However, an overemphasis on potential sanctions can be superfluous and even counterproductive. Employees may rebel against programs that stress penalties, particularly if they are designed and imposed without employee involvement or if the standards are vague or unrealistic. Management may talk of mutual trust when unveiling a compliance plan, but employees often receive the message as a warning from on high. Indeed, the more skeptical among them may view compliance programs as nothing more than liability insurance for senior management. This is not an unreasonable conclusion, considering that compliance programs rarely address the root causes of misconduct.

Even in the best cases, legal compliance is unlikely to unleash much moral imagination or commitment. The law does not generally seek to inspire human excellence or distinction. It is no guide for exemplary behavior—or even good practice. Those managers who define ethics as legal compliance are implicitly endorsing a code of moral mediocrity for their organizations. As Richard Breeden, former chairman of the Securities and Exchange Commission, noted, "It is not an adequate ethical standard to aspire to get through the day without being indicted."

Integrity as a Governing Ethic

A strategy based on integrity holds organizations to a more robust standard. While compliance is rooted in avoiding legal sanctions, organizational integrity is based on the concept of self-governance in accordance with a set of guiding principles. From the perspective of integrity, the task of ethics management is to define and give life to an organization's guiding values, to create an environment that supports ethically sound behavior, and to instill a sense of shared accountability among employees. The need to obey the law is viewed as a positive aspect of organizational life, rather than an unwelcome constraint imposed by external authorities.

Management may talk of mutual trust when unveiling a compliance plan, but employees often see a warning from on high.

An integrity strategy is characterized by a conception of ethics as a driving force of an enterprise. Ethical values shape the search for opportunities, the design of organizational systems, and the decision-making process used by individuals and groups. They provide a common frame of reference and serve as a unifying force across different functions, lines of business, and employee groups. Organizational ethics helps define what a company is and what it stands for.

Many integrity initiatives have structural features common to compliance-based initiatives: a code of conduct, training in relevant areas of law, mechanisms for reporting and investigating potential misconduct, and audits and controls to insure that laws and company standards are being met. In addition, if suitably designed, an integrity-based initiative can establish a foundation for seeking the legal benefits that are available under the sentencing guidelines should criminal wrongdoing occur. (See the insert "The Hallmarks of an Effective Integrity Strategy.")

But an integrity strategy is broader, deeper, and more demanding than a legal compliance initiative. Broader in that it seeks to enable responsible conduct. Deeper in that it cuts to the ethos and operating systems of the organization and its members, their guiding values and patterns of thought and action. And more demanding in that it requires

The Hallmarks of an Effective Integrity Strategy

There is no one right integrity strategy. Factors such as management personality, company history, culture, lines of business, and industry regulations must be taken into account when shaping an appropriate set of values and designing an implementation program. Still, several features are common to efforts that have achieved some success:

• *The guiding values and commitments make sense and are clearly communicated.* They reflect important organizational obligations and widely shared aspirations that appeal to the organization's members. Employees at all levels take them seriously, feel comfortable discussing them, and have a concrete understanding of their practical importance. This does not signal the absence of ambiguity and conflict but a willingness to seek solutions compatible with the framework of values.

• *Company leaders are personally committed, credible, and willing to take action on the values they espouse.* They are not mere mouthpieces. They are willing to scrutinize their own decisions. Consistency on the part of leadership is key. Waffling on values will lead to employee cynicism and a rejection of the program. At the same time, managers must assume responsibility for making tough calls when ethical obligations conflict.

• *The espoused values are integrated into the normal channels of management decision making and are reflected in the organization's critical activities*: the development of plans, the setting of goals, the search for opportunities, the allocation of resources, the gathering and communication of information, the measurement of performance, and the promotion and advancement of personnel.

• *The company's systems and structures support and reinforce its values.* Information systems, for example, are designed to provide timely and accurate information. Reporting relationships are structured to build in checks and balances to promote objective judgment. Performance appraisal is sensitive to means as well as ends.

• *Managers throughout the company have the decision-making skills, knowledge, and competencies needed to make ethically sound decisions on a day-to-day basis.* Ethical thinking and awareness must be part of every managers' mental equipment. Ethics education is usually part of the process.

Success in creating a climate for responsible and ethically sound behavior requires continuing effort and a considerable investment of time and resources. A glossy code of conduct, a high-ranking ethics officer, a training program, an annual ethics audit—these trappings of an ethics program do not necessarily add up to a responsible, law-abiding organization whose espoused values match its actions. A formal ethics program can serve as a catalyst and a support system, but organizational integrity depends on the integration of the company's values into its driving systems.

---

an active effort to define the responsibilities and aspirations that constitute an organization's ethical compass. Above all, organizational ethics is seen as the work of management. Corporate counsel may play a role in the design and implementation of integrity strategies, but managers at all levels and across all functions are involved in the process. (See the chart, "Strategies for Ethics Management.")

During the past decade, a number of companies have undertaken integrity initiatives. They vary according to the ethical values focused on and the implementation approaches used. Some companies focus on the core values of integrity that reflect basic social obligations, such as respect for the rights of others, honesty, fair dealing, and obedience to the law. Other companies emphasize aspirations—values that are ethically desirable but not necessarily morally obligatory—such as good service to customers, a commitment to diversity, and involvement in the community.

When it comes to implementation, some companies begin with behavior. Following Aristotle's view that one becomes courageous by acting as a courageous person, such companies develop codes of conduct specifying appropriate behavior, along with a system of incentives, audits, and controls. Other companies focus less on specific actions and more on developing attitudes, decision-making processes, and ways of thinking that reflect their values. The assumption is that personal commitment and appropriate decision processes will lead to right action.

Martin Marietta, NovaCare, and Wetherill Associates have implemented and lived with quite different integrity strategies. In each case, management has found that the ini-

tiative has made important and often unexpected contributions to competitiveness, work environment, and key relationships on which the company depends.

Martin Marietta: Emphasizing Core Values

Martin Marietta Corporation, the U.S. aerospace and defense contractor, opted for an integrity-based ethics program in 1985. At the time, the defense industry was under attack for fraud and mismanagement, and Martin Marietta was under investigation for improper travel billings. Managers knew they needed a better form of self-governance but were skeptical that an ethics program could influence behavior. "Back then people asked, 'Do you really need an ethics program to be ethical?'" recalls current President Thomas Young. "Ethics was something personal. Either you had it, or you didn't."

The corporate general counsel played a pivotal role in promoting the program, and legal compliance was a critical objective. But it was conceived of and implemented from the start as a companywide management initiative aimed at creating and maintaining a "do-it-right" climate. In its original conception, the program emphasized core values, such as honesty and fair play. Over time, it expanded to encompass quality and environmental responsibility as well.

Today the initiative consists of a code of conduct, an ethics training program, and procedures for reporting and investigating ethical concerns within the company. It also includes a system for disclosing violations of federal pro-

Strategies for Ethics Management

Characteristics of Compliance Strategy

Ethos	conformity with externally imposed standards
Objective	prevent criminal misconduct
Leadership	lawyer driven
Methods	education, reduced discretion, auditing and controls, penalties
Behavioral Assumptions	autonomous beings guided by material self-interest

Characteristics of Integrity Strategy

Ethos	self-governance according to chosen standards
Objective	enable responsible conduct
Leadership	management driven with aid of lawyers, HR, others
Methods	education, leadership, accountability, organizational systems and decision processes, auditing and controls, penalties
Behavioral Assumptions	social beings guided by material self-interest, values, ideals, peers

Implementation of Compliance Strategy

Standards	criminal and regulatory law
Staffing	lawyers
Activities	develop compliance standards train and communicate handle reports of misconduct conduct investigations oversee compliance audits enforce standards
Education	compliance standards and system

Implementation of Integrity Strategy

Standards	company values and aspirations social obligations, including law
Staffing	executives and managers with lawyers, others
Activities	lead development of company values and standards train and communicate integrate into company systems provide guidance and consultation assess values performance identify and resolve problems oversee compliance activities
Education	decision making and values compliance standards and system

curement law to the government. A corporate ethics office manages the program, and ethics representatives are stationed at major facilities. An ethics steering committee, made up of Martin Marietta's president, senior executives, and two rotating members selected from field operations, oversees the ethics office. The audit and ethics committee of the board of directors oversees the steering committee.

The ethics office is responsible for responding to questions and concerns from the company's employees. Its network of representatives serves as a sounding board, a source of guidance, and a channel for raising a range of issues, from allegations of wrongdoing to complaints about poor management, unfair supervision, and company poli-

cies and practices. Martin Marietta's ethics network, which accepts anonymous complaints, logged over 9,000 calls in 1991, when the company had about 60,000 employees. In 1992, it investigated 684 cases. The ethics office also works closely with the human resources, legal, audit, communications, and security functions to respond to employee concerns.

Shortly after establishing the program, the company began its first round of ethics training for the entire workforce, starting with the CEO and senior executives. Now in its third round, training for senior executives focuses on decision making, the challenges of balancing multiple responsibilities, and compliance with laws and regulations critical to the company. The incentive compensation plan for executives makes responsibility for promoting ethical conduct an explicit requirement for reward eligibility and requires that business and personal goals be achieved in accordance with the company's policy on ethics. Ethical conduct and support for the ethics program are also criteria in regular performance reviews.

Today top-level managers say the ethics program has helped the company avoid serious problems and become more responsive to its more than 90,000 employees. The ethics network, which tracks the number and types of cases and complaints, has served as an early warning system for poor management, quality and safety defects, racial and gender discrimination, environmental concerns, inaccurate and false records, and personnel grievances regarding salaries, promotions, and layoffs. By providing an alternative channel for raising such concerns, Martin Marietta is able to take corrective action more quickly and with a lot less pain. In many cases, potentially embarrassing problems have been identified and dealt with before becoming a management crisis, a lawsuit, or a criminal investigation. Among employees who brought complaints in 1993, 75% were satisfied with the results.

Company executives are also convinced that the program has helped reduce the incidence of misconduct. When allegations of misconduct do surface, the company says it deals with them more openly. On several occasions, for instance, Martin Marietta has voluntarily disclosed and made restitution to the government for misconduct involving potential violations of federal procurement laws. In addition, when an employee alleged that the company had retaliated against him for voicing safety concerns about his plant on CBS news, top management commissioned an investigation by an outside law firm. Although failing to support the allegations, the investigation found that employees at the plant feared retaliation when raising health, safety, or environmental complaints. The company redoubled its efforts to identify and discipline those employees taking retaliatory action and stressed the desirability of an open work environment in its ethics training and company communications.

Although the ethics program helps Martin Marietta avoid certain types of litigation, it has occasionally led to other kinds of legal action. In a few cases, employees dismissed for violating the code of ethics sued Martin Marietta, arguing that the company had violated its own code by imposing unfair and excessive discipline.

Still, the company believes that its attention to ethics has been worth it. The ethics program has led to better relationships with the government, as well as to new business opportunities. Along with prices and technology, Martin Marietta's record of integrity, quality, and reliability of estimates plays a role in the awarding of defense contracts, which account for some 75% of the company's revenues. Executives believe that the reputation they've earned through their ethics program has helped them build trust with government auditors, as well. By opening up communications, the company has reduced the time spent on redundant audits.

The program has also helped change employees' perceptions and priorities. Some managers compare their new ways of thinking about ethics to the way they understand quality. They consider more carefully how situations will be perceived by others, the possible long-term consequences of short-term thinking, and the need for continuous improvement. CEO Norman Augustine notes, "Ten years ago, people would have said that there were no ethical issues in business. Today employees think their number-one objective is to be thought of as decent people doing quality work."

NovaCare: Building Shared Aspirations

NovaCare Inc., one of the largest providers of rehabilitation services to nursing homes and hospitals in the United States, has oriented its ethics effort toward building a common core of shared aspirations. But in 1988, when the company was called InSpeech, the only sentiment shared was mutual mistrust.

Senior executives built the company from a series of aggressive acquisitions over a brief period of time to take advantage of the expanding market for therapeutic services. However, in 1988, the viability of the company was in question. Turnover among its frontline employees—the clinicians and therapists who care for patients in nursing homes and hospitals—escalated to 57% per year. The company's inability to retain therapists caused customers to defect and the stock price to languish in an extended slump.

> # At NovaCare, executives defined organizational values and introduced structural changes to support those values.

After months of soul-searching, InSpeech executives realized that the turnover rate was a symptom of a more basic problem: the lack of a common set of values and aspirations. There was, as one executive put it, a "huge disconnect" between the values of the therapists and clinicians and those of the managers who ran the company. The therapists and clinicians evaluated the company's success in terms of its delivery of high-quality health care. InSpeech management, led by executives with financial services and venture capital backgrounds, measured the company's worth exclusively in terms of financial success. Management's single-minded emphasis on increasing hours of reimbursable care turned clinicians off. They took management's performance orientation for indifference to patient care and left the company in droves.

CEO John Foster recognized the need for a common frame of reference and a common language to unify the diverse groups. So he brought in consultants to conduct interviews and focus groups with the company's health care professionals, managers, and customers. Based on the results, an employee task force drafted a proposed vision statement for the company, and another 250 employees suggested revisions. Then Foster and several senior managers developed a succinct statement of the company's guiding purpose and fundamental beliefs that could be used as a framework for making decisions and setting goals, policies, and practices.

Unlike a code of conduct, which articulates specific behavioral standards, the statement of vision, purposes, and beliefs lays out in very simple terms the company's central purpose and core values. The purpose—meeting the rehabilitation needs of patients through clinical leadership—is supported by four key beliefs: respect for the individual, service to the customer, pursuit of excellence, and commitment to personal integrity. Each value is discussed with examples of how it is manifested in the day-to-day activities and policies of the company, such as how to measure the quality of care.

To support the newly defined values, the company changed its name to NovaCare and introduced a number of structural and operational changes. Field managers and clinicians were given greater decision-making authority; clinicians were provided with additional resources to assist in the delivery of effective therapy; and a new management structure integrated the various therapies offered by the company. The hiring of new corporate personnel with health care backgrounds reinforced the company's new clinical focus.

The introduction of the vision, purpose, and beliefs met with varied reactions from employees, ranging from cool skepticism to open enthusiasm. One employee remembered thinking the talk about values "much ado about nothing." Another recalled, "It was really wonderful. It gave us a goal that everyone aspired to, no matter what their place in the company." At first, some were baffled about how the vision, purpose, and beliefs were to be used. But, over time, managers became more adept at explaining and using them as a guide. When a customer tried to hire away a valued employee, for example, managers considered raiding the customer's company for employees. After reviewing the beliefs, the managers abandoned the idea.

NovaCare managers acknowledge and company surveys indicate that there is plenty of room for improvement. While the values are used as a firm reference point for decision making and evaluation in some areas of the company, they are still viewed with reservation in others. Some managers do not "walk the talk," employees complain. And recently acquired companies have yet to be fully integrated into the program. Nevertheless, many NovaCare employees say the values initiative played a critical role in the company's 1990 turnaround.

The values reorientation also helped the company deal with its most serious problem: turnover among health care providers. In 1990, the turnover rate stood at 32%, still above target but a significant improvement over the 1988 rate of 57%. By 1993, turnover had dropped to 27%. Moreover, recruiting new clinicians became easier. Barely able to hire 25 new clinicians each month in 1988, the company added 776 in 1990 and 2,546 in 1993. Indeed, one employee who left during the 1988 turmoil said that her decision to return in 1990 hinged on the company's adoption of the vision, purpose, and beliefs.

Wetherill Associates: Defining Right Action

Wetherill Associates, Inc.—a small, privately held supplier of electrical parts to the automotive market—has neither a conventional code of conduct nor a statement of values. Instead, WAI has a *Quality Assurance Manual*—a combination of philosophy text, conduct guide, technical manual, and company profile—that describes the company's commitment to honesty and its guiding principle of right action.

Creating an organization that encourages exemplary conduct may be the best way to prevent damaging misconduct.

WAI doesn't have a corporate ethics officer who reports to top management, because at WAI, the company's corporate ethics officer *is* top management. Marie Bothe, WAI's chief executive officer, sees her main function as keeping the 350-employee company on the path of right action and looking for opportunities to help the community. She delegates the "technical" aspects of the business—marketing, finance, personnel, operations—to other members of the organization.

Right action, the basis for all of WAI's decisions, is a well-developed approach that challenges most conventional management thinking. The company explicitly rejects the usual conceptual boundaries that separate morality and self-interest. Instead, they define right behavior as logically, expediently, and morally right. Managers teach employees to look at the needs of the customers, suppliers, and the community—in addition to those of the company and its employees—when making decisions.

WAI also has a unique approach to competition. One employee explains, "We are not 'in competition' with anybody. We just do what we have to do to serve the customer." Indeed, when occasionally unable to fill orders, WAI salespeople refer customers to competitors. Artificial incentives, such as sales contests, are never used to spur individual performance. Nor are sales results used in determining compensation. Instead, the focus is on teamwork and customer service. Managers tell all new recruits that absolute honesty, mutual courtesy, and respect are standard operating procedure.

Newcomers generally react positively to company philosophy, but not all are prepared for such a radical departure from the practices they have known elsewhere. Recalling her initial interview, one recruit described her response to being told that lying was not allowed, "What do you mean? No lying? I'm a buyer. I lie for a living!" Today she is persuaded that the policy makes sound business sense. WAI is known for informing suppliers of overshipments as well as undershipments and for scrupulous honesty in the sale of parts, even when deception cannot be readily detected.

Since its entry into the distribution business 13 years ago, WAI has seen its revenues climb steadily from just under $1 million to nearly $98 million in 1993, and this is an industry with little growth. Once seen as an upstart beset by naysayers and industry skeptics, WAI is now credited with entering and professionalizing an industry in which kickbacks, bribes, and "gratuities" were commonplace. Employees—equal numbers of men and women ranging in age from 17 to 92—praise the work environment as both productive and supportive.

WAI's approach could be difficult to introduce in a larger, more traditional organization. WAI is a small company founded by 34 people who shared a belief in right action; its ethical values were naturally built into the organization from the start. Those values are so deeply ingrained in the company's culture and operating systems that they have been largely self-sustaining. Still, the company has developed its own training program and takes special care to hire people willing to support right action. Ethics and job skills are considered equally important in determining an individual's competence and suitability for employment. For WAI, the challenge will be to sustain its vision as the company grows and taps into markets overseas.

At WAI, as at Martin Marietta and NovaCare, a management-led commitment to ethical values has contributed to competitiveness, positive workforce morale, as well as solid sustainable relationships with the company's key constituencies. In the end, creating a climate that encourages exemplary conduct may be the best way to discourage damaging misconduct. Only in such an environment do rogues really act alone.

Lynn Sharp Paine is associate professor at the Harvard Business School, specializing in management ethics. Her current research focuses on leadership and organizational integrity in a global environment.

MANUFACTURING

Industrial Evolution

Bill McDonough has the wild idea he can eliminate waste. Surprise! Business is listening

Fabrics you can eat. Buildings that generate more energy than they consume. Factory with wastewater clean enough to drink. Even toxic-free products that, instead of ending up as poison in a landfill, decompose as nutrients into the soil. No more waste. No more recycling. And no more regulation.

Such a world is the vision of environmental designer William McDonough. You might think he's half a bubble off level—until you realize that he's working with powerhouses like Ford, BP, DuPont, Steelcase, Nike, and BASF, the world's largest producer of chemicals, to make it happen. And in the process, he's actually helping them produce substantial savings. "This is not environmental philanthropy," Ford Motor Co. CEO William Clay Ford Jr. said in 1999 when he hired McDonough to lead the $2 billion renovation of the Ford Rouge plant outside Detroit. "It's sound business."

Over the past 15 years, McDonough, former dean at the University of Virginia's architecture school, and his business partner Michael Braungart, a top European chemist and a founder of Germany's Green Party, have been busy launching what they call a new industrial revolution. The problem that has long obsessed them: How do you manufacture products safely that are of comparable quality as the original stuff without stifling productivity or cutting profits? Their solutions—which have already had some remarkable success—are fast turning front man McDonough, 51, into one of Corporate America's leading gurus of green growth. His and Braungart's ideas are sure to spark even more debate with the publication this month of their new book, *Cradle to Cradle*.

Indeed, there's a growing awareness among CEOs of the unsustainability of manufacturing as it's done today, using so many potentially dangerous chemicals and producing so much toxic waste. Nearly every item you use—from the car you drive to the computer you surf with to the CD player you use at the gym—contains chemicals that often haven't been tested for human safety. When these substances first hit the manufacturing plant, they are labeled as hazardous. But once they turn into consumer products, the warnings disappear. The average mass-produced water bottle or polyester shirt, for example, con-

tains small amounts of antimony—a toxic heavy metal known to cause cancer. A pair of shoes has rubber soles that are loaded with lead. You can throw the shoes away. But their environmental footprints can last decades.

Sure, no one has been killed by a sneaker. But McDonough and Braungart have been devising manufacturing processes in which factories don't contribute to greenhouse gases and consumer products don't emit carcinogenic compounds. Says Peter J. Pestillo, chairman of auto-parts maker Visteon Corp. (VC): "Bill is getting us to believe that if we start early enough, we can avoid environmental problems altogether rather than correcting them little by little."

What's more, *Cradle to Cradle*, the duo's manifesto on their eco-effective strategies, will hit the stores just as momentum grows behind critical new regulation in Europe. Two years ago, the European Union passed "end-of-life" legislation, which requires auto makers to recycle or reuse at least 80% of their old cars by 2006. But end-of-life rules won't stop with autos and are already aimed at computers and electrical gear. "Any idea which takes hold in Europe is less than a generation away from taking hold here," says Pestillo, who is working with McDonough on a toxin-free car interior.

Pressure, too, is growing on executives to find alternatives to the standard industry practice of pumping toxic waste into the air, junking valuable materials in landfills, and complying with thousands of complex regulations. McDonough believes companies can innovate their way out of regulation. He has been so persuasive that Ford, who is trying to remake the auto company his great-grandfather founded into a model of sustainable business, has put him in charge of transforming the carmaker's hulking Rouge plant. McDonough is attempting to turn this icon of dirty manufacturing into a showcase clean factory, flooded with natural light, topped with a grass roof, and surrounded by reconstructed wetlands that keep storm water from going into the public system. These wetlands alone will save the company up to $35 million. "It's not about doing things that don't make economic sense," says Timothy O'Brien, Ford's vice-president for real estate. "These things are saving us money. We're already at work on establishing Bill's guidelines in the rest of our real estate portfolio."

SOLE FOOD:

Nike makes sneakers virtually free of PVCs and is developing one that can biodegrade safely into soil

McDonough and Braungart have also helped develop a material for Nike sneakers whose soles safely biodegrade into soil. Already on the market are Nikes that are virtually free of PVC and volatile organic chemicals. The pair have also helped BASF devise the concept for a new nylon that's infinitely recyclable. And for Steelcase Inc., they have created a fabric with the company's Designtex Inc. subsidiary that is so free of toxins that you can eat it (table). Lufthansa is now putting the fabric on the seats of its planes.

One of McDonough's first achievements was in Zeeland, Mich., where he built a nearly transparent factory for Herman Miller Inc. that is bathed in sunlight and whose solar heating-and-cooling system helps cut energy costs by 30%. McDonough says productivity at the factory is up 24%, enabling the company to increase annual sales by $60 million a year with the same number of employees. And the factory only cost $15 million to build. Herman Miller is taking McDonough's ideas one step further this year by implementing a protocol whereby its engineers will be required to use materials in new furniture that have either very low or zero toxicity.

Certainly, the movement toward sustainable business practices is just beginning. And there are plenty of companies that genuinely work at changing but merely wind up replacing one harmful practice with another. The obstacles to moving toward McDonough's methods are monumental. Experts note it's often difficult to determine up front the business case for doing such things. Often, it requires companies to make a leap of faith that changing will not only be good for the environment but actually save them money. And of course, many attempts can and do fail. "It's absolutely legitimate skepticism," says Sloan School of Management professor Peter Senge. Still, given the world's depleting resources and the specter of regulation, Senge believes it's not a matter of if companies will turn more in this direction, but when. "There's a growing awareness that we are on a path that can't continue. Do we really think a billion and a half Chinese are going to generate a ton of waste every two weeks like Americans do? It will never happen. There's no place to put it."

McDonough's system tackles these problems by creating two manufacturing loops. In the first, carcinogens are designed out of the process in favor of safe ingredients that can become biological nutrients. The second loop allows the use of potentially harmful substances—what McDonough calls "technical nutrients." But in contrast with current practices, McDonough designs systems that allow these technical nutrients to be disassembled or reused indefinitely—so they never enter the ecosystem. Taking nature as the inspiration for his operating system, waste becomes food—either literally for the soil in the first loop, or figuratively for new products in the second.

As it functions today, says McDonough, industry is based on a linear, cradle-to-grave model that creates unnecessary waste. In fact, 90% of materials extracted for durable goods become garbage almost immediately. By completely remaking the industrial process—from the way factories are built to the choice of materials—McDonough is showing companies how to reinvent production from "cradle to cradle." By following nature's laws, growth can be good, McDonough believes. A system centered on depletion and pollution can be transformed into one based on regeneration and nutrition. "I don't care if you drive around in a car visible from the moon," says McDonough. "If it's all made of reusable materials and tires that become safe food for worms, and it is powered by solar energy—then hey, no problem."

Until recently, the reigning solution to environmental ills has been recycling, but McDonough believes doing less of a bad thing doesn't make it good. Recycled products are still full of toxic chemicals. "We feel good when we recycle plastic bottles containing heavy metals and carcinogens into clothes," says McDonough. "But guess what—you're still wearing cancer."

FABRIC YOU CAN EAT

Steelcase subsidiary Designtex wanted to make an ecologically safe fabric and hired environmental designers McDonough and Braungart to tackle the effort. Highlights of the project:

- 60 chemical companies were invited to join the project. All declined except for one, Ciba-Geigy.

- Ciba-Geigy's 4,500 dye formulas were evaluated for heavy metals, toxins, and carcinogens.

- 16 passed the test—enough to make the fabric.

- Under the new manufacturing process, which turns the textile mill into a water filter, the effluent is safe enough to drink.

- Fabric trimmings, which before were labeled hazardous waste, are now used as mulch.

- McDonough and Braungart are opening the new manufacturing secrets to any company that wants them.

Data: Susan Lyons, William McDonough & Partners, and Michael Braungart

That's not to mention another downside: Recycling still creates waste. McDonough calls it "downcycling"—that is, turning waste into a different product of lower quality. But that product, too, eventually winds up in a landfill. It all adds up to a costly way of doing business. Complying with federal environmental regulations alone eats up an estimated 2.6% of gross domestic product, according to the Environmental Protection Agency.

A few companies are already escaping some regulation by using McDonough's loop. BASF, for example, has designed a carpet called Savant that the company will take back and make into new carpet when you're done with it—with a guarantee that it won't be tossed into a landfill. In McDonough parlance, the carpet is a "product of service." Explains Ian Wolstenholme, BASF's sales and marketing manager for carpets: "It's like an ice cube. We can freeze and unfreeze it as many times as we like." And the carpet has the added advantage of giving BASF a potentially lifelong link to customers.

Perhaps part of McDonough's success with CEOs is that he doesn't bash them. He has the more charitable view that most executives, like technophobes at the birth of the Internet, suffer from environmental illiteracy. Patagonia Inc. Chairman Yvon Chouinard recalls that he didn't know that the polyester the outdoor outfitter used in its clothing contained antimony until McDonough told him so in their first meeting three years ago. Chouinard thought he had been doing the noble thing by avoiding cotton, which is full of pesticides. "Society is going along sort of ignorant of the damage we're doing, so it takes somebody like McDonough, who is asking the questions and seeking the answers, to offer people the choice," Chouinard says. Patagonia is now developing clothing with a new, antimony-free polyester.

Chouinard and others credit McDonough with fusing two seemingly opposing world views—environmentalism and capitalism. As a person, he's also a seeming contradiction—preppy and crunchy at the same time. At a recent opening of a documentary about his and Braungart's work, *The Next Industrial Revolution*, McDonough ascended the stage at New York's Guggenheim Museum like a Zen master in a bow tie, staring in silence at the crowd for several minutes before speaking. When he does speak, his sentences often sound like haikus. "What do you want to grow?" asks McDonough. "Health or sickness? Stupidity or intelligence? Do you want to love children for all time or destroy them?"

For years, many environmentalists thought the answer to that question was to restrain growth by scolding people about their wasteful ways. But even as they did so, it seemed as if SUVs and subdivisions just kept proliferating. If McDonough is right, conspicuous consumption may even one day turn out to be politically correct.

By Michelle Conlin and Paul Raeburn in New York

Reprinted with special permission from *Business Week*, April 8, 2002, pp. 70-72. © 2002 by The McGraw-Hill Companies, Inc.

100 BEST

Corporate Citizens

America's most responsible and profitable major public companies

Mary Miller

It's one of the oldest questions in the field of business ethics: Does socially responsible behavior pay off on the bottom line? New research shows it does, based on last year's list of the 100 Best Corporate Citizens. The overall financial performance of the 2001 list of the 100 Best firms was "significantly better" than the remaining companies in the S&P 500, according to recent analysis by Elizabeth A. Murphy and Curtis C. Verschoor, professors in the School of Accountancy and Management Information Sciences at De Paul University in Chicago. The difference was "strikingly large," Verschoor wrote in *Strategic Finance* magazine, January 2002. Using *Business Week*'s ranking of firms by financial performance (based on factors like sales growth, profit growth, and return on equity), the mean ranking of the 100 Best was "more than 10 percentile points higher" than other firms. The 100 Best Corporate Citizens also had a "significantly better reputation among corporate directors, security analysts, and senior executives, based on the 2001 *Fortune* magazine survey of 'most admired companies,'" Verschoor wrote. "This may be the most concrete evidence now available that good citizenship really does pay off on the bottom line."

What's telling is that financial performance gets only one-seventh weight in the ranking of the 100 Best Corporate Citizens. Companies make the list for serving seven stakeholder groups well, and stockholders are just one. The other six are employees, the community, the environment, overseas stakeholders, minorities and women, and customers. (Social ratings were provided by KLD Research and Analytics. See "Getting There" for methodology).

If the *Strategic Finance* study is right, what we have uncovered with the 100 Best is a model of superior management. That makes this year's list all the more intriguing for what it tells us about these firms' management styles. Indeed, by studying the cutting-edge practices of these firms, we find model business strategies in a variety of areas of concern—from layoffs and sweatshops to predatory lending and the environment. These firms show there are better ways to handle these issues than the ruthless practices that are too often the norm.

Mapping the 100 Best

Geographically, California is home to 21 of this year's best corporate citizens. On the other coast, New York boasts 12 of the best, and in the Midwest, eight are found in Minnesota and seven in Illinois. And of Indiana's two representatives, **Cummins Engine** made it into the top tier at No. 7 (up from 62 in 2000).

One study found that, compared to others in the S&P 500, the 100 Best firms outperformed financially by a margin "strikingly large."

Looking at the list over the past three years, we've noticed a good number of companies continue to make the grade year after year. Forty-nine have maintained a spot on the list all three years. Five sterling firms have been in the Top 10 the entire time: **Fannie Mae, Hewlett-Packard, Herman Miller, Procter & Gamble,** and **IBM**. IBM captured the No. 1 position two out of three years, Fannie Mae has been holding third place for two years, and

Business Ethics' 100 Best Corporate Citizens

1998-2000 Standardized values 3-year KLD averages

Rank	Overall Score	Company	2000 Revenue (millions)	2000 Net Income (millions)	1998-2000 Average Total Return to Shareholders	Community	Minorities & Women	Employees	Environment	Non-U.S. Stake-holders	Custom-ers
1	1.586	IBM	$88,396	$8,073	24.73%	2.561	3.804	1.137	1.626	0.206	1.517
2	1.233	Hewlett-Packard	$48,870	$3,697	15.95%	1.095	2.989	1.524	1.251	0.206	1.517
3	1.230	Fannie Mae	$44,088	$4,327	19.62%	2.072	3.804	0.750	0.126	0.206	1.517
4	1.179	St Paul Cos	$8,608	$993	17.56%	5.494	1.360	0.750	0.126	0.206	0.226
5	1.154	Procter & Gamble	$39,951	$3,542	3.48%	1.095	1.360	1.524	0.126	3.547	0.656
6	1.144	Motorola Inc.	$37,580	$1,318	30.53%	-0.372	2.175	2.685	0.126	0.206	2.808
7	1.099	Cummins Engine	$6,597	$8	-5.90%	3.539	0.275	1.911	-0.249	2.433	0.226
8	1.033	Herman Miller	$2,010	$140	3.65%	-0.372	1.903	2.685	2.376	0.206	0.656
9	0.989	General Mills, Inc.	$6,700	$614	11.65%	4.028	1.632	0.750	0.126	0.206	0.226
10	0.981	Avon Products	$5,715	$478	23.60%	1.095	2.446	-0.799	0.126	3.547	0.226
11	0.912	Intel Corp.	$33,726	$10,535	27.08%	0.117	0.818	1.911	2.376	0.206	0.656
12	0.909	State Street Corp.	$5,921	$595	32.52%	1.095	1.360	-0.412	0.126	3.547	0.226
13	0.891	H B Fuller	$1,353	$49	-3.81%	1.095	0.275	1.524	1.251	3.547	-1.065
14	0.880	Timberland	$1,091	$122	87.84%	2.561	0.275	-0.025	1.251	0.206	0.226
15	0.843	Bank of America	$57,772	$7,511	-5.77%	2.561	2.718	0.750	1.814	0.206	-1.710
16	0.840	Amgen	$3,629	$1,139	76.47%	2.072	1.089	0.750	0.126	0.206	0.226
17	0.830	Lucent Technologies	$28,904	$1,219	43.85%	0.117	2.446	1.524	-0.249	0.206	1.087
18	0.829	Qualcomm	$3,197	$670	857.65%	-0.372	-0.133	0.750	0.126	0.206	0.226
19	0.820	Sun Microsystems	$15,721	$1,854	116.16%	1.583	0.546	0.750	0.126	0.206	0.226
20	0.809	Southwest Airlines	$5,650	$603	51.09%	-0.372	0.275	3.073	0.126	0.206	1.517
21	0.807	Starbucks	$2,178	$95	38.38%	-0.372	0.818	0.750	0.126	3.547	0.226
22	0.760	Fed Ex Corp.	$18,257	$688	11.82%	1.095	-0.268	2.685	0.126	0.206	1.517
23	0.744	Brady Corp.	$551	$47	1.78%	1.095	1.089	0.750	1.251	0.206	1.087
24	0.722	Northern Trust Corp.	$3,548	$479	34.73%	1.095	2.175	0.750	0.126	0.206	0.226
25	0.717	UnumProvident	$9,432	$564	-16.56%	1.095	2.718	1.330	0.126	0.206	0.226
26	0.714	Freddie Mac	$29,839	$2,367	25.77%	1.583	0.546	0.750	0.126	0.206	1.517
27	0.713	JP Morgan Chase	$60,065	$5,631	11.37%	2.561	2.718	0.750	0.126	-0.908	-0.204
28	0.711	Adolph Coors	$2,414	$110	40.49%	1.095	1.632	-0.412	1.626	0.206	0.226
29	0.706	Whirlpool	$10,325	$367	-0.40%	2.561	0.003	0.750	2.376	0.206	-0.635
30	0.699	Tellabs	$3,387	$731	34.98%	-0.372	-0.268	1.911	0.126	0.206	2.808
31	0.690	Corning Inc.	$7,273	$422	78.84%	-0.372	0.275	3.073	1.251	0.206	-1.065
32	0.684	Medtronic Inc.	$5,016	$1,084	35.62%	1.583	0.546	0.750	0.126	0.206	1.087
33	0.681	Cisco Systems	$18,928	$2,668	83.99%	-0.372	1.089	1.911	0.126	0.206	0.226
34	0.676	3M	$16,724	$1,782	18.85%	1.095	0.546	0.750	0.501	0.206	1.517
35	0.647	Pitney Bowes	$3,881	$623	-1.78%	1.095	1.360	0.363	1.626	0.206	0.226
36	0.634	AT&T Corp.	$55,854	$2,650	-12.28%	2.561	1.903	0.750	-0.624	0.206	0.226
37	0.614	American Express	$23,675	$2,810	26.20%	0.606	2.446	-0.025	0.126	0.206	0.656
38	0.606	Gillette	$9,295	$392	-9.10%	-0.372	0.275	0.750	2.376	0.206	1.517
39	0.604	Symantec Corp.	$746	$170	41.87%	-0.372	1.496	1.911	0.126	0.206	0.226
40	0.601	Baxter International	$6,896	$740	26.11%	-0.372	1.903	-0.412	2.376	0.206	0.226
41	0.591	Merck & Co.	$40,363	$6,822	25.17%	2.072	2.175	0.750	-1.374	1.319	-1.065
42	0.588	Solectron Inc.	$14,138	$497	66.53%	-0.372	1.089	0.363	0.126	0.206	1.517
43	0.588	Golden West Financial	$3,957	$546	35.67%	1.095	1.089	-0.412	0.126	0.206	1.517
44	0.581	Scholastic Corp.	$1,403	$51	33.83%	0.117	2.446	-0.799	0.126	0.206	1.517
45	0.571	Oneok	$6,643	$109	21.70%	0.606	0.003	1.524	1.251	0.206	0.226
46	0.567	3Com Corp.	$4,334	$674	-4.56%	1.095	0.818	1.911	0.126	0.206	0.226
47	0.560	Lexmark International	$3,807	$285	64.51%	-0.372	0.682	1.911	0.126	0.206	0.226
48	0.560	Compaq Computer	$42,383	$569	-10.17%	0.606	0.546	1.137	0.876	0.206	1.087
49	0.528	Ecolab	$2,264	$206	17.79%	1.583	-0.540	-0.412	1.251	0.206	1.517
50	0.527	Texas Instruments	$11,875	$3,058	71.86%	-0.372	1.360	-0.025	0.126	0.206	1.087

Rank	Overall Score	Company	2000 Revenue (millions)	2000 Net Income (millions)	1998-2000 Average Total Return to Shareholders	Community	Minorities & Women	Employees	Environment	Non-U.S. Stake-holders	Custom-ers
51	0.525	Eastman Kodak	$13,994	$1,407	-7.44%	1.095	2.446	2.298	-2.124	0.206	0.226
52	0.517	Tennant Co.	$454	$28	15.12%	-0.372	1.360	0.750	0.126	0.206	1.517
53	0.516	Eli Lilly and Co.	$10,862	$3,058	15.59%	1.095	1.903	1.911	0.126	1.319	-2.786
54	0.510	Northwest Natural Gas	$532	$48	1.37%	-0.372	-0.540	3.073	1.251	0.206	0.226
55	0.503	Merix Corp.	$156	$7	35.13%	-0.372	1.632	0.363	0.126	0.206	1.087
56	0.499	Network Appliance	$579	$74	159.22%	-0.372	-0.133	0.169	0.126	0.206	0.226
57	0.497	Nucor	$4,586	$311	-2.61%	-0.372	-1.083	3.073	0.501	0.206	1.517
58	0.495	Sonoco Products	$2,711	$166	-8.56%	-0.372	-0.540	1.524	1.626	0.206	1.517
59	0.491	Wells Fargo	$27,568	$4,009	16.34%	1.095	2.718	-0.992	0.126	0.206	0.226
60	0.485	MBNA Corp	$7,869	$1,313	28.57%	2.561	-0.811	0.750	0.126	0.206	0.226
61	0.483	Clorox	$3,989	$394	2.90%	2.561	0.275	-0.412	1.626	0.206	-0.635
62	0.483	Modine Manufacturing	$1,139	$65	-11.20%	-0.372	-0.540	0.750	2.376	0.206	1.517
63	0.481	Home Depot	$38,434	$2,320	48.02%	2.072	-0.540	-0.412	-0.249	0.206	1.517
64	0.478	Deere & Co.	$13,137	$486	0.21%	-0.372	0.275	1.524	0.501	0.206	1.517
65	0.474	New York Times	$3,489	$398	10.63%	1.095	1.632	-1.186	0.126	0.206	1.517
66	0.470	Peoplesoft	$1,736	$146	12.39%	-0.372	1.089	0.750	0.126	0.206	1.517
67	0.469	Arrow Electronics	$12,959	$358	-3.28%	-0.372	0.275	1.911	0.126	0.206	1.517
68	0.468	Autodesk	$848	$10	-7.86%	1.095	1.360	0.750	0.126	0.206	0.226
69	0.458	Apache	$2,283	$693	36.81%	-0.372	-0.540	1.911	1.251	0.206	0.226
70	0.455	Delphi Automotive	$29,139	$1,062	-21.77%	-0.372	1.903	1.330	0.689	0.206	0.226
71	0.444	Microsoft	$22,956	$9,421	40.04%	0.117	1.089	0.750	0.126	0.206	0.226
72	0.436	Harman International	$1,678	$73	22.65%	-0.372	-0.540	1.911	0.126	0.206	1.517
73	0.424	Devry Inc.	$491	$48	51.57%	-0.372	0.275	0.363	0.126	0.206	1.517
74	0.423	FirstFed Financial	$322	$38	33.57%	0.117	1.089	0.750	0.126	0.206	0.226
75	0.419	Airproducts & Chemicals	$5,496	$124	3.20%	0.117	-0.540	1.911	1.251	0.206	0.226
76	0.416	Rouse Company	$634	$170	-1.53%	2.561	0.546	-0.412	0.126	0.206	0.226
77	0.412	Nordson Corp.	$741	$55	5.87%	2.561	0.003	-1.186	1.251	0.206	0.226
78	0.410	Tektronix	$1,121	$349	27.46%	0.117	-0.540	1.137	0.126	0.206	1.517
79	0.407	CIGNA Corp	$19,994	$987	36.27%	3.050	0.003	-0.412	0.126	0.206	-0.635
80	0.406	Charles Schwab	$5,788	$718	49.87%	-0.372	1.089	0.750	0.126	0.206	0.226
81	0.400	Energen	$556	$53	27.10%	0.606	-0.540	0.750	1.251	0.206	0.226
82	0.396	Guidant	$2,549	$374	25.68%	-0.372	0.275	0.750	0.126	0.206	1.517
83	0.395	PNC Financial Services	$7,623	$1,279	17.58%	1.095	0.275	0.750	0.126	0.206	0.226
84	0.377	Oracle Corp	$10,130	$6,297	128.93%	-0.372	0.275	-0.412	0.126	0.206	0.226
85	0.375	Analog Devices	$2,578	$607	73.27%	-0.372	-0.811	1.911	0.126	0.206	0.226
86	0.374	Oxford Health Plans	$4,112	$191	64.07%	0.606	0.003	0.750	0.126	0.206	-0.204
87	0.368	McDonald's Corp.	$14,243	$1,977	17.38%	0.606	1.903	-0.412	1.251	0.206	-1.065
88	0.368	Graco	$494	$70	20.35%	1.095	-0.54	-0.412	0.126	0.206	1.947
89	0.367	Marriott International	$10,017	$479	6.80%	-0.372	1.360	0.750	0.126	0.206	0.656
90	0.366	Xilinx	$1,021	$652	88.82%	-0.372	-1.354	0.750	0.126	0.206	1.517
91	0.364	MBIA Inc.	$1,025	$529	7.78%	1.095	0.275	0.750	0.126	0.206	0.226
92	0.355	Washington Gas & Light	$1,031	$83	4.79%	-0.372	2.175	-0.799	1.251	0.206	0.226
93	0.353	Safeco	$7,118	$115	-2.77%	2.072	-0.540	0.750	0.126	0.206	0.226
94	0.353	Emerson Electric	$15,545	$1,422	15.68%	-0.372	-0.540	0.363	1.251	0.206	1.517
95	0.352	PPG Industries	$8,629	$620	-2.89%	-0.372	0.003	1.524	1.251	0.206	0.226
96	0.346	Adobe Systems	$1,266	$288	91.81%	-0.372	-0.268	0.750	0.126	0.206	0.226
97	0.345	Wendys International	$2,237	$170	5.23%	-0.372	0.546	0.750	1.251	0.206	0.226
98	0.345	Tribune Company	$4,910	$201	17.67%	1.583	-0.268	-0.412	0.126	0.206	1.087
99	0.344	Kroger	$49,000	$877	23.47%	0.606	0.275	0.750	0.126	0.206	0.226
100	0.342	Applied Materials	$9,564	$2,064	66.25%	-0.372	0.275	0.750	0.126	0.206	0.226

Source: Morningstar for 2000 sales & net income, CRSP for total return to shareholders.

This year's ranking incorporates KLD data for six stakeholder groups in addition to investors: community, members of minority groups (KLD's diversity measure), employees, global suppliers and sources (KLD's non-U.S. stakeholders measure), customers (KLD's product measure), and environment.

Hewlett-Packard maintains a second place stronghold for the third year in a row.

More than a dozen firms have made substantial progress in moving up in their ranking during their three years on the list. **Timberland** made the most progress, moving from No. 92 in 1999 to No. 14 this year. In November 2001, Timberland was also honored with a Business Ethics Award, for its community service partnerships and volunteerism. (See www.business-ethics.com) Among other firms making substantial progress were the **St. Paul Companies**, No. 4 this year, up from 85 in 2000; **General Mills**, moving from No. 67 in 2000 to No. 9 this year; and **Avon Products**, advancing from No. 64 two years ago to No. 10 today.

Fannie Mae's practices represent a striking contrast to other financial firms, which prey upon rather than help low-income borrowers.

Twenty-six of this year's top 100 are making their first-ever appearance on the list. Among newcomers we welcome this year are Bank of America (No. 15), Lucent Technologies (No. 17) and Federal Express (No. 22).

Serving minorities and women— inside and outside

Looking at firms that were "best in class" in service to various stakeholders, we find inspiring cutting-edge management practices. For example, tying for top honors in service to minorities and women this year were Fannie Mae (No. 3) and IBM (No. 1). Fannie Mae serves these stakeholders externally while IBM's approach is internal—but both represent model strategies in their own way.

The purpose of Fannie Mae, a private company with an unusual federal charter, is to spread home ownership among Americans. Its ten-year, $2 trillion program—the American Dream Commitment—aims to increase home ownership rates for minorities, new immigrants, young families, and those in low-income communities.

In 2001, over 51 percent of Fannie Mae's financing went to low- and moderate-income households. "A great deal of our work serves populations that are underserved, typically, and we've shown that it's an imminently bankable proposition," said Barry Zigas, senior vice president in Fannie Mae's National Community Lending Center. "It is our goal to keep expanding our reach to impaired borrowers and to help lower their costs."

That represents a striking contrast to other financial firms, many of which prey upon rather than help low-income borrowers. To aid the victims of predatory lenders,

Fannie Mae allows additional flexibility in underwriting new loans for people trapped in abusive loans, if they could have initially qualified for conventional financing. In January the company committed $31 million to purchasing these type of loans.

At IBM, the commitment to women and minorities is internal, focused on policies for employees and suppliers—such as manager incentives for hiring and promoting women and minorities, diversity councils, loans and technical assistance to minority suppliers, child care centers in 58 locations, and adoption aid grants of $2,500 each. Programs for families are particularly strong, with up to 56 weeks of family leave and two weeks paid leave for new fathers. It's little wonder in 2001 IBM was ranked in the top ten of *Working Mother* magazine's best workplaces for mothers.

The company also placed first among 50 companies ranked by *Careers & the Disabled* magazine for accommodating the disabled. One example is IBM's Entry Point program, which places individuals with disabilities in business through internships. That's how Tim Scamporinno came to work for IBM in San Jose, Calif., where he leads a 20-member team of computer professionals. "As a result [of Entry Point], my talents have been recognized, not overshadowed by my disability," he was reported saying on the Entry Point web site.

Good Citizens of the Community

In the area of service to communities, Minnesota-based St. Paul Companies topped its peers for the second consecutive year—in large part because of its innovative and generous giving (2 percent of net earnings), for programs that increase teachers of color, support affordable housing, or promote voluntary civic activity.

The company's Minneapolis-based neighbor, General Mills, (No. 9)—also from "Minnesota Nice" territory—took second place in community service. In fiscal 2001, General Mill's overall corporate giving reached $45 million, exceeding the target of 3 percent of domestic pretax earnings. Going beyond cash, the firm's strategy combines money with volunteering, often focusing both in the company's area of expertise: food. General Mills donated the equivalent of two semi-trailer loads of food each day in 2001, placing it among the top three U.S. food contributors to people in need.

More innovatively, in 1997 the food giant helped establish Siyeza, a frozen soul-food processing company in the inner-city community of North Minneapolis, with an initial $600,000 commitment. That was followed by a $1.5 million no-interest loan to Siyeza, accompanied by help from 100 General Mills volunteers. Alfred Babington-Johnson, Siyeza board chair, told *Worth* magazine recently, "They've volunteered their expertise in every conceivable facet of the operation, from developing marketing plans to package design." Siyeza's current workforce of 80 employees—four out of five of them from poor neighborhoods—is expected to grow to 175 at peak capacity.

Leading Green Corporations

In service to the environment, this year saw an impressive six-way tie, with identical head-of-the-class scores for **Herman Miller** (No. 8), **Intel Corp.** (No. 11), **Whirlpool** (No. 29), **Gillette** (No. 38), **Baxter International** (No. 40), and **Modine Manufacturing** (No. 62).

Furniture maker Herman Miller offers a good illustration of how these environmentally superior firms operate. In 2001, it won the Waste Wise Program Award from the EPA for recycling in one year 23 million pounds of waste, and reusing another 21 million pounds for fuel to heat the main site. But environmental manager Paul Murray says that's just the tip of the environmental iceberg.

The environmental department Murray heads is small for a company the size of Herman Miller—2000 revenues of $2 billion—but he says that's intentional because of the firm's team approach to sustainability. "We're trying to get a well-rounded group involved that are not just made up of my environmental professionals," said Murray.

He's accomplished that with the Environmental Quality Action Team (EQAT), a volunteer effort directly involving 300 employees, which provides oversight for environmental activities. It's headed by a central steering committee that includes leaders of six teams. The teams concentrate on issues like setting strategies, communicating environmental objectives to constituencies, considering the impact of the buildings and grounds, and examining new products for environmental impact.

In April the company will unveil a new environmental initiative called Design for the Environment, created with eco-efficiency experts William McDonough and Michael Braungart, offering policies for engineers on issues like designing for disassembly (using staples instead of glue, for example), and using a high proportion of recycled content.

When asked for his definition of sustainability, Murray answers, "Something that's profitable," and laughs. "Besides the typical definition that our company adheres to—which is not doing business where it will harm future generations—if we aren't making money at this, we will be out of business. And then we won't be doing anybody any good."

Employees as Partners

With service to employees, four firms tied for top score: **Southwest Airlines** (No. 20), **Corning** (No. 31), **Northwest Natural Gas** (No. 54), and **Nucor** (No. 57).

An exemplar here is Southwest Airlines, the Dallas-based airline whose 27,000 employees are 83 percent unionized, and which is known to be employee-centered

and non-hierarchical. What's striking about this firm is its no-layoff policy. In the wake of the Sept. 11 terrorist attack when the industry faced significant losses, many airlines cut schedules and reduced workforces by up to 20 percent. Southwest did not lay off employees then, nor has it ever in its 31-year history.

Taking a creative approach to the crisis, the firm maintained a full flight schedule, cut fares, and expanded into markets that other airlines were pulling out of. The company also received voluntary commitments from employees to take pay cuts, forego profit-sharing, and donate hours.

For surviving the crisis with an intact workforce, spokesperson Linda Rutherford credits the "indomitable spirit of Southwest employees' keen attention to being a low-cost operation." Also important, she said, was the fact senior management quickly communicated what it was doing to avoid layoffs. "There's a lot of psychic value in that. It created a sense of stability that allowed our employee team to focus more quickly."

The creativity shown in the firm's approach to layoffs shines through in many other aspects of the airline. As the leader in value pricing, the airline offers no assigned seats, no meals, and no first class travel. Yet with its cost-cutting approach, it is known for having the quickest turnaround time in the industry and has ranked first in several quality studies. Southwest Airlines offers one more illustration that good corporate citizenship indicates superior management.

Serving Stakeholders Across the World

Often overlooked stakeholders are overseas factories and suppliers, plus the communities around them. Tying for top marks in service to these non-U.S. stakeholders are five firms: **Procter & Gamble** (No. 5), **Avon Products** (No. 10), State Street Corp. (No. 12), **H.B. Fuller** (No. 13), and **Starbucks** (No. 21).

Avon offers a good example of the cutting-edge practices at work here. In an era when many firms outsource work to sweatshops, Avon ensures employees at its suppliers have the best working conditions possible. The company's Suffern, N.Y. manufacturing plant was the first recipient of Social Accountability 8000 certification, an independent program that establishes social standards and monitors factories for compliance, on issues like safety, wages, and the right to join unions. Fitzroy Hilaire, director of supplier development and global sourcing, said he now requires all Avon factories and suppliers—both here and abroad—to pass an SA800 audit.

"SA8000 allows a company to have an improved social atmosphere. If implemented properly, it should make for a happy employee and, as such, give the company an advantage in that the employees would be more suited and more adaptable to doing work," Hilaire said.

Getting There

The methodology behind the corporate citizenship rankings

By Samuel P. Graves, Sandra Waddock, and Marjorie Kelly

In the world following the collapse of Enron, corporate citizenship is more important than ever, with companies under increasing scrutiny from friends and foes alike. Managers who believe they can continue to manage by a single measure—shareholder value—are likely to find themselves under challenge. Our complex world calls for a redefinition of corporate success to mean service to a variety of stakeholders. That is the essence of our definition of corporate citizenship. It is what the 100 Best Corporate Citizens list is about.

In a classic definition, stakeholders are those who have a stake in, or are affected by, a firm's activities. There is no single indicator of good citizenship, for by its nature it is measured from the perspectives of multiple stakeholders.

We use a synthesis of seven measures, reflecting quality of service to seven stakeholder groups: stockholders, community, minorities and women, employees, environment, non-U.S. stakeholders, and customers. All data covers the three-year period 1998-2000. Stockholder data represents a three-year average of total return to shareholders (capital gains plus dividends), using figures from CRSP, COMPUSTAT, and Morningstar. Any companies with losses in 2000 were eliminated.

Social data comes from KLD Research and Analytics in Boston, which collects and synthesizes a broad array of research—lawsuits, regulatory problems, pollution emissions, philanthropic contributions, staff diversity counts, union relations, employee benefits, awards, and so forth. KLD uses this to rate 650 public companies, including the S&P 500 plus another 150 firms chosen for social strengths. In the six social categories, KLD indicates whether each company has "strengths" and "concerns." There can be up to two of each. To arrive at a net score in a category, we subtracted concerns from strengths. Thus a firm with a score of "two" in employee strengths and a "one" in employee concerns would have a net score of "one" in the employee category.

Since all seven variables have different scales, we standardize them. We subtract the mean score for all companies from the mean for a particular company. Then we divide this difference by the standard deviation (typical difference from the mean score) for all companies. This places all seven stakeholder ratings on a common scale, called the standard deviation from the mean. In the final step, we take an unweighted average of the seven measures to yield a single score for each company. The fact that the scale is unweighted means all stakeholders have equal status.

The scores on the chart indicate a company's standard deviation from the overall mean score for that item. Technically a score could go higher than four but that's unlikely. The vast majority of companies fall within plus or minus three standard deviations from the mean.

After initial rankings are established, we do a Lexis database search of news sources on each company, to look for significant scandals or improprieties not detected in the KLD data. A handful of companies are dropped.

As with any ranking, the 100 Best Corporate Citizens list is not about perfection. It is about progress toward better treatment of stakeholders, with a goal of encouraging corporations toward ever-better practices in corporate citizenship.

Sandra Waddock is Professor of Management and Samuel Graves is Associate Professor of Management, Carroll School of Management, Boston College, Chestnut Hill, MA 02467; phone 617/552-0477; Waddock@bc.edu KLD Research and Analytics, 530 Atlantic Ave., 7th Floor, Boston MA 02210; phone 617/426-5270; www.kld.com; Socrates@kld.com.

In other service to overseas stakeholders, Avon has been a strong supporter of women's health initiatives, contributing to fundraising for breast cancer awareness in the U.K, AIDS awareness in Thailand, and self-esteem workshops for women with cancer in Australia.

That's just one company's approach to serving non-U.S. stakeholders. Starbucks and Procter & Gamble take a different tack, both focusing on supporting overseas small-scale suppliers, but in different ways. Starbucks takes the "fair trade" approach, which returns higher profits to selected indigenous coffee growers. P&G, which markets the Folgers brand, in early 2002 announced a $1.5 donation to kick off a new long-term alliance with TechnoServe, which supports small-scale coffee producers through education, remodeling schools, and donating computers.

Corporate Social Responsibility— Part of Day-to-Day Business

What marks these companies is how they embed corporate social responsibility (CSR) in strategy, often outlining it in policy. Hewlett-Packard has made CSR one of seven corporate objectives. General Mills has a policy statement encouraging employees to volunteer and a volunteerism department at the General Mills Foundation, which helps explain why 70 percent of the workforce volunteers. Environmental commitment is a bullet point in Herman Miller's Blueprint for Corporate Community.

These are a rare breed of committed companies. Getting on the list isn't easy, and staying on it is hard. Thirty-one companies on last year's list dropped off, including **Polaroid, Honeywell, Apple Computer, Dell Computer, Gap** and **Nordstrom**. Companies that never made the list include the much-admired **General Electric**—and **Enron**.

That's not to say these 100 companies are perfect. In reviewing concerns about these firms, we've seen lawsuit settlements in the millions, layoffs of thousands of employees, and other charges leveled about unfair business practices. In some cases *Business Ethics* pulled companies who might otherwise have made the list—as with **Dollar General**, which in January made a substantial restatement of earnings for 1998 to 2000. Or with **Providian Financial Corp.**, which in December 2001 paid $150 million to settle class action lawsuits alleging cheating of credit card holders. No matter how glowing their three-year record of stakeholder service, these incidents said these firms did not belong on the list.

The rest are here for a reason. The list itself is here because it's important to catch companies in the act of doing good. When that is done, perhaps other corporations will catch on to what it means to be a good corporate citizen.

Double *Yield*
The Best Corporate Citizens Perform Better Financially

A new academic study based on the 2001 100 Best Corporate Citizens list found a strong link between good citizenship and superior financial performance. As study co-author Curtis Verschoor wrote in the January 2002 *Strategic Finance* magazine (where he is editor), "This may be the most concrete evidence now available that good citizenship really does pay off on the bottom line."

In the study, researchers Vershoor and Elizabeth Murphy at DePaul University compared the 100 Best with the performance of the rest of the S&P 500. This was done by comparing the citizenship rankings given by *Business Ethics* with financial rankings done by *Business Week*. The latter rankings used eight criteria of financial performance: one- and three-year total return, one- and three-year sales growth, one- and three-year

profit growth, net profit margins, and return on equity. Since firms with a 1999 loss were excluded from the Best Corporate Citizens list, they were likewise excluded from the financial list.

The study showed that firms in the *Business Ethics* list had significantly better overall financial performance. The mean placement for the 100 Best Citizens, on *Business Week's* financial list, was more than 10 percentile points higher than the mean ranking of other S & P companies.

Elizabeth Murphy, Assistant Professor, School of Accountancy and MIS, DePaul University, 1 E. Jackson Blvd., Chicago, IL 60604; emurphy@depaul.edu.

UNIT 5

Developing the Future Ethos and Social Responsibility of Business

Unit Selections

Key Points to Consider

• In what areas should organizations become more ethically sensitive and socially responsible in the next 5 years? Be specific, and explain your choices.

• Obtain codes of ethics or conduct from several different professional associations (for example, doctors, lawyers, CPAs, etc.). What are the similarities and differences between them?

• How useful do you feel codes of ethics are to organizations? Defend your answer.

 **Links: www.dushkin.com/online/**
These sites are annotated in the World Wide Web pages.

International Business Ethics Institute (IBEI)
http://www.business-ethics.org/index.asp
Sheffield University Management School
http://www.shef.ac.uk/uni/academic/I-M/mgt/research/research.html
UNU/IAS Project on Global Ethos
http://www.ias.unu.edu/research/globalethos.cfm

Business ethics should not be viewed as a short-term, "knee-jerk reaction" to recently revealed scandals and corruption. Instead, it should be viewed as a thread woven through the fabric of the entire business culture—one that ought to be integral to its design. Businesses are built on the foundation of trust in our free-enterprise system. When there are violations of this trust between competitors, between employer and employees, or between businesses and consumers, the system ceases to run smoothly.

From a pragmatic viewpoint, the alternative to self-regulated and voluntary ethical behavior and social responsibility on the part of business may be governmental and legislative intervention. From a moral viewpoint, ethical behavior should not exist because of economic pragmatism, governmental edict, or contemporary fashionability—it should exist because it is morally appropriate and right.

This last unit is composed of seven articles that provide some ideas, guidelines, and principles for developing the future ethos and social responsibility of business. In the first article, Archie Carroll discusses some of the ethical challenges that will be faced in the new millennium. The next article discloses how trust, integrity, and fairness are crucial to the bottom line. The third article explains that the effect of the current scandals is that job seekers are going to greater lengths to gauge would-be employers' ethical standards and practices. The fourth selection, "Old Ethical Principles: The New Corporate Culture," analyzes 10 old ethical principles and applies them to the new corporate culture. In the next article, Jeffrey Seglin explains why an ethical business is a profitable one. Then, in "Profits From Principle," Bennett Daviss reflects on why corporations are finding that social responsibility pays off. The last article reflects on the findings of a recent study that when it comes to having a high-powered career and a family, the painful truth is that women in the United States don't "have it all."

ETHICAL CHALLENGES FOR BUSINESS IN THE NEW MILLENNIUM: CORPORATE SOCIAL RESPONSIBILITY AND MODELS OF MANAGEMENT MORALITY

Abstract: As we transition to the 21st century, it is useful to think about some of the most important challenges business and other organizations will face as the new millennium begins. What will constitute "business as usual" in the business ethics arena as we start and move into the new century? My overall thought is that we will pulsate into the future on our current trajectory and that the new century will not cause cataclysmic changes, at least not immediately. Rather, the problems and challenges we face now we will face then. Undoubtedly, new issues will arise but they will more likely be extensions of the present than discontinuities with the past.

Archie B. Carroll

As we transition to the 21st century, it is useful to think about some of the most important challenges business and other organizations will face as the new millennium begins. As I write this essay, the public seems to be more concerned with the Y2K problem and whether their computers will keep working, their power will stay on, their investments will be secure, there will be food in the pantry, airplanes will still fly, and that life as we know it will continue as usual. Optimistically, by the time this is published we will all look back and conclude that technology is amazing, humans are survivors, and we will wonder why we got all worked up about Y2K bug in the first place. This is my hope and expectation, so I approach this writing with the optimism that the world will not end in a technological Armageddon but that the transition will be relatively smooth, though perhaps jerky, and that we will return to business as usual soon thereafter.

This raises the question in my mind as to what will constitute "business as usual" in the business ethics arena as we start and move into the new century. My overall thought is that we will pulsate into the future on our current trajectory and that the new century will not cause cataclysmic changes, at least not immediately. Rather, the problems and challenges we face now we will face then. Undoubtedly, new issues will arise but they will more likely be extensions of the present than discontinuities with the past.

Questions have been raised in the past about ethics in business and they will continue to be raised in the future. The public's perception of business ethics has not wavered much over the past 30 years or so and there is no reason to think this will dramatically change. When the Gallup Poll first asked the public to rate the honesty and ethical standards of business executives in 1977, only 19 percent of those surveyed ranked them as "very high" or "high." When the same question was asked again in October, 1998, the figure was 21 percent. This is slightly better but statistically insignificant over this period of two decades (*American Enterprise*, March/April 1999). To be sure, some groups of businesspeople rank lower, such as stockbrokers, contractors, real estate agents, insurance and car salesmen, and advertising practitioners, but their numbers are pretty stable over this 30-year period as well. There is not much happening to cause us to think this will change.

There are a number of different ways we could approach this task of thinking about ethical challenges in the new millennium. We could think of them in terms of what new issues will arise or what specific industries will be affected. Such an approach would likely cause us to speculate about the impact of technology—computers, the Internet and World Wide Web, electronic commerce, or genetic engineering and human cloning. *Time* magazine has already hailed the 21st century as the "biotech century" (*Time*, January 11, 1999), so we could easily speculate about the business and ethical implications of this new reality we will face. Alternatively, but related, we could think of specific industries that are likely to pose ethical challenges. This approach, of course, would likely take us into medicine and health care (we do have an aging population), insurance, financial services, and telemarketing, just to mention a few.

Another important point is that all issues and topics will become more global in concern. What were once regional and national concerns have quickly become global concerns. George Soros has outlined the "crisis of global capitalism" (Soros 1999) and this doubtless will carry further ethical implications than we have initially thought.

Another approach to this task would be to look at some enduring or generic management challenges that touch the business sector, business organizations, and managers, for that is an arena which will be vital to business ethics regardless of topic, issue, industry, level of global analysis, and so on. In this connection, I have written about two topics over the past twenty years that touch upon managers and organizations, and I would like to spend the balance of this essay reviewing them and thinking about changes, if any, we are likely to see with respect to them: corporate social responsibility (CSR) and models of management morality.

Trends in Corporate Social Responsibility

Twenty years ago I proposed a definition of corporate social responsibility that has been found useful in thinking about businesses' responsibilities to society and has served as a workable base point in theoretical development and research on this topic (Carroll 1979). The four-part definition held that corporations had four responsibilities to fulfill to society: economic, legal, ethical, and discretionary (later referred to as philanthropic). This definition sought to embrace businesses' legitimate economic or profit-making function with responsibilities that extended beyond the basic economic role of the firm. It sought to reconcile the idea that business could focus either on profits or social concerns, but not both. It sought to argue that businesses can not only be profitable and ethical, but that they should fulfill these obligations simultaneously. Though I have described previously each of these four responsibilities that comprise CSR (1991, 1995), it is useful to briefly recap each as we think about the future.

The *economic responsibility* refers to businesses' fundamental call to be a profit-making enterprise. Though profit making is not the purpose of business (from a societal perspective), it is essential as a motivation and reward for those individuals who take on commercial risk. Though it may seem odd to think of this as a "social" responsibility, this is, in effect what it is. The socio-capitalistic system calls for business to be an economic institution, and profit making is an essential ingredient in a free enterprise economy. While we may think of economics as one distinct element of the CSR definition, it is clearly infused or embedded with ethical assumptions, implications, and overtones.

As we transition to the new millennium, the economic responsibility of business remains very important and will be-

come an ever more significant challenge due to global competitiveness. The new century poses an environment of global trade that is complex, fast-paced, and exponentially expanding into capital, enterprise, information, and technology markets (Kehoe 1998). Hamel and Prahalad (1994) have told us that "competing for the future" will be different. They pose the economic challenges of business as tantamount to a revolution in which existing industries—health care, transportation, banking, publishing, telecommunications, pharmaceuticals, retailing, and others—will be profoundly transformed (p. 30). In addition, these challenges will be global.

In addition to economic responsibilities, businesses have *legal responsibilities* as well, as part of their total corporate social responsibility. Just as our society has sanctioned our economic system by permitting business to assume the economic role of producing goods and services and selling them at a profit, it has also laid down certain ground rules—laws—under which business is expected to pursue its economic role. Law reflects a kind of "codified ethics" in society in the sense that it embodies basic notions of fairness or business righteousness, at least as agreed upon by our legislators. As Boatright has concurred, business activity takes place within an extensive framework of law, and all business decisions need to embrace both the legal and the economic though he agrees that the law is not enough (1993, p. 13). In the 21st century, as we usher in the millennium, we will likely see the continuing expansion of the legal system. There will be no relief in sight as the growing number of lawyers being produced annually in our nation's law schools will ensure that the supply will drive the demand. There is no diminishment in Congress of legislators with law degrees. As long as these individuals continue to be instrumental in controlling our legal system, things may well get more litigious rather than less so. Factors in the social environment such as affluence, education, and awareness will continue to produce rising expectations, an entitlement mentality, the rights movement, and a victimization way of thinking. All of these feed into and drive a litigious society (Carroll 1996, pp. 10–16). Many laws are good and valid and reflect appropriate ethical standards, however, and we will continue to see the legal responsibility of business as a robust sphere of activity.

In addition to fulfilling their economic and legal responsibilities, businesses are expected to fulfill ethical responsibilities as well (Carroll 1979). Ethical responsibilities embrace those activities, practices, policies, or behaviors that are expected (in a positive sense) or prohibited (in a negative sense) by societal members though they are not codified into laws. Ethical responsibilities embrace a range of norms, standards, or expectations of behavior that reflect a concern for what consumers, employees, shareholders, the community, and other stakeholders regard as fair, right, just, or in keeping with stakeholders' moral rights or legitimate expectations.

As we transition to the new millennium, this category of CSR will be more important than ever. Business has embraced the notion of business ethics with some conscious degree of enthusiasm over the past decade, and this trend is expected to continue. Organizations such as the Ethics Officers Association and Business for Social Responsibility provide testimony to the institutionalization of this quest. Another statistic is relevant and impressive: corporations now spend over $1 billion per year on ethics consultants (Morgan and Reynolds 1997). A major research firm, Walker Information of Indianapolis, Indiana, markets new and innovative products: business integrity assessments and stakeholder management assessments, side-by-side with more traditional products such as customer satisfaction studies. What was once relegated to writings in obscure academic journals has now made the transition into practitioner books by the dozens. One such example is *The Ethical Imperative* (1998) by consultant John Dalla Costa, wherein he argues that ethics is becoming the defining business issue of our time, affecting corporate profits and credibility, as well as personal security and the sustainability of a global economy. He argues that by conservative estimates yearly losses to corporations due to unethical behavior equal more than the profits of the top forty corporations in North America and that such economic waste and moral loss requires more than a PR Band-Aid.

But there is a possible down side to this obsession that we should be sensitive to as the ethics industry grows and matures and we move into the new century. Morgan and Reynolds (1997) have argued that for two decades now we have engaged in "a vast campaign to clean up our ethical act" in the workplace, politics, and communities. We have crafted mountains of regulations, created vast networks of consultants and committees, and have made terms such as "conflicts of interest" and "the appearance of impropriety" part of our everyday language. However, they argue, the public's confidence in business people and politicians to "do the right thing" has plummeted to an all-time low. They claim we have made legitimate ethical concerns into absurd standards and have wielded our moral whims like dangerous weapons. We have obscured core truths. Now, inflated misdemeanors are the stuff by which careers and reputations are ruined. In this climate, real integrity has been lost to this obsession with wrongdoing. In summary, they have argued that the ethics wars have "undermined American government, business, and society." As we move into the early 2000s, their concerns pose some serious problems for thought and reflection.

The fourth part of the CSR definition is the discretionary, or philanthropic, responsibility. Whereas the economic and legal accountabilities are required of business and ethical behaviors, policies, and practices are expected of business, philanthropy is both expected and desired. In this category we include the public's expectation that business will engage in social activities that are not mandated, not required by law, and not generally expected of business in an ethical sense, though some ethical underpinnings or justification may serve as the rationale for business being expected to be philanthropic. The subtle distinction between ethical and philanthropic responsibilities is that the latter are not expected with the same degree of moral force. In other words, if a firm did not engage in business giving to the extent that certain stakeholder groups expected, these stakeholders would not likely label the firm as unethical or immoral. Thus, the philanthropic expectation does not carry with it the same magnitude of moral mandates as does the ethical category. Examples of philanthropy might include business giving,

community programs, executive loan programs, and employee voluntarism. I have depicted the normative prescription of philanthropy to "be a good corporate citizen." This, however, is a narrow view of corporate citizenship. On another occasion, I proposed a wider view by portraying all four of the CSR categories to constitute the "four faces of corporate citizenship" (Carroll 1998). Upon deeper reflection, I came to think that a wider view which included being profitable, obeying the law, being ethical, and "giving back" to the community, was more fully reflective of what corporate citizenship was all about.

As we transition to the 21st century, I expect the current trend toward "strategic philanthropy" to remain the guiding philosophy. Businesses will continue to strive to align their philanthropic interests with their economic mandates so that both of these objectives may be achieved at the same time. One of business's most significant ethical challenges will be to walk the fine line between conservative and liberal critics of its philanthropic giving. It is becoming increasingly difficult to direct corporate philanthropy without being offensive to some individual or group. Jennings and Cantoni (1998) provided several vivid illustrations of how this might happen. Apparently, retailer Dayton-Hudson made a contribution to Planned Parenthood only to find right-to-lifers outside its stores cutting their credit cards. They did an about-face and made contributions to right-to-life groups only to subject themselves to pro-choice protestors. In other illustrations, U.S. West gave money to the Boy Scouts of America and was flogged by gay-rights activists. Levi Strauss withdrew support from the Boy Scouts, and drew a backlash from religious leaders. This type of dilemma will pose significant and continuing problems for businesses in the future as our special-interest society flourishes.

In summary, as businesses, in their quest to be socially responsible, seek to concurrently (1) be profitable, (2) obey the law, (3) engage in ethical behavior, and (4) give back through philanthropy, they will face new and continuing ethical challenges in the new millennium. I have only touched on some of the relevant issues, but they will doubtless extend beyond what I have chosen to discuss here.

Models of Management Morality

In 1987, I embarked on a "search for the moral manager." Pertinent questions then and now included "are there any?" "where are they?" and "why are they so hard to find?" (Carroll 1987). The thesis of my discussion was that moral managers were so hard to find because the business landscape was so cluttered with immoral and amoral managers. At that time I articulated three models of management morality: Immoral Management, Moral Management, and Amoral Management. The purpose of describing these three moral types was to delineate, define, and emphasize the amoral category and to provide models of management morality that I thought would better convey to businesspeople the range of moral types in which managerial ethics might be classified. I believed that through description and example managers would be able to better assess their own ethical behaviors and motivations and that of other organizational members as well—their supervisors, subordinates, and colleagues. I was moved to emphasize the Amoral Management category by virtue of my observational world that did not seem to fit under the category of Immoral Management. As I recap each of these moral types, I will comment on their relevance as we transition into the 2000s. Immoral and Moral Management are easier to describe and are more traditional, so I will start with them.

Immoral Management (or Managers) is a good place to start, for without them we would have no field known as business ethics. Positing that unethical and immoral are synonymous in the organizational context, I defined Immoral Management as that which is not only devoid of ethical principles or precepts but also positively and actively opposed to what is right or just. In this model, management decisions, actions, and behavior imply a positive and active opposition to what is ethical or moral. Decisions here are discordant with ethical principles and the model implies an active negation of what is moral. Management motives are selfish. They are driven by self-interest wherein management cares only about itself or about the organization's gains. The goal is profitability and success at any price, and legal standards are seen as barriers that must be overcome. The Immoral Management strategy is to exploit opportunities and cut corners wherever it is helpful (Carroll 1987, 1991). In short, the Immoral Managers are the bad guys. It is doubtful that ethics education or more ethical organizational climates will change them.

As we enter the new millennium, I have no strong reason to argue that this group will change significantly. There are still immoral managers and they will likely always be with us. If the initiatives of business ethics scholars, teachers, and consultants have had any impact, combined with initiatives from the business community itself, it is logical to argue that they will be a diminishing if not a vanishing breed.

By contrast, *Moral Management (or Managers)* represents the exemplar toward which I could well argue our teaching and research is directed. That is, as educators and business leaders, we are striving to create Moral Managers. John Boatright, in his 1998 presidential address to the Society for Business Ethics, spoke of a Moral Manager Model, wherein the manager both acted and thought morally, and Boatright concurred that the goal of business ethics is to turn out moral managers. In Moral Management, business decisions, attitudes, actions, policies, and behavior conform to a high standard of ethical, or right, behavior. The goal is conformity to lofty professional standards of conduct. Ethical leadership is commonplace and represents a defining quality. The motives of Moral Managers are virtuous. The motives are directed toward success within the confines of the law and sound ethical precepts (e.g., fairness, justice, due process). The goal of Moral Management is success within the letter and spirit of the law. The law is regarded as a minimum and the Moral Manager prefers to operate well above what the law mandates. The strategy is to live by sound ethical standards and to assume ethical leadership. If Immoral Managers were the bad guys, Moral Managers are the good guys.

There seems to be an inclination toward emphasizing Moral Management as we move into the new century and millennium. Obviously, it is the underlying premise or implicit goal of the business ethics field and much of its literature. For example, Moral Management is similar to Paine's "integrity strategy" in which she argues that ethics should be the driving force of the organization (Paine 1994). The model fits well with Ciulla's and Gini's discussions of ethics as the heart of leadership (Ciulla 1998, Gini 1998), and it is consistent with Aguilar's recommendations for leadership in ethics programs that can contribute substantially to corporate excellence (Aguilar 1994). The Moral Management model follows logically with Wilson's "moral sense" (1993), and is the underlying model for ethical leadership in Hood's "heroic enterprise" (1996). Moral Management is harmonious with Badaracco's belief that executives can use defining moments as an opportunity to redefine their company's role in society (1998). Finally, it must be argued that the Moral Manager is the prototype for "understanding stakeholder thinking" (Nasi 1995) and for managing "the stakeholder organization" (Wheeler and Sillanpaa 1997). Like the other models, the trends here are global (Carroll and Meeks 1999). All of these writings, and many others, suggest a bright future for the Moral Management Model and its associated characteristics.

The third conceptual model is *Amoral Management (or Managers)*. I distinguish between two types of amoral managers— those that are intentional and those that are unintentional. *Intentional Amoral Management* is characterized by a belief that moral considerations have no relevance or applicability in business or other spheres or organizational life. Amoral management holds that management or business activity is outside of or beyond the sphere in which moral judgments apply. These managers think that the business world and the moral world are two separate spheres and never the twain should meet. Intentional Amoral Managers are a vanishing breed as we enter the new millennium. We seldom find anymore managers who think compartmentally in this way. There are a few left, but those who are left seem reluctant to admit that they believe in this way. I do not anticipate that they will be as much of a problem in the next century. Richard DeGeorge (1999) also has been concerned with this group in his discussions of the myth of amoral business in several editions of his *Business Ethics* textbook. As he points out, most people in business do not act unethically or maliciously; they think of themselves, in both their private and their business lives, as ethical people. They simply feel that business is not expected to be concerned with ethics. He describes them as amoral insofar as they feel that ethical considerations are inappropriate in business—after all, business is business (p. 5).

On the other hand, there is *Unintentional Amoral Management*, and it deserves closer scrutiny. These managers do not factor ethical considerations into their decision making, but for a different reason. These managers are well-intentioned but are self-centered in the sense that they do not possess the ethical perception, awareness, or discernment to realize that many of their decisions, actions, policies, and behaviors have an ethical facet or dimension that is being overlooked. These managers are ethically unconscious or insensitive; they are ethically ignorant. To the extent that their reasoning processes possess a moral dimension, it is disengaged. Unintentional Amoral Managers pursue profitability within the confines of the letter of the law, as they do not think about the spirit of the law. They do not perceive who might be hurt by their actions.

The field of managers to whom the Unintentional Amoral Management characteristics apply is large and perhaps growing as the new decade arrives. These managers are not hostile to morality, they just do not understand it. They have potential, but have not developed the key elements or capacities that Powers and Vogel (1980) argue are essential for developing moral judgment. Key among these capacities are a sense of moral obligation, moral imagination, moral identification and ordering, moral evaluation, and the integration of managerial and moral competence. The good news is that this is the group that should be most susceptible to learning, changing, and becoming Moral Managers. Of the three moral management models presented, I would maintain that the Unintentional Amoral Managers probably dominate the managerial landscape. An alternative view is that within each manager, each of the three models may be found at different points in time or in different circumstances, but that the Amoral Management model's characteristics are found most frequently. If these are correct assessments, this represents a huge challenge for business ethics educators, consultants, and organizations seeking to brink out the Moral Management model in the new millennium.

Conclusion

There will be many challenges facing the business community and organizational managers as we transition into the new millennium. Many industries and business sectors will be affected. Products and services as well as channels of distribution may be revolutionized and with these changes will come the usual kinds of ethical issues that commercial activity inevitably generates. Though it is impossible to predict all the arenas that will be affected, the safest conclusion is that many of the issues we have faced in the latter half of the twentieth century will endure for some time to come. Corporate social responsibility will continue to be a meaningful issue as it embraces core concerns that are necessary to the citizenry and business alike. Companies will be expected to be profitable, abide by the law, engage in ethical behavior, and give back to their communities through philanthropy, though the tensions between and among these responsibilities will become more challenging as information technology continues to push all enterprises toward a global-level frame of reference and functioning.

With respect to the three models of management morality, it is expected that Immoral Management will diminish somewhat as values and moral themes permeate and grow in the culture and the commercial sphere. Immoral Management will become an endangered species but will not disappear. Greed and human nature will ensure that Immoral Managers will al-

ways be with us. Our goal will be to minimize their number and the severity of their impact. The Moral Management model will grow in importance as an exemplar toward which business and organizational activity will be focused. The great opportunity will be in the vast realms of Unintentionally Amoral Managers. As the public and many private schools and educational systems continue to eliminate a concern for virtue and morals from classroom teaching, or alternatively, promote values clarification or ethical relativism, a ready supply of amoral young people entering business and organizational life will be guaranteed. In recent years, however, there have been the beginnings of a moral awakening in society, and I would like to believe that this optimistic paradigm will succeed, grow, and survive, but it will be facing major obstacles. At best, unintentional amorality will continue to be with us, and thus we ethics professors and consultants will continue to be employed and to have a challenging task ahead of us as the new millennium arrives.

Bibliography

Aguilar, Francis J. 1994. *Managing Corporate Ethics*. New York: Oxford University Press.

American Enterprise. 1999. "Opinion Pulse." May/June, p. 90.

Badaracco, Joseph L., Jr. 1998. "The Discipline of Building Character." *Harvard Business Review*, March–April, pp. 115–124.

Boatright, John R. 1993. *Ethics and the Conduct of Business*. Englewood Cliffs, N.J.: Prentice-Hall.

Boatright, John R. 1998. "Does Business Ethics Rest on a Mistake?" San Diego: Society for Business Ethics Presidential Address, August 6–9.

Carroll, Archie B. 1979. "A Three-Dimensional Conceptual Model of Corporate Social Performance." *Academy of Management Review* 4: 497–505.

_____. 1987. "In Search of the Moral Manager." *Business Horizons*, March–April. pp. 7–15.

_____. 1991. "The Pyramid of Corporate Social Responsibility: Toward the Moral Management of Organizational Stakeholders." *Business Horizons* 34: 39–48.

_____. 1995. "Stakeholder Thinking in Three Models of Management Morality: A Perspective with Strategic Implications." In *Understanding Stakeholder Thinking*, ed. Juha Nasi. Helsinki: LSR-Publications, pp. 47–74. Also in Clarkson 1998, pp. 139–172.

_____. 1996. *Business and Society: Ethics and Stakeholder Management*, 3rd ed. Cincinnati: South-Western College Publishing/International Thompson Publishing.

_____. 1998. "The Four Faces of Corporate Citizenship." *Business and Society Review* 100/101: 1–7.

_____ and Meeks, Michael D. 1999. "Models of Management Morality: European Applications and Implications." *Business Ethics: A European Review* 8, no. 2: 108–116.

Clarkson, Max B. E., ed. 1998. *The Corporation and its Stakeholders: Classic and Contemporary Readings*. Toronto: University of Toronto Press.

Ciulla, Joanne B. 1998. *Ethics, the Heart of Leadership*. Westport, Conn.: Praeger.

Costa, John Dalla. 1998. *The Ethical Imperative: Why Moral Leadership is Good Business*. Reading, Mass.: Addison-Wesley.

DeGeorge, Richard T. 1999. *Business Ethics*. 5th ed. Upper Saddle River, N.J.: Prentice-Hall.

Gini, Al. 1998. "Moral Leadership and Business Ethics." In *Ethics, the Heart of Leadership*, ed. Joanne Ciulla, pp. 27–45.

Hamel, Gary and Prahalad, C. K. 1994. *Competing for the Future.* Boston: Harvard Business School Press.

Hood, John M. 1996. *The Heroic Enterprise: Business and the Common Good.* New York: The Free Press.

Isaacson, Walter. 1999. "The Biotech Century." *Time,* January 11, pp. 42–43.

Jennings, Marianne and Cantoni, Craig. 1998. "An Uncharitable Look at Corporate Philanthropy." *Wall Street Journal,* December 22, p. A8.

Kehoe, William J. 1998. "GATT and WTO Facilitating Global Trade." *Journal of Global Business,* Spring, pp. 67–76.

Morgan, Peter W. and Reynolds, Glenn H. 1997. *The Appearance of Impropriety: How the Ethics Wars Have Undermined American Government, Business, and Society.* New York: The Free Press.

Nasi, Juha, ed. 1995. *Understanding Stakeholder Thinking.* Helsinki, Finland: LSR Publications.

Paine, Lynn Sharp. 1994. "Managing for Organizational Integrity." *Harvard Business Review,* March–April, pp. 106–117.

Powers, Charles W. and Vogel, David. 1980. *Ethics in the Education of Business Managers.* Hastings-on-Hudson, N.Y.: The Hastings Center, pp. 40–45.

Soros, George. 1998. *The Crisis of Global Capitalism.* New York: Public Affairs.

Wheeler, David and Sillanpaa, Maria. 1997. *The Stakeholder Corporation.* London: Pitman Publishing.

Wilson, James Q. 1993. *The Moral Sense.* New York: The Free Press.

After Enron: The Ideal Corporation

Following the abuses of the '90s, executives are learning that trust, integrity, and fairness do matter—and are crucial to the bottom line

By John A. Byrne

Every summer for the past 10 years, Jack Stack has been going to Massachusetts Institute of Technology's Sloan School of Management to speak with young chief executives about the ideals and values of the engine manufacturing company he helped to make a management paragon. In the late 1980s, Stack's Springfield ReManufacturing Corp. emerged as a model for how management and labor could successfully work together in a culture of trust and ownership. Thousands of managers flocked to his company to hear his ideas while others gathered to hear him during his annual trek to MIT for its Birthing of Giants program for new CEOs.

But as the dot-com era took hold in the late 1990s, Stack saw a change in the attitudes of the business leaders who showed up at MIT. They seemed far more ambitious for themselves than for their companies. They were building organizations to flip, not to last. They were more interested in the value of their stockholdings than the profits of their companies. They told him his ideas for tapping into the enthusiasm, intelligence, and creativity of working people were antiquated. And they said he was out of touch.

Stack says that even he began to think of himself as a dinosaur. "So many young CEOs were mesmerized by getting a $1 million or $2 million pop, selling out, and then getting out of town," he says. "They forgot that business is all about values."

Suddenly, leaders like Stack—people who take concepts like ethics and fairness seriously—are back in vogue in a big way. In the post-Enron, post-bubble world, there's a yearning for corporate values that reach higher than the size of the chief executive's paycheck or even the latest stock price. Trust, integrity, and fairness do matter, and they are crucial to the bottom line. The corporate leaders and entrepreneurs who somehow forgot that are now paying the price in a downward market roiled by a loss of investor confidence. "The chasm that separates individuals and organizations is marked by frustration, mistrust, disappointment, and even rage," says Shoshana Zuboff, a Harvard Business School professor and co-author of a new book called *The Support Economy*.

The realization that many companies played fast and loose with accounting rules and ethical standards in the 1990s is leading to a reevaluation of corporate goals and purpose. Zuboff and many other business observers are optimistic that the abuses now dominating the headlines may result in healthy changes in the post-Enron modern corporation. What's emerging is a new model of the ideal corporation.

Business leaders say corporations will likely become far more transparent—not only for investors, but also for employees, customers, and suppliers. The single-minded focus on "shareholder value," which measured performance on the sole basis of stock price, will diminish. Instead, companies will elevate the interests of employees, customers, and their communities. Executive pay, which clearly soared out of control in the past two decades, is already undergoing a reassessment and will likely fall back in an effort to create a sense of fairness. And corporate cultures will change in a way that puts greater emphasis on integrity and trust.

The new agenda, say management observers, will require greater investment in financial systems, ethics training, and corporate governance. It may also demand a resetting of expectations so that investors are more realistic about the returns a company can legitimately and consistently achieve in highly competitive markets. Growth rates of 20% and up, even in technologically-driven industries, are likely to be a thing of the past.

In the anything-goes 1990s, too many companies allowed performance to be disconnected from meaningful corporate values. "A lot of companies simply looked at performance in assessing their leaders," says Larry Johnston, CEO of Albertson's Inc. (ABS), the food retailer. "There have to be two dimensions to leadership: performance and values. You can't have one without the other."

This and other changes will be driven less by the threat of government intervention and more by the stigma of being branded an unethical enterprise. That's why the government's newfound zeal to indict individuals and even companies carries such power, regardless of how the cases are resolved. "Social sanctions may eclipse the law in imposing penalties for misconduct and mischief," says Richard T. Pascale, a management authority and author of *Surfing the Edge of Chaos*. "The corporation of the future has to think about this new development as an increasingly formidable factor to be reckoned with."

That's a change from the 1990s, when pressure from Wall Street and the dot-com mania led to much of the corporate excess. During those years, when Stack found his ideas decidedly out of favor, he stuck with the "open-book management" culture that had made him something of a celebrity years earlier. By sharing all of the company's financials with all employees and giving them an ownership stake in the company, Stack had built a level of mutual trust and respect unusual in business.

There were other organizations that clung to similar beliefs, from Southwest Airlines Co. (LUV) to Harley-Davidson (HDI). "We all stayed close together because we knew the dot-com model didn't have legs," says Stack. "But many of us wondered if the world would get back to companies with real values." Right now, Stack's ideas about leadership and management are resonating with many who feel disillusioned about business.

If there's one change that nearly everyone foresees today, it's a move to make the corporation far more transparent. That's obvious when it comes to investors, who are demanding truth in the numbers and clarity in disclosure. But it's also important for employees if they're to have a true sense of ownership in their company's affairs. At Stack's company, there are weekly huddles with workers and managers, prominent scorecards on factory walls charting work progress, and ongoing emphasis by managers on building a company and not just a product. Workers undergo training so they can understand the numbers on a balance sheet and an income statement.

That need to make the inner workings of the corporation visible to all constituencies is expected to drive lots of change. "In some sense, there aren't going to be many secrets in business anymore," believes consultant James A. Champy, chairman of Perot Systems Corp.'s (PER) consulting practice. "Even customers are calling for it today. Wal-Mart Stores Inc. (WMT) wants to know what the costs of its suppliers are." The end result: It will put greater pressure on companies to clean up their management processes and become more efficient, and it will cause yet another reexamination of less-profitable businesses.

Corporate cultures, which in many cases veered out of control in the 1990s by emphasizing profit at any cost, are also in for an overhaul. More than anything else, those beliefs and attitudes are set by the top execs. The values they espouse, the incentives they put in place, and their own behavior provide the cues for the rest of the organization. "The CEO sets the tone for an organization's culture," says Alfred P. West Jr., founder and CEO of financial-services firm SEI Investments Co. (SEIC), which operates the back-office services for mutual funds and bank trust departments.

Like Stack, West is a rather uncommon CEO. As the company's founder, he does not take stock options and pays himself a sober $660,000 a year. Rather than a spacious corner office, he has the same open-plan office space and desk as anyone else at company headquarters in Oaks, Pa., and he shuns the perks that are commonly demanded in the executive contract. Why? "If you separate yourself from everybody else with corporate aircraft and enormous stock options, your employees are going to get the wrong message," says West.

To make sure they get the right message, West spends a lot of time banging home his vision of the company to the people who work there. His goal of building an open culture of integrity, ownership, and accountability is a harbinger for what organizations will look like in the future. "We tell our employees a lot about where the company is going. We overcommunicate the vision and the strategy and continually reinforce the culture." Companies are also using that kind of openness to make it easier for their employees to report ethical lapses and unfair practices with whistle-blower hotlines and open procedures for airing grievances. And to give employees an incentive to use all that newly available information, many companies will help them acquire stakes through discounted stock plans. And even stock options are in for a revamping—with longer vesting periods and perhaps mandatory holding periods as well.

Through the current dark period, there's reason for optimism. Harvard's Zuboff notes that capitalism has avoided devastating crises because it is a robust economic system that changes and adapts. The unprecedented economic expansion of the 1990s was widely seen as the triumph of managerial capitalism. Highly motivated business people used public capital to bring to life creative ideas and concepts for new companies and products. Corporate ownership was dispersed among many shareholders, but control and the lion's share of rewards were concentrated at the top of the managerial hierarchy—whether the company was a startup or an incumbent.

The next stage, believes Zuboff, will be something she calls "distributed capitalism," in which ownership will be more widely spread and organizations will be as responsive to their employees and communities as they have been to their shareholders in the past decade.

Wishful thinking? Perhaps. But the first task of the post-Enron corporation is to acknowledge that a company's viability now depends less on making the numbers at any cost and more on the integrity and trustworthiness of its practices. In the future, leadership that preaches this new ethos and reinforces it through value-driven cultures will be far more likely to reap the rewards of the changing marketplace.

Reprinted with special permission from *Business Week*, August 26, 2002, pp. 68–70, 74. © 2002 by The McGraw-Hill Companies, Inc.

Wanted: Ethical Employer

Job Hunters, Seeking to Avoid An Enron or an Andersen, Find It Isn't Always Easy

BY KRIS MAHER

AN ATTRACTIVE title and good pay weren't Kathleen Britton's only priorities during her recent job hunt. She says she was equally keen to find a new employer with a squeaky-clean reputation.

Ms. Britton, 45 years old, was an assistant vice president at a New York brokerage house and was laid off in December, she says, partly because she raised concerns about certain practices in the investment-banking unit. Regulators later interviewed her for a related investigation.

When Ms. Britton joined the firm in 1995, she says she ignored her qualms about a questionable prior dealing, which had been settled with authorities, because the brokerage house enjoyed widespread respect in the industry. She says she expects to accept a position next month at a big financial-services firm, and this time, she says, she checked her new employer much more thoroughly. "I trusted my ethics and my judgment," she says.

The current wave of corporate scandals is leading more job seekers to go to greater lengths to gauge would-be employers' ethical standards and practices. They are poring over Internet message boards looking for staffers' appraisals of management, checking financial histories and seeking meetings with present and past employees. The downside: It is impossible to uncover everything about a corporation's moral weak spots in advance.

Gun-shy candidates say they fear that joining an unethical employer could endanger their tenure, retirement savings and self-esteem. As countless **Arthur Andersen** LLP staffers are discovering, working for a business with a damaged reputation also can impede future job prospects by leaving a black mark on a résumé.

Many companies have begun to notice heightened concerns about ethical standards among both job seekers and recent hires. "With respect to new employees that have come in the last few months, I've had seven to nine who've said to me that one of the reasons they came to UTC is that they had researched our ethics program," says Patrick Gnazzo, vice president of business prac-

tices for manufacturer **United Technologies** Corp. in Hartford, Conn. "I haven't noticed that before in any great degree."

Mr. Gnazzo anticipates a further increase in ethics-related inquiries when United Technologies recruits at business schools in the fall. Describing the company's dedication to high ethical standards "is a great recruiting tool," he says. In 1986, United Technologies started an "ombudsman/dialog" program that lets employees inquire anonymously about ethics issues. The program has received nearly 56,000 inquiries.

Some job seekers figure out how well a company puts its values into practice from clues they collect during job interviews. A red flag should go up, for instance, if a hiring manager promises an excessive severance package following a layoff without first consulting a higher-level executive. "That tips you off about a lack of controls," says Richard Bayer, chief operating officer of the Five O'Clock Club, a career-counseling organization based in New York.

Despite their more extensive checks, some new hires don't discover corporate-ethics shortcomings until after they arrive. Mark Tremont says he thought he had thoroughly investigated a West Coast start-up before he became its chief financial officer several months ago. The 54-year-old executive consulted his personal network to learn about the company's finances and business practices. He also spent about two weeks in face-to-face discussions with top managers there.

Once he started work, however, Mr. Tremont says that he grew uncomfortable with how the chief executive had handled several past financial transactions. The CEO "didn't lie, he didn't do anything illegal," Mr. Tremont says. "He just dealt in a gray area I didn't want to deal in."

Mr. Tremont says he quit three weeks after he arrived. "My personal reputation was worth more than anything," he says. Now, the Bellevue, Wash., resident says he is doing volunteer work part-time while he searches for another position.

Other applicants putting would-be employers under a microscope feel frustrated by how little information they can glean in

A Job Seeker's Ethics Audit

Some probing questions to ask about a prospective employer:

- Is there a formal code of ethics? How widely is it distributed? Is it reinforced in other formal ways such as through decision-making systems?
- Are workers at all levels trained in ethical decision making? Are they also encouraged to take responsibility for their behavior or to question authority when asked to do something they consider wrong?
- Do employees have formal channels available to make their concerns known confidentially? Is there a formal committee high in the organization that considers ethical issues?
- Is misconduct disciplined swiftly and justly within the organization?
- Is integrity emphasized to new employees?
- How are senior managers perceived by subordinates in terms of their integrity? How do such leaders model ethics behavior?

Source: Linda K. Trevino, chair of the Department of Management and Organization, Smeal College of Business, Pennsylvania State University

advance. "From the outside, it's really hard to tell," says a former television producer for a public-relations agency in New York.

She says questionable billing practices and "an accumulation of inappropriate behavior" led her to quit the agency in April 2001 without lining up another position. The 34-year-old producer says she now is seeking a corporate-communications position at a pharmaceutical company in part because the drug industry is considered to be highly regulated.

Some businesses resist prospects' inquiries about their less-than-comprehensive ethics programs, though. Job hunters should view such hesitation as another reason to look elsewhere, experts say. "If an organization is uncomfortable with you asking questions, then I would say that that's a sign right there," says Linda K. Trevino, a professor of organizational behavior at Pennsylvania State University's Smeal College of Business.

Ms. Trevino gives her business students a list of questions to help clarify a company's culture and the effectiveness of its ethics program. She believes it is more important than ever to conduct this "ethical culture audit." The list includes: "Is integrity emphasized to recruits and new employees?" and "Are people of integrity promoted? Are means as well as ends important?"

At the nation's biggest companies, it is relatively simple for applicants to find out official ethics policies. Most have adopted ethics codes and describe their ethics programs on corporate Web sites.

But job seekers shouldn't be overly impressed simply because a company has a code, cautions Edward Petry, executive director of the Ethics Officer Association, a professional group in Belmont, Mass., with 805 members. According to Mr. Petry, it is more important to find out how easily employees can get guidance on ethics issues and what kind of ethics training a company offers.

Mr. Petry also urges candidates to ask whether a potential employer has an ethics officer—and whether that individual reports to the chief executive and the board audit committee. Another thing to watch for is whether a company integrates its purported values into performance appraisals and compensation plans. "You'll find that very few do," he reports.

Old Ethical Principles

THE NEW CORPORATE CULTURE

Address by WILLIAM J. BYRON, S. J., Distinguished Professor of Management, McDonough School of Business, Georgetown University, Washington, D.C.
Delivered to the Annual Luncheon of the Duquesne University NMA Students Association, Pittsburgh, Pennsylvania, April 21, 1999

It would be an interesting exercise if you attempted, right now as I begin to address the topic, "Old Ethical Principles for the New Corporate Culture," to jot down on a notepad (on a mental notepad, at least) what you would regard as old or "classic" ethical principles—the time-honored, enduring principles that should always be there to guide the business decision maker.

I've come up with ten and will attempt to apply them to the new corporate culture. Without waiting for you to give me yours, I'm going to proceed to list mine. Here they are: (I) the principle of human dignity; (II) the principle of participation; (III) the principle of integrity; (IV) the principle of fairness (justice); (V) the principle of veracity; (VI) the principle of keeping commitments; (VII) the principle of social responsibility; (VIII) the principle of subsidiarity; (IX) the principle of pursuit of the common good; and (X) the ethical principle of love.

Principles are initiating impulses—they are internalized convictions that produce action. Principles direct your actions and your choices. Your principles help to define who you are. Principles are beginnings, they lead to something.

How do the old ethical principles outlined above play themselves out today in the new corporate culture? First a word about both "culture" and what is new in the "new" corporate culture.

A culture is a set of shared meanings, principles, and values. Values define cultures. Where values are widely shared, you have an identifiable culture. There are as many different cultures as there are distinct sets of shared meanings, principles, and values. This is not to say that everyone in a given culture is the same. No, you have diversity of age, wealth, class, intelligence, education, and responsibility in a given culture where diverse people are unified by a shared belief system, a set of agreed-upon principles, a collection of common values. They literally have a lot in common and thus differ from other people in other settings who hold a lot of other things in common. You notice it in law firms, hospitals, colleges, corporations—wherever people comment on the special "culture" that characterizes the place.

The old corporate culture in America was characterized by values like freedom, individualism, competition, loyalty, thrift, fidelity to contract, efficiency, self-reliance, power, and profit. If not controlled by self, or by social norms, or by public law, pursuit of some of these values could be fueled by unworthy values like greed and the desire to dominate. You have to remember that for some people greed is a value (a supreme value!), so is revenge; the list of negative destructive values could run on.

The new (or newer, or most recent) corporate culture is defined by many, but not all, of these same values, although they are interpreted now somewhat differently. And there are some new values emerging in the new corporate context. Think of this new context in terms of what might be called the new corporate contract.

What was once presumed to be a long-term "relational contract" can no longer be relied upon to sustain an uninterrupted employment relationship over time. What brings employees, even managerial employees, and their employers together in corporate America is now more of a 3 transactional contract; the transaction and the concomitant employment may be short-lived. Both parties to the employment transaction (the new corporate contract) negotiate the arrangement in a new way. The middle manager, for example, wanting to be hired says, in effect,

"If you hold me contingent, I'll hold you contingent." He or she will settle in, but not too comfortably; other options will always be explored, front-end financial considerations will be more important than they were in more stable times, and severance packages will be filled and neatly wrapped before the job begins. Not only will other options be considered as the ink is drying on the new employment contract, but actual offers will be entertained at any time.

Another term for this approach is free-agent management. The free agent will not jump unless a safe landing is assured, and he or she is well aware that the best way to get a new job is to be effective, and appear to be content, in the old one. But contingency, not loyalty, is the thread that ties the contracting parties together today. Let me continue the comparison now with the way things used to be.

Whereas the old (say, fifty years ago) corporate culture would tolerate an employer's not looking much beyond the interests of a firm's shareholders, the new corporate culture is growing comfortable with the notion of "stakeholder" and sees an ethical connection between the firm and not only its shareholders, but all others who have a stake in what that firm does: Employees, suppliers, customers, the broader community, and the physical environment, to name just a few. The corporate outlook is more communitarian, more attentive to the dictates of the common good. There was some of this in the past, a "social compact" between employer and employee that was somewhat paternalistic and relatively free of both the deregulation and foreign competition that have caused much of the present economic dislocation in America, but the dominant value of the old corporate culture was individualism, not communitarianism. There is evidence now that individualism is again on the rise. As that happens, you have to begin to wonder about the fate of a few of those "old" ethical principles.

What is "new" in the new corporate culture is more easily examined these days through the lens of employment contracts (written or unwritten). People have been getting fired since hired hands were first employed to extend an owner's reach and productivity. But now there is something new in the old reality of layoff or separation from payroll. In that "something new" lies the difference between firing and downsizing. There is more to the difference than a simple distinction between blue and white collars. Today's wilted white collars were never so plentiful, and their wearers' hopes for quick and permanent reinstatement have never been so thin.

Typically, organizations are "downsized" at the end of a process that has come to be known as delayering, restructuring, or reengineering. The machine-tool metaphors veil the psychological pain felt by men and women who are set adrift. Not all that long ago, those who bounced back quickly were leaving organizations that were not shrinking, just experiencing turnover. This was before the days of what the Economist of London, in describing the contemporary American economy, called "corporate anorexia."

Multiplication of managerial positions was then taken for granted as technology developed, markets expanded, and the economy grew. Now technology keeps on expanding, many old markets (and lots of new ones) continue to grow along with the economy. But layers of management, like so many rugs, are being pulled out from under the well-shod feet that, until recently, walked with confidence along the corridors of corporate America. Now they are out and looking—many could be looking for quite awhile unless they understand themselves and the new corporate culture. As their organizations shrink, displaced managers themselves have to expand personally. They have to enlarge their outlook and their personal ensemble of employable skills.

Now with all of this said, I want to line up the old ethical principles over against the ethical challenges presented by this new corporate culture.

I. The Principle of Human Dignity.

This is the bedrock principle of both personal and social ethics. In the new corporate culture, human dignity is taking a beating. In some corporations, workers at all levels are being treated as if they were disposable parts. Although employees will, regrettably, but for sound economic reasons, continue to be separated from their jobs, they must never be viewed by those making the downsizing decisions as disposable parts.

II. The Principle of Participation.

Every human person in any workplace has a right to have some say in the decisions that affect his or her livelihood. To be shut out of all discussion is to be denied respect for one's human dignity. The ethical thing to do in this new corporate culture, in cases either of layoff or of career continuation in the same organization, is to involve the employee in planning and in the execution of the plan. This means preparation for separation, should that have to happen; it also means enhancing the "value added" potential and the productivity of employees who will remain.

III. The Principle of Integrity.

Honesty is always the best policy on both sides of the employer-employee hyphen; it is also the best policy to guide relations with all the organization's stockholders.

It is one thing to take severe measures to guarantee the survival of the enterprise, it is quite another to deceive others and even worse to reduce employment in order to improve a balance sheet or boost a stock price. After downsizing, some who remain and occupy positions of power at the top of the organization will benefit economically; they should be honest about the extent of that benefit and the uses they intend to make of what might well be regarded as a windfall.

IV. The Principle of Fairness (Justice).

Everyone knows what fairness is. At least we think we know, and we are usually convinced that we are absolutely right. We just know it! Sometimes, a few additional facts or the recognition of our own biases will prompt us to reset our fairness clock, but we have a way of just knowing when unfair treatment occurs.

A strong sense of justice will safeguard a person of integrity from violating any trust. If no trusts are violated, if no injustice is involved, a downsizing in response to economic necessity can be justified. But there is such a deep feeling of injustice, of unfair treatment, in so many downsized corners of our new corporate culture that those in control must examine their corporate conscience for evidence of injustice done to millions of separated employees in recent years.

V. The Principle of Veracity.

Why "veracity" when you've just noted that "integrity" belong on your list? Integrity means living truthfully, while veracity, of course, means speaking truthfully.

Veracity is truthfullness, and the truth will always set you free. There may be unpleasant consequences for you if you tell the truth. But, as the saying goes, "the truth will always out," and the truth teller will always have a place to stand, a soul to claim, and a peace of mind that can never be taken away. Truth not just when convenient, truth in all circumstances is the only compass that works in an age of ambiguity. Truth telling, as difficult as it may be at times, is the only way to preserve an ethical corporate culture.

VI. The Principle of Keeping Commitments.

Here again the issue of trust is in the foreground. Inevitably, when journalistic accounts of the new corporate culture touch upon the human side of downsizing, you will read that corporate loyalty is a thing of the past. Corporations no longer keep their commitments, the story usually goes. And often that is exactly the case.

Commitments are the cement of social relationships. If commitments are kept in the workplace, morale and a sense of security will be high. If a firm simply cannot make commitments to its employees, uncertainty, anxiety, and the individual's commitment to self-preservation will increase in the best of hearts and the best of workplaces. Since fewer and fewer firms are able in this new corporate culture to promise permanent employment, closer and completely honest communication is all the more necessary if trust is to be preserved in the workplace.

VII. The Principle of Corporate Social Responsibility.

This principle relates to the economic, the legal, the ethical, and the positive discretionary or philanthropic categories of a firm's behavior. The good corporate citizen will make a profit and abide by the law. Just to remain within the law, however, is not the sum and substance of corporate responsibility; not everything that is required by ethics is also required by law.

Corporate ethical responsibility stretches all the way from respect for individual human dignity (in employees, customers, suppliers, colleagues, competitors) all the way out to respect for the physical environment that is necessary to sustain life on this planet.

Countless ethical considerations come to mind in the context of downsizing and this new corporate culture of economic uncertainty and contingent employment. One that I see as crucial belongs in the category of "employability" and applies to both employer and employee. Keeping an employee employable is an ethical responsibility of both employer and employee in the new corporate culture.

In a knowledge economy (not simply an "information economy") like ours in this new corporate culture, the ethical imperative points not only to the care of casualties, but also to the advancement of education for the cultivation of new ideas, new creativity, new technology, new products, services, and eventually, jobs.

VIII. The Principle of Subsidiarity.

Those who say the care of economic casualties and the creation of jobs should be "left to government," risk violating the principle of subsidiarity, which would allow neither decisions nor actions at a higher level of organization that could be taken just as effectively and efficiently at a lower level. This principle would push decision making down to lower levels, but sometimes government must act in the interest of the common good. And there will be instances when only government can address an issue properly and effectively.

The principle of subsidiarity should also apply in private sector organizations, in ordinary workplaces. This ties in with the principle of participation and, as is so often the case, is reducible to the principle of human dignity. Individuals are not to be ground under by impersonal, anonymous decision makers at higher levels in the organization.

IX. The Principal of Pursuit of the Common Good

Is a basic principle of ethical behavior; it is a bedrock principle like the principle of human dignity. Without it, social chaos would prevail. The "Common Good" is a catch-all phrase that describes an environment that is supportive of the development of human potential while safeguarding the community against individual excesses.

It looks to the general good, to the good of the many over against the interests of the one.

It is important that there be agreement in the community that the common good should always prevail over individual, personal interests. To promote and protect the common good is the reason why governments exist—a point worth noting here just after a discussion of the principle of subsidiarity, the principle that has a way of keeping government in its proper place.

X. Love.

One reason why the old ethical principles have continuing relevance in this new corporate culture, is the fact that they are rooted in a human nature that does not change all that much from age to age. Underlying human nature in any circumstance is the law of love. The challenge today is not to find a replacement for the law of love, which is always applicable, of course, to God, self, family, neighbor, and workplace associates, the challenge is just to let love happen in this new, but still very human corporate culture. The challenge is also there to be clear about the meaning of love; it means sacrifice, the willingness to be and do for others.

Now go back to your mental notepad and compare the "old" ethical principles you listed there with the ones outlined in this presentation. It would be regrettable, wouldn't it, if all those old principles just grow older as newer and greater challenges appear in the corporate culture and in the other activity centers of contemporary American life. That could happen. It will certainly happen if those who still recognize the old principles do nothing to apply them.

From *Vital Speeches of the Day*, July 1, 1999, pp. 558–561. © 1999 by City News Publishing Company, Inc. Reprinted by permission of *Vital Speeches of the Day* and the author.

DO IT RIGHT

A noted author explains why an ethical business is a profitable business.

BY JEFFREY L. SEGLIN

Business ethics? Isn't that one of those celebrated oxymorons, like military intelligence or jumbo shrimp? Oh, sure, every business school likes to make noise about the ethics courses in its curriculum. But the wizened professors who teach those courses, even at top MBA programs, often make snide comments about feeling marginalized. It's like being that lump of spinach lying on a plate next to a big juicy steak.

26: PERCENTAGE OF B-SCHOOL STUDENTS WHO WOULD LET A GIFT SWAY A COMPANY PURCHASING DECISION

ALL STATS FROM AN EXCLUSIVE SURVEY OF 445 U.S. BUSINESS SCHOOL STUDENTS BY *MBA JUNGLE*, 2001.

So why bother doing the right thing? Why bother even thinking about doing the right thing? It's a question I've been asked by CEOs and students alike. After all, few employers are likely to grill recruits about their grades in an ethics class. Why should you apportion any of your intellectual appetite to something as abstract—and as seemingly intangible—as ethics, when you could be devouring the things that really matter to the bottom line: an entrepreneurial finance text, say, or the arcane details of trading currency futures?

The answer depends on whom you ask. A philosopher might wax lofty about how doing right is its own reward. A priest might invoke heaven and hell. But a business professor will likely tell you this: Ethics and profits are not mutually exclusive. In fact, a growing body of research suggests they are inseparable. The companies—and businesspeople—with the highest ethical standards tend to greatly outperform the Machiavellian wanna-bes. In other words: no spinach, no steak. It's that simple.

Ethical Management Is Better Management

Over the years, I've found that one of the challenges of any discussion about business ethics, whether it occurs in the class-

room, in executive offices, or on the shop floor, is that the mere mention of the topic conjures up unpleasant images: phalanxes of finger-wagging Naderites getting their jollies at the expense of those trying to make an honest buck; armies of oversensitized poetry majors who'd sooner forfeit every worldly possession than harm one scale on a snail darter's back. And let's face it, nobody wants to be lectured, particularly by the likes of them. But the notion that business ethics is primarily about passing judgment, that it always focuses on determining absolute rights and wrongs, is flawed. A more informed view acknowledges that the choices a person makes are seldom black and white. In fact, managers are often faced with a choice between two equally right—or wrong—options.

PERCENTAGE WHO WOULD LOOK AT AN EXAM THEY FOUND THE DAY BEFORE HAVING TO TAKE IT: 34

Broadly speaking, I've come to think of practicing business ethics as weighing the impact of our decisions—and working through all their implications—on the various constituencies involved. What, exactly, are those constituencies? In my book, *The Good, the Bad, and Your Business: Choosing Right When Ethical Dilemmas Pull You Apart*, I categorized them as Money, People, and the Common Good. The money sector should be obvious: What financial impact will a decision have? The people you need to consider are employees, customers, and other individuals who might be affected by your decisions. And the common good involves the greater community in which you operate the business—not just the physical neighborhood and its residents but also the network of vendors and suppliers you use. If you think of these three areas as a Venn diagram with each category represented by a circle, the point of overlap for the three is where the interests of each have been addressed for the most positive outcome. Of course, you can't always completely satisfy each constituency's needs, but in the decision-making process you've fully thought through the implications of your actions and tried your best to understand their impact. It's really no different from what a chess master does—playing out every move, every contingency in his head before lifting his finger from the piece.

If that sounds remarkably similar to the way you've been taught to make management decisions, that's because, frankly, it is. The reason ethical decision making is such a powerful business tool is that it forces us to calculate and reflect upon the effects of our actions. In other words, ethical management is good management.

But what about the bottom line? Isn't that where good management begins and ends? After all, as no less a light than Milton Friedman, Nobel laureate in economics, observed, a business's social responsibility is to its stockholders. Therefore, its objective should be to increase profits. Period. That's tough to argue with, but consider the research of John Kotter and James Heskett, two Harvard Business School professors who studied decision making and performance in 207 large American firms over an 11-year period. Their study, published in 1992, found that the more single-minded a company's focus on the putative needs of the stockholders, the less return those stockholders are likely to get. Ironic, isn't it?

Heskett and Kotter concluded that those firms that both paid attention to the needs of all constituencies—customers, employees, and stockholders—and emphasized leadership from managers at all levels, actually "outperformed firms that did not have those cultural traits by a huge margin." If you're looking for bottom-line impact, consider the numbers: Over the 11-year period studied, companies whose focus extended beyond the balance sheet "increased revenues by an average of 682 percent versus 166 percent for those companies that didn't, expanded their work forces by 282 percent versus 36 percent, grew their stock prices by 901 percent versus 74 percent, and improved their net incomes by 756 percent versus 1 percent." That's more than slightly significant.

Of course, paying attention to how your business decisions will affect constituencies like employees and customers requires exactly the kind of ethical decision-making process I'm talking about. But merely thinking things through is not enough. What's critical is how you act on that analysis. If, for example, you calculate the damaging effects of your actions but then decide, "Screw it, let's steal money from our customers, rip off our suppliers, nuke the whales, and burn the pension plan," you've acted unethically—and from a long-term management perspective, you've shot yourself in the foot.

That's because customers and colleagues alike recognize when they're working with people who practice good ethics—and they value them. Released last year, the results of KPMG Consulting's first Organizational Integrity Survey offered compelling evidence that management's ethical behavior can dramatically affect employees' estimation of their company's attractiveness to prospective customers and employees. Overall, KPMG found that 69 percent of the 2,390 working adults surveyed believed their current customers would recommend their company to others. Among those who believed that management would uphold the company's ethical standards, that number shot up to 80 percent. It fell to 40 percent among employees who believed that management would turn a blind eye to improper behavior. And when it comes to recruiting word of mouth, the differences are staggering. More than 66 percent of employees would recommend their company to prospective employees. Among those who believed management would walk the ethical line, that number rose to 81 percent. But of those who believed their boss's ethics to be questionable, only 21 percent said they would recommend their company. When you think about how much customer referrals add to the balance sheet, and then heap on what amounts to tremendous savings in recruiting costs, you start to get a sense of the impact that ethical decisions have on the bottom line.

Shades of Gray

Even with stark numbers like these, the belief that business and ethics make for an awkward marriage is not easily dispelled. And to be fair, practicing good ethics isn't an automatic slam dunk for the bottom line. Several years ago, while I was hashing over these very issues with Jon P. Gunnemann, a professor of social ethics at Emory University, he said something that I won't soon forget. While you can argue that smart, responsible management and doing the right thing often go hand in hand, he said, you can't make the assumption that doing the right thing will always be good for the company. In fact, he added, sometimes doing the right thing can have tragic results for a business.

79: PERCENTAGE WHO HAVE TAKEN OFFICE SUPPLIES FROM WORK FOR HOME USE

Of course, he's correct. The point was driven home when I talked with Ed Shultz, the former chief executive of Smith & Wesson, the gun manufacturer based in Springfield, Massachusetts. Faced with lawsuits from 29 different municipalities that accused handgun manufacturers of responsibility for various violent crimes, Shultz decided in March 2000 to enter into an agreement with the federal government to make some changes: Smith & Wesson would start including locks on its handguns and continue to research "smart gun" technology intended to prevent a weapon from being operated by anyone but its owner. Shultz describes himself as an enthusiastic gun owner but told me that he made his decision because when he asked himself, "Would I put locks on our guns if it might save one child? the answer was yes." The company's customers and retailers, however, reacted with fury, and the National Rifle Association came out with both barrels blazing. Sales plummeted. Shultz ended up leaving Smith & Wesson in September of last year, and by October the company had been forced to lay off 125 of its 725 Springfield employees.

But such awkward results are the exception. Consider Shultz's position. He was in a uniquely politicized industry, and there was simply no point of intersection between the interests of his customers (die-hard gun consumers and their uncompromising lobbyists) and those of the common good (as repre-

HOW ETHICAL ARE YOU?

Close the door and lower the shades. It's just you and your conscience. Choose A, B, or C, then tally the score to gauge your values in school, business, and life.

1 AN EMPLOYEE YOU MANAGE TELLS YOU HE'S ABOUT TO PUT A DOWN PAYMENT ON A HOUSE. YOU KNOW HE'S GOING TO BE LAID OFF BEFORE THE MONTH IS OUT, BUT YOU'VE BEEN TOLD THIS INFORMATION IN STRICT CONFIDENCE. HE WANTS YOUR ADVICE ON THE STABILITY OF THE COMPANY. YOU:

○ **A.** Tell him the company is doing just fine, and wish him well.
○ **B.** Tell him that he's about to be laid off.
○ **C.** Suggest he wait until the end of the month before making a decision.

2 DURING YOUR ANNUAL REVIEW, YOUR BOSS GOES ON AND ON ABOUT HOW WONDERFUL A JOB YOU DID ON A PARTICULAR PROJECT. YOU KNOW THAT THE BULK OF THE WORK WAS DONE BY A COLLEAGUE WHOSE CONTRIBUTIONS HAVE GONE UNNOTICED. WHEN THE BOSS STOPS GUSHING, YOU:

○ **A.** Thank him but let him know that your colleague was the chief contributor to the project.
○ **B.** Thank him and let him know that it was a team effort.
○ **C.** Thank him, and smile.

3 YOU GET THE FINAL EXAM BACK FROM YOUR FINANCE PROFESSOR, AND YOU NOTICE THAT HE'S MARKED CORRECT AN ANSWER THAT YOU GOT WRONG. REVEALING HIS ERROR WOULD MEAN THE DIFFERENCE BETWEEN AN A- AND A B+. YOU:

○ **A.** Tell the professor about his mistake.
○ **B.** Say nothing, figuring you shouldn't be penalized for his oversight.
○ **C.** Tell the professor, but make the case that he should still give you the higher grade since you could have said nothing.

4 A BELEAGUERED CLASSMATE OFFERS YOU A NICE CHUNK OF CHANGE IF YOU'LL WRITE HIS FINAL PAPER FOR HIM. YOU HEAR HIM OUT AND THEN:

○ **A.** Politely decline.
○ **B.** Decline, but offer to edit his paper for a fee.
○ **C.** Turn him in.

5 YOU'RE THE ONLY ONE AT THE OFFICE WORKING LATE. AS YOU PASS BY THE BOSS'S OFFICE, YOU NOTICE HIS E-MAIL IS STILL UP ON HIS SCREEN. YOU:

○ **A.** Pass on by. It's none of your business.
○ **B.** Pass on by. You might get caught.
○ **C.** Pop in, and read as much as you can.

6 COMPANY POLICY IS NOT TO PAY FOR IN-ROOM MOVIES WHEN YOU'RE ON THE ROAD. NEVERTHELESS, YOU CALL UP A FEW FILMS ON THE HOTEL SET, AND AN $18 CHARGE APPEARS ON YOUR BILL. YOU:

○ **A.** Decide not to request reimbursement for the $18, and instead pay for the movies out of your own pocket.
○ **B.** Choose not to request reimbursement for the movies, but add $18 to your expense account disguised as another expense.
○ **C.** Insist to the hotel front desk that you never saw the movies and you've been billed incorrectly.

7 BIDS COME IN FROM THREE EQUALLY QUALIFIED VENDORS FOR A PROJECT YOU'RE MANAGING ON A TIGHT BUDGET. YOUR COMPANY HAS A POLICY AGAINST ACCEPTING GIFTS FROM VENDORS, BUT THE HIGH BIDDER HAS OFFERED TO SLIP YOU WORLD SERIES TICKETS. YOU:

○ **A.** Give the job to the high bidder—telling yourself that the tickets are a sign he wants your business more than the others.
○ **B.** Give the job to the low bidder, and ignore the high bidder's ticket offer.
○ **C.** Give the job to the lowest bidder and tell the high bidder that company policy forbids you to take gifts.

8 YOU'VE WAITED IN LINE FOR 10 MINUTES TO BUY COFFEE AND A MUFFIN. WHEN YOU ARE A COUPLE OF BLOCKS AWAY, YOU REALIZE THAT THE CLERK GAVE YOU CHANGE FOR $20 RATHER THAN FOR THE $10 YOU GAVE HIM. YOU:

○ **A.** Go back to the coffee shop, and tell the clerk that he gave you too much change.
○ **B.** Wait until the next time you're at the coffee shop, and return the difference then.
○ **C.** Savor your coffee, muffin, and free $10.

9 A CLASSMATE TELLS YOU THAT SHE HAS BEEN SEXUALLY HARASSED BY SOMEONE IN HER STUDY GROUP. YOU:

○ **A.** Encourage her to report the harassment incident to the dean.
○ **B.** Report the harassment incident to the dean yourself.
○ **C.** Suggest that she switch into another study group.

10 YOU'VE DONE SOME INDEPENDENT CONSULTING WORK DURING THE YEAR. WHEN TAX TIME ROLLS AROUND YOU REALIZE ONE CLIENT NEGLECTED TO ISSUE A 1099 FORM FOR THE $4,500 HE PAID YOU. WHEN YOU'RE CALCULATING YOUR TAXES, YOU:

○ **A.** Report the $4,500.
○ **B.** Let your client know you haven't received a 1099 but that you're going to report the $4,500 to the IRS.
○ **C.** Don't report the $4,500.

11 YOUR COMPANY IS SERIOUSLY CONSIDERING ENTERING A NEW MARKET, AND YOU WANT TO FIND OUT HOW MUCH ITS COMPETITORS CHARGE FOR THEIR VARIOUS GOODS AND SERVICES. YOU:

○ **A.** Pose as a prospective customer and get as much pricing material as you can from the competitors.
○ **B.** Call the competitors, identify yourself, and see if they'll share pricing information with you.
○ **C.** Pay a graduate student to call the competitors and tell them that he'd like their pricing information for a research paper he's working on.

12 A HIGHLY TALENTED MEMBER OF THE TEAM YOU MANAGE MISSES A CRITICAL MEETING WITH YOUR COMPANY'S LARGEST CUSTOMER. AS A RESULT, YOU LOSE $100,000, HALF OF THE EXPECTED FEE. THREE DAYS LATER, YOU DISCOVER THAT THE EMPLOYEE HAS STARTED DRINKING AFTER HAVING BEEN SOBER FOR FIVE YEARS. YOU:

○ **A.** Fire him on the spot.
○ **B.** Get him to agree to go through rehab, and give him another chance.
○ **C.** Forget about it. He's too talented to lose, and in the long run he'll more than make up for this one lost customer.

13 YOU'RE TAKING A QUIZ TO GAUGE HOW ETHICAL YOU ARE. YOU:

○ **A.** Answer the questions honestly.
○ **B.** Figure out what the most ethical choice is and choose it, regardless of what you'd actually do.
○ **C.** Peek ahead at the scoring to see what it will take to ace the quiz.

—QUIZ BY JEFFREY L. SEGLIN

FOR AN ANALYSIS OF YOUR SCORE, SEE "THE RESULTS ARE IN." OR TAKE THE TEST ONLINE AT WWW.MBAJUNGLE.COM/ETHICS, AND COMPARE YOUR SCORE WITH OTHER RESPONDENTS.

THE RESULTS ARE IN

SCORING: points according to choice

1.	A-2	B-1	C-0
2.	A-0	B-1	C-2
3.	A-0	B-2	C-1
4.	A-0	B-2	C-1
5.	A-0	B-1	C-2
6.	A-0	B-1	C-2
7.	A-2	B-1	C-0
8.	A-0	B-1	C-2
9.	A-0	B-1	C-2
10.	A-1	B-0	C-2
11.	A-1	B-0	C-2
12.	A-2	B-0	C-1
13.	A-0	B-1	C-2

18 POINTS OR MORE
GONE ASTRAY

Given the choice between taking the honest path and a less honorable road, you are drawn to the latter. While you might justify your decision as a short-term boost to your company's—or your own—bottom line, ethics be damned, such decisions could have a disastrous effect on long-term performance. If you find yourself tempted to stray, a widely used self-test to gauge ethical behavior goes like this: If you won't be able to sleep at night after you've done something,

then there's a good chance you've crossed an ethical line. Of course, this test is only as good as the people taking it. Joseph Badaracco points out in his book, *Defining Moments*, that "if people like Hitler sometimes sleep well and people like Mother Teresa sometimes sleep badly, we can place little faith in simple sleep-test ethics."

8 TO 17 POINTS
ETHICALLY CHALLENGED

You try to make the right choice, but sometimes your curiosity or insecurity draws you to an action that on a better day you might not have chosen. No one said making ethical decisions was ever going to be easy, especially when doing the right thing can be costly: Good ethical behavior, after all, does not always have a positive payback. Sometimes, it takes courage to keep your wits about you when everyone else has lost theirs. Chances are, it will pay off for you.

FEWER THAN 8 POINTS
HIGHLY PRINCIPLED

You have a well-developed sense of right and wrong—and the integrity to veer toward the former. There's ample temptation in the classroom, business, and personal life, so it takes some resolve to walk the ethical line. Part of the process of being an ethical person is thinking through your actions. At the end of the day, all you can hope for is to know that you've done your thoughtful best to do the right thing.

sented by an aggressive government). He considered all the options, all the contingencies, and did what his conscience dictated. Ethical management? Yes. Good management? Milton Friedman might not think so. But then again, what constitutes good management in a no-win situation? Perhaps the course that causes the least harm? More than 100 workers lost their jobs as a result of Shultz's actions. But how many lives may have been saved?

PERCENTAGE WHO HAVE INCLUDED A NONBUSINESS EXPENSE ON A COMPANY EXPENSE REPORT: 27

Nobody pretends that ethical decisions are simple matters. More often than not, managers are faced with choices that reflect the world's ambiguity and subtle shadings. Take lying, for example: In abstract terms, it's generally agreed that lying is somehow bad or unethical. But listen to what Joseph L. Badaracco Jr., a Harvard Business School ethics professor and the author of *Defining Moments: When Managers Must Choose Between Right and Right*, says about lying: "Not telling the full truth is different from outright lying. If you're going to run a big company or run the country, you can't put all your cards on the table; that's simply naive." A CEO once told me about the time he decided to be candid with his employees about his com-

pany's financial straits. He called the employees together, explained the circumstances, and asked if they could wait a week before cashing the paychecks he was handing out. "All 40 employees ran to the bank that day," he says. Given the same circumstances, the CEO said, he would be less forthcoming the next time. So is that unethical? Certainly not, particularly when you consider that the employees' actions could jeopardize the health of the company and, by extension, their own well-being.

Now More Than Ever

These days, the New Economy looks increasingly like the Old Economy cleverly hidden behind an office masseuse, ergonomic chairs, and the promise of stock options. But one thing will be different going forward: Ethics will matter more than ever.

4: PERCENTAGE WHO HAVE CHEATED ON A TEST WHILE IN B-SCHOOL

At a time when many businesses are driven by Wall Street's hunger for short-term performance, it takes strong resolve to recognize that some practices favored by analysts and shareholders can wreak havoc on a company in the long term. Inflating growth projections is one such practice, obscuring the source of profits another. But massive layoffs may be an even worse offender, and not only because firings are often carried out unethically, with too little concern for the employees being let go; there's compelling evidence that in the long term cross-company firings are simply bad business. Earlier this year, Mercer Management Consulting conducted a survey of companies that used cost cutting as their primary strategy during the recession years of 1989 to 1991 and found that 71 percent failed to achieve growth in the five prosperous years that followed.

PERCENTAGE WHO WOULD BUY STOCK ON INSIDE INFORMATION RECEIVED FROM A FRIEND: 52

In the current economic slowdown, the same cost-cutting temptations exist. Thinking carefully, however, about their impact on employees, customers, vendors, the community, and stockholders can result in choices that will benefit not only those constituencies but also the long-term performance of the business.

Beyond the immediate economic climate, future managers will have plenty of ethical problems to wrestle with. The rise of technology, for instance, has brought with it new sets of moral quandaries—from employee and customer privacy concerns to enhanced incentives and greater abilities to engage in corporate espionage to new twists on old antitrust issues. What's more, the Internet makes it easier for a company's customers, no matter how far-flung, to share experiences and information. Negative word of mouth like that engendered by, say, the use of sweatshops in faraway countries travels faster and to more potential customers than ever before. That's all the more reason why business ethics are so important right now—and why they'll continue to be a driving force in the future. So go ahead, try the spinach. Then enjoy the steak.

FOR MORE SURVEY RESULTS, GO TO:
www.mbajungle.com/ethics

Five Forces Redefining Business

Profits from Principle

Corporations are finding that social responsibility pays off.
This realization will change the very nature of business.

By Bennett Daviss

Ray Anderson built Interface, Inc., a billion-dollar international carpet manufacturer based in Atlanta, on a simple precept: A corporation's purpose is to earn a good return for shareowners while complying with the law. Then, in 1994, during a struggle to regain lost market share and shore up his company's sagging stock price, Anderson read eco-entrepreneur Paul Hawken's book, *The Ecology of Commerce*, which documents industry's profligate squandering of natural resources and sketches a vision of environmentally sustainable business.

Anderson took it personally. His company was chewing up more than 500 million pounds of raw material each year and excreting more than 900 tons of air pollutants, 600 million gallons of wastewater, and 10,000 tons of trash.

Reading the book was Anderson's epiphany—"a spear in my chest"—the CEO recalls. It also put a spur in his backside: Anderson set out to make his corporation's 26 factories on four continents the world's

first environmentally sustainable manufacturing enterprise, recycling everything possible, releasing no pollutants, and sending nothing to landfills. "We're treating all fossil fuel energy as waste to be eliminated through efficiencies and shifts to renewable energy," he says.

Idealistic? Definitely. Unbusinesslike? Definitely not.

"In just over two years, we've become 23% more efficient in converting raw stuff into sales dollars—and we've only scratched the surface," Anderson notes. That efficiency has cut not only waste, but also a cumulative $40 million in costs. The savings, which were projected to grow to $76 million by the end of 1998, helped Interface make the winning low bid in 1997 to carpet The Gap Inc.'s new world headquarters in San Francisco. The Gap invited Interface to bid specifically because of the carpet company's environmental initiatives.

"We've found a new way to win in the marketplace," Anderson believes, "one that doesn't come at the

expense of our grandchildren or the earth, but at the expense of the inefficient competitor."

Anderson's crusade is one example among countless others proving a new rule in business: Profits and social responsibility are becoming inseparable.

Helping Workers Work

Just ask Donna Klein, director of work/life initiatives for Washington, D.C., based hotelier Marriott International. Her industry depends on the low-wage workers who change sheets and scrub tubs. They often live below the poverty line and spend less than a year on the job.

The company couldn't afford to simply hike wages in an effort to retain more of its approximately 150,000 low-wage workers. Casting about for a way to reduce turnover, and thereby the extra costs involved in training and supervising new employees, Klein discovered that the workers were usually driven from their jobs by personal prob-

INTERFACE, INC.

Ray Anderson of Interface saved his carpet manufacturing company $40 million through measures such as recycling and cutting waste.

lems: domestic violence, scrapes with immigration authorities, becoming homeless, or an inability to master English, among others. Supervisors reported spending as much as half their working time trying to help employees straighten out their personal lives.

In 1992, Klein set up a 24-hour, multilingual hotline staffed by trained social workers whom hotel employees could call for help and referrals to aid agencies. By 1997, the project had cut Marriott's turnover to 35%, compared with the hotel industry's average of 100% or more.

The hotline is handling more than 2,000 employee calls each year. "It costs well over $1 million a year to run it, but it saves us more than $3 million a year in hiring, training, and other costs," Klein says. In 1997, Klein's office documented 600 cases in which the hotline was the key factor that kept an employee from quitting, saving an estimated $750,000 for that year, she reports. "We've documented increases in productivity, morale, and better relations with

managers and co-workers as a result of the hotline. But we're not able to quantify the gain in managers' time. The hotline frees them to focus on customer service instead of employees' problems."

Such examples are legion. After the Malden Mills factory in Lowell, Massachusetts, burned during the 1995 Christmas season, owner Aaron Feuerstein continued to pay workers' salaries and benefits until a new plant was built. In the new factory, worker productivity reportedly improved by 25% and quality defects have dropped by two-thirds. Although some of the gains are attributable to newer equipment, Feuerstein believes it's "a direct result of the good will of our people." San Francisco's Thanksgiving Coffee Company invests a share of its revenues in community development among the Central American villages that grow its beans, ensuring loyal suppliers and reasonable prices during times of small harvests. Mercedes-Benz has

designed its new S-class sedans and 500/600SEC luxury coupes to be entirely recyclable, giving it and its dealers a new source of low-cost used parts.

The evidence that social responsibility swells profits appears in studies as well as stories. Returns for the Domini 400 Social Index—a roster of 400 publicly traded, socially responsible firms tracked by the Boston investment advisory firm of Kinder, Lydenberg, Domini & Co.—have outpaced those for the Standard & Poor's 500 for each of the last three years. In 1992, UCLA business professor David Lewin surveyed 188 companies and found that "companies that increased their community involvement were more likely to show an improved financial picture over a two-year time period." A 1995 Vanderbilt University analysis found that in eight of 10 cases low-polluting companies financially outperform their dirtier competitors. And the U.S. General Accounting Office reports that employee stock-

INTERFACE, INC.

Skylights supply daytime lighting at Interface's new plant.

option plans and participatory management schemes hike productivity an average of 52%.

"We're going through a mind-change," says Marjorie Kelly, editor of the Minneapolis-based *Business Ethics* magazine. "Most of us still carry around the subliminal idea that ruthless behavior beats the competition and good behavior is money out of pocket. But the data shows that the traditional idea is wrong. Social responsibility makes sense in purely capitalistic terms."

Five Forces Redefining Business

Conservative economists, most notably Nobel laureate Milton Friedman at the University of Chicago, have long argued that the sole mission of a corporation is to maximize profits for the benefit of shareholders and that spending on social causes violates that prime directive. But the new marketplace is proving that profits can best be maximized by embracing, rather than forswear-

ing, social concerns. The idea that profitability and social awareness are not antagonistic but interdependent redefines the purpose of business.

Five forces are converging to shape business's new social imperative: consumer conscience, socially conscious investing, the global media, special-interest activism, and expectations of corporate leadership.

1 First, today's consumers have learned by experience that societies and economies—like nature—are closed systems. Automobile exhaust doesn't disappear into the sky; it transforms the atmosphere and consequently our climate. When employers don't make health insurance available to workers, the cost of health care for those workers isn't saved, but is shared among all of us in higher health-care costs and taxes that support public emergency rooms.

Two decades ago, if a company made cars with exploding gas tanks

or marketed U.S.-banned pesticides in Third World countries, it could view these as purely financial issues. Then, as the flower children of the 1960s became the consumers of the 1980s, such issues were recast in a moral light. Those consumers began speaking out—with their voices, their votes, and their wallets.

The result: By 1992, a survey by the Public Relations Society of America identified social-issues marketing—that is, celebrating a company's commitment to public issues as well as to its products and customers—as the leader among the industry's 10 hottest trends. The same year, the quarterly *Business and Society Review* reported in its summer issue that "corporate social responsibility is now a tidal wave of the future."

"People judge corporations today by their social performance as much as by their financial performance—their impact on the environment, their role in aggravating or relieving social problems," explains Richard Torrenzano, president of the Torren-

Reflective surfaces on the outside of Interface's new plant minimize the need for air conditioning, thereby reducing the company's energy consumption.

INTERFACE, INC.

zano Group, a New York consulting firm. "People indicate by their purchases not just the value of a product or service, but how they view the company's role in their communities." Because ethical probity shapes consumer choices, a company's deportment has become a crucial bottom-line concern.

For example, a 1980s boycott of Burger King for its use of beef raised on pasture slashed from South American rain forests damaged sales enough to force the company to change its purchasing habits. On the other hand, New Hampshire's Stonyfield Farm yogurt company has been able to expand its share of the stagnant retail yogurt market by touting its steady financial support for organic and family farms.

2 Consumers' new conscience has complemented, and cultivated, the second factor—the rise of socially conscious investing. The movement gained momentum during the 1970s and 1980s as institutions and investment funds were pressured to shed their South African holdings to pro-

test apartheid. According to the Social Investment Forum, a New York-based nonprofit information clearinghouse, in the last 10 years the value of U.S. socially aware investments has grown from $50 billion to more than $500 billion and is one of the financial industry's strongest growth areas.

"If I don't invest in companies with actual or potential social and environmental liabilities, I'm reducing my risk of owning a company that suddenly owes huge fines or settlements in damage suits," says Hugh Kelley, president of the Social Responsibility Investment Group, an Atlanta advisory firm. Neither will his companies be rocked by boycotts and bad publicity. "Those kinds of problems go right to the bottom line."

3 Those potential problems are exacerbated by the third factor: a competitive, unsparing, and technologically endowed media—especially television—that makes once-abstract concepts like global warming or sweatshop labor personal to consumers. Once discovered, a com-

pany's ethical lapse can now be flashed to news outlets and brokerage firms globally before a CEO can hurry back from lunch. "Journalists today are much more sophisticated," Torrenzano adds. "They ask tougher questions, and they give no slack when someone has a problem. It motivates companies."

A company's deportment has become a crucial bottom-line concern.

4 Fourth, zealous special-interest groups have become deft at using the media to link corporate practices with social and environmental problems and solutions. Burger King's troubles began in 1986 when the upstart Rainforest Action Network called on the world to boycott the chain, claiming it used "rain-forest beef" grazed on pastures carved from South America's imperiled tropical forests. At first, the company ignored the allegation. Within two years, Whopper sales slumped—as much as 17% by some reports—and the burger giant capitulated with a statement forswearing ecologically incorrect meat. "Activists are becoming increasingly effective in forcing corporations to cooperate in their vision of social change," noted the late Rafael Pagán, a pioneering corporate social-policy adviser.

5 Fifth, the public is transferring its expectations of leadership in solving social problems from government to business. Over the past two decades, the failure of federal "Great Society" programs and increasing partisan gridlock has exacerbated public demand for action against society's lingering ills. As a result, while Congress dithers, commercial firms pressured by consumers' new concerns are enacting social policy ranging from environmental cleanup to flexible work policies, from Third World economic development to new product safety standards. By those actions, companies not only gain a competitive edge but also ratify a new moral compact between business and society.

Increasingly, companies are embracing that new compact deliberately. The San Francisco-based group Business for Social Responsibility has grown from 45 members in 1993 to more than 1,400 today. "The companies joining the group aren't just the Ben and Jerrys of the world," says charter member Gary Hirshberg, co-founder of Stonyfield Farm. "We're getting divisions of Kraft, the Fortune 500, and investment bankers out to make a killing who recognize that this is the way to success. We don't just have the oddball New Age companies any more. We've got the suits." BSR's members now include giants such as General Motors and Coca-Cola and boast combined annual sales of more than $1 trillion—a seventh of the entire U.S. economy.

"These companies aren't joining just to say they're members," says Cliff Feigenbaum, editor and publisher of the *Green Money Letter*, a quarterly newsletter tracking the new business conscience. "They're joining because they want help."

Drawing a New Balance

Companies that venture into this new territory are learning that profiting by principle demands an unequivocal commitment to both conscience and cash flow. But the new compact also is forcing companies to calibrate a new and delicate—even precarious—balance between the two. Consumers United Insurance Company and The Body Shop have provided object lessons.

Founded in 1969, Consumers United was a company ahead of its time. It offered unisex insurance rates and covered policyholders' unwed domestic partners before either became a public issue. Founder Jim Gibbons turned full ownership of the firm over to the employees, who controlled corporate policy and could overrule his decisions with a majority vote. The wage structure ensured that the lowest-paid worker would be able to support a family of four. This experiment in controlled chaos thrived, and by 1986 the company managed $47 million in invested assets.

Gibbons deployed his clients' funds with the same earnest idealism with which he managed the company. The firm bought 26 vacant acres in Washington, D.C., and built low-income housing. It funded a local youth group and promised each of the 70 children who joined that, if they stayed drug-free and didn't make babies, Consumers United would pay their way through college.

Such largesse drew the attention of insurance industry regulators in Delaware, the state in which Consumers had incorporated. The regulators weren't convinced that big-hearted gestures such as paying poor kids' college bills guaranteed enough future cash to pay claims. Finally convinced that Gibbons wasn't being prudent enough with policyholders' money, the regulators felt they had no alternative but to seek a court order declaring Consumers insolvent. In 1993, the state seized control of its assets and shut the company down. "It provides a cautionary tale for any business that pays more attention to its social mission than to its bottom line," *Business Ethics* writer Bill Gifford noted in an obituary article.

If Consumers did too much of a good thing, The Body Shop did too little. In the 1980s, promotional materials for the British-based body-care products company featured photos of co-founder Anita Roddick sitting in rain-forest clearings dickering with natives to buy their renewable products. It avowed that none of its products were tested on animals. Body Shop catalog covers promoted progressive causes. Roddick and husband Gordon became celebrated symbols of business with a conscience.

Then, in 1994, a six-page expose in the pages of *Business Ethics* detailed evidence that native peoples supplied less than 1% of the company's raw materials, that many of its ingredients were being tested on animals (although not by The Body Shop itself), and that its "natural" products included generous amounts of petroleum. The article also hinted that the corporation's well-publicized concern for social betterment was prompted as much by greed as by conscience. After the public glimpsed the gap between rhetoric and reality, the company's stock prices plunged and sales slumped.

"They were making claims that didn't exactly match their practices, and it came back to bite them," says Dan McKenna, president of Principle Profits Asset Management in Amherst, Massachusetts, an investment advisory firm serving the socially conscious. "They saw their financial position suffer when the reality didn't live up to the image."

Shoe giant Nike is busy teaching itself a similar lesson. Widely accused of using child labor in Third World sweatshops to make its high-priced sneakers, the company has launched a number of initiatives to improve the lot of foreign workers. In October 1996, Nike tried to polish its image by releasing an independent study showing that its workers in Indonesia and Vietnam were buying VCRs and otherwise living well. Three weeks later, an audit by accounting firm Ernst & Young detailing unsafe working conditions in one of Nike's Vietnamese factories made the front page of the *New York Times*. According to one report, in 1996 Nike paid Michael Jordan more for his endorsement—at least $30 million—than it did its 19,000 non-U.S. factory workers combined.

"That can be read as a statement of the way Nike balances marketing with human dignity," McKenna says. "It seems that Nike hasn't yet committed to the full meaning of social responsibility."

Business Ethics editor Marjorie Kelly agrees. "Social responsibility can't follow the catalytic converter model," she admonishes. "In a car, you can leave the engine unchanged and just bolt on a new part to take out the pollutants. But in a business you can't just open an ethics office down the hall and leave the company's culture and practices unchanged. A genuine commitment to social responsibility transforms not just what a company does, but also how it thinks."

What's Ahead: Four Trends

That commitment will continue to be tested in the next decade. Today's demands and pressures for corporate social leadership are redrafting the tacit contract between business and society. Four trends are shaping the terms of the new covenant:

1. Good works and financial gain must balance. During the cash-rich 1980s, socially involved corporations and pressure groups coined the term "the double bottom line" to describe a company's attempts to better its profits and its community at the same time. But the '80s are over and the double bottom line still has to be derived from a single balance sheet. In the future, each company will define its social role in terms of self-interest and fund good works only to the extent that the company gains financially from them.

For those reasons, social and environmental initiatives will focus largely within companies themselves. For example, a corporation may be willing to underwrite an alternative-energy program, but only in its own factory and only if the scheme doesn't add to costs, compromise product quality, or lengthen delivery times. A proposal for an on-site day-care center, flextime program, or employee gym will win favor only by showing evidence that it will reduce turnover and absenteeism enough to pay its own way.

Privately owned companies will have more flexibility but still must align social programs to profits. Stonyfield Farm plants forests to offset its factory's carbon-dioxide emissions—an investment that also strengthens its brand identity and consumer loyalty in an increasingly competitive industry.

2. Activists gain leverage by becoming advisers, not adversaries. Because financial self-interest will circumscribe corporations' social initiatives, the role of the activist is expanding from adversary to adviser. As long as there are corporations, there will be a place for corporate watchdogs. But in the years ahead, activists will gain greatest leverage by working directly with companies to help executives make the links between profit and social and environmental probity—helping them see the connections between life-cycle product engineering and cost cutting, or between better treatment of workers and money saved from turnover, lawsuits, boycotts, government fines, and public-relations expense. Adversarial groups will still prod with sticks, but activist-advisers will entice companies by dangling the carrots of cost savings and competitive advantage.

3. Corporations will be audited socially just as they now are financially. Progressive companies have begun to hire specialized consultants to rate their social and environmental performance; in the future, shareholders and activists will place all corporations under greater pressure to open their doors to these outside consultants. The ISO 9000 standards for industrial quality management, promulgated by the International Organization for Standardization (ISO), sparked the ISO 14000 standards for environmental systems management. Recently, the Council on Economic Priorities promulgated the SA 8000 standards (for "social accountability"), setting forth criteria by which companies' treatment of domestic and foreign workers can be assessed, rated, and publicized. Look for outside social and environmental auditing to become a new norm as companies seek to ingratiate themselves with savvy and discerning consumers.

4. Corporate social identity will be as important as brand identity. As people come to expect corporations to take a larger social role, companies will develop a social identity that consumers respond to as strongly and readily as they do a brand identity.

That shift links a corporation's behavior to its product image and, therefore, to its profits. When Texaco's corporate culture was accused of racial prejudice, millions of people boycotted the firm's gas stations. After Johnson & Johnson's open, thorough, and cooperative response to deadly tamperings with its Tylenol tablets, the pain remedy actually increased its market share.

As these and other companies have learned, a corporation will not be able to choose whether to have a social identity; the public will fashion one for it based on a company's social and environmental actions—or lack thereof. Companies sculpt brand identities by manipulating images in the public mind, but businesses will find their social identity harder to control. There are too many prying journalists, activists, and shareholders to avoid.

As companies learn that social or environmental gaffes gnaw at profits, they also will realize that there is only one way to guard against the financial losses that these kinds of blunders can lead to. Companies must "walk the talk": From the boardroom to the loading dock, they must adopt policies and practices that enact the new, nobler norms of corporate conduct that corporate

precedents and public expectations are imposing.

Traditionalists have long argued that business's only social obligation is to maximize profit. The new social contract between business and society inverts that principle: In the new century, companies will grow their profits only by embracing their new role as the engine of positive social and environmental change.

About the Author

Bennett Daviss is an independent journalist who writes, speaks, and consults

on education reform, socially responsible business, and other issues of sustainability. His articles have appeared in more than 40 magazines on four continents. With Nobel physicist Kenneth Wilson, he is co-author of the book *Redesigning Education*. His address is Walpole Valley Road, Walpole, New Hampshire 03608.

Portions of this article first appeared in *Ambassador Magazine*. Reprinted courtesy of *Ambassador Magazine* and Trans World Airlines.

Executive Women and the Myth of

Having It All

A disturbing new study reveals that, 30 years into the women's movement, female executives still don't have what they want—and probably never will.

by Sylvia Ann Hewlett

THERE IS A SECRET OUT THERE—a painful, well-kept secret: At midlife, between a third and a half of all successful career women in the United States do not have children. In fact, 33% of such women (Business executives, doctors, lawyers, academics, and the like) in the 41-to-55 age bracket are childless—and that figure rises to 42% in corporate America. These women have not chosen to remain childless. The vast majority, in fact, yearn for children. Indeed, some have gone to extraordinary lengths to bring a baby into their lives. They subject themselves to complex medical procedures, shell out tens of thousands of dollars, and derail their careers—mostly to no avail, because these efforts come too late. In the words of one senior manager, the typical high-achieving woman childless at midlife has not made a choice but a "creeping nonchoice."

Why has the age-old business of having babies become so difficult for today's high-achieving women? In January 2001, in partnership with the market research company Harris Interactive and the National Parenting Association, I conducted a nationwide survey designed to ex-plore the professional and private lives of highly educated, high-earning women. The survey results are featured in my new book, *Creating a Life: Professional Women and the Quest for Children*.

In this survey, I target the top 10% of women—measured in terms of earning power—and focus on two age groups: an older generation, ages 41 to 55, and their younger peers, ages 28 to 40, as defined for survey purposes. I distinguish between high achievers (those who are earning more than $55,000 in the younger group, $65,000 in the older one) and ultra-achievers (those who are earning more than $100,000). I include a sample of high-potential women—highly qualified women who have left their careers, mainly for family reasons. In addition, I include a small sample of men.

The findings are startling—and troubling. They make it clear that, for many women, the brutal demands of ambitious careers, the asymmetries of male-female relationships, and the difficulties of bearing children late in life conspire to crowd out the possibility of having children. In this article I lay out the issues underlying this state of affairs, identify the heavy costs involved, and suggest some remedies, however preliminary and modest. The facts and figures I relate are bleak. But I think that they can also be liberating, if they spur action. My hope is that this information will generate workplace policies that recognize the huge costs to businesses of losing highly educated women when they start their families. I also hope that it will galvanize young women to make newly urgent demands of their partners, employers, and policy makers and thus create more generous life choices for themselves.

The Continuing Inequity

When it comes to career and fatherhood, high-achieving men don't have to deal with difficult trade-offs: 79% of the men I surveyed report wanting children—and 75% have them. The research shows that, generally speaking, the more successful the man, the more likely he will find a spouse and become a father. The opposite holds true for women, and the disparity is particularly striking among corporate ultra-achievers. In fact, 49% of these women are childless. But a mere 19% of their male colleagues are. These figures underscore the depth and scope of the persisting, painful inequities between the sexes. Women face all the challenges that men do in working long hours and withstanding the up-or-out pressures of high-altitude careers. But they also face challenges all their own.

Slim Pickings in Partners.

Let's start with the fact that professional women find it challenging even to *be* married—for most, a necessary precondition for childbearing. Only 60% of high-achieving women in the older age group are married, and this figure falls to 57% in corporate America. By contrast, 76% of older men are married, and this figure rises to 83% among ultra-achievers.

Consider Tamara Adler, 43, a former managing director of Deutsche Bank in London. She gave her take on these disturbing realities when I interviewed her for the study. Adler was the bank's most senior woman, and her highly successful career had left no room for family. She mentioned the obvious reasons—long hours and travel—but she also spoke eloquently about how ambitious careers discriminate against women: "In the rarified upper reaches of high-altitude careers where the air is thin... men have a much easier time finding oxygen. They find oxygen in the form of younger, less driven women who will coddle their egos." She went on to conclude, "the hard fact is that most successful men are not interested in acquiring an ambitious peer as a partner."

It's a conclusion backed up by my data: Only 39% of high-achieving men are married to women who are employed full time, and 40% of these spouses earn less than $35,000 a year. Meanwhile, nine out of ten married women in the high-achieving category have husbands who are employed full time or self-employed, and a quarter are married to men who earn more than $100,000 a year. Clearly, successful women professionals have slim pickings in the marriage department—particularly as they age. Professional men seeking to marry typically reach into a large pool of younger women, while professional women are limited to a shrinking pool of eligible peers. According to U.S. Census Bureau data, at age 28 there are four college-educated, single men for every three college-educated, single women. A decade later, the situation is radically changed. At age 38, there is one man for every three women.

The Time Crunch.

Now add to that scarcity of marriage candidates a scarcity of time to spend nurturing those relationships. My survey results show that women are dealing with long and lengthening workweeks. Twenty-nine percent of high achievers and 34% of ultra-achievers work more than 50 hours a week, and a significant proportion of these women are on the job ten to 20 more hours a week than they were five years ago. Among ultra-achievers, a quarter are away on business at least five nights every three months. According to research by sociologists Jerry Jacobs and Kathleen Gerson, the percentage of women working at least 50 hours a week is now higher in the United States than in any other country.

Think of what a 55-hour week means in terms of work-life balance. If you assume an hour lunch and a 45-minute round-trip commute (the national average), the workday stretches to almost 13 hours. Even without "extras" (out-of-town trips, client dinners, work functions), this kind of schedule makes it extremely difficult for any professional to maintain a relationship. Take Sue Palmer, 49, managing director of Grant Thornton, the London-based global accounting firm, and the only woman on its management committee. "Ten years ago," she said, "an assistant of mine told me at the end of a particularly grueling 70-hour week, 'You know, Sue, you couldn't have a torrid love affair if you wanted to.' And I shot back, 'I couldn't have a *tepid* love affair if I wanted to.'"

Of course, long hours aren't unique to women. They're a fact of life in corporate America, where management is under intense pressure to use its professional workforce for as many hours a week as possible. The reasons for this go back to 1938 when Congress passed the Fair Labor Standards Act, which institutionalized the 40-hour workweek and required employers to pay overtime for additional hours worked. One provision, however, exempted managers and professionals and still does. For those workers, extra hours carry no marginal costs to employers. The temptation for companies to take advantage of that provision might not have been so problematic back in 1938 when only 15% of employees were exempt, and most of them were men with stay-at-home spouses. But it

The Sobering Facts

In January 2001, in partnership with Harris Interactive and the National Parenting Association, I conducted a nationwide survey targeting the top 10% of women—measured in terms of earning power—and a small sample of men for comparative purposes. Responding were 1,168 high-achieving career women ages 28 to 55; 479 high-achieving, noncareer women ages 28 to 55; and 472 high-achieving men ages 28 to 55. (The group of ultra-achieving men was not large enough to disaggregate.) The sample was drawn from the Harris Poll on-line database of cooperative respondents. Data were weighted for key demographic variables to reflect each sample's national population. My analysis delineated an older generation, 41 to 55, and that group's younger peers, 28 to 40. I also distinguished between high achievers (those earning more than $65,000 or $55,000, depending on age), ultra-achievers (those earning more than $100,0000), and high-potential women—highly qualified women who have left their careers, mainly for family reasons. Corporate women were defined as working in companies with more than 5,000 employees. The two charts below contain some of the startling—and sobering—findings.

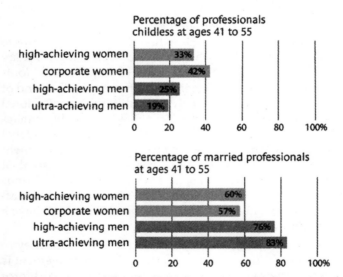

The survey was carried out by Harris Interactive under the auspices of the National Parenting Association, a nonprofit research organization. Funding for the survey and the associated research was provided by Ernst & Young, Merck, the Annie E. Casey Foundation, and the David and Lucile Packard Foundation. For more about the methodology and findings, go to www.parentsunite.org.

produces significant overload today when close to 30% of employees are in the exempt category, many of them women who rarely have the luxury of a spouse at home tending to domestic responsibilities.

An Unforgiving Decade.

Women pay an even greater price for those long hours because the early years of career building overlap—almost perfectly—the prime years of childbearing. It's very hard to throttle back during that stage of a career and expect to catch up later. As policy analyst Nancy Rankin points out, the career highway has all kinds of off-ramps but few on-ramps.

In fact, the persistent wage gap between men and women is due mainly to the penalties women incur when they interrupt their careers to have children. In a recent study, economists Susan Harkness and Jane Waldfogel compared that wage gap across seven industrialized countries and found it was particularly wide in the United States. For example, in France, women earn 81%, while in the United States, women continue to earn a mere 78% of the male wage. These days, only a small portion of this wage gap can be attributed to discrimination (getting paid less for doing the same job or being denied access to jobs, education, or capital based on sex). According to recent studies, an increasingly large part of the wage gap can now be explained by childbearing and child rearing, which interrupt women's—but not men's—careers, permanently depressing their earning power. If the gap between what men and women earn in this country is wider than elsewhere, it isn't because this country has done an inferior job combating discrimination. It is because it has failed to develop policies—in the workplace and in society as a whole—that support working mothers.

Ironically, this policy failure is to some extent the fault of the women's movement in the United States. Going back to the mid-nineteenth century, feminists in this country have channeled much of their energy into the struggle to win formal equality with men. More recently, the National Organization for Women has spent 35 years fighting for a wide array of equal rights, ranging from educational and job opportunities to equal pay and access to credit. The idea is that once all the legislation that discriminates against women is dismantled, the playing field becomes level and women can assume a free and equal place in society by simply cloning the male competitive model.

In Europe, various groups of social feminists have viewed the problem for women quite differently. For them, it is not woman's lack of legal rights that constitutes her main handicap, or even her lack of reproductive freedom. Rather, it is her dual burden—taking care of a home and family as well as holding down a job—that leads to her second-class status.

The Second Shift.

The problem with the notion that American women should be able to successfully clone the male competitive

Primary Child Care and Household Responsibilities
High-achieving Men and Women

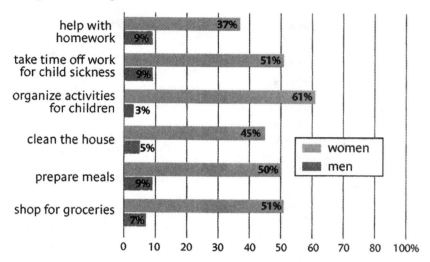

Source: National Parenting Association

model is that husbands have not picked up a significant share of women's traditional responsibilities on the home front. Even high-achieving women who are married continue to carry the lion's share of domestic responsibilities. (See the exhibit "Primary Child Care and Household Responsibilities.") Only 9% of their husbands assume primary responsibility for meal preparation, 10% for the laundry, and 5% for cleaning the house. When it comes to children, husbands don't do much better. Only 9% of them take time off from work when a child is sick, 9% take the lead in helping children with homework, and 3% organize activities such as play dates and summer camp.

Yes, these percentages have grown over the years—but not much. At the end of the day, the division of labor at home boils down to one startling fact: 43% of the older, high-achieving women and 37% of the younger, high-achieving women feel that their husbands actually create more household work for them than they contribute. (Thirty-nine percent of ultra-achieving women also feel this way, despite the fact that half of them are married to men who earn less than they do.)

Stubborn Biology.

So this is the difficult position in which women find themselves. According to Lisa Benenson, former editor of *Working Woman* and *Working Mother* magazines, "The signals are very clear. Young women are told that a serious person needs to commit to her career in her 20s and devote all her energies to her job for at least ten years if she is to be successful." But the fact is, if you take this advice you might well be on the wrong side of 35 before you have time to draw breath and contemplate having a

child—exactly the point in life when infertility can—and overwhelmingly does—become an issue.

Media hype about advances in reproductive science only exacerbates the problem, giving women the illusion that they can delay childbearing until their careers are well established. My survey tells us that 89% of young, high-achieving women believe that they will be able to get pregnant deep into their 40s. But sadly, new reproductive technologies have not solved fertility problems for older women. The research shows that only 3% to 5% of women who attempt in vitro fertilization in their 40s actually succeed in bearing a child. This kind of information is hard to come by because the infertility industry in this country likes to tout the good news—with dire consequences. Too many career women put their private lives on the back burner, assuming that children will eventually happen for them courtesy of high-tech reproduction—only to discover disappointment and failure.

A Costly Imbalance

I can't tell you how many times over the course of this research the women I interviewed apologized for "wanting it all." But it wasn't as though these women were looking for special treatment. They were quite prepared to shoulder more than their fair share of the work involved in having both career and family. So why on earth shouldn't they feel entitled to rich, multidimensional lives? At the end of the day, women simply want the choices in love and work that men take for granted.

Instead, they operate in a society where motherhood carries enormous economic penalties. Two recent studies lay out these penalties in very specific terms. In her study, economist Waldfogel finds that mothers earn less than

213

Creeping Nonchoice
Reality and Regret

The findings presented in this article are compelling in the way that brutal statistics can be. But for men, the most powerful evidence of a problem came from the personal stories I heard while conducting the research. Going into the interviews, I had assumed that if accomplished women were childless, surely they had chosen to be. I was prepared to believe that the exhilaration and challenge of a megawatt career made it easy to opt out of motherhood.

Nothing could be further from the truth. When I surveyed these women about children, their sense of loss was palpable. Consider Lisa Polsky, who joined Morgan Stanley in 1995 as managing director after successful stints at Citibank and Bankers Trust; she managed to make it on Wall Street, the ultimate bastion of male market power. But when we met in 1999, our conversation focused on what she had missed. Polsky was 44 then, and her childbearing days were over. She said, "What gnaws at me is that I always assumed I would have children. Somehow I imagined that having a child was something I would get to in a year or so, after the next promotion, when I was more established."

Kate, 52, a member of the medical faculty at the University of Washington, felt the same way. "Looking back, I can't think why I allowed my career to obliterate my 30s," she told me. "I just didn't pay attention. I'm only just absorbing the consequences."

And there is Stella Parsons, 45, who had just been offered a chairmanship at Ohio State University the day I interviewed her. But she waved my congratulations away. "I wish some of this career success had spilled over to my private life. I just didn't get it together in time." Then she whispered, "I'm almost ashamed to admit it, but I still ache for a child."

other women do even when you control for marital status, experience, and education. In fact, according to her research, one child produces a "penalty" of 6% of earnings, while two children produce a wage penalty of 13%. In a more recent study, economists Michelle Budig and Paula England find that motherhood results in a penalty of 7% per child.

Given such a huge disincentive, why do women persist in trying to "have it all"? Because, as a large body of research demonstrates, women are happier when they have both career and family. In a series of books and articles that span more than a decade, University of Michigan sociologist Lois Hoffmann has examined the value of children to parents and finds that, across cultures, parents see children as enormously important in providing love and companionship and in warding off loneliness. Children also help parents deal with the questions of human existence: How do I find purpose beyond the self? How do I cope with mortality?

Thus, the fact that so many professional women are forced to sacrifice motherhood is patently unfair, and it also has immense implications for American business, since it causes women intent on motherhood to cut short their careers. This is, of course, the flip side of the same coin. For if a large proportion of women who stay on track in their careers are forced to give up family, an equally large proportion who opt for family are forced to give up their careers. According to my survey, 66% of high-potential women would like to return to full-time jobs.

The cost to corporations and to our economy becomes monumental in the aggregate. Our nation needs professional women to stay in the labor force; we can ill afford to have a quarter of the female talent pool forced out of their jobs when they have children. But in 2000, at the height of the labor crunch, Census Bureau data showed that fully 22% of all women with professional degrees (MBAs, MDs, PhDs, and so on) were not in the labor market at all. What an extraordinary waste of expensively educated talent!

At the same time, we need adults at all income levels to become committed, effective parents. When a parent devotes time, attention, and financial resources to help a child become a well-adjusted person—one who succeeds in school and graduates from college—not only do parents feel deeply fulfilled, but society, of course, is graced with productive workers who boost the GDP, obey the law, and pay their taxes. Thus, we are all stakeholders in parents' ability to come through for their children.

And when women come to understand the value of parenthood to the wider community, they can quit apologizing for wanting both a career and a family. A woman can hold her head high when she goes into her boss and asks for a schedule that fits her needs.

The Challenge to Business

The statistics I've laid out here would be bearable if they were purely historical—the painful but isolated experience of a pioneering generation—but they are not. My survey shows that younger women are facing even more difficult trade-offs. (The sidebar "The Delusions of a Younger Generation" suggests that younger women may be more dangerously complacent than their elders.) Can we reverse these pernicious trends and finally create the possibility of true work-life balance? I believe we can.

The first challenge is to employers, to craft more meaningful work-life policies. Professional women who want both family and career know that conventional benefit packages are insufficient. These women need reduced-

The Delusions
of a Younger Generation

One professional woman, a 29-year-old lawyer, told me: "The pioneer women of the 1970s and 1980s paid some kind of special price for their careers. For us, things are different. We plan on having it all."

But is such easy confidence warranted? I think not. In fact, women in their 20s and 30s are dealing with the same cruel trade-offs. If anything, the choices younger women must make are more difficult than ever. Let's start with the fact that they are marrying even later. My data show that the high-achieving women of the older generation tended to marry young: 75% of them were married by 25, but only 54% of the younger generation are married by that age.

Young women are delaying childbirth even longer, too. If you compare women in the two age groups by calculating what proportion had a child by 35, younger women seem to be in worse shape. Only 45% of the younger women have had a child by 35, while 62% of the older women had a child by that age. (Indeed, among ultra-achievers, no one in the older group had her first child after 36.)

It's easy to speculate that these women are delaying childbirth because they don't feel a sense of biological urgency. The hype around the miracle babies of high-tech reproduction is falling on eager ears. Amy, 29, is just embarking on her career. Her story is probably typical. "I figure I've got 14, 15 years before I need worry about making babies," she e-mailed me. "In my mid-30s, I'll go back to school, earn an MBA, and get myself a serious career. At 40, I'll be ready for marriage and family. I can't tell you how glad I am that this new reproductive technology virtually guarantees that you can have a baby until 45. Or maybe it's even later. Go doctors!"

Modern medicine notwithstanding, the chances of Amy's getting pregnant in her 40s are tiny—in the range of 3% to 5%. The luxury of time she feels is, unfortunately, an illusion.

hour jobs and careers that can be interrupted, neither of which is readily available yet. And more than anything, they need to be able to partake of such benefits without suffering long-term damage to their careers.

High-achieving women make it abundantly clear that what they want most are work-life policies that confer on them what one woman calls "the gift of time." Take Joanna, for example. At 39, Joanna had worked for five years as an account executive for a Chicago head-hunter. She believed her company had great work-life policies— until she adopted a child. "My main problem," Joanna said, "is the number of hours I am expected to put in. I work 60 hours a week 50 weeks of the year, which leaves precious little time for anything else." Joanna asked for a reduced schedule, but it was a "no go. The firm didn't want to establish a precedent," she said. Joanna began looking for another job.

According to my survey, some employers take family needs into account: 12% offer paid parenting leave and 31% job sharing. Many more, however, provide only time flexibility: 69% allow staggered hours, and 48% have work-at-home options. These less ambitious policies seem to be of limited use to time-pressed, high-achieving women.

So, what do professionals want? The high-achieving career women who participated in my survey were asked to consider a list of policy options that would help them achieve balance in their lives over the long haul. They endorsed the following cluster of work-life policies that would make it much easier to get off conventional career ladders and eventually get back on:

A Time Bank of Paid Parenting Leave. This would allow for three months of paid leave, which could be taken as needed, until the child turned 18.

Restructured Retirement Plans. In particular, survey respondents want to see the elimination of penalties for career interruptions.

Career Breaks. Such a leave of absence might span three years—unpaid, of course, but with the assurance of a job when the time came to return to work.

Reduced Hour Careers. High-level jobs should be created that permit reduced hours and workloads on an ongoing basis but still offer the possibility of promotion.

Alumni Status for Former Employees. Analogous to active retirement, alumni standing would help women who have left or are not active in their careers stay in the loop. They might be tapped for advice and guidance, and the company would continue to pay their dues and certification fees so they could maintain professional standing.

Policies like these are vital—though in themselves not enough to solve the problem. In particular, companies must guard against the perception that by taking advantage of such policies, a woman will tarnish her professional image. Outside the fiction of human resource policies, a widespread belief in business is that a woman who allows herself to be accommodated on the family front is no longer choosing to be a serious contender. Top management must work to banish this belief from the corporate culture.

The good news is that, where top management supports them, work-life policies like the ones I've listed do pay off. My survey data show that companies offering a rich array of work-life policies are much more likely to hang on to their professional women than companies that don't. High-achieving mothers who have been able to stay in their careers tend to work for companies that allow them access to generous benefits: flextime, telecommuting, paid parenting leave, and compressed workweeks. In contrast, high-achieving mothers who have been forced out of their careers tended to work for companies with inadequate work-life benefits.

I heard a wonderful example of the loyalty these kinds of policies engender when I spoke with Amy, 41, a marketing executive for IBM. Her son had just turned three, and Amy was newly back at work. "People don't believe me when I tell them that my company offers a three-year personal leave of absence," she said. As she described the policy, it applies not only to mothers; others have used it to care for elderly parents or to return to school. The leave is unpaid but provides continuation of benefits and a job-back guarantee. "IBM gave me this gift," she said, "and I will always be grateful." Clearly, in the aggregate, business leaders hold the power to make important and constructive change.

Because companies can't be expected to craft all the policies that will make a difference in women's lives, government should also take action. I have urged policy makers at the national level, for example, to extend the Family and Medical Leave Act to workers in small companies and turn it into paid leave. State and federal governments could also accomplish much by providing tax incentives to companies that offer employees flextime and various reduced-hour options. And we should promote legislation that eliminates perverse incentives for companies to subject their employees to long-hour weeks.

The Challenge to Women

My book focuses on what women themselves can do to expand their life choices. In a nutshell, if you're a young woman who wants both career and family, you should consider doing the following:

Figure out what you want your life to look like at 45. If you want children (and between 86% and 89% of high-achieving women do), you need to become highly intentional—and take action now.

Give urgent priority to finding a partner. My survey data suggest that high-achieving women have an easier time finding partners in their 20s and early 30s.

Have your first child before 35. The occasional miracle notwithstanding, late-in-life childbearing is fraught with risk and failure. Even if you manage to get one child "under the wire," you may fail to have a second. This, too, can trigger enormous regret.

Choose a career that will give you the gift of time. Certain careers provide more flexibility and are more forgiving of interruptions. Female entrepreneurs, for example, do bet-

ter than female lawyers in combining career and family—and both do better than corporate women. The key is to avoid professions with rigid career trajectories.

Choose a company that will help you achieve work-life balance. Look for such policies as reduced-hour schedules and job-protected leave.

That's an easy list to compile, but I have no illusions that it will change the world, because identifying what each women can do is only half the battle. The other half is convincing women that they are entitled to both a career and children. Somehow the perception persists that a woman isn't a woman unless her life is riddled with sacrifice.

An End to Self-Sacrifice

In February 2001, I conducted an informal focus group with young professionals at three consulting firms in Cambridge, Massachusetts. During that session, a young woman named Natalie commented, "This is the third consulting firm I've worked for, and I've yet to see an older, more senior woman whose life I would actually want."

Natalie's colleague Rachel was shocked and asked her to explain. She responded, "I know a few hard-driving women who are climbing the ladder at consulting firms, but they are single or divorced and seem pretty isolated. And I know a handful of working mothers who are trying to do the half-time thing or the two-thirds-time thing. They work reduced hours so they can see their kids, but they don't get the good projects, they don't get the bonuses, and they also get whispered about behind their backs. You know, comments like, 'If she's not prepared to work the client's hours, she has no business being in the profession.'"

This is the harsh reality behind the myth of having it all. Even in organizations whose policies support women, prevailing attitudes and unrelenting job pressures undermine them. Women's lives have expanded. But the grudging attitudes of most corporate cultures weigh down and constrain what individual women feel is possible.

Sylvia Ann Hewlett is an economist and the author of several books, including Creating a Life: Professional Women and the Quest for Children *(Talk Miramax Books, 2002), from which this article is adapted. She is the founder and chairwoman of the National Parenting Association in New York.*

To further explore the topic of this article, go to www.hbr.org/explore

---

Index

Index

Test Your Knowledge Form

We encourage you to photocopy and use this page as a tool to assess how the articles in *Annual Editions* expand on the information in your textbook. By reflecting on the articles you will gain enhanced text information. You can also access this useful form on a product's book support Web site at *http://www.dushkin.com/online/*.

NAME: _____ DATE: _____

_____

TITLE AND NUMBER OF ARTICLE:

_____

BRIEFLY STATE THE MAIN IDEA OF THIS ARTICLE:

_____

_____

LIST THREE IMPORTANT FACTS THAT THE AUTHOR USES TO SUPPORT THE MAIN IDEA:

_____

_____

WHAT INFORMATION OR IDEAS DISCUSSED IN THIS ARTICLE ARE ALSO DISCUSSED IN YOUR TEXTBOOK OR OTHER READINGS THAT YOU HAVE DONE? LIST THE TEXTBOOK CHAPTERS AND PAGE NUMBERS:

_____

_____

LIST ANY EXAMPLES OF BIAS OR FAULTY REASONING THAT YOU FOUND IN THE ARTICLE:

_____

_____

LIST ANY NEW TERMS/CONCEPTS THAT WERE DISCUSSED IN THE ARTICLE, AND WRITE A SHORT DEFINITION:

_____

We Want Your Advice

ANNUAL EDITIONS revisions depend on two major opinion sources: one is our Advisory Board, listed in the front of this volume, which works with us in scanning the thousands of articles published in the public press each year; the other is you—the person actually using the book. Please help us and the users of the next edition by completing the prepaid article rating form on this page and returning it to us. Thank you for your help!

ANNUAL EDITIONS: Business Ethics 03/04

ARTICLE RATING FORM

Here is an opportunity for you to have direct input into the next revision of this volume.
We would like you to rate each of the articles listed below, using the following scale:

1. Excellent: should definitely be retained
2. Above average: should probably be retained
3. Below average: should probably be deleted
4. Poor: should definitely be deleted

Your ratings will play a vital part in the next revision.
Please mail this prepaid form to us as soon as possible.
Thanks for your help!

RATING	ARTICLE
	1. Thinking Ethically: A Framework for Moral Decision Making
	2. Appreciating, Understanding, and Applying Universal Moral Principles
	3. Defining Moments: When Managers Must Choose Between Right and Right
	4. Managing by Values
	5. Improper Behavior
	6. Doing Well by Doing Good
	7. Best Resources for Corporate Social Responsibility
	8. HR Must Know When Employee Surveillance Crosses the Line
	9. Cut Loose
	10. Enough Is Enough
	11. Unjust Rewards
	12. Harassment Grows More Complex
	13. Is Wal-Mart Hostile to Women?
	14. Racism in the Workplace
	15. The Unifying Force of Diversity
	16. The Kindest Cut
	17. Downsize With Dignity
	18. A Hero—and a Smoking-Gun Letter
	19. Speaking Out Has High Cost
	20. Where Do You Draw the Line?
	21. Was the Threat Real, or a Hoax?
	22. Leaders as Value Shapers
	23. The Parable of the Sadhu
	24. Trust in the Marketplace
	25. Ethics in Cyberspace
	26. Adding Corporate Ethics to the Bottom Line
	27. Corporate Social Audits—This Time Around
	28. Scandals Shred Investors' Faith
	29. How to Fix Corporate Governance
	30. America Addresses Work Force Diversity
	31. Virtual Morality: A New Workplace Quandary
	32. Values in Tension: Ethics Away From Home
	33. Global Standards, Local Problems
	34. The Perils of Doing the Right Thing

RATING	ARTICLE
	35. Ethical Marketing for Competitive Advantage on the Internet
	36. Designing a Trust-Based e-Business Strategy
	37. Managing for Organizational Integrity
	38. Industrial Evolution
	39. 100 Best Corporate Citizens
	40. Ethical Challenges for Business in the New Millennium: Corporate Social Responsibility and Models of Management Mor
	41. After Enron: The Ideal Corporation
	42. Wanted: Ethical Employer
	43. Old Ethical Principles: The New Corporate Culture
	44. Do It Right
	45. Profits From Principle: Five Forces Redefining Business
	46. Executive Women and the Myth of Having It All

(Continued on next page)

ANNUAL EDITIONS: BUSINESS ETHICS 03/04

|||||

NO POSTAGE
NECESSARY
IF MAILED
IN THE
UNITED STATES

BUSINESS REPLY MAIL
FIRST-CLASS MAIL PERMIT NO. 84 GUILFORD CT

POSTAGE WILL BE PAID BY ADDRESSEE

McGraw-Hill/Dushkin
530 Old Whitfield Street
Guilford, Ct 06437-9989

ABOUT YOU

Name _____ Date _____

Are you a teacher? ☐ A student? ☐
Your school's name _____

Department _____

Address _____ City _____ State ____ Zip ____

School telephone # _____

YOUR COMMENTS ARE IMPORTANT TO US!

Please fill in the following information:
For which course did you use this book?
_____

Did you use a text with this ANNUAL EDITION? ☐ yes ☐ no
What was the title of the text?
_____

What are your general reactions to the *Annual Editions* concept?
_____

Have you read any pertinent articles recently that you think should be included in the next edition? Explain.
_____

Are there any articles that you feel should be replaced in the next edition? Why?
_____

Are there any World Wide Web sites that you feel should be included in the next edition? Please annotate.
_____

May we contact you for editorial input? ☐ yes ☐ no
May we quote your comments? ☐ yes ☐ no